"Matthew Barrett has the ev tested, deeply traditional biblic book is the story of his joy in fi aside some rubble and debris th ....u on top of it in recent years. *Simply Trinity* p ...s the good news of the unmanipulated doctrine of the triune God."

Fred Sanders, Torrey Honors College, Biola University

"Matthew Barrett's book is perfect for students of theology in the evangelical tradition. In clear and readable chapters Barrett draws his readers to appreciate classical trinitarian theology as the foundation of biblical faith. Readers are led away from the rocks of those who have sought to convince us that such theology needs radical change, and into the calm, wide sea that is the Christian community's historic faith."

Lewis Ayres, Durham University

"Matthew Barrett exposes those tinkering with the Trinity and provides a great antidote to them. He offers a sane and sober recovery of the church's exegesis of Scripture to explain that the three persons of the Godhead share in one substance, power, and eternity without hierarchies or other heresies. Barrett provides an informative mix of exegesis, church history, and systematic theology to defend the Christian doctrine of the Trinity against its unwitting saboteurs."

Michael F. Bird, Ridley College, Melbourne, Australia

"*Simply Trinity* delivers an accessible scholarly introduction to historic and biblical understandings of the Trinity and demonstrates how much is at stake in the trinitarian debates that have recently roiled the evangelical community. I recommend it highly."

Thomas S. Kidd, Baylor University

"I was blown away by this book, a clear, powerful intervention into trinitarian controversy. The critique of evangelical subordinationists alone is fantastic, and no attentive reader should miss their connections with social trinitarianism. Evangelical theology is in serious trouble, and I think many of us have known that for years, but this book will be impossible to ignore. We simply must turn this trend around or evangelicalism will lose its hold on the gospel."

Craig Carter, Tyndale University

"I hope this accessible book is widely read and discussed, especially by evangelicals. It will challenge some things taught in recent decades. But Barrett's arguments from Scripture and tradition are to be taken seriously, since we all long for our speech and worship of the triune God to be faithful."

Kelly M. Kapic, Covenant College

"Matthew Barrett has written a stormer of a book. He meets head-on the major turn away from the historic Christian account of the triune God to the post-enlightenment account that favored redefinition and novelty tending toward unorthodoxy. In the twentieth century evangelicals adopted this new strategy and have sought to redefine God in favor of their social agendas. I am grateful to God for this book and for the service Professor Barrett has done the church of Christ."

Liam Goligher, Tenth Presbyterian Church

"Barrett glorifies the infinitely simple Father, Son, and Holy Spirit with deep wisdom. This would be reason enough to read, but most doctrinally rich books about the Trinity are boring. By contrast, this book sings! From the get-go, Barrett captures one's attention and doesn't let go. The result is urgently needed nourishment for both head and heart."

Matthew Levering, Mundelein Seminary

"Matthew Barrett provides the church with a valuable resource, introducing a pro-Nicene account of the Trinity peppered with stories, illustrations, and examples that will make *Simply Trinity* both engaging and understandable for students and for Christians in the pew. This work is solidly biblical, consciously pro-Nicene, and the ideal replacement for the various social trinitarian treatments of the Trinity that have been popular in the local church in recent decades."

Glenn Butner, Sterling College

"Immediately convinced of the need for this book, readers become acquainted with the history of Trinity drift as well as the history of its antidote. Barrett's style is both inviting and accessible, utilizing first-person narrative and cogent theological explanation to communicate rigor and depth. He presents a biblically and historically thorough case for the simple triune God differentiated only by eternal generation and spiration. I will value this book as a scholarly dialogue partner and pedagogical teaching text, showing that if we fail to submit ourselves to the image of our gracious God consistent in text and tradition, we will have no foundation from which to think and live theologically in such a demanding time as this."

Amy Peeler, Wheaton College

"Matthew Barrett is a theologian who delights in the Trinity, a man who perceives the Trinity's importance. Because of his love of the Trinity, Barrett is flustered by the fact that many twentieth-century evangelical theologians have used and distorted the Trinity for their own social and political agendas. They have misinterpreted the Scriptures. They are ignorant of the church fathers and much of the Christian theological tradition. They have set the Trinity adrift. Barrett's book is a refutation of such trinitarian drift, but more so, it is a clear, creative, robust, and scholarly presentation of the Trinity, a presentation that will bring joy to the minds and love to the hearts of all who read it. In so doing, all will give praise to the Father, honor to the Son, and glory to the Holy Spirit."

Thomas G. Weinandy, Capuchin College, Washington, DC

"The Trinity is one of the Bible's more challenging doctrines, and yet Matthew Barrett ably guides readers through the issues to present clear and cogent teaching. He opens the treasures of the past and draws on patristic, medieval, Reformation, and contemporary theologians to explain the doctrine of the Trinity. But he also usefully shows where some have gone astray and charitably speaks the truth in love. People would do well to read this book and plumb the depths of the Bible's teaching on the nature of our triune God."

J. V. Fesko, Reformed Theological Seminary, Jackson, MS

"*Simply Trinity* could be a game changer. By writing a book for laypersons on the doctrine of the Trinity and the contributions of the church fathers, Matthew Barrett has gone a long way in helping to banish popular errors that continue to persist about the very nature of God. But this book is so much more. Complex doctrines and historical terms are brought out of the halls of academia and given back to the laity. As I read, there were moments when I shut my eyes and gave thanks to the God whose essence and perfections are beyond words. Please read this book."

Todd Pruitt, Covenant Presbyterian Church, Harrisonburg, VA; cohost, *Mortification of Spin* podcast

"*Simply Trinity* successfully aims to put the church back on the path of confessional fidelity. Matthew Barrett helps us understand that how we read the Bible and whom we read it with is imperative to beholding the triune Author who reveals himself to us in his Word. You will see how our understanding of God affects our understanding of salvation and what we forfeit if we get it wrong."

Aimee Byrd, author of *Recovering from Biblical Manhood and Womanhood*

"*Simply Trinity* will help nudge readers to a more scriptural and historically orthodox formulation of the doctrine of the Trinity; it will also help in doing the same for various attributes of God. If you are interested in what Scripture teaches about God and Trinity, how the early creeds of Christianity formulated Scripture's teaching into creedal statements, and how many in our day have left the old paths on this issue, this book is for you."

Richard C . Barcellos, Grace Reformed Baptist Church, Palmdale, CA; IRBS Theological Seminary, Mansfield, TX

SIMPLY TRINITY

THE **UNMANIPULATED** FATHER, SON, AND SPIRIT

MATTHEW BARRETT

BakerBooks

a division of Baker Publishing Group
Grand Rapids, Michigan

© 2021 by Matthew Barrett

Published by Baker Books
a division of Baker Publishing Group
PO Box 6287, Grand Rapids, MI 49516–6287
www.bakerbooks.com

Printed in the United States of America

Library of Congress Cataloging-in-Publication Data
Names: Barrett, Matthew, 1982– author.
Title: Simply Trinity : the unmanipulated Father, Son, and Spirit / Matthew Barrett.
Description: Grand Rapids, Michigan : Baker Books, a division of Baker Publishing Group, [2021]
Identifiers: LCCN 2020035463 | ISBN 9781540900074 (paperback) | ISBN 9781540901521 (casebound)
Subjects: LCSH: Trinity.
Classification: LCC BT111.3 .B355 2021 | DDC 231/.044—dc23
LC record available at https://lccn.loc.gov/2020035463

21 22 23 24 25 26 27   7 6 5 4 3 2 1

TO ELIZABETH.
Your resilience is like a budding gerbera daisy after the rain.
The sun shines bright and so do you.

"How precious is your steadfast love, O God!
The children of mankind take refuge
in the shadow of your wings. . . .
For with you is the fountain of life;
in your light do we see light." (Psalm 36:7, 9)

Contents

Contents

Acknowledgments

Lord knows my pilgrimage writing this book has not been undertaken alone. After I finished *None Greater* (Baker, 2019), John Fesko encouraged me to keep writing on the doctrine of God, because the church and academy alike need to retrieve orthodox trinitarianism. Kelly Kapic was also an inspiration, believing this project was timely considering the confusion he has seen firsthand. I especially want to thank Scott Swain. He has been a conversation partner, always full of trinitarian acumen, always checking the guardrails for safety. Thank you, Scott, for writing the foreword and conveying just how critical it is to get the Trinity right. I am also full of gratitude for Fred Sanders. Fred not only read and endorsed the manuscript but offered wisdom on accuracy and tone. His seasoned experience was invaluable. I must pay the same compliment to the other endorsers who provided valuable feedback. Of course, any residual shortcomings are mine.

I am also grateful to Brian Vos and the team at Baker who believe theology is too important not to be accessible. I am thankful to the Baker team, especially Amy Nemecek, for their hard work smoothing out the rough edges. One of these days I will write a book less complicated than the Trinity. And the marketing team will rejoice with one voice.

I wrote this book while on sabbatical. Samuel Powell and Point Loma hosted my family during the summer of 2019. I must say, nothing beats writing on the Trinity with the Pacific coastline between your toes. Thank you for your hospitality; my family still raves about our time on your campus.

I am blessed to teach at Midwestern Baptist Theological Seminary and am blessed still more that those in leadership value writing. Thank you, Jason Allen, for not only initiating this sabbatical but encouraging me to write on the Trinity for the church. I pray this book helps the church find its way home. Jason Duesing has also cheered me on. How rewarding it is to teach at a school where colleagues support one another. Last, to my students: your enthusiasm was fuel in my tank. Whether it was in a seminar or over sweet tea at Anselm House, your probing reminded this fatigued writer why he writes in the first place. Special thanks to Ronni Kurtz, Sam Parkison, Joseph Lanier, Jen Foster, and Timothy Gatewood for their many hours on the bibliography and manuscript.

But few proved as inspirational as my own children. I will never forget those nights when we sang (sometimes even rapped!) the Nicene Creed. Thanks to you, orthodoxy now has rhythm. Most of all, I must thank my wife, Elizabeth. Like she does with every book, Elizabeth begins and ends each pilgrimage with me. What wife stays up in bed until midnight to discuss the intricacies of eternal generation? Mine does, and there is none quite like her. For that reason, I dedicate this book to her.

Foreword

SCOTT R. SWAIN

Matthew Barrett wants to take you on a journey in his time-traveling DeLorean. He wants to take you back to a time when pastors, theologians, and Christians read the Bible differently than we often read it today, to a time when the orthodox doctrine of the Trinity was birthed, by means of God's sovereign Word and Spirit, in the church's theology and piety. Why is such a journey necessary? Why should you consider joining him? Dr. Barrett is no mad scientist, and his time-traveling quest does not stem from sentimentalism for a bygone golden age of the church. To quote Huey Lewis and the News, Dr. Barrett wants to take you "back in time" because he believes that the future of the church's doctrine, piety, witness, and worship is at stake.

Classical Protestant theologians spoke of two foundations of the church's doctrine and life. They identified Holy Scripture as the *cognitive foundation*, the supreme source and norm of all that the church is called to believe and to practice, the foundation of "the truth, which accords with godliness" (Titus 1:1). In addition to this cognitive foundation, they identified the triune God as the

13

ontological foundation of the church's doctrine and life. As all things are "from" and "through" and "to" the triune God in the order of being (Rom. 11:36), so, they judged, all things are from and through and to the triune God in the order of theological understanding and Christian living. The doctrines of creation and providence, the person and work of Jesus Christ, the church and sacraments, salvation and the last things—each of these doctrines rests on the doctrine of the triune God for its meaning and significance, and the life of godliness that builds on these doctrines directs us to the triune God as our supreme good and final end. The confession that Jesus is the Christ, the Father's Spirit-anointed Son, is the foundation of the Christian confession (Matt. 16:16; 28:19; Mark 12:1–12; Eph. 2:20). For this reason, the doctrine of the Trinity is the foundation of Christian teaching and living. Without the doctrine of the Trinity, there is no Christianity.

Dr. Barrett wants to take you back in time because many Reformed and evangelical churches in North America and the United Kingdom have lost touch with this foundational doctrine in recent days. How did this happen? Unfortunately, our contemporary predicament does not arise from simple amnesia, simple forgetfulness of something we once knew. Our contemporary predicament arises from the fact that churches have been wrongly catechized in basic Christian teaching on the Trinity.

For reasons Dr. Barrett explores in the pages that follow, a number of late-twentieth-century evangelical theologians neglected and/or rejected several common features of classical Christian teaching about the Trinity and, in place of those features, introduced a new and significantly distorted account of the Trinity, what Dr. Barrett calls a *manipulated Trinity*. Though this approach preserved the distinction between the persons of the Trinity, it wrongly divided the singular being and essence of the Trinity, ascribing different attributes to different persons (e.g., authority to the Father, submission to the Son) and thereby dividing God's supreme and singular will. Over the past several decades, this approach to the Trinity gained significant traction in evangelical circles through popular study Bibles, textbooks, journals, and conferences and through its promotion in some of the largest, most influential schools of pastoral training in North America and the United Kingdom. Sadly, this largely revisionist work of catechesis has been largely successful. Many evangelical Christians today have come to believe that the manipulated Trinity is orthodox Christian teaching.

It is not. And this is why we should welcome Dr. Barrett's invitation to travel back in time. If we have lost touch with the supreme foundation of Christian teaching, if we have received poor training from our contemporaries, then we must find better, more faithful teachers, even if that means looking to the past. By God's grace, such teachers exist, and they can help us better appreciate who, what, and how the triune God has revealed himself to be in Holy Scripture.

That said, our journey to the past is not for the sake of the past but for the sake of a better future. When something as valuable as orthodox Christian teaching on the Trinity has been lost, we must seek to retrieve it so that we, our children, and our churches might reestablish our faith on a more solid foundation, that we might redirect our piety by the light of a more brilliant star, and that we might renew our witness according to the measure of a more reliable standard. We should welcome Dr. Barrett's invitation to travel back in time so that, by the help of God's sovereign Word and Spirit, we too might join the chorus of saints in heaven and earth throughout all ages in offering the thrice-holy Trinity the worship that he alone deserves.

So buckle up and enjoy your trip. Dr. Barrett is a skillful driver and a reliable guide.

Which brings me to one final reason you should accept Dr. Barrett's invitation to (re)discover the unmanipulated Trinity. One of the major missteps recent trinitarian theology took was to suggest that the Trinity is only meaningful insofar as we can demonstrate its usefulness for various practical, social, and political ends. But this is to get things utterly backward. The Trinity does not exist for our sake or for the sake of our agendas. The triune God is not a means to an end. We exist for him (1 Cor. 8:6). The Trinity is an end in himself (Rom. 11:36). Therefore, studying the Trinity—seeking better to know and understand, to cherish and adore, to worship and serve the triune God—needs no justification beyond itself. The reason for studying the triune God is not to bend the Trinity to our various social programs. The reason for studying the triune God is to bend our minds, wills, actions, and communities to the Trinity, confident that, in doing so, we will discover in him both the reason for our existence and the fullness of joy (Ps. 16:11; John 15:11; 17:13).

Scott R. Swain, President and James Woodrow Hassell
Professor of Systematic Theology, Reformed
Theological Seminary, Orlando, Florida

Trinity Drift

Therefore we must pay much closer attention to
what we have heard, lest we drift away from it.

HEBREWS 2:1

All that is gold does not glitter,
Not all those who wander are lost;
The old that is strong does not wither,
Deep roots are not reached by the frost.

J. R. R. TOLKIEN,
THE FELLOWSHIP OF THE RING

Dagon and Ebenezer

"Dad, what's an Ebenezer?"

It was an honest question. Our family had sung that famous hymn "Come Thou Fount" a thousand times, but this time when we sang "Here I raise my Ebenezer, hither by Thy help I've come," my daughter Georgia interrupted, confused by this strange word.

"It's a rock," I responded.

"A rock?"

"Let me tell you a story. A long time ago, before Jesus, even before King David, there was a prophet named Samuel."

"The boy in the temple? Didn't God keep calling his name when he was sleeping?"

"Yes, but in this story, he was much older. Samuel had a tough job. He had to tell God's people, Israel, to repent, and they wouldn't. They wanted to worship false gods instead."

"Idols?"

"That's right. Except it was so out of control that God let Israel's enemy, the Philistines, conquer his people in war. But that's not the worst of it. The Philistines took the most holy thing God's people had: the ark of the covenant. The ark sat in the house of God, and when God wanted to be with his people, his presence came down on the ark. When the ark was captured and taken away, it was as if Israel had lost God himself. It was the worst thing that could ever have happened."

"Did they get it back?"

"They did. The Philistines put the ark in the temple of their god, Dagon. In the morning, Dagon had fallen down face-first in front of the ark. Embarrassing, right? The Philistines propped Dagon back up, but the next morning he was on his face again in front of the ark, and this time his head had fallen off. Not just his head, but his hands too, like they'd been cut right off. Are you laughing?"

"Yes," Georgia said with a smile she was trying to hide.

"It is kind of funny. Anyway, the Philistines got the message. They sent the ark back. Samuel couldn't believe it: just when it appeared God had left his people for good, he came back to save them from their enemy. That's so like God, isn't it? But Samuel knew how unworthy the people were to receive the ark back. So he summoned all of them to put away their false gods and serve the one true God. Believe it or not, Israel listened and obeyed. When the ark arrived, Samuel took a stone, set it in a spot where Israel would see it for generations to come, and he called that stone—"

"Ebenezer!"

"That's right. He called it Ebenezer because he said, 'Till now the Lord has helped us.' From that day forward, for hundreds and hundreds of years, every time a little boy or girl, just like you, asked their mom or dad why there was a giant stone in the middle of town, they heard this story. The stone was just a stone, but it was so much more: it helped the people always remember who this great God is and what he has done; it helped them never to forget their story, their family heritage."

"What a great story."

"Isn't it? One of my favorites. Don't forget, it's your story too."

First Samuel 6 and 7 really is one of my favorite stories. But it took my little girl to help me see why: *God deeply cares about heritage.*

Your heritage matters. It's your story, and one day it will be the story of your sons and daughters, a story they will in turn tell to their sons and daughters. And on and on it will go. The stories of our lives, the stories we inherit and find ourselves in, leave us a heritage that more or less defines who we are and who we will become.

But have you ever considered what kind of *theological* heritage you have inherited or will leave behind? If you are reading this book, your heritage, like my own, may be an *evangelical* one. There are many reasons to be proud of our evangelical heritage: its insistence that one must be born again to be a Christian, its commitment to the Bible as our supreme authority, its determination to keep the cross of Jesus central, and its zeal to take the good news of Jesus's sacrificial death to the nations. These marks define our evangelical story.

But our evangelical heritage is cut short if it's not also a *catholic* heritage—catholic with a small *c*, referring to those universal beliefs the church has confessed from its inception. Due to their biblical fidelity, the church has put these beliefs in creed form to be confessed by the church universal (in all times and in all places) and to guard the church against the threat of heresy, which more often than not poses as scriptural teaching. For this reason, they are called *orthodox* beliefs. Question is, do our beliefs as evangelicals align with those biblical, orthodox beliefs the church has cherished and confessed since its beginning, and will our identity moving forward be characterized by those same beliefs?

I didn't tell you, but the four marks I mentioned above make up the evangelical quadrilateral: conversionism, biblicism, crucicentrism, and activism. According to historians, these four marks define and determine whether one is an evangelical.

But notice, no Trinity. Wherever did the Trinity go?

Young, Restless, Reformed . . . but Trinitarian? Trinity Drift

Perhaps the Trinity is assumed with each mark of the evangelical quadrilateral. I hope so. But you must admit the Trinity's absence as a mark in its own right parallels its absence within evangelical culture today. I have been an evangelical for decades now, and I've never met anyone or heard of anyone outside the evangelical fold who has said, "Those evangelicals may be many things, but there's no question they are trinitarians through and through." I've heard them call us by many names, but trinitarians? Never.

Granted, many evangelical churches and pastors know they are supposed to affirm the Trinity, and so they do. But if they're being honest, they have no idea why other than to say, "The Bible says so somewhere, right?"—though they're not sure what verse that might be. Ask them to articulate that same Trinity *according to biblical orthodoxy*, and they will return a blank stare. You may be giving me one right now.

"Hold on, professor," you might object. "Haven't we experienced a resurgence of theology in recent years?" We have. Malnourished and hungry for meat rather than just milk, young folks at the turn of the century dug deep to resurrect theology in the church, and not just any theology but *Reformed* theology. But two decades have passed, and we now have the advantage of looking back to recognize gaping holes we did not see before—blind spots. Here is one too big to ignore: with all our focus on the bigness of God in salvation history, somehow who our triune God is in eternity was left out. How ironic. The story of *salvation* is a story that reveals not only what our triune God has accomplished but who he is in and of himself as Father, Son, and Holy Spirit. How telling. Perhaps our Reformed resurgence is not all that *Reformed* after all, or at least not as Reformed as it should be.

But it's not just that the Trinity has received little attention among the young, restless, and Reformed. There is reason to believe that in the middle of our Reformed resurgence—and all the excitement it brought—we've drifted away from the *biblical, orthodox* doctrine of the Trinity. Trinity drift, as I like to call it, was not sudden and explosive but gradual, like a couple on a sailboat enjoying each other's company in the blue sea breeze, congratulating each other on the fine outing they've prepared, only to look up and realize they no longer see the shore. Worse still, they have no idea how to get back.

Don't believe me? Let's revisit our story; let's go back in time to determine what our future holds.

Back to the Future

One of the best moments of my life was the day my dad and I first watched *Back to the Future*. I had just turned twelve, and little did I know I was about to watch a classic.

Marty McFly and Doc—and let's not forget Einstein the dog—transcend the limits of time thanks to the DeLorean, a chic time machine if there ever was one. But as Doc and Marty learn the hard way, time travel is littered with danger, so much so that Doc wishes he had never invented the flux capacitor in the first place. To alter the past, even in the slightest, is to put the future at risk. When Marty leaves 1985 and travels back to 1955, he makes a terrible mistake, one that puts his own future existence in jeopardy.

We can't go back in time to change our evangelical future, as much as I'd jump at the opportunity to glide through history in the DeLorean. But we can look back in time and see where the future might go . . . if things don't change in the present. What will the future look like for evangelicals if our present trajectory continues to mimic our recent past? To answer that question, we need to take a hard, honest look at the last three decades if we are to understand why the future of trinitarian theology might be in jeopardy.

If Doc's DeLorean took you back to the turn of the century and to any evangelical college campus, what would you see? You'd see me—the much younger me, that is—sitting in the college cafeteria highlighting the pages of a thick blue hardcover book with a square picture of Moses facing the desert. If it weren't for Moses, you'd think this tome was a medical encyclopedia. But we all know the book: it's Wayne Grudem's *Systematic Theology*, popular among evangelicals for its clear and trusted summary of Bible doctrine.

But let's say your DeLorean is sophisticated enough to jump forward in time and drop you off not just on any ol' college campus, but one with a seminary community. If that's the case, then as you leave the DeLorean for the coffee cart and library carrels, you'd spot me again, lost in a book just as thick, but this time with a cover that looked like blue and red stained glass and featured a cross down the middle. It's Millard Erickson's *Systematic Theology*, popular for the philosophical flavor it brings to doctrine, reasoning its way to conclusions with rigorous, logical prose.

These were some of my first introductions to the doctrine of the Trinity. Sure, I believed in the Trinity; I was a Christian, after all. But I had no idea why. So, as a young, aspiring student, eager to learn Christian theology, I jumped in headfirst, yellow and pink highlighters and all. I was sure to pay attention in class, too, looking for opportunities to learn more about this Trinity so central to my Christian identity.

The way I was taught to approach the Trinity, however, was more or less like a hard science. The Trinity was treated like a conundrum, even a problem, but one that could be solved with the proper formula. Since no verse in the Bible taught the Trinity, one had to get mathematical. First, add up and list the verses that say God is one. Next, add up and list the verses that say Father, Son, and Spirit are each fully God. And . . . *voila!* We know God is one essence and three persons. Done.

Or so I thought.

At the time, I remember thinking this approach felt somewhat forced, even foreign to how I first met the Trinity of the Bible. I came to know the Trinity at a young age, but I should clarify that it was the other way around: the Trinity came to know me. The extraordinary thing about my conversion was that it was so . . . ordinary. My parents were faithful to read me the Bible, and they had a special affection for the Gospel of John. After reading texts like John 3, the Holy Spirit opened my eyes to Jesus as the Son of God, and when I trusted in him as my Savior, I knew I had been forgiven by the Father. I do not remember ever hearing a sermon on the Trinity, nor did my parents sit down with me and explain the Trinity. But as I encountered the gospel, I met the Trinity. As I said, however, it was the other way around: the Trinity met me . . . the Trinity even saved me. I loved the Trinity because the Trinity first loved me.

But when I read about the Trinity in these textbooks, the Trinity not only felt forced—the sum total of a long list of random proof texts—but the result of a magic trick. It was as if the Trinity came out of nowhere. *Poof.* Like a rabbit out of a black hat.

I also noticed something peculiar, even a bit unsettling. Both in college and in seminary, each textbook I read made a point to reject an old Christian belief I had never heard of before: the eternal generation of the Son from the Father. And it wasn't just well-loved textbooks, but some of the most highly recommended books on the doctrine of God by evangelical theologians and philosophers— John Feinberg, Bruce Ware, Robert Reymond, William Lane Craig, J. P. Moreland, and others. These thinkers, and others like them, were helpful in different ways, and their books were assigned by professors I had good reasons to trust. But they shared this weakness: they rejected this ancient doctrine called eternal generation because they were unable to find a text to support it. Without a chapter and verse, it couldn't be included in their list; it just didn't fit into their formula. Others rejected this churchy belief because it just didn't make rational sense, and if it wasn't reasonable, it couldn't be sensible.[1]

If you don't know what eternal generation is, don't worry. It sounds more complicated than it really is. In fact, it's something almost too simple to say. Ask yourself this question: *Why does the Bible use the names Father, Son, and Spirit to describe the Trinity?* Answer: in the Bible, especially in a book like the Gospel of John, the Father is called *Father* because he is, well, the Father of his Son. As Fathers do, he begets his Son. That is, after all, what it means to be a Father. But since this is God we're talking about, not a mere mortal, he does so from all eternity. He eternally begets his Son, though he himself is begotten by no one (he is unbegotten). That's because he is the source or origin. This is called *paternity*.

The Son is called Son in Scripture because he has a Father. Think of it this way: he is from his Father, begotten by his Father from all eternity. Or we might say the Son is generated (the words begotten and generated are synonyms) from the Father's divine nature from all eternity. That is, after all, what it means to be a Son. This is called *filiation*.

The Spirit is called Spirit in Scripture because he proceeds from the Father and the Son from eternity. He is not another Son (a brother) nor a grandson—that would be weird—so we should not say he is eternally begotten or generated. Rather, he is spirated from the Father and the Son. This is called *spiration*, a label that captures the biblical meaning of the word "Spirit."

Since we're talking about key words, I should also mention that there is a phrase that sums up all three of these biblical names: *eternal relations of origin*. That is a phrase to remember. Highlight it. Underline it. Circle it. It sounds sophisticated, but its meaning is quite simple really. The word "origin" is fitting because we are describing where these three persons come from (e.g., the Son is *from* the Father). The word "eternal" is appropriate since this is God we have in view. And the word "relation" is another way of referring to the *persons* of the Trinity, specifically what is so unique about each of them (e.g., the Father is unbegotten, the Son is begotten, the Spirit is spirated).

Now, back to the DeLorean. As I did some digging of my own, I discovered that this ancient way of describing the Trinity was— well, how do I put it—*the norm*. For two thousand years the church's best Bible interpreters believed this was the biblical way to define the Trinity. This made my jaw drop. The textbooks and teachers introducing me to the Trinity acted as if their scientific, mathematical approach, an approach that happily showed eternal generation the door, was just . . . standard. Everyone around me assumed it was too. But it wasn't. Not even close. It's only been in the last century, in *our* generation, that the Trinity has been reformulated in radical ways.

But my deep digging uncovered more: not only had Christianity's best Bible interpreters confessed a doctrine like eternal generation ever since the church's conception, but they believed such a doctrine safeguarded the deity of Christ from the most dangerous of heresies. To be clear, we are talking about a belief so essential to the Trinity, distinguishing the Son *as Son* from the Father *as Father*, that when the deity of Christ was questioned in the fourth century, the church fathers gathered at the Council of Nicaea (325)—perhaps the most important council in all of Christian history—and wrote a creed to affirm eternal generation as a condition of true orthodoxy (see chapter 2). If the Son is not begotten from the Father's divine essence from all eternity, they argued, then the Son is not equal to the Father in deity. The doctrine not only distinguished the person of the Son from the person of the Father but ensured the two were coeternal and coequal in divinity, power, will, glory, and authority. *To affirm eternal generation was equivalent to confessing oneself to be a Christian, and a Bible-believing Christian at that. To deny eternal generation was to align yourself with heresy.*

Again, my jaw hit the floor. How can such a belief be dismissed today by evangelicals, the same people who claim to be crucicentric? It was unnerving, to say the least, that such a trinitarian basic had been cut out of evangelical textbooks and erased from the whiteboards of evangelical classrooms—classrooms where I was supposed to be learning about the Trinity. And then it occurred to me: we have and still are experiencing Trinity drift.

But wait, things get worse. The drift continues . . .

The ~~Beach Is~~ Books Are Calling . . . and I Must Go

Since I am a Los Angeles native by birth, you won't be surprised to hear me say that wherever I go, my spirit tends to wander back to the City of Angels. It may seem strange to those who crave the open plains of the Midwest—which I also love, by the way—but

I feel at home whenever I fly back to that concrete city with its spaghetti freeways.

Southern California is a paradox: its sunburned concrete stretches for miles on end, but you can always count on any stretch of concrete leading to a beach with golden sand and white-capped waves. Each summer our family escapes the oppressive humidity of the Midwest for sunny SoCal, known for its immutable weather of seventy-five degrees. It's always worth it: each day I read and write, but in the afternoons and evenings we trek on down to the beachfront to cool off in the Pacific and watch the sunset show off its orange, pink, and yellow canvas as if it were one of LA's fashion models walking down the runway. One summer, this habit became so customary to us beach bums that my daughter swore she'd buy the T-shirt she kept seeing that read, *The beach is calling, and I must go.* Unfortunately for mom and dad, kids have a way of turning the tables. When the trash needed an exit, or when little sister needed a bowl of cereal, my oldest would say with that cunning smile of hers, "Sorry, Mom. Sorry, Dad. Books are calling, and I must go."

That summer it was mostly the beach that kept calling, and we were all too willing to be summoned. But every once in a while, the summons flipped, and I'd skip writing and find a local bookstore to peruse. This is my habit no matter what town our family inhabits—I'm incurable. At the end of every vacation, the kids pack up seashells while Dad tries, hopelessly, to shove a stack of books in an already full suitcase.

One afternoon I discovered a hole-in-the-wall shop filled with books from floor to ceiling. Here's what I did: I started in fiction, picking out those classics I have yet to read, knowing that in the far corner was a neglected section called "theology" that awaited me like the cherry on top of an ice cream sundae. But to my surprise, this particular bookstore had a warehouse full of cherries. There on the wall before me was a story, each shelf of books telling me what ideas had been engaged over the last fifty to seventy years.

Like a child in a candy store, I started grabbing books by the handfuls. But after four hours it was time to go. I purchased my big stack of books from the lady at the cash register and walked outside to be greeted by the salty smell of fish and chips.

When my family returned from vacation, with tan lines and enough vitamin D to survive the winter, I hid myself away in my study and cleared an entire bookcase to view all the books I had purchased, as well as a slew of others I had collected over the years. I won't trouble you with the author and title of each book I opened—we'll meet some of them in chapter 3 anyway. But I must share with you what I discovered. Book after book revealed a pattern, and each shelf told a story.

First, I took up a book by one of the most influential theologians of the late twentieth century. His agenda was explicit: the Trinity is our master plan for *politics*. Just as the Trinity is a community or society of equal persons cooperating with one another, so too power structures in human society should favor a community of cooperation and equality. God is not a unitary monarch (monotheism) nor is the Trinity a hierarchy (with the Father as the authority), both of which result in a dictatorship in society. Rather, there is an equality among the persons, and that equality in community is our model for a socialist society. *Who knew the Trinity could be so political?*

Next, I got grabby, taking a handful all at once, since each had the word "ecumenical" sprinkled across their pages. These authors also appealed to the cooperative unity between the persons of the Trinity, but this time as a master plan for ecumenism, unity between different religions. Like the Trinity, the distinctions of each religious party need not be lost; nevertheless, cooperation and interdependence are primary, as each party (person) embraces unity with others, in this case for the sake of missions. Some even believed that the plurality that exists in this unified society we call Trinity is our blueprint for embracing religious pluralism in the world. *Who knew the Trinity could be so inclusive?*

I put this stack of books down, both for its sheer weight and because I spotted a few outliers hiding in the upper right-hand corner of the bookshelf. At first, I thought these books and papers were misplaced because they had a lot to say about environmentalism. But I was mistaken. These authors had transfigured the Trinity for the sake of ecology. They warned against ecological heresies that treat humans as superior to the environment and subordinate nature to man's power. Creation and humankind share the same essence, imaging the Son's equality with the Father in the Trinity. *Who knew the Trinity could be so green?*

Next came a slew of brightly colored books in shades of blue and green, but still a few in plain white or black. Again, I was convinced these books must be misplaced, for in each of them gender and sexual identity occupied the author's attention. But again, I was mistaken. Looking at one book after another, I quickly learned that there is no agenda as sexy as gender identity in theology. These authors were convinced that the equality between the persons of the Trinity is our justification for equality between the sexes in church as well as society. Just as there is a society of equal persons in the Trinity, so too are the sexes, male and female, equal in human society. An egalitarian Trinity should result in an egalitarian society. Some books on this shelf were so bold as to call God a woman. *Who knew the Trinity could be so feminist?*

Other books on this same shelf were written by evangelicals, but instead of using the Trinity to argue for gender equality, these authors used the Trinity to introduce hierarchy. They appealed to a functional subordination of the Son to the Father in eternity as justification for the subordination of wives to their husbands and women to their pastors. Just as the Father and Son are equal in essence but distinct in their roles, so too the wife is equal as a person but subordinate in role to the authority of her husband. Like many before them, these authors redefined orthodox trinitarianism, substituting orthodox categories (like simplicity and eternal generation) for social categories (roles as relation*ships*). *Who knew the Trinity could be so patriarchal?*

Just when I thought I'd seen it all, I picked up a book that had the word "sexuality" right there in the title. While the books I'd just put down used subordination to support hierarchy, this book used a similar method but appealed instead to the mutual love between the Father and Son to support homosexuality. These authors defended gay and lesbian marriages on the basis of functional roles within the Godhead. Just as the differences between the persons of the Trinity do not preclude their equality, so too the differences between heterosexual and homosexual do not preclude the equality between different sexual orientations. They remain equal and at the same time distinct, retaining their personal identity (like the Trinity). *Who knew the Trinity could be so sexual?*

Socialism, ecumenism, pluralism, environmentalism, egalitarianism, complementarianism, homosexuality . . . as I put the books down, my theological soul felt a little nauseous.[2] These were the books cherished by the past two generations of churchgoers, pastors, students, and professors. These were the books the church and academy turned to in order to understand the Trinity. And most of all, these were the books that taught the next generation how to use the Trinity to meet whatever social agenda they believed mattered most. There has been no end to the ways we use (abuse) the Trinity to meet our social agendas. And then it hit me: not only are we experiencing *Trinity drift*, but our redefinition of the Trinity has given us a license to *manipulate the Trinity*.

For evangelicals and liberals alike, the Trinity has become a wax nose, twisted and molded at will until the biblical, orthodox Trinity is beyond recognition. With the best of intentions, modern thinkers have transformed theology into anthropology. The Trinity has become a mirror in which we see our own reflection; we hold up our doctrine of the Trinity, and we might as well be holding up a picture of ourselves. We are no longer made in the image of the Trinity, but the Trinity is reinterpreted and refashioned until it is now made in our own image. The result: there are as many Trinities as there are social agendas. The Trinity itself has even been redefined as social to ensure these social agendas have traction. Our endless quests to make the Trinity relevant to society result in one thing: the triune God in eternity has been swallowed up by who we want him to be for us in history.

The Trinity is our social program.

All the Air We Breathe but Cannot See

For all my talk about SoCal, I should confess that I actually grew up in San Francisco. For those unfamiliar, San Fran is at the top of California while Los Angeles is at the bottom. It makes for one of the most scenic road trips. From start to finish—if you don't sightsee, which is not likely—the trip takes six hours to drive from Lombard Street to Hollywood. But if you fall asleep on your way in, you may miss a disturbing paradox, one that any honest California native knows to be true but more often than not shocks tourists.

In SoCal, when you sit in traffic moving as slow as molasses on Interstate 5 (which Californians just call *The 5*), take a seat in Dodger Stadium with a ten-inch Dodger Dog, or ride the Matterhorn at Disneyland with your screaming kids, you do not see all the smog you're inhaling. But for those who first visit the Golden Gate Bridge, Alcatraz Island, and Fisherman's Wharf in San Fran and then drive all the way down to SoCal, a different picture emerges. By the time you tap your brakes flying down the Grapevine and look up to see the City of Angels for the first time, you might just gasp at all the smog you now see—it's anything but angelic.

It's possible for everyone in society to go about their busy lives and never question all the air they cannot see. That is, until they are given a new perspective. Vantage point can make all the difference.

So too with the Trinity and our Christian heritage. The evangelical air we've been breathing for the last three decades is modern in every way. We don't know it, because everyone is breathing the same air and seems fine. We assume the Trinity we breathe in and out is the biblical one, even the Trinity of our fathers. *But it's not.* The trinitarian air we inhale and exhale has been blown into our evangelical hemisphere by the winds of modernity, and these smoggy winds are as far away from the Bible and Christian orthodoxy as can be.

We have drifted from biblical orthodoxy by exchanging the Trinity of our fathers for a social Trinity, one that can be manipulated to meet our social agenda. We have redefined the Trinity as a society of relationships in which each person cooperates by means of his (or her) own center of consciousness and will (what a previous generation labeled the heresy of tritheism) so that we can use the Trinity as our prototype for the type of human society we think best.

And evangelicals, whether we always realize it or not, have also breathed in the air of social trinitarianism, all the while convinced our Trinity is straight-up, unadulterated, mountain-air Bible. Nothing more, nothing less. But when the smog clears—and some of it has in recent years—it becomes apparent that the evangelical doctrine of the Trinity is a far cry from biblical orthodoxy. Think of it this way: the smog (modern theology) engulfs Los Angeles like a thick blanket covering its residents. But in response, we've either chosen to ignore it (*What smog?*) or convinced ourselves that it is quality air after all (*I'm sure it's fine*), despite what others are telling us on their way into town.

Which means not only do we need a new vantage point to see all the trinitarian smog we breathe, but we need new air. And that air can only be provided by the old winds of biblical orthodoxy. Nicene orthodoxy, to be exact. It is time the real Trinity stands up. It is time the church comes face-to-face with the God who is *simply Trinity.*

Unadulterated. Uncorrupted. *Unmanipulated.*

The Dream Team

I have written this book to wake us up, to give us a new vantage point, to summon new winds with fresh air that can help us breathe again. I don't say that out of pride, but out of humility . . . and a bit of embarrassment of my own. As I tell my story in the following pages, you'll see that I have a past; I too have been inhaling the smog of modern theology just like everyone else. But after years of digging deep into our family story, it has become clear to me that the Trinity I was taught by well-meaning evangelicals is not the Trinity of the Scriptures, nor the one our Christian fathers confessed and bled for, even died for under the threat of heresy. To remain silent seems irresponsible. We are drifting, and it's time for the church to find its way home.

If you will join me on this quest, I'd like to take you back in time, long before our modern era, and reintroduce you to your story, your Christian heritage. That will, I'm thrilled to say, require a trip in the DeLorean. But it may be the most important trip we could ever take. For if we don't know our own story, a story that will revisit not only our church fathers but the ancient voices we hear in Scripture, then our evangelical future will remain in jeopardy.

As you've probably guessed by now, I've been a Los Angeles Lakers fan as long as I can remember. Purple and gold have flowed through my family's veins for generations. My father and his twin brother used to sit on the court, under the hoop, at Lakers games when they were boys. Back in the 1960s and '70s, their idol was Jerry West, whose silhouette is worn on every NBA jersey to this day. He was better known as Mr. Clutch for his last-second game-winning shots. He once hit a sixty-foot Hail Mary to send the Lakers into overtime against the Knicks in Game 7 of the 1970 NBA Finals. I could go on and talk about Wilt Chamberlin and Kareem Abdul-Jabbar and their unstoppable sky hooks, about Earvin "Magic" Johnson's fast breaks and the beginning of "Showtime," about Shaquille O'Neal, a Hercules in the paint if there ever was one. And who can forget Kobe Bryant, who came as close as anyone to stealing Michael Jordan's reputation as the GOAT (greatest of all time).

But then there was a ten-year drought. No championships. No rings. The Lakers tried throwing money at the players, recruiting veteran soon-to-be-hall-of-famers to make up a team that looked, on paper at least, like a dream. It didn't work. As basketball purists know, there's more to a championship team than all-stars. However, there is one giant exception: the Dream Team. In 1992, the NBA put together an all-star lineup to compete in the Olympics. The team to compete in Barcelona, Spain, was like no other, including guards like Michael Jordan and Magic Johnson, forwards like Larry Bird and Charles Barkley, and centers like Patrick Ewing and David Robinson. And it worked: the Dream Team took home the gold.

Why mention the Dream Team in a book about the Trinity? *If we are to resist the temptation to manipulate the Trinity to*

The Dream Team

Point guards	Magic Johnson	Athanasius
	John Stockton	Hilary of Poitiers
Small guards	Michael "Air" Jordan	Augustine of Hippo
	Clyde "the Glide" Drexler	Gregory of Nyssa
Small forwards	Chris Mullin	Basil of Caesarea
	Scottie Pippen	Anselm
	Larry Bird	Thomas Aquinas
Power forwards	Charles Barkley	Gregory of Nazianzus
	Christian Laettner	John of Damascus
	Karl "the Mailman" Malone	Francis Turretin
Centers	David Robinson	John Owen
	Patrick Ewing	John Gill

serve whatever social program we wish, if we are to find our way home to the orthodox God of the Bible, then we need help. Not just any help, but an all-star team, one that cannot be beaten. To assemble this theological Dream Team, we must go back in time to the greats of the Great Tradition, those church fathers who battled with heretics and even put their lives on the line to ensure the church remained *faithful to the Scriptures*.

Why Can't I Just Quote the Bible?

Faithful to the Scriptures—now that is the key phrase. Our Dream Team is not a replacement for the Bible but a time-tested guide to interpreting the Bible. The Bible alone is our final, infallible authority. But as the saying goes, *every heretic has a Bible verse*. And, as we will see in chapter 2, the most dangerous heretics knew how to quote the Bible better than anyone, so it was essential to use extrabiblical words to safeguard the Bible's Trinity from manipulation.

It will not do then to have a Bible verse contest, as if whoever can quote the most verses wins. That's not how we come to know the Trinity anyway: there is no verse in the Bible that spells out the Trinity, but the Trinity is revealed to us in the story of the gospel (see chap. 4). But given how many times this gospel story has been used by heretics to distort our triune God, we must not be so prideful to think we don't need help interpreting the Bible. *We do need help.*

Acknowledging our need for help is the first step to approaching the Bible with *humility* and a faith that seeks understanding rather than the other way around. We will learn from the Bible-interpreting mistakes of the past so that we don't create a Trinity made in our own image (see chap. 3). We will gaze at the Bible with Christians who've come before us, asking them to open our eyes to the beauty of a Trinity we might not otherwise see. In doing so, we call on a tradition, the Great Tradition, that is deeply grounded *in the Scriptures*. Here's the point: interpreting the Bible with humility as God intended means interpreting the Bible *with the church*.

Many today will respond with a shout of protest: *No creed but the Bible!* That shout, however, is a selfish individualism, or what I call a crude, narrow biblicism, that masks itself in the name of biblical authority. *Sola scriptura* has been misunderstood, even radicalized, to mean *me* and *my* Bible alone. But that is a mindset captive to our culture's god: autonomous individualism. It fails to recognize that everyone who picks up a Bible is located within history and embedded within a specific tradition. That is not a bad thing; it should be celebrated, in fact.[3] The only question is

What Does *Sola Scriptura* Really Mean?

Sola scriptura is often misunderstood to mean the Bible is the *only* authority. But that is *solo scriptura*, a view held by radicals. *Sola scriptura* does not preclude other authorities in the church (creeds, councils, pastors, etc.). Rather, it means that Scripture alone is divine revelation and without error, and therefore our *final* authority. *Sola scriptura* is not anti-tradition but affirms a right view of tradition.

Tradition 0—Radicals and Rationalists
Since the apostles, the church has been lost and must be reinvented. Tradition is worthless and wicked; at best it carries little value. Only the Bible is the authority and source of theology.

Tradition 1—Protestant Reformers
The church has not been lost but needs reform. Tradition is essential to reform, helping us interpret the Bible properly, and carries authority in the church. But Scripture is the final authority.

Tradition 2—Roman Catholics
Tradition is a second source of infallible revelation, on par with or even above Scripture.

whether it is the right tradition or not, whether it is a tradition that helps or detracts from reading the Bible as God intended.

But more important still, such an individualistic approach to the Bible is not *biblical*. Now that is ironic. In a plethora of ways, the apostle Paul, for example, says the gospel he "received from the Lord" he then "delivered" or "handed on" (Latin: *trado*) to the church (1 Cor. 11:23). Later, he again reminds the church that he preached and handed down the gospel that they "received" (15:1). Paul also tells the church that if they are to "stand firm," then they must "hold to the traditions that you were taught by us, either by our spoken word or by our letter" (2 Thess. 2:15). And when Paul trains Timothy, he reminds Timothy that he first believed in the triune God of the Bible because his grandmother Lois and his mother Eunice were faithful to pass on the faith that they also received from others (2 Tim. 1:5; cf. 3:15). Paul reassures Timothy that the Spirit will "guard the good deposit entrusted to you" (2 Tim. 1:14). And like Paul, Jude commands the church to "contend for the faith that was once for all delivered to the saints" (v. 3).

"Delivered to the saints"—that sounds like a tradition. For this reason, the saints started using the Latin word *traditio*, which means "to hand down to another." They recognized that the gospel Jesus gave to his apostles was then given by the apostles to the church, just as Jesus intended. It should go without saying, but that gospel was trinitarian through and through. This trinitarian gospel tradition became known as the *rule of faith*, and it was recited with earnest joy whenever the church gathered together. It even took on written form, as seen in the Apostles' Creed. And when heresy threatened the trinitarian heart of this gospel summary, this rule of faith, the church universal met and wrote another creed—the Nicene Creed. The creed was faithful to Scripture, and for that reason was authoritative for Christians everywhere and always. *To depart from the Nicene Creed was to depart from biblical teaching itself. To abandon the Nicene Creed was to abandon the God of the gospel himself.*

The creed then is a ministerial authority, holding Christians accountable to the ultimate (magisterial) authority of the Bible. And no one so faithfully interpreted Scripture and the Nicene Creed like the Great Tradition—the theological Dream Team. By rigorous attention to the text of Scripture, they developed a well-thought plan that taught the church how to construct a doctrine of the Trinity from the Scriptures. In doing so, they helped the church stay faithful to the Trinity of the Bible over against Trinities distorted by manipulation.

And they still can. But I must warn you, it will involve a little time travel.

To the DeLorean!

I hope you're as excited as I am to travel in the DeLorean once more. But before we start punching numbers into the flux capacitor, allow me to tell you where we're going.

First, as I said, we need to hear a voice no longer heard today—that is, the voice of our church fathers. We will go back in time to the fourth century to understand why our fathers chose certain words and phrases to protect the Trinity of the Bible from heresy. We will also discover that they left us with a trinitarian grammar—a language, to be exact—that teaches us how to distinguish between Father, Son, and Holy Spirit as Scripture does but without compromising the oneness (simplicity) of our triune God. In the next chapter, we will meet these fathers who make up this Great Tradition, this theological Dream Team. And despite bad press, they are a team, for in their own ways they each retrieve that biblical teaching of the Nicene Creed. We will watch the Dream Team pass the ball, noticing how they work as one, the whole team assuming the same Nicene rules of the game, and each team member having his Nicene fundamentals down to ensure we remain faithful to the Scriptures.

Second, the DeLorean will take us back to the future to compare the biblical orthodoxy of our fathers with the radical changes to the Trinity by modern thinkers—and they are radical changes, to be sure. But not just modern thinkers; evangelical thinkers, too. Despite what we've been told, it will become conspicuous that many modern and evangelical portrayals of the Trinity are antithetical to the creeds and confessions the church has confessed as true to Scripture.

Third, the DeLorean will take us way, way back to the Scriptures themselves, where we will spend most of our time. When we arrive, a first-century Hebrew woman named Zipporah will guide us. We will hear what she first heard when she encountered Jesus speaking about his Father, and we will see what she first saw when she witnessed the Spirit descend at Pentecost. Through her eyes and ears, with careful exegesis and theological precision, we will approach the Bible *as a whole* and read the Bible *with the church* to understand how God has revealed himself as Father, Son, and Holy Spirit. But as we do, we will fight the temptation to manipulate who God is in himself with who we want him to be for the sake of our social programs.

By the end of this journey, this quest, the real Trinity will stand up, and you will encounter the *unmanipulated* Trinity, the One who is *simply Trinity*. Should you have a faith that seeks understanding, then you will believe simply when you see him who is simply Trinity.[4]

And now . . . I've always wanted to say this: *To the DeLorean!*

PART 1

HOW DID WE DRIFT AWAY?

I find that a lot of Protestant churches are embarrassed by things that are traditional, that as things become generationally older they lose relevance. . . . There's not just a great deal of loss but misrepresentation of what we are.

MARILYNNE ROBINSON

One generation shall commend your works to another, and declare your mighty acts.

PSALM 145:4

Can We Trust the God of Our Fathers?

Retrieving Biblical Orthodoxy

[With the Trinity], nowhere is erring more dangerous,
seeking more toilsome and finding more fruitful.

AUGUSTINE, *THE TRINITY*

If Christian theology today is sometimes in disarray—as,
indeed, I believe it is—then one of the major reasons is . . . its
lack of roots. . . . There can be few things more necessary for
the renewal of Christian theology than the promotion of awed
reading of classical Christian texts, scriptural and other.

JOHN WEBSTER, *THE CULTURE OF THEOLOGY*

TO THE DELOREAN!

Where we're going: The Nicene Creed, fourth century AD

Key point: Heretics used the Bible to subordinate the Son. The church fathers used extrabiblical words to protect the Trinity of the Bible. Each person is a "subsistence" of the same "simple" essence. Only eternal relations of origin (unbegotten Father, begotten Son, spirated Spirit) distinguish the persons. The Son is both distinct and equal to the Father because he is begotten from the Father's essence.

My Grandmother's Bible

On my desk sits an old Bible. To most people, it's just another Bible. But to me, it's much more. It's my grandmother's Bible, and before she died, she gave it to me. Every time I see it, I am reminded how God used my grandmother, and especially my own mother, to tell me about Jesus. If it weren't for them, I might not be a Christian at all.

Did you know that young Timothy felt the same way? *Don't forget who first shared the gospel with you,* the apostle Paul once wrote to Timothy. Who did first share Christ with Timothy? It wasn't Paul. It wasn't even an apostle. It was Timothy's grandmother Lois and his mother Eunice (2 Tim. 1:5). When Timothy remembered his heritage, he became bold for the gospel, unashamed (1:7–8). Timothy's heritage equipped him to guard the deposit entrusted to him (1:14).

Whether it's my grandmother or Timothy's, our faithfulness to the gospel of Jesus Christ more often than not depends on those who come before us. If they get Jesus wrong, so might we. If they misread their Bibles, so might we. Everything is at stake: if we are not faithful to the Scriptures and if we are not faithful to teach sound doctrine to the next generation, all could be lost.

I do not say that lightly but speak from personal experience. As I shared in the last chapter, I was a young student once, hungry to learn the Bible and its theology. But the standard textbooks my evangelical teachers put in my hands questioned, even rejected the biblical doctrine of the Trinity taught by the church for almost two thousand years. I was presented with a Trinity I was told I could trust, but as I dug deep, I discovered that the Trinity I was taught was novel in many ways, manipulated for a variety of agendas. I had been robbed of an inheritance that should have been passed down to any normal Christian. It's scary to think that I almost lost the Trinity altogether.

It's not an overstatement to say that all was almost lost once upon a time, just a few centuries after Paul wrote to Timothy. One pastor read the Bible incorrectly and passed on a heretical view of the Trinity to the next generation. He sparked a forest fire that threatened to destroy the heart of the Christian faith. Thankfully, some of the players on our Dream Team stood up to guard the good deposit entrusted to them. In this chapter, we will sit at their feet as they teach us how to read our Bible in a way that is faithful to the Trinity of the Bible.

It All Began with a Bible Study: Arius, the Spark That Lit the Forest on Fire

At the beginning of the fourth century AD, when the Christian church was still young, a dispute erupted that threatened the survival of Christianity as we know it. Sometime around the year 318, the bishop of Alexandria, whose name was Alexander, asked the presbyters (pastors) under his care to pick a hard text in the Old Testament and explain it. Not a bad idea. But no one guessed this basic Bible study would set the whole world on fire.

The pastor who lit the forest on fire was an older man by the name of Arius.[1] It's hard to be sure what text Arius expounded. It may have been Proverbs 8, a text that personifies wisdom, which the church before and after Arius interpreted as Christ.[2] Christ is the wisdom of God, and through wisdom God created the cosmos.

45

Except Arius took a different take on wisdom/Christ in Proverbs 8:22–25. When the text says God begat wisdom, Arius concluded that the Son was begotten or created (Arius treated these two words as synonyms). The Son may be begotten/created before time or the creation of the cosmos, but he has a beginning, a point at which he came into existence. While God has always existed, the Son has not, which means there was a point at which God became a Father.

That interpretation did not sit well with Alexander. In his sermons, Alexander taught, like many before him, that the biblical names—Father, Son, Spirit—are not random, meaningless inventions; rather, these names reveal who this Trinity is. The Son, for example, is Son because he is *from* the Father from all eternity, *begotten* by the Father before all ages, the *eternal* Son of God. This is what Scripture means whenever it calls Christ the *Son*.

But Arius was deeply disturbed by such a teaching.[3] It violated the central tenet of monotheism, producing not one but two gods. Arius was committed to the monarchy of God: God is not just one, but the one and only one who is *principle*. There can be, therefore, no other principle but him. For God to be God, he must be unbegotten. He alone is the *anarchos* (Greek), the one without a cause and beginning. But the Son is the *arche*, caused and brought into existence, having a beginning.[4]

Arius was also convinced Alexander had violated the Creator-creature distinction. The one monarch, God, is infinite, eternal, immutable, impassible, and therefore incomprehensible to created beings who are finite, temporal, mutable, and passible. By claiming that the Son, who became incarnate, is also God, one with the Father, Alexander had introduced change into the very nature of God. And not just any change, but the worst kind: passibility (emotional change and suffering). After all, we know that Jesus died on a cross; so the Son cannot be God as the Father is God, said Arius. Yes, the Son is begotten by the Father, and he is begotten

The Subordination of the Son

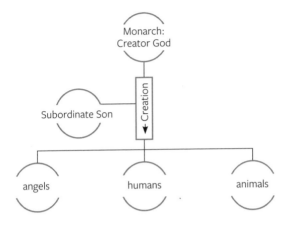

timelessly—Arius was no adoptionist, as if the man Christ Jesus was declared to be God's Son at the start of his incarnation. But, for Arius, the Son is not begotten from eternity either. He has a beginning. That way change and suffering may be characteristic of the Son but kept at bay from the Father. The two—Father and Son—must remain separate; they cannot be from the same divine nature, otherwise the divine nature would be vulnerable to change and suffering.

Additionally, if the Son is not begotten from the Father from all eternity, then he must, said Arius, be begotten/created *out of nothing* (Latin: *ex nihilo*). He is not, then, one with the monarch (God) in nature but exists in the created realm, though in between God and the rest of creation as the first one to be created. He is creation's Mediator before God. He is not from the very *being* of God, but the effect (or product) of God's *will*, external to God. As privileged as he is as the first of creation, the glory of God is bestowed upon him as a gift. The one monarch, God, remains incomprehensible to the Son, for he is not a Son by nature but by grace.

That said, a question lingers:

Question: With Arius's emphasis on the subordination of the Son, what is it then that unites the Father and the Son?

Arianism's answer: The unity cannot be a unity of being but can only be a unity of will.

What Does It Mean for God to Be One? Unity of Being versus Unity of Will

For Arius, the Son is not *eternally* begotten nor is he eternally begotten from the Father's *divine nature*; therefore, he cannot be consubstantial (from the same nature or substance) with the Father in divinity. If he is not coeternal with the Father as the Son, who is eternally begotten by the Father, then he cannot be coequal either. As one who is not generated from the Father's divine nature, neither coeternal nor coequal with the Father, the unity the Son has with the Father can never be a unity of being, nature, or essence, or what theologians like to call *ontology*. At best, the Son shares a unity of will, the Son cooperating with the will of his Father; the unity is merely *functional*.

The Son, then, is not in a different category from the rest of creation; he is merely the best and first of creation. Generated by the Father, he is the pinnacle of the created order, but nonetheless still part of the created order, still an effect of the divine will as is the rest of the cosmos. Generated/created by the Father, the Son does not share the same divine attributes as the Father. The divine nature is characterized by infinitude (God is immeasurable), eternity (God is timeless), immutability (God does not change), impassibility (God is not vulnerable to emotional fluctuation; he does not suffer), etc. But the same cannot be said of the Son. For he is a creature, and creatures do not share such divine attributes. Like the rest of creation, the Son is not infinite and eternal (there once was a time when the Son was not), immutable (he changes), or impassible (he suffers).

If the Son is attributed divinity in any sense, it is only in this sense: divinity is not his by nature but is bestowed on him by grace. Since he was the first to be created, he is unique, granted a special participation in the glory of God. Nevertheless, that grant is a gift, something the Son receives; it is not something intrinsic to his nature.[5] He is Son by grace, not by nature. *Grace rather than nature*—that is the nucleus of the problem. Which is why Arius cannot say that the unity in the Trinity is one of nature; it can only be a unity of will. Don't miss this: with such an emphasis on will, Arianism is not only an *ontological* subordination but a *functional* subordination of the Son. In other words, the Son is inferior not only as a person but in his actions.

Begotten, Not Created: Nicaea

The teachings of Arius and his supporters proved as explosive as dynamite, and the blast ruptured unity in the church. In an effort to regain lost unity, the emperor Constantine called a church council, recruiting theologians from the East and the West to represent the church universal. In AD 325, a year that would go down in history, bishops and delegates assembled in Nicaea, which is in modern-day Turkey. Alexander of Alexandria, the one Arius first reacted to with consternation, was sure to attend, and some deacons were welcome too, including Alexander's up-and-coming theologian, Athanasius.

Did Arius show up? He did, along with other like-minded colleagues such as Eusebius of Nicomedia.[6] But the council did not side with the Arians. After an in-depth evaluation, they decided Arianism was contrary to Scripture, even a heresy. They also wrote a creed to help the church know what Scripture does teach about the Trinity, a creed to be confessed in churches everywhere. The creed read as follows:

> We believe in one God, the Father All Governing, creator of all things visible and invisible.

And in one Lord Jesus Christ, the Son of God, begotten from the Father as only begotten, that is, from the essence of the Father [*ek tēs ousias tou patros*], God from God, Light from Light, true God from true God, begotten not created, of the same essence as the Father [*homoousion tō patri*], through whom all things came into being, both in heaven and in earth; Who for us men and for our salvation came down and was incarnate, becoming human. He suffered and the third day he rose, and ascended into the heavens. And he will come to judge both the living and the dead.

And [we believe] in the Holy Spirit.

But, those who say, Once he was not, or he was not before his generation, or he came to be out of nothing, or who assert that he, the Son of God, is of a different *hypostasis* or *ousia*, or that he is a creature, or changeable, or mutable, the Catholic and Apostolic Church anathematizes them.[7]

Notice, first of all, the emphasis on the eternal generation of the Son. He is begotten from the Father. But by "begotten," the Nicene fathers did not mean what the Arians meant, that the Son is created. No, the Son is begotten, not made. There's a difference. For us creatures, to be begotten is to come into existence for the first time. Arius was so literal in his thinking that he could not understand that the biblical metaphor, when applied to God, defies any limitations it might have in our world. Yes, the Son is begotten—that is the very definition of a Son. But since this is the eternal, infinite, immutable, and impassible God we are talking about, the Son's generation is eternal, infinite, immutable, and impassible, meaning he can have no beginning as creation does.

Also notice—and this is extremely important—the creed says the Son is begotten from the *ousia* of the Father. What does that mean? They used this Greek word *ousia* to refer to the essence of God. Excuse the pun, but that word *ousia* gets at the essence of divinity. Remember, Arius thought the Son was begotten as a creature, a product of the Father's will, and therefore cannot be of the same essence as the Father. But the Nicene fathers argued that the Son is begotten from the same essence of the Father. Eternal generation does not undermine the Son as coeternal and coequal; eternal

> **Key Word** | **Essence**
>
> *ousia* = God's essence (nature)
>
> The Son is begotten from the Father's *ousia* (essence). For that reason, he is *homoousios,* from the same essence as the Father.

generation safeguards the Son as coeternal and coequal. Only if he is eternally begotten from the Father's essence is he wholly divine.

This is often missed in presentations of Nicaea, as if all the council said was that the Son is equal to the Father. But the council said more—way more. The Son is equal to the Father *because* the Son is "begotten . . . of the same essence as the Father." It's not enough to focus on terms like *ousia,* as if we could do enough word studies to come up with a trinitarian formula. That approach leaves the door of manipulation open to read whatever concept of the Trinity we want into words like *ousia.* A far better approach, a far more Nicene approach, is to read these terms in context. For Nicaea, the context of words like *ousia* is in plain sight: it is eternal generation.[8] "Begotten" is the first thing the creed says about the Son. Only after "begotten" is addressed does the creed apply the word *homoousios* to the Son, a word we will learn about soon. For unless the Son is begotten from the Father's essence, he cannot be said to be equal in divinity to the Father.

The Nicene fathers appealed to biblical imagery to establish the Son as the begotten one. When they confess the Son to be Light from Light, passages like John 1 and Hebrews 1 are in view, leading the Nicene fathers to conclude that the Son is true God of true God. As light is from light, so the Son is from the Father.[9] Yes, the Son is distinguishable as a begotten person, but the fact that he is begotten also conveys he is from the same essence, accentuating his coequality. If the Son is Light from Light, then it is appropriate to call him *homoousios* as well. It's a Greek word, *homo* meaning "same" and *ousia* meaning "essence." The Son is not from a different essence as the Father. Nor is the Son from a similar but not identical essence as the Father. As one who is begotten from the *ousia* or essence of the Father, the Son must be from the *same* (identical) essence as the Father.

Think of it this way: the Son is *coessential*, meaning he shares the same divine essence; he is *consubstantial*, meaning he shares in the same divine substance. Begotten from the Father's essence from all eternity, the Son's existence originates from the same eternal, divine essence as the Father, which means he is coequal, true God of true God. Lest we doubt that, Nicaea leads us to consider the works of God: the Father creates the world *through his Son*. Unlike Arius, who positions the Son on the side of the created order, Nicaea identifies the Son with the Creator himself, indeed as the Creator himself.

In the end, Arius rejected the creed, as did two other bishops who took Arius's position. The detractors were sent into exile, and it appeared Constantine had achieved the unity he was after. However, the decades after Nicaea were tumultuous as controversy moved beyond Arius.[10] Arius sparked the controversy, but many others fueled the flames.

Looking for Trouble, Finding It Everywhere: After Nicaea

Comedian Groucho Marx once said, "Politics is the art of looking for trouble, finding it everywhere, diagnosing it incorrectly, and applying the wrong remedies." I doubt Groucho had the aftermath of Nicaea in mind, but he might as well have. At first the Arians were exiled; then Nicene supporters like Athanasius were exiled. And back and forth it went, depending on who was in political power.

But it wasn't just politics that got messy; so did theology. Everyone loves a good story about good versus evil, the good guys coming out on top over those maleficent bad guys. But such neat categories don't always make for reliable history. In all the ruckus there emerged a cluster of competing positions, and it was not always clear which one would prevail in the end.[11] For example, some took the Arian view to its logical end and argued that the Son is from a different essence than the Father. They became known as Neo-Arians, and they stressed that the Son is unlike the Father, subordinating the Son to the Father.[12]

But others protested, saying the Son is like the Father. Nevertheless, they drew a hard line: the Son is like the Father . . . but only in *activity*.[13] Their camp (known as *Homoians*) grew in popularity; after all, they appeared to be biblical, focusing on what the Son does in salvation history, functionally subordinating the Son.

Still others wanted to say more: the Son is not only like the Father in function, he is like the Father in essence. That was the Father's intention, to beget a Son *like* himself.[14] But they were not willing to say, with Nicaea, that the Son is begotten from the Father's essence (*homoousios*). They worried that might confuse the Son with the Father, as if there is no difference between them. Instead, the Son must only be similar or like the Father in essence (*homoiousios*).[15] You need not be an expert in Greek to recognize that the difference came down to one single letter: *i*. Who knew one little Greek letter could be the difference between orthodoxy and heresy?

Is your head spinning yet? If it is, that's a good sign. It means you, too, see the need for clarity. Athanasius and three wise men from the East also saw this need. Let's meet them and find out what they did to help the church out of this fog.

It's Greek to Me

Ousia = essence

Homoousios = same essence (Nicaea)
Homoiousios = similar/like essence
Heteroousios = different/unlike essence

Simply Trinity

One important step forward can be credited to Athanasius, who defended the eternal generation of the Son from the Father by appealing to divine *simplicity*. In theology, simplicity does not mean God is elementary or basic. It means God is not made up of, composed of, or compounded by parts. For example, God does not merely possess attributes, as if his attributes are different parts of his essence, each part compatible with every other part. That is not simplicity but merely congruence. Rather, simplicity means that God's essence just *is* his attributes, and his attributes his essence. Scripture, for instance, does not merely say God possesses love, but that he *is* love. God does not merely perform good acts, but he *is* good. In other words, God's attributes are not one thing and his essence another thing, but all that is in God *is* God. Incorporeal and immutable, God is identical with his perfections.[16] This is what it means for God to be one.

Why would Athanasius appeal to simplicity when he is talking about the Trinity? To show that the Son is begotten from the *Father's* essence. That's what it means for the Son to be *homoousios* with the Father: begotten from the Father's divine essence (*ousia*) from all eternity.

Here the title of our book is relevant: we avoid heresies like Arianism when we affirm God to be *simply Trinity*—simplicity in essence, Trinity in persons. To say that the triune God is simple is to say that all that is true of the divine essence (eternity, immutability, etc.) is true of each and every person of the Godhead. The Son is no exception to that rule; he, too, is "simply God," as Stephen Holmes says, "equally identical with all the divine properties."[17]

What does simplicity have to do with doctrines like eternal generation? A lot. Simplicity helps us differentiate, for example, between human generation and divine generation. Listen to Athanasius: "As then men create not as God creates, as their being is not such as God's being, so men's generation is in one way, and the Son is from the Father in another. For the offspring of men are portions of their fathers, since the very nature of bodies is not uncompounded, but in a state of flux, and composed of parts; and men lose their substance in begetting,

| Key Word | Simplicity |

God's essence is without parts. There is no composition in God. All that is in God is God. Simplicity is true of each person in the Trinity, since each person is a subsistence of the divine essence. The persons are not "parts" that compose God, nor is one person a "portion" of another person.

and again they gain substance from the accession of food. And on this account men in their time become fathers of many children."[18]

What is Athanasius saying? Generation cannot apply to the Trinity in the same way it applies to humanity. The reason why: the triune God is *simple.* "God, being without parts, is Father of the Son without partition or passion; for there is neither effluence of the Immaterial, nor influx from without, as among men; and being uncompounded in nature, He is Father of One Only Son."[19]

Later on, Athanasius gets more specific: why is it, for instance, that Scripture says the Son is *from* the Father? Nicaea answered that question: to be *from* the Father is to be begotten from the essence of the Father. The Arians looked at Scripture and assumed the Son is "from God" as a creature is from God, as if "the Word of God differed nothing from us." In contrast, Nicaea used *ousia* (essence) language when referring to eternal generation to differentiate between the Son and the rest of creation. "For though all things be said to be from God, yet this is not in the sense in which the Son is from Him," said Athanasius. "Since He is not a creature, He alone is . . . 'from the Father.'" We must "say that the Son is 'from the essence of the Father.'"[20]

So whenever we hear that phrase "one in essence," we should not "imagine partitions and divisions of the Godhead," as if something material is in view. Rather, "having our thoughts directed to things immaterial, let us preserve undivided the oneness of nature and the identity of light; for this is proper to a son as regards a father, and in this is shewn that God is truly Father of the Word."[21]

In the decades after Nicaea, Athanasius would not be alone in his appeal to simplicity in the Trinity. Three theologians from Cappadocia offered support: Gregory of Nyssa, Basil of Caesarea, and Gregory of Nazianzus. For the Cappadocians, affirming simplicity in the Trinity not only meant the persons held the essence in common. It meant more: the persons were consubstantial with one another because they were one in *will* and *power*.[22] Will and power are not separate from the essence, as if they can be divided up in different degrees among the persons, for example. No, will and power are to be identified with the one essence. We mortals tend to distinguish between essence, will, and power for the sake of comprehension and clarity, but we must remember that they are *not* parts in God. Indeed, they are one and the same. God is one, the three persons having one essence, will, and power.

As we will see in the next chapter, many in the modern era rejected God's simplicity, evangelicals included.[23] "It doesn't make sense!" they protested. "Plus," they grumbled, "we should not focus on simplicity (oneness) but on the persons of the Trinity instead (threeness)." Many then said there is no simplicity in God at all but three separate centers of consciousness and will. Each person is his own self-determining, self-willing subject. Some so divided the persons from one another that they created gradations of authority within God (see chap. 8).

Ahead of their time, the Cappadocians will have none of this. It's inconceivable. For example, Gregory of Nazianzus, responding to those Arians who said the Son has a different *will* than the Father, counters, "We have one Godhead, so We have one Will."[24] If there is but one essence, so too must there be one will, otherwise the persons are divided (tritheism) or subordinated (Arianism). "For I cannot see how that which is common to two [Father, Son] can be said to belong to one alone [Father]."[25]

Can the same be said of *power*? It must. "For one is not more and another less God; nor is One before and another after; nor are They divided in will or parted in power." Gregory then concludes by asserting their simplicity: "But each of these Persons possesses Unity, not less with that which is United to it than with itself, by reason of the identity of Essence and Power."[26]

If the persons of the Trinity are one in essence, will, and power—*simply* Trinity—then it also follows that they work inseparably in creation and salvation. Indivisible in essence, indivisible in operation, the church fathers liked to say. Singular in nature and will, the persons perform a singular action. Separate, individual centers of consciousness and will may be true of created persons but cannot be true of divine persons, otherwise the Godhead would be divided.[27] What theologians call *inseparable operations* was so indispensable in the Cappadocian defense of Nicaea that Gregory of Nyssa said we should infer the oneness of the Trinity's nature from the identity of their single operation, and Gregory of Nazianzus made the Trinity's simplicity his launching pad to then discuss what distinguishes the persons.[28]

This idea of inseparable operations is so important that we will devote all of chapter 10 to exploring it. It is a core component of orthodoxy, to be sure. When Lewis Ayres, a world-renowned expert on the Trinity, lists the three essential conditions for one to be pro-Nicene, a belief in inseparable operations is one of them.[29]

Simply *Trinity*

A second essential step on the road to further clarity occurred when the church fathers decided that for all the good found in the creed of Nicaea, one sentence proved ambiguous and needed further clarification: the anathema at the end of the creed. It condemns Arianism outright, quoting Arian phrases even. So far, so good. But it also condemns those who say the Son "is of a different *hypostasis* or *ousia*" than the Father. At the time of Nicaea, these two Greek terms were treated as synonyms, which created much confusion and debate after Nicaea. To some, it sounded like Nicaea was saying that the person of the Son is the same person as the Father. Some thought the creed had succumbed to Sabellianism, an early church heresy that said there is only one divine person (not three) who merely reveals himself in three different ways.[30] In an attempt to emphasize the equality of the Son with the Father through eternal generation, had the creed confused the Father and the Son, as if they are the same person?[31]

Nicaea, however, was not advocating Sabellianism, and in the years ahead it became crucial to overcome such an accusation. Remember, Nicaea distinguished between the persons when it said the Son is begotten from the Father. By contrast, Sabellianism viewed the persons as mere *functions*, as if what makes God Father, Son, and Spirit are the diverse forms he takes when he creates or saves humanity. However, since the creed of Nicaea used the two Greek words *ousia* and *hypostasis* as synonyms, many struggled to take the creed seriously. Like throwing down an ace of spades just when everyone thought the game was lost, the Cappadocians made a major contribution at precisely this point. On the one hand, they persuaded many to stick with the original language of the creed—the Son is *homoousios* (one in essence) with the Father. But! The Son is not the same person as the Father. While there is only one essence (*mia ousia*), there are three persons (*treis hypostaseis*). This distinction did wonders and even brought opponents together.

That's not the only contribution the Cappadocians made. Not only did they distinguish between the essence and the persons, but

How Does Scripture Distinguish the Persons?

Unbegotten = Father
Begotten = Son
Spiration (procession) = Spirit

they also introduced a vocabulary, along with the Great Tradition
that followed, that kept the church from confusing the persons
with each other. This vocabulary was not speculative but was just
another way of explaining what the Bible means when it calls God
Father, Son, and Holy Spirit:

> The Father is *unbegotten*: the Bible calls the Father *Father*
> because he begets his Son (paternity), though he himself is
> begotten by no one.
>
> The Son is *begotten* (*generated*): the Bible calls the Son *Son*
> because he is begotten by his Father (filiation).
>
> The Spirit is *spirated*: the Bible calls the Spirit *Spirit* because
> he is breathed out by the Father and Son (spiration).

To sum up these distinctions, the church thought hard about
phrases it could use to describe these biblical names. The Nicene
fathers and the Great Tradition that followed came up with three
phrases:

1. Modes of subsistence (existence)[32]
2. Eternal relations of origin
3. Personal properties[33]

These phrases may sound strange, but they are essential. Some
called these *modes of subsistence (existence)*, the word "subsistence" referring to the way the one essence of God "subsists" or
"exists" in a unique way in each person. Others used the phrase
eternal relations of origin, "relations" referring not to relation-
ships (which is a modern, psychological category) but to each
person's everlasting provenance. Some even combined the two,
calling the persons subsisting relations. Still others said paternity, filiation, and spiration are properties unique to each person. The persons are identical in all things *except* these personal
properties.[34]

Three to Remember

Modes of subsistence (existence)
Eternal relations of origin
Personal properties

These phrases are different ways of referring to the Father as unbegotten, the Son as begotten, and the Spirit as spirated. These *alone* distinguish the persons.

For example, consider one of the Cappadocians: Gregory of Nyssa. Gregory defends the Trinity's simplicity, but then he asks what it is that distinguishes the persons. Answer: their "mode of existence." When, for example, we say that the Father is unbegotten, we are "taught in what mode He exists." When we say that the "Son does not exist without generation," we are taught to say that this is the Son's "mode of existence."[35]

On the one hand, the "question of existence is one" (simplicity); on the other hand, the "mode of existence is another" (Trinity). For example, consider the Spirit. "Every excellent attribute is predicated of the Holy Spirit just as it is predicated of the Father and of the Son [simplicity], with the exception of those by which the Persons are clearly and distinctly divided from each other."[36] Gregory is distinguishing between *essential* properties, those attributes synonymous with the divine essence (power, holiness, etc.), attributes all three persons hold in common, and *personal* properties, the Father as unbegotten, the Son as begotten, the Spirit as spirated, which alone distinguish the persons. That word "alone" is key. Perhaps you've used that word when referring to the five *solas* of the Reformation (like *sola gratia*, grace alone). But the word *sola* could also be applied here: the only thing that marks each person in distinction from the others are modes of subsistence, eternal relations, or personal properties.

Despite this breakthrough by the Cappadocians, some still had questions: if the Son is a different person from the Father, what is it that makes him one in essence (*homoousios*) with the Father?

Why Is the Son One in Essence with the Father?

To answer that question, we must set the record straight: the phrase "one essence, three persons" wasn't a motto all on its own, as if to be Nicene all one had to do was say the magic words. Remember, the distinction itself was embedded within a context: eternal generation. The reason the Son is one in essence with the Father is because he is eternally begotten from the Father's essence. (How about that: eternal generation not only distinguishes the Son but ensures his equality.)

As Athanasius said, "The Son is ever the proper offspring of the *Father's essence.*"[37] That is basic to the biblical metaphor itself: "A man by counsel builds a house, but *by nature [essence]* he begets a son . . . the son is proper offspring of the *father's essence*, and is not external to him."[38] The Cappadocians said the same. Gregory of Nyssa writes, the "Only-begotten" Son "is in the Father, and so, *from His nature [essence],*" and for that reason there never was a time when the Son "existed not."[39] Did those in the West agree? They did. After all, they were articulating the same creed. For example, Augustine wrote that in eternal "generation the Father *bestows being* on the Son without any beginning in time, without any changeableness of nature." And not just eternal generation, but eternal spiration too: "so does procession from them both [Father and Son] *bestow being* on the Holy Spirit without any beginning in time, without any changeableness in nature."[40] After Augustine, countless others said the same.[41]

Through eternal generation, the one essence is communicated from the Father to the Son.[42] The Father can do so because he has the divine essence from himself; he does not receive the essence from another person but is unbegotten.[43] While the Arians

protested that such a generation must subordinate the Son
(a charge still leveled today
by critics), these fathers responded by pointing out what
the Nicene Creed before them
had also said: generation from
the Father's *ousia* (essence) is
eternal and immutable. It is
not like human generation.

The point is this: as much
as we distinguish between essence and persons, we dare not

Key Word	Subsistence

Latin: *subsistentia* (translated
into Greek as *hypostasis*)

The divine essence has three
modes of subsistence. Each
person is a subsistence of the
divine nature. Example: the Son
is begotten from the Father's
essence. For that reason, he is
one in essence (*homoousios*),
coequal, and coeternal with the
Father.

separate them. We can keep them together if we use one of those
trusty phrases to say that the one, simple essence has three modes
of subsistence, or the one essence subsists in three persons. Or, if
we get uber nerdy and start mixing phrases, we might even say each
person is a subsisting relation. Why use all this technical jargon?
We use it to say our God is simply Trinity.

The Spirit Under Fire

The Cappadocians, however, not only defended the Son against
subordinationism, but the Spirit as well, which brings to the surface one of their finest moments.

The struggle over the Trinity was complicated further when a
group sprouted out of an already tumultuous ecclesiastical and
political soil and applied the Arian logic to the Holy Spirit. They
became vocal in the 370s in particular and were called the "fighters
against the Spirit," or *Pneumatomachi*, contesting the coequality and
coeternality of the Spirit and claiming that the Spirit cannot be called
homoousios. He is but a creature, inferior to the Father and the Son.

Their claims ignited a literary backlash from the Cappadocians, who defended not only the eternal generation of the Son

but the eternal spiration of the Spirit as well. The Spirit is not a second Son, for he is not generated. Instead, as the biblical name for Spirit (*pneuma*) indicates, he is *spirated*, proceeding from the Father from all eternity, and given to us in history for the sake of our salvation. The Spirit is a gift.

The Spirit's spiration or procession was considered the Spirit's personal property or eternal relation of origin, and it not only distinguished the Spirit as a *hypostasis* but protected the Spirit as coeternal and coequal with the Father and the Son. For the Spirit did not proceed from a different or merely similar divine nature, but from the Father and the Son's divine nature. His spiration ensures he holds the same divine nature in common as the Father and the Son. At points, the Cappadocians did not use the language of *homoousios* with the Spirit, but only because they sought to win over those who might stumble over the vocabulary.

Nevertheless, the Cappadocians embarked on an apologetic defense of the Spirit's coequality by appealing not only to divine titles applied to the Spirit but especially to divine works—creation, salvation—attributed to the Spirit. Since the Spirit is not a lesser deity nor a created entity, the Spirit is to be worshiped alongside the Father and the Son, otherwise our worship is not fully trinitarian. As with the Son, the Cappadocians believed the consequences for salvation were significant: "Were the Spirit not to be worshiped, how could he deify me through baptism?" asked Gregory of Nazianzus. "From the Spirit comes our rebirth, from rebirth comes a new creating, from new creating a recognition of the worth of him who effected it."[44]

At Last: Constantinople

These advances on Nicaea—connecting simplicity and Trinity, distinguishing between essence and person, affirming the eternal procession of the Spirit—begged for another council, one that would reaffirm the creed of Nicaea but this time with a more elaborate statement on the Spirit.[45]

Constantinople was ripe for just such a council, thanks to the emperor Theodosius. In AD 381, bishops were summoned once more, this time in Constantinople (modern-day Istanbul). Unfortunately, Athanasius and Basil of Caesarea had died by then. Nevertheless, their contributions were not forgotten but echoed and celebrated by the Eastern bishops who arrived in Constantinople. In many ways, Constantinople retrieved and reaffirmed the creed of Nicaea (AD 325) as binding and authoritative. But the creed Constantinople gave birth to is known as the Nicene-Constantinopolitan Creed, or more concisely, the Nicene Creed.

The Nicene Creed (AD 381)

We believe in one God, the Father All Governing, creator of heaven and earth, of all things visible and invisible.

And in one Lord Jesus Christ, the only-begotten Son of God, begotten from the Father before all time, Light from Light, true God from true God, begotten not created, of the same essence as the Father [*homoousion tō patri*], through Whom all things came into being; Who for us men and because of our salvation came down from heaven, and was incarnate by the Holy Spirit and the Virgin Mary and became human. He was crucified for us under Pontius Pilate, and suffered and was buried and rose on the third day, according to the Scriptures; and ascended to heaven, and sits on the right hand of the Father, and will come again with glory to judge the living and the dead. His kingdom shall have no end.

And in the Holy Spirit, the Lord and life-giver, Who proceeds from the Father, Who is worshiped and glorified together with the Father and Son, Who spoke through the prophets; and in one, holy, catholic, and apostolic Church. We confess one baptism for the remission of sins. We look forward to the resurrection of the dead and the life of the world to come. Amen.

(John H. Leith, ed., *Creeds of the Churches*, 30–31)

That is fitting: Constantinople was not writing a new creed, only reaffirming what was said at Nicaea but with further clarifications now in view.

Constantinople proved a major advance for the cause of Nicaea. By no means did debate cease after 381. However, the Nicene Creed further solidified the cause of orthodoxy first defended by Athanasius and advanced by the Cappadocians, only to be perpetuated and celebrated by the Great Tradition, both East and West, that we will explore throughout the rest of our quest.

That said, what kind of authority did the Great Tradition believe the Nicene Creed should have in the church? That is a question relevant for the church today.

The Authority of the Nicene Creed for the Apostolic Church, Yesterday and Today

We should not overlook that second-to-last line of the Nicene Creed: "We believe . . . in one, holy, catholic, and apostolic Church." That is no throwaway line. This is not a reference to the Roman Catholic Church; that would be anachronistic, since it did not yet exist as we know it today. Rather, it is a reference to the church universal, and this church is not only universal but holy and apostolic. It is universal *because* it is holy and apostolic. The fathers are claiming, in other words, that this Trinity they confess is none other than the Trinity of the Scriptures, the same Scriptures penned by the apostles. For that reason, the creed carries authority in the church, and not just the church of the fourth century but the church *universal*, across all lands and spanning all eras, East and West.

That said, the Nicene Creed is not a dead letter; rather, it carries authority to this day. No, it is not on par with Scripture; it is not a source of divine revelation. But since it conforms to Scripture, it is to be adhered to, confessed, and celebrated in the church to this day. *To depart from the creed is to depart from scriptural teaching itself.*

As we will see in chapters 3 and 8, too many evangelicals today—some with an agenda to make the Trinity relevant, others out of a biblicist spirit of individualism—reject parts of the creed, like eternal generation. That is not to be taken lightly. Our roots are catholic in every way, reaching all the way back to the church fathers and their apostolic confes-

Key Word	Heresy

Heresy is a belief that contradicts, denies, or undermines a doctrine that an ecumenical church council has declared biblical and essential to Christianity. What makes heresy so subtle and dangerous? It is nurtured *within* the church and is wrapped within Christian vocabulary. Its representatives even quote the Bible. It often presents itself as the whole truth when it is a half-truth.

sions. Our default instinct should not be a hermeneutic of suspicion but a hermeneutic of trust, one that breeds humility, an eagerness to sit as a pupil at the feet of orthodoxy rather than stand over it as its lord. So that any time we hear anyone—no matter how many degrees they have attached to their name—dismiss or reject the creed, our natural *apostolic* instincts should kick in and we should ask, "Brother, sister, why is your first instinct to distrust the God of our fathers and their *credo*?"

If we are to default in one direction or the other, it should be in the direction of orthodoxy, not heresy. Unfortunately, with the arrival of the modern era came a hailstorm of modern theologians pelting the church with a hermeneutic of distrust toward the God of our fathers, determined to either dispose of orthodoxy altogether or modify the Trinity of orthodoxy so that it could meet their social agenda.

To that story we now turn.

Since When Did the Trinity Get Social?

The Manipulated Trinity

I see the twentieth-century renewal of Trinitarian theology as depending in large part on concepts and ideas that cannot be found in patristic, medieval, or Reformation accounts of the doctrine of the Trinity. In some cases, indeed, they are points explicitly and energetically repudiated as erroneous—even occasionally as formally heretical.

STEPHEN HOLMES, *THE QUEST FOR THE TRINITY*

Would it not be wise to accept the doctrine
of the immanent trinity of God?

KARL BARTH,
LETTER TO JÜRGEN MOLTMANN, 1964

TO THE DELOREAN!

Where we're going: Twentieth century—our recent past.

Key point: Trinity drift. Social trinitarianism has redefined the biblical, orthodox Trinity. Danger: tritheism. Social trinitarianism has manipulated the Trinity for a myriad of social agendas. Danger: a Trinity made in our own image.

Haunted by the Ghost of Orthodoxy Past

There is one day of the year my family looks forward to with relentless anticipation. Once bellies are full from a week's worth of Thanksgiving leftovers, I announce to my kids that it's time, it's finally time. They look at me with eyes as big as acorns, jump off the couch, and scramble to throw on their winter coats and lace up their hiking boots. We all know it's cold, but it's worth it.

When we arrive at the Christmas tree farm, the contest begins: who will find this year's perfect Christmas tree? It's the one plump with needles and tall enough to wear three, maybe four strands of colored lights, but not too tall that it cannot be capped by an angel before it reaches the living room ceiling. Once we spot that angelic pine, the heavens open and God himself looks down and sees that it is good. It is the one.

That's what's supposed to happen. Most years I'm yelling at the kids to stop fighting over which tree they want while I publicly embarrass myself with my total inability to saw a tree trunk no thicker than six inches. But once I've conquered nature and have enough sap on my hands to prove it, once Mom and Dad have scarred the kids for life with all their Christmas cheer, we drive back home, plant that tree in our living room, and the decorating begins.

Afterward, Mom makes everyone hot chocolate, and we sit down by the fireplace to listen to a Christmas story while staring at a tree now blushing red, orange, blue, and green. There are many fine stories to choose from, but few as fitting as Charles Dickens's *A Christmas Carol*. The story begins with Scrooge, a heartless businessman if there ever was one. Scrooge was not always this way, but through a series of life decisions, his heart was arrested by the love of money at the expense of relationships, and Scrooge became "hard and sharp as flint." And no season of the year made him so uncomfortable as the season of giving itself.

But one Christmas Eve, Scrooge is visited by the ghost of Marley, his old business partner. And what an awful, fearful ghost he is. The very sound of him is tortuous: chains wrapped around his legs like snakes, clinking and clanging with every step. "I wear the chain I forged in life," says Marley. "I made it link by link, and yard by yard; I girded it on of my own free will, and of my own free will I wore it." And so, too, has Scrooge. Soon enough, like Marley, he will go to a place where there is "no rest, no peace" but "incessant torture of remorse."[1] Before he leaves, Marley promises three ghosts will visit Scrooge to haunt him about his past, present, and future.

Later that night, Scrooge is woken by a "bright clear jet of light"; it is the Ghost of Christmas Past, wearing a "great extinguisher for a cap." Back in time they travel and stop just at that point in life when Scrooge is in his prime. A young woman, with tears in her eyes, sits next to the young Scrooge, lamenting that a golden idol has displaced her. Try as she might, she can no longer compete with this idol; wealth has become his one passion. Watching his cold self prefer this one passion to a woman who could have been his wife is too much to bear, and Scrooge begs the Ghost of Christmas Past to take him away. So he does, but only to transfer him in time to yet another haunting memory from his past. Try as he might to extinguish the ghost's radiant light with its snuffer hat, Scrooge discovers that he cannot escape his past; it has forever shaped who he is and what he will inevitably become.

The story of Scrooge, read afresh each year at Christmas, reminds us what to live for, what it is in life that really matters. What could be worse than a life lived and nearly finished only to be full of regrets, haunted by the past? Thanks to the Ghost of Christmas Past, Scrooge is scared sober, with still enough time to change his ways. And change he does.

But it's not just individuals who can be haunted by the past; entire movements and historical eras can be too. Sometimes we are so nearsighted that we cannot see the big picture of where we've been and where we're headed. And so, the haunting begins—that's if we're lucky enough for a ghost to show up and scare us stiff.

I don't want to get creepy—we are, after all, talking about Christmas, not Halloween. But consider this chapter the Ghost of Orthodoxy Past. Lewis Ayres, one of today's leading experts on the Trinity, tells us that there is a great divide between the biblical, orthodox doctrine of the Trinity, which can be traced back to the Nicene Creed, and the modern understanding of the Trinity over the last hundred years. However, this modern Trinity has snuffed out the biblical, orthodox Trinity, even pretended to be the orthodox Trinity, until there is little of orthodoxy that remains. It's not merely that "modern Trinitarianism has engaged with pro-Nicene theology badly." The situation is way worse: "it has barely engaged with it at all." "As a result the legacy of Nicaea remains paradoxically the *unnoticed ghost at the modern Trinitarian feast.*"[2]

Not that long ago, this ghost went unnoticed at the trinitarian party, but now it haunts us, and its moans are only growing louder, its blinding light so bright no candle snuffer can extinguish it. To see why, we must walk through the rooms in this haunted house we call *modern Christianity*, rooms that explain and expose the recent past. But don't be fooled, it's *our* recent past. It's *my* recent past too. As I shared, I was once taught a modern view of the Trinity as if it was the Bible's view of the Trinity. But the Ghost of Orthodoxy Past kept haunting me. What I discovered in these haunted rooms will be frightening for us to see: *the Trinity of the Bible, our Trinity, has been manipulated beyond recognition. The guest of honor at the trinitarian feast is not the biblical, orthodox Trinity at all. Trinity drift is real. And we are its victims.*

Question is, how did we get here? That is a question the Ghost of Orthodoxy Past can answer.

Room #1: The Trinity Is Speculative and Irrelevant to Society—Protestant Liberalism Abandons Biblical Orthodoxy

For sixteen hundred years, the Great Tradition believed that God revealed himself as Trinity in the Scriptures. That assumption was thrown into question with the arrival of the eighteenth century and an intellectual revolution known as the Enlightenment. The revolution began when thinkers taught that there was an ugly broad ditch separating absolute truth (located in human reason) from contingent truth (located in history). While our reason can give us universal truth, history cannot; it is capricious. Why? It cannot be demonstrated. The "accidental truths of history can never become the proof of necessary truths of reason."[3] Even if you were the world's greatest Olympic long jumper, the ditch cannot be crossed. It's impossible.

Christianity fell headfirst into this ditch, and with it fell the doctrine of the Trinity. For the Bible's claims about the Trinity are rooted in a revelation that was transmitted through historical persons and events, from Moses to Jesus to the apostle Paul. But history is unreliable, giving us no access to universal truth. Universal truth can come from our reason alone. Whatever parts of Christianity float to the top of the ditch after the wreckage and seem reasonable—that is, universally sensible—might be retrieved for safekeeping. Yet none of these parts included doctrines like the Trinity, but only the Bible's ethics, as found in Jesus's teachings, for example. As for the Trinity, it lay at the bottom of the ditch and should be kept there.

With this ditch in the way, what was the Christian to do? Many tried to play by the Enlightenment's rules of the game: we just need to apply enough reason to prove God is reasonable, sensible to the human intellect. But that mentality resulted in a deistic God, a God stripped of the supernatural, for the supernatural is anything but sensible. Others said the Trinity can't be known by our reason, so we must close our eyes, get a running start, and take a blind leap of faith.[4] Still others said the answer is far more pietistic: it's not out there somewhere, but within; we must look to our religious experience or feeling of absolute dependence on that which is divine.

It's this last answer that proved influential—so influential it has not only occupied Christianity up to the present day but moved Christianity and its doctrine of the Trinity into the land of theological Liberalism. Or, shall I say, the *room* of theological Liberalism, where the Ghost of Orthodoxy Past continues to haunt us.

Liberalism's founding father was a man named Friedrich Schleiermacher, and he believed there was one word that captured the nucleus of the Christian faith and life: *Gefühl*. It's a German word and refers to a "self-conscious feeling of absolute dependence."[5] Dependence on what? On whom? The infinite, the divine, or what some call God.[6] The *Gefühl* set Jesus apart, for example. He was the ultimate example of a man who came into contact with the infinite, the poster boy for that self-conscious feeling of absolute dependence.[7]

Traditional doctrines and dogma, however, get in the way. Take the "eternal distinction in the Supreme Being" between the persons of the Trinity: the Father unbegotten, the Son begotten, the Spirit spirated. Such distinctions do not concern the "religious consciousness, for there it could never emerge."[8] Such distinctions are speculative, out of reach, knowledge not innate to the self-conscious feeling of absolute dependence. Nor are they the concern of Scripture, which has to do with Christian piety, not doctrinal speculation about God's being and essence. Even if "we had no knowledge of any such transcendent fact" like the Trinity, and even if the orthodox view of the Trinity was heresy itself, still "our faith in Christ and our living fellowship with Him would be the same."[9] According to Schleiermacher, the Trinity has "no use in Christian doctrine."[10]

But let's just say, for the sake of argument, that the Trinity is not speculative, that it can be known. Even then, Schleiermacher is convinced the Trinity is chock full of internal contradictions. For example, if one distinguishes between persons, then equality is lost. Schleiermacher takes issue with eternal generation because it makes the unbegotten Father superior to the begotten Son. He acknowledges that the church fathers believed generation is eternal, but still, he protests, it conveys the Son is dependent, and if dependent then inferior. Likewise with the Spirit. In sum, if "such distinctions are made, the equality of the Persons is lost."[11] By contrast, Schleiermacher chooses the side of equality. In fact, he goes further, wondering whether the heresy of Sabellianism might be the right view of the Trinity after all.[12] The church should not be so quick to condemn Unitarianism either. Not only have they preserved the oneness of God, but they "by no means parted with all those spiritual affections which spring from God-consciousness."[13] That is what really matters in the end.

Schleiermacher's mindset was accelerated by many others in the nineteenth century.[14] Some gave Liberalism a moralistic agenda like no other. Christianity does not concern itself with speculative dogmas like the Trinity but with the ethics of God's kingdom and how those ethics might transform society. The Trinity is irrelevant because it has nothing to contribute to society's moral advancement in Christian values. Christianity is not about *who God is*—that's a metaphysical obsession that occupied the church fathers—so much as *what God does* in society and what society ought to do in cooperation with God. In short, Christianity is not about dogmas but ethics, not about doctrine but values.

This mindset entered the twentieth century through the Social Gospel as put forth by Walter Rauschenbusch.[15] With Rauschenbusch, unless the Trinity proves necessary for social concerns in the church and the wider community, it is not needed at all. There the Trinity lay, rotting like dead wood on a fallen, decaying tree. *Wormwood.* All because it is irrelevant to one's feeling of absolute dependence or the ethics of social justice.

Room #2: We Can Make the Trinity Relevant Again— Moderns Substitute a Social Trinity for Orthodoxy

Just when the Trinity seemed lost for eternity (or lost in eternity), dismissed with an outcry (*Speculation!*), a new wind blew into the corridors of the academy and the pews of the church, one that said the Trinity did matter after all. And like that, a Trinity renaissance was launched.

Observing the disconnect between the doctrine of God and the church's agenda for society, modern theologians believed they had the answer. If Liberals said the Trinity was irrelevant unless proven expedient to ethics and social justice, theologians in the twentieth century exclaimed, "It is relevant; it really, really is!"

But to prove it, they needed a Trinity radically different from the historic, orthodox model; they needed a *social* Trinity that matched their vision for society. The theologians and pastors who took up this new challenge are innumerable and sometimes diverse. But before we wade into those choppy waters, let's take a short tangent to understand why Trinity and society became so interlinked in the first place.

The Rule to Change All Rules

In the 1960s, somewhere in between bell-bottoms and Beatlemania, the Roman Catholic theologian Karl Rahner wrote a book on the Trinity, declaring that it is now high time to throw off the shackles of scholastic speculation and liberate the Trinity. Rahner, like almost every modern theologian, is critical of those in the West, from Augustine to Aquinas, because, he claims, they start with the one essence of God. By contrast, Rahner says he will side with the East by beginning with the three persons, the Father in particular.

Even when the West does focus on the three persons, Rahner complains that they only contemplate the persons in *eternity* rather than the Trinity in *history*.[16] They have "locked" the Trinity "within itself," in "splendid isolation," and we creatures are "excluded."[17] Rahner protests, *Rationalism!*[18] Is this not the reason the Trinity became irrelevant in the first place?

But Rahner claims he has the antidote to this Western virus, this Latin epidemic: the Trinity is not to be incarcerated in eternity

East versus West? Myth Busting

Many modern theologians have erected a wall between East and West, as if East and West took two antithetical approaches to the Trinity. Social trinitarians claim that the Greeks (East) started with the three persons and moved to the one essence, while the Latins (West) started with the abstract notion of one essence and moved to the three persons. And they side with the East, blaming those in the West, especially Augustine, for centuries of emphasis on unity and simplicity. This reading of history and approach to the Trinity, popularized recently by Colin Gunton, can be traced back to Theodore de Régnon (nineteenth century). But after much investigation, historians have discerned that this modern paradigm is mistaken, lacking real evidence. As we've seen, Athanasius and the Cappadocians (the East) appealed to simplicity (the one essence) to make their case for the Son's eternal generation. As for Augustine, he did not craft a different Trinity from Nicaea, but retrieved the Nicene doctrine of the Trinity. Patristic scholars today are now criticizing this false paradigm, but theologians are slow to catch up and have not paid attention to their research.

but set free in history. How so? Rahner has the answer: "The 'economic' Trinity is the 'immanent' Trinity and the 'immanent' Trinity is the 'economic' Trinity."[19]

Time out. What is the difference between immanent and economic? The *immanent* Trinity refers to who the triune God is in himself, apart from creation or the economy of salvation. The *economic* Trinity refers to how the triune God acts in relation to creation and in the economy of salvation. In the past, theologians were careful to distinguish between immanent and economic, lest the two be confused, conflated, or collapsed. We would not want to project qualities in creation onto the Creator, creating a God in our own image.

But Rahner challenges the received paradigm with his thesis (or rule, as it is called). He does not go into great detail, fleshing out his thesis in all its specifics, so there has been some debate how to interpret Rahner. A generous reader might say he only meant to communicate that the economic Trinity is our only access to

Karl Barth

There was no theologian so influential in the twentieth century as Karl Barth. Reacting against the Liberalism of his day and its overemphasis on divine immanence, which Barth believed transformed theology into anthropology, Barth turned the church's attention back to God's transcendence. And yet, Barth's doctrine of the Trinity has been a matter of debate. On the one hand, he can sound orthodox. On the other hand, some have accused him of Sabellianism because he reacted against the word "person," thinking it too modern. Barth's entire program, including his view of the Trinity, centers on God's self-revelation in the Word, Christ Jesus. With his focus on the incarnation, Barth concludes that obedience defines not only the Son's economic mission but the immanent Trinity. For this reason, some critics charge Barth with succumbing to subordinationism.

the immanent Trinity. But many believe Rahner meant more.[20] In some sense, Rahner equates the immanent and the economic, so that the two are one and the same. "No adequate distinction can be made between the doctrine of the Trinity and the doctrine of the economy of salvation."[21]

But what is not up for debate is this fact: Rahner's Rule gave modern theologians the opportunity to rethink everything, and most importantly, to close the gap between Creator and creature.[22] In the name of Rahner, some today go so far as to reject the immanent Trinity altogether. *God is as God does.* Nothing more. Function is everything. As one modern author has argued, "The eternal begetting of the Son and the breathing forth of the Spirit take place in God's economy."[23] *God becomes Trinity when he acts like one in history.*

With the gap between immanent and economic closed, the Trinity and society were linked together, so that who society is must be who the Trinity is, and who the Trinity is must be who society is. But if this link was to stick, an even more radical move became necessary: the very DNA of the Trinity had to be redefined. No longer could historic orthodoxy be followed, but a new doctrine, a *social* doctrine of the Trinity, was now expedient, at least if the Trinity was to be relevant for the *social* concerns of society. While a vortex of examples might be considered, let's focus on one of Rahner's brightest students.

The Trinity Goes Social

One of the most influential theologians of the past century—and that is no exaggeration—is Jürgen Moltmann, well-known for his belief in a God who suffers.[24] As it turns out, two Karls—Karl Rahner and Karl Barth—taught him the Trinity when he was a student.[25] But Moltmann believes his mentors got the Trinity wrong: by starting with "the sovereignty of the One God" they were "then able to talk about the Trinity only as the 'three modes of being' or the 'three modes of subsistence' of that One God."[26] (In chapter 2 we learned that "modes of subsistence" is a phrase that refers to the way the one essence exists in the Father as unbegotten, the Son as begotten, and the Spirit as spirated.) He concludes that the two Karls, much like Schleiermacher himself, are in grave danger of Sabellianism due to their focus on the oneness of God.[27]

Moltmann may detest Barth's trinitarianism the most because it prides itself on the way God reveals himself as *Lord*. This obsession with lordship can only be the outcome of a Western, individualistic preoccupation with the one divine substance and monarch. Moltmann even criticizes the Nicene Creed, that historic standard of orthodoxy, as "ambivalent where the question of God's unity is concerned." For it "suggests a unity of substance between Father, Son, and Spirit" with all its talk about the Son being *homoousios* (of the same essence) with the Father, begotten from the Father's essence from all eternity.[28]

Moltmann bucks against this Western emphasis on lordship because it stems from an unwavering commitment to *monotheism*—a most terrible word in Moltmann's opinion.[29] The "unity of the absolute subject is stressed to such a degree that the trinitarian Persons disintegrate into mere aspects of the one subject"; this stress on unity leads "unintentionally but inescapably to the reduction of the doctrine of the Trinity to monotheism."[30] By contrast, he has "decided in favour of the Trinity." No one who calls themselves a Christian decides in *disfavor* of the Trinity, so what does Moltmann mean exactly? "I have developed a *social doctrine of the Trinity*, according to which God is a community

---

What Is a *Social* View of the Trinity?

"I have developed a *social doctrine of the Trinity*, according to which God is a community of Father, Son, and Spirit, whose unity is constituted by mutual indwelling and reciprocal interpenetration." —Jürgen Moltmann

of Father, Son, and Spirit, whose unity is constituted by mutual indwelling and reciprocal interpenetration."[31]

Notice what word social trinitarians like Moltmann use to define the Trinity: *community*. The Trinity is a *community* or *society*, a cooperation of divine persons, each with his own center of consciousness and will. Since each person in this society is equal to the next, equality is distributed and hierarchy eliminated. Moltmann appeals to the concept of *perichoresis*, but not in the way the Great Tradition did—each person one with each other due to the simple essence they hold in common. That would be a return to monotheism and metaphysics (ontology)—again, two notorious words in Moltmann's estimation. By contrast, Moltmann gives perichoresis a strong social emphasis: the Trinity is a community with mutual reciprocity between persons in relationship with one another. The focus is not ontological (simplicity; modes of subsistence) but communitarian, the Trinity a cooperative society of love.

By redefining the Trinity as *social*, Moltmann now has the solution for the evils that plague society. "It is only when the doctrine of the Trinity vanquishes the monotheistic notion of the great universal monarch in heaven, and his divine patriarchs in the world, that earthly rulers, dictators and tyrants cease to find any justifying religious archetypes any more."[32] If his social Trinity is the way to go, then "we find the earthly reflection of this divine sociality, not in the autocracy of a single ruler but in the democratic community of free people, not in the lordship of the man over the woman but in their equal mutuality, not in an ecclesiastical hierarchy but in a fellowship church."[33] Moltmann rejoices that feminist theologians can now fight for the equality of the sexes thanks to the Trinity being an equal society of persons—God himself is no longer patriarchal but bisexual, giving matriarchy a divine voice. Moltmann cheers on a liberation gospel as well. We can now champion the cause of the oppressed in society over against "political monotheism" thanks to the lack of hierarchy in the triune community.[34]

Swear Words?

In this book, we will use the terms *ontology* (ontological) and *metaphysics* (metaphysical) as synonyms. They refer to the *whatness* of something or someone. In theology, these words refer to God's essence and how his essence exists (subsists) in three persons. For all kinds of weird reasons, Christians today have been taught to assume these words are swear words. But the Great Tradition disagrees: these words fight against domesticating God and imposing our social experience on the Creator.

Moltmann's first step to freedom is a rejection of the opening line in the Apostles' Creed: "I believe in God, *the Father Almighty*." Here is the problem wrapped up in one phrase. The way forward is not to think of God or the Trinity in terms of *power* but *love*, self-communicating, suffering (passible) love.[35] While power is the weapon of the one ruler over the oppressed in society (what he calls monotheistic monarchianism), love is the medicine that restores community, both in God and in society. What kind of community, you ask? A *socialist* community. It's "not the monarchy of a ruler that corresponds to the triune God; it is the community of men and women, without privileges and without subjugation." Again, the Trinity is our paradigm: "The three divine Persons have everything in common, except for their personal characteristics. So the Trinity corresponds to a community in which people are defined through their relations with one another and in their significance for one another, not in opposition to one another, in terms of power and possession."[36]

Is Moltmann alone in his social agenda? As it turns out, he launched a social crusade, a crusade carried on by one of his own students and one of today's most popular thinkers: Miroslav Volf.

The Trinity Is Our Social Program

Miroslav Volf is from Croatia, but he has been influential in America—so influential, in fact, he was even invited to advise that department of the White House devoted to faith-based partner-ships. Much of his career has been devoted to political and public theology, so it is not surprising that Volf has something to say about the Trinity and society. In fact, the title of his book says it all: *After Our Likeness: The Church as the Image of the Trinity.* Volf is just as convinced that the historic doctrine of the Trinity must be modified or even rejected, at least if the Trinity is to serve as a model for church and society, which it must. The Trinity, in some sense at least, is to be our social program.[37] With his aim set on the church in particular, Volf concludes that there must be a direct correspondence between the type of community we see in the church and the Trinity.[38] Question is, what type?

To answer that question, we must understand what Volf is re-sponding to. Some social trinitarians say the secret to the Trinity is this: we must redefine God's being as communion.[39] *Being as communion*—whatever does that mean? Rather than defining the "being" of the Trinity as the Great Tradition did, as an essence with three modes of subsistence (metaphysics alert!), it is argued instead that "being" refers to the interpersonal love relationships or communion that the persons have with one another. Except this society of love has the Father at the top. Imagine drawing a straight line from the Trinity to church and society. Just as there is hierarchy in the Trinity, the Father at the top, so too, this group argues, there is hierarchy in the church, the bishop at the top. Can you hear Moltmann dragging his nails across the chalkboard yet?

Now, back to the Croatian thinker, Volf. Here is something ironic: he, too, is a social trinitarian. "Amen!" he says to inter-personal, societal relationships of love. "Amen!" he says to being as communion. But the trinitarian communion is one of equality rather than hierarchy, and since the Trinity is the paradigm for church and society, then so too should the church's polity reflect such equality. Authority rests in the gathering of the whole, not in a single patriarch or bishop at the top. In a word, the church is to be as congregational as the Trinity and the Trinity as congregational as the church. With all this talk about church, don't miss the real issue: *to meet the agenda of the church, the Trinity has been redefined.* But don't miss the irony either: *social trinitarians are coming to opposite conclusions; some want hierarchy, others want equality.*

To see such revisionism with crystal clarity, let's travel to Brazil and meet a theologian whose name just happens to sound similar to Miroslav Volf. His name is Leonardo Boff. What's so unique about Boff is this: he believes the Trinity is the prototype not only for the church but for politics as well. Boff has been a long-standing voice for liberation theology, especially in South America. Liberation theologians read the Bible and conclude that its main message is the promise and hope that the oppressed in society will be set free from their oppressors. The gospel is not the triune God's plan to send his Son, as if Jesus substituted himself for us, taking the penalty for our sin so that we can be forgiven and receive eternal life. Rather, the gospel is social and political liberation, setting free those pushed down in society from those in power. So why did Jesus die? "The incarnate Son died as a protest against the slaveries imposed on God's sons and daughters."[40] That redefinition of the gospel assumes a redefinition of the Trinity, to be sure.

Redefining the Trinity begins with swapping out the orthodox definition of *person* for a modern one: "The modern notion of person is basically that of *being-in-relationship*; a person is a subject existing as a *centre of autonomy*, gifted with consciousness and freedom."[41] In this one sentence, Boff sums up social trinitarianism. But Boff anticipates an objection: if this modern redefinition of person is applied to the Trinity, how can it not result in tritheism? Boff is convinced he escapes this heresy because the "stress is laid on *relationship*, the complete openness of one person to another."[42] Boff admits—in a moment of total honesty about his intentions—that there is a real danger in being misunderstood as heretical: "When classical theology used the term 'person,' it did not understand it in the same way that we do now. So without explaining this to people every time we use the term, we risk their understanding our words in a heretical sense."[43] Nevertheless, Boff is convinced the charge of heresy is worth the risk.

Redefining person as one who is in relation*ship* with others, Boff then redefines the Trinity as a *society* and a *community*. Boff looks to the *human* society for help. "Society is not just the sum total of the individuals that make it up, but has its own being woven out of the threads of relationships among individuals, functions and institutions, which together make up the social and political community." The outcome: "Cooperation and collaboration among all produce the common good."[44] So too, then, with the Trinity: it is a divine society where the individuals are persons in relationships with one another, persons who cooperate and collaborate as would a human community. Human society is a "pointer" to the Trinity, and the Trinity is the "model" for society.[45] The Trinity is a "community vision": "God is a community of Persons and not simply the One; God's unity exists in the form of communion (common-union)."[46] Only this redefinition of the Trinity "prevents any totalitarianism ostensibly based on divine monotheism and any paternalism based on the monarchy of the Father to whom all must submit and on whom all depend." In short, the "domination model is replaced by the communion model."[47] Such community means there is "total reciprocity" between the Father, Son, and Spirit, a "loving relationship" one to another.[48]

That phrase "loving relationship" is key. The persons "are not embodiments of One (nature or substance or absolute Spirit or Subject)," as many in the Great Tradition said, "but three Subjects

How Do Social Trinitarians Redefine the Persons of the Trinity?

"The modern notion of person is basically that of *being-in-relationship*; a person is a subject existing as a *centre of autonomy*, gifted with consciousness and freedom." —Leonardo Boff

Is a Social Trinity a Political Hope or a Danger to the World?

"Direct translation of the Trinity into a social programme is problematic because, unlike the peaceful and perfectly loving mutuality of the Trinity, human society is full of suffering, conflict and sin. Turned into a recommendation for social relations, the Trinity seems unrealistic, hopelessly naïve, and for that reason perhaps even politically dangerous. To a world of violent, corrupt and selfish people, the Trinity seems to offer only the feeble plan, 'Why can't we all just get along?'"—Kathryn Tanner, "Social Trinitarianism and Its Critics"

in eternal (and therefore essential) communion, always united and interpenetrating one another."[49] If they are three separate subjects, can they really be one God? Boff thinks so: the "eternal communion of love makes these Three one God."[50] The Beatles would have been proud: for Boff, all you need is love. But notice, for social trinitarians *love* becomes a second, additional distinction or mark within the immanent Trinity, not just eternal relations of origin (unbegotten Father, begotten Son, spirated Spirit).

Redefining the Trinity in social categories, Boff has his model in place for society. A social Trinity condemns capitalist societies, the "dictatorship of the property-owning classes with their individualistic and business interests always shored up by mechanisms of state control." Boff warns that these "regimes have produced the greatest divisions in history between rich and poor, between the races and between the sexes." But it's not just division that's the problem; capitalism is to blame for the misery of the disenfranchised across the globe.[51] A capitalist society is by definition out of step with the Trinity: "Capitalist regimes contradict the challenges and invitations of trinitarian communion."[52]

What kind of society then can lead us to the Trinity? "Societies with a socialist regime are founded on a right principle, that of communion between all and the involvement of all in the means of production."[53] That's because the Trinity itself is socialist, a community where power is absent and all things are distributed in equal measure. Follow Boff's logic:

> *How the Trinity works:* "In the Trinity there is no domination by one side, but convergence of the Three in mutual acceptance and giving. They are different but none is greater or lesser, before or after."

Ergo . . .

> *How society works:* "Therefore a society that takes its inspiration from trinitarian communion cannot tolerate class differences, dominations based on power (economic, sexual or ideological) that subjects those who are different to those who exercise that power and marginalizes the former from the latter."[54]

This unbreakable link between socialism and social trinitarianism could not be more relevant for Boff's liberation gospel. "Society is not ultimately set in its unjust and unequal relationships, but summoned to transform itself in the light of the open and egalitarian relationships that obtain in the communion of the Trinity, the goal of social and historical progress. If the Trinity is good news, then it is so particularly for the oppressed and those condemned to solitude."[55] As we look around this cruel world, we see the Trinity wherever the oppressed rise up like a phoenix from the ashes and protest their injustice against the superpowers of this world. "The Trinity communicates itself whenever . . . the oppressed and their allies fight against tyranny and oppression."[56] Where do the oppressed find the strength and courage to do so? Where do they look to know what kind of society to build instead? "The communion of the Trinity is then their source of inspiration, plays a part in their protest, is a paradigm of what they are building."[57] Boff sums it all up when he concludes, the Holy Trinity is "our liberation program."[58]

But wait, the Ghost of Orthodoxy Past is not finished. One more room will haunt us yet.

Room #3: The Historicizing Family

We have now explored those figures prominent at the heart of the twentieth century. But there is another group of influencers who have joined the trinitarian renaissance. I like to call them the *historicizing family*. Though I admit, many in the previous two rooms have family ties to the historicizing family as well.

To meet the first theologian in our historicizing family we pass through the orange and yellow autumn leaves of New Haven, Con-

Marks of a Social Trinity

Social trinitarianism is diverse, and some versions are more radical than others, but most hold some or all of the following eight marks in common:

1. Starting point (or at least emphasis) is not simplicity but the three persons; some reject simplicity altogether.
2. Trinity is redefined as a society and community, analogous to human society.
3. Persons are redefined as three centers of consciousness and will.
4. Persons are redefined according to their relationships: focus on mutuality, societal interaction.
5. Unity is redefined as interpersonal relationships of love between persons (redefinition of perichoresis).
6. Large overlap (sometimes collapse) of immanent and economic Trinity.
7. Sets East over against West, appealing to Eastern fathers.
8. Social Trinity is a paradigm for social theory (ecclesiology, politics, gender, etc.).

Accusation: Social Trinity = Tritheism

necticut, home to Yale University. During the second half of the twentieth century, Hans Frei could be heard from the Ivy League's lecterns. Frei so shaped a generation that his thought simply became synonymous with the Yale School of Theology. Frei's school of thought has also been labeled *narrative theology*, due to its emphasis on Scripture's narrative.[59] In the aftermath of Liberalism, which disregarded the reliability of the Gospel stories and their historical accounts of Jesus, Frei was a refreshing, postliberal voice. He warned against Liberalism's eclipse of the biblical narrative.[60]

Despite Frei's commendable critique of Liberalism, his own approach has negative consequences for the classic Christian doctrine of God. For example, Frei believes the Great Tradition before him was misleading, guiding the church and academy into theological speculation with its emphasis on who God is in himself. Instead, our attention should be on the *narrative* the Bible presents. Frei does not think the focus point is to be Jesus's teachings, not even his teachings about himself. Instead, we must zero in on the narrative that describes what action Jesus took, especially in his passion. If you want to know who the person of Christ is, look no further than what Christ does. Discussions about the immanent Trinity and the person of the Son are the stuff of creeds and councils. "*Metaphysics! Ontology!*" Frei protests, whereas the Bible's attention is on the works of God in history, specifically the works of the incarnate Christ in history.

Notice, Frei has drawn our attention to a good thing: narrative. And specifically the Bible's stories about Jesus's human experience. So what's the problem? The problem is, Frei has focused *merely* on narrative. As a result, he has ignored other parts of Scripture—including other narratives!—that tell us who God is apart from humanity. As Bible readers, we pay attention to not only what Jesus does but what he says, especially what he says about who he is prior to creation and incarnation (see his many "I Am" sayings, for example). If we only focus on Jesus's human experience, we risk undermining the divine and eternal identity not only of the Son but of the entire Trinity. In short, we humanize God by *merely* focusing on history, losing patience, as Frei does, with any and all discussions about the immanent Trinity. In sum, emphasis is everything. An overemphasis on the human experience of Jesus can lead to a negligence or outright revision of God's deity apart from humanity.

To meet the second theologian in our historicizing family, we leave Yale for Princeton, but this time to meet a Lutheran: Robert Jenson. At the turn of the century, Jenson joined the Center for Theological Inquiry, associated with Princeton Theological Seminary. He, too, made a beeline for the incarnation. In Christ and him crucified, we receive the revelation of God—or, to use Jenson's phrase, God's self-identification. Naturally, then, our focus is to be on the narrative of Scripture, examining what the incarnate Son does, how he functions.[61] We are not, then, to focus on an immanent Trinity, as if we can know who the triune God is apart from the world (*ad intra*). Shame on the Great Tradition, East and West, from Nicaea to Augustine, for doing so. Instead, we must "accommodate the gospel," and to do so we must "reinterpret [God's] being."[62] The eternal relations of origin, for example, are not timeless and immutable, fixed to be what they are apart from creation. No, what the triune God does in history *constitutes* who he is in eternity.[63] The relations *become* relations as they take place within creation. The persons of the Trinity are, in a real sense, *temporal*.[64] "[The] identity of the eternal Son is the human person Jesus."[65]

Is there a danger to such an extreme emphasis on what God has done in history? Yes. "Exclusive focus on historical description thus runs the risk of reductionism."[66] As we've witnessed since the inception of Rahner's Rule, the immanent is collapsed into the economic and, in Jenson's case, the economic is said to constitute the immanent. Who God is in eternity is reduced to his acts in history; indeed, his acts in history even make him who he is as Trinity. God's triune relations become temporal; his being is in becoming. No longer do we have an immutable and eternal Trinity. For all Jenson's emphasis on the gospel, the Trinity has been reduced to the gospel, and its identity collapsed into the history of salvation.[67]

The Tip of the Social Iceberg: Evangelicalism No Exception

Have evangelical Christians escaped the influence of social trinitarianism? They have not. They, too, have contributed to Trinity drift.

A Game of One-on-One		
	Nicene Orthodoxy	**Social Trinitarianism (some evangelicals)**
When?	Early church fathers to the Post-Reformation Reformers (first to eighteenth centuries)	Enlightenment to present day (eighteenth to twenty-first centuries)
What distinguishes the persons in the Trinity?	Eternal relations of origin: Father is unbegotten, Son is begotten, Spirit is spirated.	Community and relationships: persons form a society, cooperating with one another in I-Thou relationships.
What is a divine person?	Person is a subsistence of the divine essence; a subsisting relation. There are three modes of subsistence: unbegotten Father, begotten Son, spirated Spirit.	Person is a distinct center of consciousness and will, a personality in mutual, interdependent relationships of love (or hierarchy) with others.
How many wills are there in the Trinity?	One will, according to the one essence. Persons are undivided, indivisible in will and operation.	*Social trinitarians*: three wills because there are three centers of consciousness (and in some models, hierarchy between persons) *Modified social trinitarians*: one will, but three different agents (and in some models, hierarchy between persons) *Accusation*: tritheism; subordinationism

For example, countless Christian philosophers today have embraced a social view of the Trinity, even at the risk of tritheism.[68] They propose a social Trinity where Father, Son, and Spirit are "distinct centers of knowledge, will, love, and action." What defines the persons as *persons*? They are "distinct centers of consciousness."[69] Together they form a "community" or "society," so that "the Holy Trinity is a divine, transcendent society or community of three fully personal and fully divine entities."[70] With such an emphasis on distinct wills and centers of consciousness, the historic Nicene affirmation of simplicity will just not do anymore. Simplicity "ends up complicating trinity doctrine quite needlessly. Its lease ought not to be extended."[71] If simplicity is affirmed in any sense, it must be "modest," and it must conform to a social view of the persons.[72]

Others are bolder still. William Lane Craig and J. P. Moreland argue that the "central commitment" of social trinitarianism is this: "In God there are three distinct centers of self-consciousness, each with its proper intellect and will."[73] Three wills, three centers of self-consciousness—this is the very DNA of social trinitarianism. No Trinity otherwise. Rejecting the classic affirmation of divine simplicity, they conclude, "God is an immaterial substance or soul endowed with three sets of cognitive faculties each of which is sufficient for personhood, so that God has three centers of self-consciousness, intentionality, and will."[74] However, they also feel the pressure to explain why three wills and centers of consciousness is not tritheism. They even acknowledge that their view contradicts many of the church's creeds, including the Athanasian Creed (discussed in chap. 5). Nevertheless, they find comfort in an appeal to *sola scriptura*.[75]

Evangelical theologians are no exception either. Take Stanley Grenz, one of the most renowned evangelical thinkers of the last century. The Trinity is a social reality, said Grenz, and the defining mark of this community is love.[76] Love is the all-controlling attribute of God and the defining mark of the society we call Trinity, binding the persons in unity. Their benevolent fellowship, bound by the Holy Spirit in particular, is what keeps the persons united as one single being. But it takes self-dedication: each person must be committed to *relationships of societal, cooperative love*. Grenz rebuked the Great Tradition for emphasizing God's *being*, a being with three modes of subsistence. According to Grenz, that creates a fourth person. Instead, we must define the persons as those who pursue eternal love relationships with one another.[77]

The New Calvinist movement is not immune to social trinitarianism either, as much as it thinks it is. As we will see in chapter 8, evangelicals like Wayne Grudem and Bruce Ware have also redefined the Trinity as a society of persons defined by societal "roles" and "relationships," cooperating with one another as distinct agents. In the twentieth century, social trinitarians redefined persons as relationships of mutuality and self-giving love to support equality in society, especially between the sexes.[78] But Grudem and Ware believe this society of relationships in the Trinity is defined by functional hierarchy. The Son, for example, is subordinate to the supreme, absolute authority of the Father *within the immanent Trinity*, a view known as EFS (eternal functional subordination). Their social agenda comes through just as strong, if not stronger, than social trinitarians before them, when they then argue that authority-submission inside the Trinity, within the eternal Godhead, is the paradigm and prototype for hierarchy in society, especially wives submitting to their husbands in the home. Critics classify EFS with the historicizing family because EFSers, whether they realize it or not, project the functional subordination of the Son to the Father during the incarnation back onto the eternal, immanent Trinity, only to return to history in order to apply their hierarchy to gender roles.

We could go on and on. What we've seen is but the tip of the social Trinity iceberg. This iceberg is so expansive that its frozen mass has swelled into the waters of evangelicalism as well. Ironically, some look at the iceberg and conclude we are experiencing a trinitarian revival, a renaissance even.

Revival or Departure?

Many who have experienced the resurgence of interest in the Trinity have drawn the conclusion that there has been a revival of trinitarian thought. The Trinity was lost but now is found, and despite the dismissive attitude of old school Protestant Liberalism, the Trinity matters after all. Through doctrinal CPR, the Trinity has been resuscitated, and never has it been more relevant for society.

But the Trinity they've resuscitated is neither the orthodox one nor the biblical one (chap. 2). To be blunt, they have not revived the orthodox Trinity, but they have killed it, only to replace it with a different Trinity altogether—a social Trinity—one that can be molded, even manipulated, to fit society's soapbox.

With the arrival of the twenty-first century, it's now conspicuous that there are as many Trinities as modern theologians. With each new Trinity arrives a new social program. Quests for the Trinity are in the end not about God but about *me* and *my* social agenda.[79] The Trinity is now a "pretext": we claim to have a new "insight into the inner nature of God" but only so that we "can use it to promote social, political or ecclesiastical regimes."[80] As I shared at the start of our journey, I have experienced this firsthand. Within evangelical circles, both in the classroom and the church, contemplating and praising the Trinity was not the end goal (as it should be), but the Trinity was used merely as a means to other ends.

I am not alone in such a conclusion. With a detailed analysis of modern thought, Stephen Holmes voices a lament just as sobering: "The explosion of theological work claiming to recapture the doctrine of the Trinity that we have witnessed in recent decades in fact misunderstands and distorts the traditional doctrine so badly that it is unrecognizable. . . . [These are] thoroughgoing departures from the older tradition, rather than revivals of it."[81] Lest you miss how serious Holmes believes these departures to be, departures that pose as revivals, he issues this warning: "I see the twentieth-century renewal of Trinitarian theology as depending in large part on concepts and ideas that cannot be found in patristic, medieval, or Reformation accounts of the doctrine of the Trinity. In some cases, indeed, they are points explicitly and energetically repudiated as erroneous—even occasionally as formally heretical—by the earlier tradition."[82]

Trinity drift is real. We have not only drifted away from the biblical, orthodox Trinity, but we have manipulated the Trinity to meet our social agendas.

Question is, how do we now find our way home?

PART 2

HOW DO WE FIND OUR WAY HOME?

[The Trinity is] to be received by faith and adored with love.

FRANCIS TURRETIN, *INSTITUTES*

The Trinity is not brought down to our level as
a model for us to imitate; our hope is that we
might one day be raised up to its level.

KATHRYN TANNER,
"SOCIAL TRINITARIANISM AND ITS CRITICS"

How Does God Reveal Himself as Trinity?

Eternity and the Mystery of the Gospel

Arian, go to Jordan, and there you will see the Trinity.

THE ANCIENT FATHERS

The doctrine of the Trinity is often represented as a speculative point, of no great moment whether it is believed or no[t] . . . but alas! it enters into the whole of our salvation, and all parts of it; into all the doctrines of the gospel.

JOHN GILL, *BODY OF DIVINITY*

TO THE DELOREAN!

Where we're going: The days when Jesus walked the earth. A (fictional) woman named Zipporah, who lived in the first century, will introduce us to the Trinity of the Bible.

Key point: The Trinity is revealed in the gospel, but we must not conflate or collapse God in himself, apart from the world (immanent Trinity), with God's actions toward creation and salvation (economic Trinity) or we will manipulate the Trinity.

Go to Jordan

It did not seem right. At least to those of us who were there, watching and staring in unbelief. Jesus baptized by John? I looked around, and those who came with me to the Jordan River that day seemed just as perplexed, foreheads crinkled and eyebrows like darts pinpointing their disbelief.

Three days earlier, I was baptized by John in those same waters after I heard the prophet Isaiah being read in synagogue. It's that section of the scroll that reads,

A voice cries:
"In the wilderness prepare the way of the Lord;
make straight in the desert a highway for our God."[1]

When I heard it, I just knew it was John. He has been preaching repentance to my people and promising us that the day is coming when the promised One, the anointed Savior of Israel, the Lord himself, will arrive to redeem Israel.

Ever since my baptism, I've been sharing John's message with as many people as I can. Each week my family, friends, and neighbors walk out to the Jordan to witness more baptisms. But what I keep hoping to see is the coming of Israel's redeemer. After much anticipation, that day arrived. John was in the Jordan baptizing again, when a man named Jesus from Galilee was spotted walking toward him. John stopped what he was doing, and after a period of awkward silence—no one sure why John had paused for so long—he pointed to Jesus and shouted, "Behold, the Lamb of God, who takes away the sin of the world! This is he of whom I said, 'After me comes a man who ranks before me, because he was before me.' . . . This is the Son of God."[2] John had told us before that when the promised One comes, the baptism the Messiah brings will be far greater than John's. For the Anointed One will baptize with the Holy Spirit and with fire. As Israel's redeemer, he will deliver both judgment against the wicked and salvation to the repentant. Now, at last, the day of salvation was at hand.

Or was it?

With all eyes fixed on Jesus, the unexpected happened. Jesus walked into the water and asked John to baptize *him*. "What is he doing, Zipporah?" my sister Naomi asked. "Why is he asking John to baptize him? Shouldn't it be the other way around?" I didn't have an answer.

Even John was confused. We heard him say, "I need to be baptized by you, and do you come to me?"[3]

Like I said, it didn't seem right; everything was backwards or upside down or sideways or something. But Jesus persisted. "Let it be so now, for thus it is fitting for us to fulfill all righteousness."[4] Who was John to say no? So he baptized Jesus. When Jesus came out of the water, the heavens opened like Jehovah himself was about to step down. That's when John saw the Spirit of God descending like a dove and coming to rest on Jesus. John also heard a voice from heaven—it was the voice of the Father himself, saying, "This is my beloved Son, with whom I am well pleased."[5]

Seeing this unfold before my own eyes uprooted all my assumptions. Jesus was baptized, but unlike me, it was not because he was a sinner. Instead, as the Lord himself, he was baptized for me and for my people. It's as if he was reliving—yes, even recapitulating—my family history all over again. Having entered into the waters, would he now, like Israel, go into the wilderness to be tempted, and then, like Moses, ascend God's mountain to teach us how to live in God's kingdom? Would he succeed where we, sons of Adam and daughters of Eve, all children of Abraham, had failed? And if so, what would his obedience to the law mean for the righteousness of Israel . . . for my righteousness? Time would tell.

But that day Jesus deconstructed another assumption of mine. As an Israelite, I know the law; at its center is my people's mantra, the Shema: "Hear, O Israel: The LORD our God, the LORD is one."[6] Unlike all the nations around us, nations that believe in many gods, we believe in one God. So how can John be right that when the heavens opened, the divine voice itself pronounced its blessing on one who is, in the words of Isaiah, *the Lord*. Are there two lords now? And not just two, but three, for John said a dove descended on Jesus. Some say this is the Spirit. John swore it must be.

Overwhelmed, I left that day with more questions than answers.

I Heard the Father, Walked with His Son, and Now Have the Spirit within Me

In the months and years ahead, I continued to follow this Jesus, sticking to the shadows, hiding myself within large crowds, but nevertheless becoming somewhat of a disciple myself. I wasn't the only one; a group of us women stuck together like that, some of us believing more than others that this Jesus was the one the Scriptures spoke about.

But I still had my questions. On the one hand, I heard him reaffirm our people's belief that God is one. On the other hand, not only did I hear Jesus pray to his Father, but I heard him claim to be *from the Father* and, for that reason, equal with God. Claims like these almost got Jesus killed. His opponents misunderstood him, as if he was claiming to be a second deity. But I gave it some thought, and in the end, I think I understand what Jesus meant: distinct as he is from his Father, he is also one with his Father. He wasn't contradicting the Shema but expanding our understanding of the Shema in light of his own identity with God.

One day, for instance, I caught up with Jesus after finishing my shopping at the market. No surprise that his opponents (more like skeptics) were after him again, though Jesus remained patient and shrewd. Just when they thought they had him tied up in one of their theological conundrums, Jesus posed an astute theological question of his own:

> How can they say that the Christ is David's son? For David himself says in the Book of the Psalms,
>
> > "The Lord said to my Lord,
> > 'Sit at my right hand,
> > until I make your enemies your footstool.'"[7]

Everyone in the crowd knew Jesus was quoting Psalm 110, a psalm recited in synagogue on a frequent basis. But the way Jesus asked about this psalm shed new light. I don't know why I had never seen these two Lords in the text before. I must have recited David's words a thousand times, yet I never paid attention to the plurality David assumes is present in the one God we worship. But Jesus did. Not only that, but Jesus gave the impression that *he* is one of those Lords—David's Lord to be exact. Apparently, David overheard a divine conversation between the Father and his Son in eternity about the victory the Father promised he would accomplish, a victory Jesus has now come to inaugurate in history. It's as if the Spirit spoke through David as David gave voice to the very person of the Father addressing his only begotten Son before all time. After all, if I remember Psalm 110 right, the Father goes on to say to his Son, "before the dawn-bearing morning star appeared, I begot you."[8]

Not long after, my paradigm shattered once and for all when Jesus did not deliver my people from the Romans like I thought he would, like I thought he should. Instead, he surrendered himself to his enemies and was crucified on a cross. I stood at the foot of that cross, looking up at Jesus, his face splattered with blood, his head bobbing up and down until he took his last breath. Tears ran down my cheeks, and though I couldn't bring myself to do it, I wanted to raise my fist at Jesus and scream. He had deceived me; I believed in him. *I believed in him.* John was wrong. Jesus was no King; he was not the promised One to sit on David's throne forever.[9]

But as my grief mixed with frustration, I once more remembered that day I first saw Jesus on the riverbank. "Behold, the Lamb of God who takes away the sin of the world!" John had shouted in excitement. I stopped sobbing, looked up at Jesus, his skin now pale and cold, and my tearful rage subsided. What if I was wrong? John said Jesus was the *lamb*, the Passover lamb. Then it occurred to me: by laying down his own life, a life meant to make a sacrifice, he had ransomed Israel. Isaiah himself said as much.[10] And Jesus knew it all along. That explains why he kept predicting he would die, why he did not resist his arrest, and why he shouted out on the cross, "It is finished!"[11]

My hesitant but newfound hope was confirmed three days later when Jesus's tomb was found empty. A group of women close to Jesus said they even saw him. Then I remembered, Jesus had predicted this too; we just didn't see it at the time. No one did. John was right all along: Jesus is the Son of God. Weeks later, I saw Jesus for myself. There are no words to describe what I saw—a dead man, whom I *saw* die, now alive? I didn't want to let Jesus out of my sight, afraid I might lose him again, afraid he might be taken away. But Jesus was intent on going away. He told us so, explaining it was time for him to return to the Father. Once again, I felt confused, but this time my confusion was accompanied by worry: *Jesus, please don't leave. Not yet at least. You just came back. We need you . . . I need you.* But Jesus said, as if he knew the worrisome thoughts within our hearts, that he had no intention of leaving us alone, like orphans to wander this world aimlessly and without a home. Wait in Jerusalem, he said, and the Helper, the Comforter, the Holy Spirit will come and be with you, even guide you.[12] He had promised this Helper before his death, but now that Jesus had risen, he reminded us once more, his words taking on fresh significance. Then Jesus left us, ascending into heaven. Never have I felt so alone, so desperate for this Comforter to descend, than at that moment.

So, we waited. And just like he said, the Comforter arrived, though not in the way I thought he would. I was in another room from the disciples when I heard a strange sound, the sound of wind hitting the walls in a fury. I rushed over to see it, and there on top of the disciples' heads was fire, except it looked like flaming tongues, as odd as that sounds. When the wind stopped beating on the house and the hovering flames faded, the disciples left the room only to be met by a crowd. "What does this mean?" someone asked, voicing the very question everyone was thinking. Seeing the confusion on everyone's faces, Peter stood up and told us about the prophet Joel who foretold this day would come, as well as many other Scriptures that pointed forward to Jesus, as if everything we had witnessed was according to the plan of God.[13]

That day Peter preached a sermon like none I've heard before. Peter himself was like a new man—explaining to us that this plan of salvation is none other than the plan of the one God who is Father, Son, and Holy Spirit. Just like Jesus, Peter went back to the Scriptures, the psalms especially, to reiterate David: "The Lord said to my Lord, 'Sit at my right hand, until I make your enemies your footstool.'"[14]

When we heard this good news, many of us—it seemed like all of us—were cut to the heart and asked what we should do next. "Repent," Peter said, "and be baptized every one of you in the name of Jesus Christ for the forgiveness of your sins, and you will receive the gift of the Holy Spirit."[15] That day three thousand people were baptized—*three thousand!*

And I was one of them. I had followed John, I had even been baptized by John, but now I was a follower of Jesus himself. I can't help but think this was what John intended all along. As Peter lowered me into the water and brought me up again, I remembered what Jesus said just before he ascended to his Father and sent the Holy Spirit: "Go therefore and make disciples of all nations, baptizing them in the name of the Father and of the Son and of the Holy Spirit, teaching them to observe all that I have commanded you. And behold, I am with you always, to the end of the age."[16]

That day is a day I will never forget. The Holy Spirit gave me faith in the crucified and risen Son, the Lord Jesus, my Mediator before the Father, the one who loved me before the foundation of the world. Washed in the blood of the Lamb, I have been his child ever since, and though I can no longer see Jesus, he continues to be with me through his Spirit of holiness, just as he promised. Some days are harder than others, but on the hard days the Comforter reassures me I am not alone, that I am being conformed more and more into the image of Jesus, the true image of the invisible God. ■

Stop Approaching the Trinity Like Rationalists and Pietists: The Gospel Is Trinitarian

Why put yourself in the shoes of a first-century woman like Zipporah? Doing so helps us see just how ingrained the Trinity is within our Christian story. From Jesus's baptism (Matt. 3:14–17; John 1:29–34), to his dying words (John 19:30), to his Great Commission (Matt. 28:19–20), to the giving of the Spirit at Pentecost (John 16:7; Acts 2:1–4), the story of salvation is trinitarian through and through. The Trinity is revealed in the redemption of the ungodly; Father, Son, and Spirit are unveiled in the salvation of humankind.[17]

For the first-century believer, to become a Christian was to embrace the salvation given and accomplished by none other than the triune God: Father, Son, and Holy Spirit. To gain access to the throne of grace, one had to come to the Father by believing in his only begotten Son, and that only happened if the Holy Spirit opened one's blind eyes to the Son's saving, resurrection life. For these early Christians, to believe the gospel was to believe that the one God of Israel was triune. Anything less was simply not Christian. A gospel that was not trinitarian was no gospel at all.[18]

I cannot emphasize this point enough. As long as we bear the label *evangelical*, we also believe in a gospel that is trinitarian through and through. However, evangelicals today forget this, plagued as we are by a type of trinitarian Alzheimer's. There may be reasons why. Sometimes we treat the Trinity like *rationalists*, as if the Trinity were some cognitive riddle to be cracked, a divine Rubik's Cube, fitting together random biblical texts until we come up with the magic mathematical formula. Once we formulate distilled propositions about each person's divinity, we add it all up and—*voila!*—Trinity. At other times, we treat the Trinity like *pietists*, dismissing the Trinity at the start of our pilgrimage because it is pure speculation that has nothing to do with the gospel or the Christian life, whether it be prayer, worship, or the preaching of the good news itself.

Either road is destructive. Either road has one end: a Trinity affirmed on paper but forever a footnote to the real matters of the Christian faith. Each road produces an evangelicalism that is "cold toward the doctrine of the Trinity, confused about its meaning, or noncommittal about its importance."[19] In my experience, many professors and pastors tend to be the former (cold, confused), while the average churchgoer in the pew tends to be the latter (noncommittal).

But as we saw with Zipporah, the Trinity defines the gospel because the gospel itself is all about the Trinity. The Father has sent his only begotten Son to accomplish our redemption, and the Father and the Son have sent the Spirit to apply that redemption within us. There is a trinitarian *descent* for the sake of our salvation.

Even our subjective reception of this objective gospel and its ongoing application to us in the life of the church is trinitarian. Regenerated to new life by the Spirit, we are called to the Son, granted faith in Christ our Savior, and, on the basis of his life, death, and resurrection, we have access to the Father's throne of grace. "For through him [Christ] we both have access in one Spirit to the Father" (Eph. 2:18). United to his Son by the power of the Spirit, our communion begins with not just one or two but all three persons of the Godhead. "In him [Christ] you also are being built together into a dwelling place for God by the Spirit" (Eph. 2:22; cf. 3:14–17). As a result, the most practical components of the Christian life are affected. We pray, for instance, to the Father through the Son by the Spirit. When we gather for worship, our liturgies (should!) lead us in the same direction, empowered by the Spirit to repent and believe in the only begotten Son sent by the Father for us and our salvation. As Paul says, "[We] worship *by the Spirit of God* and glory in *Christ Jesus*" (Phil. 3:3). "Enlightened by the Spirit," says Basil of Caesarea, we look "upon the Son, and in Him as in the Image, behold the Father."[20] If the gospel reveals a trinitarian descent, our reception of that gospel involves an *ascent* into the triune life of God.

Furthermore, the trinitarian nature of the gospel also means that this gospel tells us something about who this triune God is in and of himself, apart from creation and salvation. The deeper we go into the mystery of the gospel of Jesus Christ, the more we discover that the mission of the Son in salvation history—the fact that he is *sent* by the Father—reflects his eternal origin from the Father in eternity. That pattern applies to the whole Trinity: the Father sending the Son, the Father and the Son giving the Spirit— these missions are not arbitrary but reveal something intrinsic about God's triunity. The Father *sends* his Son into the world because it is the Son who is eternally *begotten* (generated) by the Father apart from the world. Likewise, the Father and the Son *give* the Spirit, who descends on the world because the Father and the Son eternally *breathe out* or *spirate* the Spirit apart from the world. Point is, the temporal missions *reveal* the eternal relations.[21]

Nevertheless, for many Christians a barrier remains. Excited to learn that the gospel is trinitarian through and through, overjoyed to discover that the missions in salvation history tell us something eternal about who this triune God is in and of himself, the Christian sprints to the Scriptures expecting to see the Trinity pop out on every page. Starting in Genesis, this newfound trinitarian zeal begins to wane as he or she reads hundreds of pages, disappointed not to see the whole Trinity making a grand appearance in any explicit way. Fatigued and frustrated, doubts set in: *Is this Trinity just an invention of the New Testament? I've been told the Trinity is the very core of the gospel I believe, so why then does it not make its grand entry until the last two hundred pages of my Bible?*

What's Interior Decorating Got to Do with It?

Have you ever noticed that history's turning points are sometimes discovered in the background of its story? The Reformation is a case in point. We love to retell the story of that obscure German monk, Martin Luther, and his Ninety-Five Theses nailed to the castle church door in Wittenberg, or that fiery William Farel, who threatened a young and impressionable John Calvin to stay and pastor in Geneva lest God curse his ivory-tower aspirations. But keep in mind that sometimes the surest markers of reform were subtle, quiet changes in the furniture. Yes, the *furniture*. If you lived in the sixteenth century, one of the first objects to confront you as you walked into one of Rome's cathedrals was the altar, front and center. For it was on the altar that the miracle of transubstantiation was said to occur: the bread and wine transformed into the body and blood of Jesus. But if you walked into a church committed to the Reformation, it was the pulpit that confronted you as well, a pulpit sometimes attached to a pillar so that all God's people could hear all God's Word. This simple (but controversial) transition in architecture communicated where final authority resided: in the Word of God. For it was in the Scriptures that the gospel itself could be found, which is why Luther said Scripture, the Old Testament in particular, is the swaddling cloth in which Christ is born.

Did you know that interior decorating matters for our doctrine of the Trinity as well? B. B. Warfield compares the revelation of the Trinity to fixtures in a room.[22] At first, the room is dimly lit, and you cannot see the objects in the room very well, if at all. But as the lights brighten, you can make out pieces of furniture, and the lighter the room gets, the more you discover just how furnished this room was to begin with. The furniture did not appear all of a sudden when the lights turned bright. No, the furniture was there the whole time. So, what changed? Our sight changed. While the dimness of the room kept us from seeing the furniture, a little illumination resulted in what appeared to be "new" furniture.

In reality, the velvet couches, the oak bookshelves, the van Gogh artwork adorning the walls were there the whole time.[23]

Interior decorating teaches us three points about how the Trinity is revealed to us in history.

1. *In between two worlds.* While there are many allusions to plurality within the one God across the Old Testament, the *fullness* of the Trinity is revealed at a unique point in history: the time between the Testaments. If the Trinity begins to come into full light with the incarnation of the Son, Christ Jesus, then God's *full* revelation of his triune identity occurs after the writing of the Old Testament but before the writing of the New Testament. With the incarnation of the Son and the descent of the Spirit, the Trinity is revealed in the salvation of God's people, which then gives the New Testament authors much to say and confess about the Father, Son, and Holy Spirit in their epistles.[24]

As Christians in the twenty-first century, we need this reminder. This side of the cross, with the full canon in hand—the canon referring to all those books we call inspired Scripture, aka the Bible—we flip pages in our Bible and move from the Old to New Testament in seconds. But don't forget, hundreds of years pass by with a flip of the page. What holds these two testaments together is none other than Christ himself. He is the christological clamp.[25] His coming means not only the fulfillment of all those covenant promises God made in the Old Testament but the full revelation of God himself as Father, Son, and Holy Spirit. Through redemption comes revelation, and through revelation comes redemption.[26] The Trinity is not a mere means to salvation; the Trinity *is* salvation for God's people.

Is the Bible Trinitarian?

"The whole book [Bible] is Trinitarian to the core; all its teaching is built on the assumption of the Trinity; and its allusions to the Trinity are frequent, cursory, easy and confident." —B. B. Warfield, "The Biblical Doctrine of the Trinity"

2. *Perfected, extended, and enlarged.* Rather than thinking, as many skeptics do, that the Trinity is an invention, the New Testament correcting the monotheism of the Old Testament, we should instead think of the Trinity coming into full view, lit up and radiant, an effulgence of triune revelation right before our eyes. "The mystery of the Trinity is not revealed in the Old Testament," says Warfield, "but the mystery of the Trinity *underlies* the Old Testament revelation, and here and there *almost comes into view*." Remember Zipporah? She stared at Christ crucified, only to recall John's words—"Behold, the Lamb of God." It was then that the lights came on: the entire sacrificial system, as well as prophets like Isaiah, had pointed forward to this dark day of redemption. For that reason, the "Old Testament revelation of God is *not corrected* by the fuller revelation which follows it, but only *perfected, extended and enlarged*."[27]

I like that word—*extended*. God's triunity was embedded in the soil of the Old Testament, and at the proper time it shot up and blossomed in the light of the Son. Is this not what Hebrews

Does the Old Testament Point to the Trinity?

Observe several traces of the Trinity in the Old Testament:

- Distinction between names: Elohim and Yahweh
- Plural form *Elohim*
- The angel of the Lord
- Wisdom personified in Job 28:12–27 and Proverbs 8
- Word of God also personified; ascribed divine attributes
- Spirit of God
- God speaks of himself in the plural
- Multiple divine persons named
- Three persons named

These and more can be found in *Reformed Dogmatics* by Geerhardus Vos.

says? "Long ago, at many times and in many ways, God spoke to our fathers by the prophets, but in these last days he has spoken to us by his Son" (1:1–2). If we think in the categories of Hebrews, then the Trinity is not an invention of the New Testament but is revealed in full color when God's promises of old are fulfilled in the coming of his own Son.[28]

3. *Brought to you courtesy of the Scriptures.* Although the Trinity is manifested, at least in full, between the testaments, the *Scriptures* are God's written, definitive revelation of his triune identity for his people. In the New Testament, the triune God of the Old Testament steps into the bright lights of this world's stage to reveal his triune identity foreshadowed prior to that point. But having done so, he then leaves a permanent witness to his triune identity by giving us the Scriptures, which, I should remind you, are inspired by the triune God himself. The Father has revealed his Word by his Spirit.

This last point should not be underestimated. Yes, it is *in the gospel* that our God reveals his triune identity in greater detail. In the incarnation we meet not only the Son but the Father and the Spirit. But how does this triune gospel come to us now that Christ has ascended to the right hand of the Father? Answer: in the Scriptures. The Bible is the triune gospel inscripturated. The written Word of God (itself a form of special revelation) is the God-appointed medium through which we receive the fullest and most definitive knowledge of the Trinity. How ingenious of God: these Scriptures are breathed out by the triune God himself for the purpose of revealing their triune Author for us and our salvation.[29]

With all this emphasis on the gospel and how that gospel reveals the Trinity, another question is raised, and one we must get right:

Q: *The Trinity is revealed to us in the economy of salvation—especially the gospel—but should we conflate who God is in eternity with his acts in salvation history?*

A: *No.*

Danger Ahead: Conflation

In all our excitement over the gift of revelation, a gift that gives us knowledge of our triune God, we might get cocky and assume that all there is to the Trinity is whatever we see happen in the incarnation (the gospel). As if who the Trinity is in and of himself is irrelevant, only to be collapsed into whatever the triune God does in creation and salvation, or whatever the man Christ Jesus does during his earthly ministry. Forget ontology; functionality is the key, says many a theologian.

If taken to an extreme, we might also assume that the triune God's actions in salvation history do not merely *reveal* but *constitute* the persons of the Trinity in eternity (see chap. 3). Either danger can be summarized in one word: *conflation*. Who the triune God is in and of himself is conflated with what happens in history. The eternal God is, to be blunt, *historicized*. All in the name of the gospel, too.

Before we start pointing the finger at others, do realize that this danger is not out there somewhere; it's a danger within our own camp. I speak from personal experience when I say that we Bible-believing, gospel-centered, Christ-saturated evangelicals are prone to this danger we've called conflation. I realize how confusing that sounds; after all, didn't I just emphasize the *gospel* and how that gospel reveals the Trinity? But notice, there is a major difference between saying (1) the gospel reveals the Trinity and (2) the gospel constitutes, even creates, the Trinity. It might sound strange to say so, but as evangelicals we can easily drift from #1 to #2, while masking our drift in gospel categories.

For all our healthy focus on what God has done to save us, we might talk and talk and talk about *our* salvation and forget to talk about the gospel's ultimate object of adoration: the triune God himself. The gospel is supposed to move us beyond *ourselves* to know God and who he is *in and of himself*. For all our focus on what God *does for us*, we sometimes forget who he *is apart from us* and why there is no gospel at all without the latter.

How Do We Avoid Conflation?

Resisting this danger of conflation demands theological precision on our part, and whenever precision is needed, so are words and phrases that can help clarify.

To begin with, let's distinguish between the *immanent Trinity* and the *economic Trinity*. The immanent Trinity refers to who our triune God is in eternity, apart from the created order. Sometimes the immanent Trinity is called the *ontological Trinity*. Remember, ontology refers to the study of being, in this case God's being, that is, his essence or nature. To refer to the immanent Trinity, then, is to refer to who the triune God is *internally*, according to himself and in and of himself, apart from creation. The economic Trinity, however, refers to how this triune God acts toward the created order. Economic describes the triune God's *external* operations in creation, providence, and redemption. Perhaps some Latin can help: when we refer to the Trinity in eternity (immanent Trinity), apart from the created order, we can refer to the *opera ad intra*, the internal operations of the Trinity. But when we refer to how the Trinity acts toward his creation (economic Trinity), we can refer to the *opera ad extra*, the external operations of the Trinity.

But the million-dollar question is this: what is the relation between immanent and economic? As we learned in chapter 3, Karl Rahner said, "The 'economic' Trinity *is* the 'immanent' Trinity, and *vice versa*." Rahner said this is the "fundamental axiom" of trinitarian theology.[30] Elsewhere, Rahner elaborates: "Both mysteries, that of our grace and that of God in himself, are the same fathomless mystery."[31]

What should we make of Rahner's Rule? If he merely means that we have not two Trinities but one Trinity, that the triune God's economic works, his external operations in relation to the world, reveal something true about who he is in and of himself (immanent Trinity), then fair enough. We should avoid the danger of bifurcating the immanent and economic. There is not, for example, a different Trinity, a second Trinity behind the curtain of God's Word that is duplicitous, contrary to the Trinity revealed to us in the Scriptures. The Trinity is not two-faced or schizophrenic.

In addition, as far as our knowledge of the Trinity is concerned, the only way we know anything true about who God is in and of himself as Father, Son, and Holy Spirit is through his revelatory acts (e.g., incarnation and Pentecost) and Word (Christ and the Scriptures). We should not become trinitarian agnostics, as if the immanent and economic distinction results in no true knowledge of God whatsoever. Nor do we desire to create a trinitarian dichotomy, as if who the triune God is toward his creation says nothing true nor resembles by analogy who this triune God is in eternity. If these variations were true, then this book would be very short indeed; I would not have much to say.

Nevertheless, there are reasons to be suspicious of Rahner's Rule.

It Depends on What the Meaning of the Word "Is" Is

Every US presidency is filled with controversy, but have you ever noticed that sometimes these notorious scandals are remembered by a single line, sometimes a single word? The Watergate scandal, for example, exposed Richard Nixon's scheme to break into the Democratic National Committee's headquarters. In an attempt to appear innocent, Nixon spoke on national television and insisted, "I'm not a crook." Or consider Bill Clinton's grand jury trial concerning his sexual relations with Monica Lewinsky. When asked about his attorney's statement—"there is absolutely no sex of any kind, manner, shape or form with president Clinton"—the president responded, "It depends on what the meaning of the word 'is' is."

There is nothing politically scandalous about Rahner's Rule. But unlike Clinton's now comical statement, Rahner's Rule does depend on what the meaning of the word "is" is. If the rule is taken to mean—as that word "is" seems to convey—that the economic is to be *equated* with the immanent, well then, we have a problem. Notice, the rule says "vice versa," which means not only is the economic the immanent but the immanent *is* the economic. Who the triune God is in himself is nothing more than who the triune God is in history. There are many reasons this is dubious.[32]

First, it distorts the purpose of revelation by conflating who our triune God is apart from creation with what he does in creation. In the end, little to no surplus remains. What God says to his creatures about his triune identity through his mighty works and words does reveal something true about the triune God in eternity (see chap. 7). But we should not assume that who God is in his revelatory actions toward the created order exhausts who he is apart from the created order. In other words, the economic, external works of the Trinity may reveal something that is true about the Trinity (though we must be careful what that something is exactly), but we dare not think who this triune God is in and of himself can be reduced to his external actions in history, actions that may even be temporary. If we do, we may impose human limitations or characteristics on God himself.

For example, take a modern thinker like Moltmann (chap. 3). Moltmann looks at the cross and assumes that if the Son suffers in his humanity, not only must he then suffer in his divinity, but the whole Trinity suffers as well. God was crucified; God died. Moltmann has collapsed the immanent into the economic, allowing the humanity of Christ during the incarnation to define and determine the deity of the entire Trinity in eternity. Or consider EFSers who look at the Son's submission to the Father during the incarnation, which is for the purpose of salvation, and then assume that the Son must be subordinate to the Father's authority in eternity too, even within the immanent Trinity (see chap. 8). The Son's inferiority defines who the Son is apart from the

Immanent and Economic Trinity

Immanent	Economic
Opera ad intra Internal operations	*Opera ad extra* External operations or missions
Triune God in and of himself	Triune God in relation to created order
The eternal life of the triune God	The triune God's acts in history: creation, providence, and redemption
Cannot be exhausted by the economic	Reveals something true about immanent but does not exhaust immanent
The hidden depths of God; known in its fullness by the Trinity alone	Revealed to creatures by the triune God's mighty acts and words

world (*ad intra*); it makes the Son a Son. Like Moltmann, EFS has taken a human quality during the incarnation—but in this case submission—and projected it back onto the divine person of the Son apart from creation so that hierarchy defines the inner life of the Trinity in eternity. These are examples of locking eternity into history, so that the characteristics and limitations of humanity are projected onto deity. What occurs in the human experience of Christ is projected onto the divinity of the entire Godhead. At its root, this is a failure to distinguish between Christ in the form of a *servant* and Christ in the form of *God*. Christology has swallowed up the Trinity. *Our triune God has been domesticated, created in our image.*

This first problem reveals an irony: Rahner attempted to liberate the Trinity, which he believed scholasticism (think the Great Tradition) had locked in eternity. But Rahner's Rule locks God in as well; the difference is that the Trinity's prison cell is not eternity but history. God in himself is no more than his earthly interactions with creatures.

Second, conflating God in eternity with his actions in history risks making God no bigger than creation itself. It reduces God's infinite, triune identity in and of himself in eternity to the *effects* of his actions toward his creatures. It is one thing to say (as we have) that the economic *reveals* the immanent to a degree and in

God Doesn't Need You . . . and That's Good News

By distinguishing between the immanent and the economic, we safeguard God's aseity. Aseity means God is life in and of himself. He does not then depend on anyone or anything for his existence or happiness (Acts 17:24–29). Creatures are derivative, dependent beings, but not the Creator. If we collapse the immanent and economic, we compromise this key difference between the Creator and creature and forfeit God's aseity.

a specific way—the sending of the Son reflecting the eternal generation of the Son, for example. But it is an altogether different thing to say that the economic *constitutes* the immanent, or that anything and everything in the economic (suffering, submission) is to be *projected* back into the immanent, as if what distinguishes Father from Son from Spirit are his actions in the world.[33] Gilles Emery warns, "The history of salvation manifests the Trinity, but it is not the economy of salvation that gives to the Father, Son, and Holy Spirit their distinct personality. . . . [The] economy does not constitute the Trinity."[34] While God's acts in history may reveal something of his triune identity, he in no way depends on history for his triune identity, nor should all that occurs in history be projected onto the Trinity's immanent, eternal identity.

Relations and Missions

With all the confusion Rahner's Rule has created, some have wondered if it is wise to use a different vocabulary than immanent and economic, a vocabulary that might be more specific and avoid the conflation and projection pitfalls of the past. If immanent and economic are misappropriated, it is easy to project just about anything under the umbrella of economic onto the immanent— suffering, subordination, change, and so on—and then claim, "The economic reveals the immanent, right? Right."

Without dumping immanent and economic language altogether, there may be wisdom in using a far more specific vocabulary like *relations* and *missions*.[35] Remember, the immanent Trinity refers to who God is in himself, the one God who is distinguished as three persons by his eternal relations of origin alone: the Father is unbegotten, the Son is begotten, and the Spirit is spirated (see chap. 2). These eternal relations of origin—and these relations *alone*—explain the internal and eternal ordering (processions) in the Trinity (paternity, filiation, spiration). But they also explain the external and temporal missions of the Trinity.

For example, it is because the Father *begets* his Son in eternity that it is fitting for the Father to *send* his Son to become incarnate in history. And it is because the Father and the Son together (as one source) *spirate* the Spirit in eternity that it is fitting for the Father and the Son to *send* (give) the Spirit in history. But let's be very clear to avoid conflation: begetting and spirating in eternity are not the same thing as sending and giving in salvation history. Begetting and spirating are *eternal* and *internal*, occurring within the triune God before all ages, apart from the world, independent of the world. Sending, however, is *temporal* and *external* in the sense that the Son and Spirit are sent into the world with a specific mission to accomplish once and for all.

Lest we think too much of ourselves, we need to sober up and remember that even if our triune God never created the universe, even if our triune God never decided to send his Son to save the world, the eternal relations of origin would still be true. The eternal relations of origin are independent of creation and salvation. Our God is Trinity regardless of whether he ever creates or redeems. We reject the modern belief that the Father sending his Son into the world constitutes his relations as the unbegotten Father who begets his Son from all eternity, or that the sending of the Spirit into the world by the Father and the Son constitutes his relation as the spirated Spirit from all eternity. In doing so, we safeguard our triune God's freedom and aseity (self-existence and self-sufficiency): he is triune whether or not he creates or saves. As the timeless eternal God, his triune identity in no way *depends* on creating or saving the world. As John Gill says, "If there had never been a creature made, nor a soul saved, nor a sinner sanctified, God would have been the same he is, three Persons in one God."[36] The triune God gives grace by choice, but he lives by nature, out of necessity.[37]

Missions Reveal Relations

Modern Theology

Orthodox Trinitarianism: Fathers, Creeds, and Reformed

That does not mean, however, that the eternal relations of origin are not *reflected* in the temporal missions of the Trinity. Missions do reveal relations, even if those same missions in no way constitute relations. For example, in chapter 6 we will focus on eternal generation, the Son's eternal relation of origin (or personal property). There we will learn that the Son's temporal mission (being *sent* by the Father) is designed to *reveal* (but not constitute) his eternal relation of origin as the only begotten Son from the Father, generated by the Father before all ages. As Augustine says, "Just as the Father, then, begot and the Son was begotten, so the Father sent and the Son was sent."[38] Likewise with the Spirit: the Father and the Son sending and giving the Spirit to perfect the work of salvation is designed to *reveal* (but not constitute) the Spirit's eternal relation of origin: spiration, proceeding from the Father and the Son from all eternity. Augustine writes that just "as for the Holy Spirit his being the gift of God means his proceeding from the Father, so his being sent means his being known to proceed from him."[39] Future chapters will capitalize on the biblical language of being sent (Son) and being given (Spirit).[40]

In summary, the temporal missions—the sending of the Son and the giving of the Spirit—can *reveal* the eternal relations of origin (eternal generation and spiration), but the temporal missions in no way *constitute* the eternal relations of origin. The temporal missions are contingent (God does not have to create and save), but the eternal relations are necessary (he cannot be triune apart from them). Similarly, do not assume that anything that occurs in the economy (human suffering of the Son on the cross, the Son's humble submission to the Father as a servant [Phil. 2] to accomplish salvation) is to be *projected* back onto the immanent. We have avoided such ambiguity and striven instead for specificity: it is the *sending* in particular that reveals the eternal *relations* in particular. Far from anything and everything in the incarnation being projected back onto eternity, the Son being sent is a reflection and extension of the Son being begotten; likewise, the Spirit being given is a reflection of the Spirit being spirated. These relations *alone* are revealed in the missions. To read anything else back into the relations is to invite conflation.

Allergies, Anyone? John 1 and the Word of God

We evangelicals are prone to conflation. We approach the text assuming history is its only focus. The result? We develop an allergy to things eternal. Ironically, this approach—a crude biblicism—is a failure to be biblical enough.

Yes, Scripture's story line does take narrative form, focused as it is on salvation history. But the biblical authors never stop there, nor is narrative an end in and of itself. Never do they shove the infinite, incomprehensible Trinity into our tiny box of history, limiting who God is to what God does, prioritizing function over being. Either in their presuppositions (consider the Psalms) or in their theological conclusions (consult Paul's letters), they intend the reader to read *theologically*. More to the point, the biblical authors have no allergy whatsoever to eternity and ontology (the being of God). The biblical authors are not so focused on the historical facts of the life of Christ that they are unconcerned with his eternal, trinitarian origin prior to the incarnation. They are not so earthly minded that they are of no heavenly good. We should not be either.

Consider the opening of John's Gospel, for example. I often hear pastors advising churchgoers to give the Gospel of John to someone they are trying to evangelize. That's for good reason, too: John's Gospel lays out the gospel with lucid conviction, bringing the unbeliever face-to-face with the crucified and risen Christ and the many gifts he gives to all recipients of his grace. That's why we love texts like John 3:16; we desire to tell the world about God's Son so that they might receive eternal life.

But in our rush to talk about eternal *life*, we sometimes skip to the second half of John 3:16 and forget to talk about the eternal *Son*. As the first half of John 3:16 says, God "gave his only begotten Son" (KJV). Let those words marinate: God . . . gave . . . his . . . only begotten . . . Son. When we rush to the benefits the Son brings and skip over the identity the Son has in eternity, we neglect not only the first half of John 3:16 but the first two chapters of John's Gospel—chapters, need I remind you, that precede John 3.

Did you know, for instance, that John begins his Gospel not with the eternal life we receive but with the life the triune God enjoys in eternity? Go back to the opening of John 1 and what do you read? "In the beginning was the Word, and the Word was with God, and the Word was God. He was in the beginning with God" (1:1–2). Before we get to the good news about Jesus and the eternal life he brings, let's take a step back and consider, as John does, where this Jesus originates from in the first place. This will be hard, but let's put off what God has done in creation and focus first on who God is apart from creation. *Why would we do that?* Here's why: unless you understand who God is *apart from you*, you will never understand the importance of what God has done *for you*, at least not in full. I realize how counterintuitive that sounds, holding off on the history of redemption—your history—to talk about things eternal. Abstract and esoteric perhaps. But John is convinced that in doing so you will have a better grasp of who this Word is and why he became flesh and dwelt among us. Furthermore, a long line of church fathers also believe that John's approach avoids a dirty swamp of heresies, many of which threaten to *conflate* who God is in and of himself (*ad intra*) with how God acts externally (*ad extra*) toward his creation.

Notice what John does first: he begins in the beginning. But what John means by the beginning is probably not what you think. He echoes the language of creation from Genesis to talk about the eternal God who made creation, and who this God must be before any rose bush or palm tree came into existence. Before all ages, there was God and nothing else. Before the cosmos existed, there was God and him alone.[41] Except *alone* may sound as if he was lonely. He was not. For in the beginning, says John, was the Word—John's way of referring to the Son. Coeternal, this Word was *with* God. Coequal, this Word *was* God. It's hard to more closely identify the Word with God than this. He was coequal with God as the one who was God himself.

As we will see in chapter 7, John's choice of language—*Word*—is strategic. For soon enough he will tell his reader that this Word is none other than the Son of God himself. A word is worded by its speaker, meaning there is a source. Likewise with the Word: as the Word of God, he comes from God from all eternity to reveal God to those in history. John will spell this out in more detail when he switches his imagery from Word to Son (1:14). As Son, he is from his Father, for that is what it means to be a son after all. Yet since this is God we are talking about, the Son is generated from the Father's nature before all ages. Never was there a time when the Father was without his Word, because never was there a time when the Father did not beget his Word. If there were, then in no way could John say the Word (the Son) was both with God and was God. In John's mind the Word (the Son) is both distinct from God (the Word was with God) and one with God himself (the Word was God). But distinction (in personhood) and identity (in essence) is only possible because of eternal generation: the Son is distinct precisely because he is begotten by the Father; the Son is coequal precisely because he is begotten from the Father's nature, the same divine nature the Son shares.

Having established the Word's eternal relation of origin in verses 1–2, John is now ready to introduce the world. It is because the Word is eternal (never was there a time when the Word was not with God) and it is because the Word's origin is divine (never was there a time when the Word was not God) that "all things were made through him, and without him was not any thing made that was made" (1:3). Through the Word, God created the cosmos *ex nihilo*. To clarify, it's not the Word who is created out of nothing; the world is created out of nothing by the Word. The Word is not created along with creation, nor is the Word created prior to the rest of creation (Arianism; see chap. 2). Rather, the creation is brought into existence through the Word whose existence never began, whose divinity never had a starting point.

But it's not just creation that is attributed to the Word; salvation is as well. No work of God is kept from the Son. Transitioning metaphors, John calls the Word the "life" and the "light" (1:4–5), the "true light" that gives life to the world (1:9). He can do that since the "world was made through him" (1:10). But here's something more remarkable still: in order to give life to the world, the Word became incarnate. "And the Word was made flesh, and dwelt among us, (and we beheld his glory, the glory as of the only begotten of the Father,) full of grace and truth" (1:14 KJV).

Extraordinary! The eternal Word, the Son of God himself, the one who is begotten from the Father from all eternity, was sent by the Father to ensure we would be recipients of his grace. On the one hand, says John, "No man hath seen God at any time" (1:18), an observation the Old Testament itself reiterates (Deut. 4:15). On the other hand, "the only begotten Son, which is in the bosom of the Father, he hath declared him" (1:18 KJV). How appropriate, then, for John to call the eternal Son the eternal Word. It is because he is the only begotten Son from the Father, begotten before all ages as the Word who was with God and was God, that he can then, at the proper time, become incarnate and *reveal* the Father to us for our salvation. He is the revelation of God in the flesh.

As we will learn in future chapters, from John 1 forward, John and Jesus will both move back and forth from eternity to history, from God in himself to God toward us, always demonstrating that the latter is contingent on the former. But never, *never* conflating the two. As Jesus claims repeatedly to be the way to salvation in John's Gospel, he will also back up his right to make that claim, especially when the religious leaders question his authority, by appealing to his eternal origin from the Father. It is only because he is begotten by the Father from all eternity that he can then claim to be sent by the Father to become incarnate in history. His eternal relation to the Father constitutes his redemptive mission to the world, but not vice versa. Get that order right, and we see the gospel in proper trinitarian perspective; get that order wrong, and we misuse the gospel to redefine the Trinity in eternity.

God Doesn't Fit in Our Box

In summary, we evangelicals can learn much from John's opening chapter. With our well-intentioned focus on the gospel, we must not privilege certain texts or events to the point that we neglect texts that speak volumes about the character and triunity of God apart from history. If we do so, we risk shoving the infinite essence of our triune God into our tiny box of history, limiting who God is to what God does, prioritizing function over being. But the biblical authors understand that who the triune God is in and of himself can in no way be conflated or manipulated.

With the dangers of conflation flagged and historicizing tendencies arrested, the Word of God sits open before us, the missions of our triune God ready to reveal who this triune God is apart from us and what his relations mean for the simplicity of his infinite being.

Why Must God Be One to Be Three?

Simply Trinity

What is meant by simple is that its being is identical
with its attributes, apart from the relation in which
each person is said to stand to each other.

AUGUSTINE, *THE TRINITY*

Simplicity in respect to essence, but
Trinity in respect to persons.

FRANCIS TURRETIN, *INSTITUTES*

TO THE DELOREAN!

Where we're going: Into eternity, to learn about the Trinity's simplicity.

Key point: Simplicity really, really matters: it ensures the Trinity is one God and each person is equal. Simplicity helps fight against social trinitarianism, tritheism, and subordinationism, which cannot preserve the unity of the Trinity.

Tell Us Plainly

Yesterday I walked all the way to temple. I made the journey to prove myself: my sister didn't think I could still do it. Not at our age anyway. When we were young, the two of us walked to temple at least three times a week. I remember those trips: we used to skip hand-in-hand across the purple ocean of hyacinth squills in the spring. Halfway, we'd lie down under an olive grove to escape the heat, shaded by those ancient arms, fed by their single offering: brown and black olives, some bitter, some sweet. Popping olives into our mouths two at a time, we'd laugh at each other's confident predictions. How certain we were that any day now a handsome young man from Jerusalem would travel so far as our little town just to ask our father for our hand in marriage.

That was a long time ago, and while no handsome suitors ever arrived, my sister and I have remained constant companions. But we don't always see eye to eye. It wasn't the distance that bothered her, but the precarious tension within Jerusalem made her feel uncertain when I told her I was on my way to temple that morning. She's my older sister, so I suppose she feels responsible for me, but I've told her many times now that I can take care of myself.

But I knew she was on to something. For when I sat down to rest my ankles, which were now blistering from the rough edges of my leather sandal straps, that man Jesus walked by, and a crowd of disciples followed behind, like ducks all headed to the same pond. Worry swept over me like a tall wave in the sea. Every time I cross paths with Jesus something happens—a miracle or a fight with the Jews, but usually both. My feet were still screaming for relief, but I put my sandals back on and limped my way into the temple, curious to see what Jesus was up to. I didn't get far before I was pushed aside by the religious leaders, a pack of wolves ready to pounce with their sharp, skeptical questions meant only to trap the rabbi.

"How long will you keep us in suspense? If you are the Christ, tell us plainly," they demanded.[1]

But they were anything but sincere. In my experience, no matter what Jesus says or does, they will not believe him. They're not open to believing him. They have been eyewitnesses to some of Jesus's most impressive miracles, but they hate him all the more for these supernatural feats; they want him dead. That was the motive behind their question, a question as fatal as it was fierce. I knew it. The crowd knew it. Still, the question had face value to those listening, to those who came without an agenda. Heads turned with all eyes on Jesus, waiting to see how he would respond now that he was being put on the spot.

"I told you, and you do not believe. The works that I do in my Father's name bear witness about me, but you do not believe because you are not among my sheep."

I looked around, trying to judge the reaction of the crowd, Israelites no doubt familiar with their Shema. Judging by the furrowed brows, Jesus's response was a shock.

"Is he claiming that he is not on his own, that he has come from his Father, that his miracles are all done in the name of his Father, that he is none other than the Father's Son and Messiah?" the man next to me asked.

But Jesus continued, this time with words that took aim at *their* identity, the identity of his critics: "You are not among my sheep," he told them. "My sheep hear my voice, and I know them, and they follow me. I give them eternal life, and they will never perish, and no one will snatch them out of my hand."

Hearing such a conclusive verdict, I looked around and could tell what they were thinking by the look on their faces: *How do you know this?* As if he knew what they were thinking, Jesus fired back and said, "My Father, who has given them to me, is greater than all, and no one is able to snatch them out of the Father's hand."

"How does he know this?" the woman to my left said in a low voice, not wanting anyone to hear.

"Haven't you been listening?" I whispered back. "He is the Son, the one to whom his Father has given these sheep."

"But didn't Jesus just say these sheep were in his hand? Now he says they are in his Father's hand. So, which is it?" she replied.

"Both," I said.

Then Jesus said something that took everyone by surprise: "I and the Father are one." Even his own followers were taken off guard by the blunt blow of those words.

After what seemed like an eternity of reticence, the religious leaders let out an audible, disgruntled groan, shaking their heads, some holding out their hands and looking around, expecting everyone else to share their disbelief.

"What is he saying?" the woman next to me asked again, now more confused than before, but this time in a quieter voice, seeing the tension between the religious leaders and Jesus escalating.

"I don't think Jesus is merely referring to the way he, the Son of God, cooperates with the plan of his Father, a plan to save his sheep," I tried to clarify. "Jesus doesn't mean anything less, but I think he means much, much more."

Was I right? Or was I reading too much into Jesus's words? What happened next revealed the answer: the Jews picked up stones from the ground, jagged and sharp enough to really hurt someone, even kill someone. The crowd started to panic when they realized that someone was Jesus. Stoning was a penalty for serious blasphemers, the type who claim that they are Israel's Messiah or God himself, or both. Just the thought of a stoning shot anxiety up and down my spine like a cold chill. This was why only last week my sister told me to stop following Jesus; she was worried I might get hurt just being near the man.

Perhaps she was right. But now was not the time to stop. I was already in the thick of it.

As I watched them take aim at Jesus, everything clicked all at once: Jesus was claiming something significant, something divine even. He was claiming an eternal identity, and his claim was so strong, so absolute, so radical, that he believed he was one with the Father himself. I must have been thinking out loud, for the woman next to me elbowed me in the ribs, as if to say, "Shut up!"

I looked back up at Jesus, then at the Jews, then at Jesus again. He was a dead man. But just when the first stone was about to launch, Jesus spoke up. "I have shown you many good works from the Father; for which of them are you going to stone me?"

The question was provocative, forcing the Jews to tell him who they thought he was. And, to my surprise, they took the bait. "It is not for a good work that we are going to stone you but for blasphemy, because you, being a man, make yourself God."

I knew it: the Jews did understand Jesus's claim to be as radical as I thought.

"If I am not doing the works of my Father, then do not believe me; but if I do them, even though you do not believe me, believe the works, that you may know and understand that the Father is in me and I am in the Father."

This second response intensified an already dire situation. Jesus could not have made a more direct claim to oneness with God. No Jew would have dared to claim such a thing, nor would even the greatest of Israel's prophets. But maybe, just maybe Jesus was something more.

The dispute went on for what seemed like the better part of half an hour until the Jews stopped debating and sought to arrest Jesus instead. Somehow, though I'm not sure how, Jesus escaped. Last thing I heard, he made his way across the Jordan and received a much better reception when he landed on the other side. I've thought about making the trip myself if my feet could endure it. But I'm afraid I've inherited my father's soft soles. ■

How Can the Son Be *in* the Father?

"The Father is in me and I am in the Father."—Jesus (John 10:38; cf. 14:10–11, 20)

"Although remaining distinct, yet they [the three persons] are never separated from each other, but always coexist; wherever one is, there the other also really is."—Francis Turretin

The Great Tradition in the East and West used different words to refer to this coexistence or mutual indwelling:

1. *Perichoresis* (Greek)
2. *Circumincessio* (Latin)

But Jesus can only affirm perichoresis if he is *homoousios*, from the same essence, as the Father. However, he is only *homoousios* if he is begotten from the Father's *ousia*. If not, then perichoresis makes little sense. As Hilary says, "Those properties which are in the Father are the source of those wherewith the Son is endowed." Hilary elaborates, "The Father is in the Son, for the Son is from Him; the Son is in the Father, because the Father is His sole Origin; the Only-begotten is in the Unbegotten because He is the Only-begotten from the Unbegotten" (*The Trinity* 3.4). John of Damascus and Thomas Aquinas (who even quotes Hilary) say the same. Unfortunately, social trinitarians have removed perichoresis from its patristic context and redefined it in societal categories.

Show Us the Father

What Zipporah witnessed in the temple, which you can read more about in John 10, was yet another sign of the accelerating hostility Jesus faced from the Jews. But what Jesus's opponents could not accept, Zipporah embraced: *Jesus is one with the Father.*

In the Gospel of John, this will not be the last time Jesus makes such an audacious claim—a claim that the church fathers believed was of no little significance for our understanding of the Trinity. For example, in John 14 Philip asks Jesus to show him and his fellow disciples the Father and that will be enough for them to believe, a request not all that different from the Jews in John 10 but without their notorious malice. Jesus's response is the same: "Have I been with you so long, and you still do not know me, Philip? Whoever has seen me has seen the Father. How can you say, 'Show us the Father'? Do you not believe that I am in the Father and the Father is in me? . . . Believe me that I am in the Father and the Father is in me, or else believe on account of the works themselves" (John 14:9–11).

What does Jesus mean? Augustine gives us insight: "When the Father is shown, the Son who is in him is shown also, and when the Son is shown, the Father who is in him is shown too."[2] As we saw in John 10, this mutual indwelling is only possible if the Son is of the selfsame essence as his Father.[3] "What is common to the divine persons," says Aquinas, "is the concept that each one of them subsists in the divine nature and is distinct from the others."[4] Whether it is the Father, the Son, or the Spirit, it is this unity in nature that defines the Trinity as one.[5]

By the end of John's Gospel, Jesus prays to his Father, knowing he will soon be raised up on the cross: "I glorified you on earth, having accomplished the work that you gave me to do. And now, Father, glorify me in your own presence with the glory that I had with you before the world existed" (John 17:4–5). Much could be said here about the cross as a type of glory, but for our purposes don't miss what's inferred: Jesus shares in a glory with the Father that predates his incarnation, that predates creation itself. It is a

Read the Bible with the Church

"[The] connection of the Father in the Son, and of the Son in the Paraclete [Spirit], produces three coherent Persons, who are yet distinct One from Another. These Three are one essence, not one Person, as it is said, 'I and my Father are One,' in respect of unity of substance, not singularity of number."—Athanasius divine glory, a trinitarian glory to be exact, one that the persons of the Godhead share one with another. Not only does Jesus refer to his preexistence as the Son of God, but he claims the unique, divine right to a glory God alone knows as Father, Son, and Spirit. And yet, as the Athanasian Creed says, there are not three glories but one.[6]

How is such unity possible? If the "Father, existing before the ages, is always in glory, and the pre-temporal Son is His glory, and if in like manner the Spirit of Christ is the Son's glory, always to be contemplated along with the Father and the Son," then there can be no "'before' in what is timeless," nor can one person be "'more honourable' in what is all essentially honourable," says Gregory of Nyssa.[7] There is but one divinity, one glory, one honor, and one authority. The Son is just as honorable as the Father, which is precisely what the Jews missed when they nailed him to a cross. They dishonored the honorable Son of God, sent from the Father yet equal to the Father in every way. For he is none other than the Father's glory.

Jesus, however, is not the only one who understood his identity in such trinitarian terms, identifying himself with the one God of Israel. The apostle Paul also has much to say, and not just about the Son but the Spirit as well, helping us envision Israel's monotheism through a trinitarian lens.

But to understand Paul, we first need to know a thing or two about Mexican food.

Chorizo, Tamales, and the Lord Who Is One

You would never know it by looking at me, thanks to my dad's side of the family, but I am half Mexican and proud to say so. As often as possible, I visit my aunts and uncles, nephews and cousins on my mom's side. Her last name has changed, but she will always be a Cervantez at heart, and so will I. Each time I leave my relatives, I wish I could stay longer. We talk for hours, sometimes all day. No agenda. No phones. No television. Just loved ones sharing, debating, reminiscing. It's the best.

I enjoy everyone in my *familia*. But I must say, my auntie Lecha holds a special place in my heart. That's because she knows the way to my heart, which is the way into every Mexican's heart: through the stomach. There is nothing like waking up in the morning to the sizzle and salty smell of chorizo crackling on the stove. There is nothing like sitting down for Thanksgiving dinner and bypassing the turkey to snag one of her legendary spicy tamales. Just when I think I couldn't eat another, she says, "*Mijo*, you're too skinny. You look like you're starving. Here, *mijo*, eat another tamale." I'm helpless. These tamales are irresistible. With *familia*, life always—and I mean *always*—revolves around food. But not just any food. Food that's been made with love and is consumed with loved ones.

My heritage has opened my eyes in countless ways to the centrality of food in the Bible, from the tree in the garden to the marriage supper of the Lamb. Of course, food could also be a source of contention in the first century. Take the Corinthians, for example. Paul must tell the Corinthians not to eat food sacrificed to idols *if* it will cause a less mature brother or sister to stumble (1 Cor. 8). For our purposes, something Paul says in the middle of this instruction is relevant for our doctrine of the Trinity. Just after Paul says an "idol has no real existence" and that "there is no God but one," he then says, "For although there may be so-called gods in heaven or on earth—as indeed there are many 'gods' and many 'lords'—yet for us there is one God, the Father, from whom are all things and for whom we exist, and one Lord, Jesus Christ, through whom are all things and through whom we exist" (1 Cor. 8:5–6). There is no question Paul has the Shema in view; he quotes from Deuteronomy 4:35, 39.[8] But who in the Old Testament ever included another name, another person, in the Shema? To do so would have been blasphemy. But Paul does. In the same breath he quotes from the Shema, he names Jesus Christ. There is "one God," he says, "the Father . . . *and* one Lord, Jesus Christ." Paul names the Father and the Son as the one God referenced and worshiped in the Old Testament.

What is more, when Paul refers to the Father as the one God, he refers to his work of creation: "from whom are all things and for whom we exist." But notice, he does the same when referring to Christ: "one Lord, Jesus Christ, through whom are all things and through whom we exist." Whether Paul has in mind John 5, where Jesus is almost killed for claiming to work on the Sabbath *just as his Father works on the Sabbath*, a prerogative reserved for God alone, Paul seems to presuppose the same concept. Jesus is not a second god, another deity that rivals the Father, as the religious leaders assumed. He is named and shares the single name of God with the Father; the divine work of creation attributed to the Father is attributed to him as well.

Paul is essentially telling these Corinthians that the one God of the Old Testament is to be confessed in trinitarian terms.[9] Paul is not adding Jesus to the Trinity, nor is he reinventing the Shema to meet his new trinitarian doctrine. Rather, Paul believes a true, right confession of the Shema is trinitarian through and through, a point that Paul takes for granted now that Christ has come. To confess that God is one is to confess Father, Son, and Holy Spirit as one Lord.

But wait, where is the Spirit in 1 Corinthians 8? The Spirit is not referenced in 1 Corinthians 8, but Paul is no binitarian. In his second letter to the Corinthians, Paul will use this same lordship language, except this time he applies it not only to the Son but to the Spirit. To understand why we must go back in time to the days of Moses. In the old covenant Moses "put a veil over his face so that the Israelites might not gaze at the outcome of what was being brought to an end" (3:13). Paul laments that "their minds were hardened" (3:14). Did anything change by Paul's day? No. Unfortunately, says Paul, "to this day whenever Moses is read a veil lies over their hearts." Although all seems lost, Paul says that there is hope: "For to this day, when they read the old covenant, that same veil remains unlifted, because only through Christ is it taken away. Yes, to this day whenever Moses is read a veil lies over their hearts. But when one turns to the Lord, the veil is removed" (3:14–16). What good news!

But wait, there's more good news, and this time it has to do with the Holy Spirit: "Now the Lord is the Spirit, and where the Spirit of the Lord is, there is freedom. And we all, with unveiled face, beholding the glory of the Lord, are being transformed into the same image from one degree of glory to another. For this comes from the Lord who is Spirit" (2 Cor. 3:17–18). The Spirit has unveiled our faces so that we are the recipients of the new covenant's blessings. But notice, the Spirit can only do so because he is the Lord himself. As the Lord, the "Spirit of God" not only awakens us to new life, opening our blind eyes, but transforms us, even sanctifies us so that we "have the mind of Christ" (consult 1 Cor. 2:10–16).

In sum, sometimes Scripture speaks of the Father, sometimes of the Son, and sometimes of the Spirit, but whenever it refers to any one person it assumes that person is consubstantial with all the others, coeternal and coequal in divinity, holding the one divine essence in common. The one God, the one Lord, is none other than Father, Son, and Holy Spirit. But in some cases, all three persons make an appearance all at once, and the beauty of triunity glistens all the more, as when Paul concludes his second letter to the Corinthians with a final blessing and benediction: "The grace of the Lord Jesus Christ and the love of God and the fellowship of the Holy Spirit be with you all" (13:14).

Yet Paul's letters to the Corinthians are but a sample of a larger pattern that pervades all his letters to the churches. For example, Paul writes to the Galatians concerning their adoption as children of God: "[We] were enslaved. . . . But when the fullness of time had come, God sent forth his Son, . . . so that we might receive adoption as sons. And because you are sons, God has sent the Spirit of his Son into our hearts, crying, 'Abba! Father!'" (4:3–6).

Or consider Paul's letter to the Ephesians, where he reminds the Ephesians that it is "through him"—that is, Christ—that "we both have access in one Spirit to the Father" (2:18). With such access, both Jews and Gentiles are like a house in which the triune God dwells (2:19), a household that has Christ as its cornerstone (2:20). In Christ, this household is "joined together" and "grows into a holy temple in the Lord" (2:21). "In him [Christ] you also are being built together into a dwelling place for God by the Spirit" (2:22). Paul is creative, using the metaphor of a building to encourage the Ephesians to unite together as one household, a unified temple. That unity is to reflect the unity of the triune God himself: "There is one body and one Spirit . . . one Lord, . . . one God and Father of all" (4:4–6). Paul is echoing Jesus's own prayer that his people would be one even as he is one with the Father (John 17:22).

Whether Paul is referring to the gospel, adoption, or the unity of the church, he assumes in each the triunity of the Father, Son, and Holy Spirit. In Paul's mind, there is but one God, one Lord, and his (one) name is Father, Son, and Holy Spirit. Paul is merely mimicking Christ before him, who commissioned his disciples by commanding them to baptize in the "name [singular] of the Father and of the Son and of the Holy Spirit" (Matt. 28:19).

As the church has confessed down through the ages, each person is a subsistence of the one divine essence, Father, Son, and Spirit holding the one essence in common, consubstantial with one another.

With Scripture's clear affirmation of triunity in view, let's get to the essence of the matter, because essence is, after all, what we most need to discuss.

Simply Trinity

To confess God as one is often taken to mean there is but one God. That is certainly true, and we should say nothing less. But there is more, far more, to say about God's oneness. To confess God as one is also to confess that God *is* one. He is one by nature, he is one in nature. He is not a God made up of parts but a God without parts. There is in him no composition, nor can he be compounded by parts. If he could, then he would be a *divided* being (parts are divisible by definition), a *mutable* being (parts are prone to change), a *temporal* being (parts require a composer), and a *dependent* being (depending on these parts as if they precede him). These attributes may define finite creatures, but they cannot characterize the immutable (unchanging), eternal (timeless), and self-sufficient God (aseity) who is without bodily form (incorporeal). As Hilary of Poitiers says, it is because God has no body—bodies being divisible by parts, as we know from experience—that he is "simple essence: no parts, but an all-embracing whole: nothing quickened, but everything living."[10]

How, then, do we describe a God without parts? Simple: we say God is simple. Not as in elementary or simplistic. Rather, he is a God of absolute simplicity. That means all that is in God *is* God. His essence and his attributes are not separate entities. His essence is his attributes and his attributes his essence. God does not merely possess love, for example; he *is* love. God does not merely possess holiness; he *is* holy. And so on and so on. His substance or essence is characterized by an intrinsic oneness. This is, at least in part, why he alone deserves to be called God, for no created being can

Simplicity and *Alice in Wonderland*

When Alice falls down the rabbit hole and returns to Wonderland, the Mad Hatter looks her over and says, "You're not the same as you were before. You were much more . . . muchier . . . you've lost your muchness." Whenever we talk about creatures, the Mad Hatter is right. But not with God. His essence never changes; he never becomes muchier than before. That's due to his simplicity. Since he is not made up of parts like us, he never loses his muchness. He is maximally alive or pure act, as the fathers liked to say.

be simple in this divine sense. "True divinity dwells in the unity of substance and the unity of substance dwells in the true divinity."[11] He is *simply* God.[12]

But some believe simplicity poses a challenge: how can God be simple if he is three persons?

How Can God Be Simple If He Is Triple?

When we confess monotheism, we are not just subscribing to any monotheism; we are not *bare* monotheists. Monotheism is not a cover-up for a God who is impersonal. Gregory of Nazianzus confronts this wrongheaded assumption: "Monotheism, with its single governing principle, is what *we* value—not monotheism defined as the sovereignty of a single person . . . but the single rule produced by equality of nature, harmony of will, identity of action, and the convergence toward their source of what springs from unity—none of which is possible in the case of created nature. The result is that though there is numerical distinction, there is no division in the substance."[13] What's Gregory after? Monotheism does not mean that God is a single person who governs the world.

Objection

How can simplicity apply to the persons if the Father acts to beget his Son? Doesn't eternal generation assume the Trinity acts and becomes something he is otherwise not (what theologians label passive potency)? Answer: no. The reason why: the persons are not agents with their own wills. Generation is not something that happens to the Son. Rather, to be the Son just *is* to be begotten. As Anselm prays, "You are so simple that there cannot be born of You any other than what You are. . . . Nor can there proceed from Your supreme simplicity what is other than that from which it proceeds. Thus, whatever each is singly, that the whole Trinity is altogether, Father, Son, and Holy Spirit" (*Proslogion*, in *Major Works*, 23).

Rather, his single rule reflects a single nature, will, and operation. Yet that can be said of three divine persons as long as they hold in common the same, single nature, will, and operation.

Perhaps our previous journey into trinitarian vocabulary should be revisited. Remember, to do justice to the way all of Scripture describes God's oneness and threeness, it was fitting for the fathers to say God is *one essence, three persons*. That is not to say essence and persons are to be divorced from one another (which would create four things, a quaternity). No, the three persons are subsistences of the one, undivided divine essence or nature, so that the three persons, distinct as they may be as Father, Son, and Spirit, nevertheless hold the one divine essence in common.

That means simplicity and Trinity are only a contradiction if God is one *in the same way* that he is three. But as we've just seen, that's not the case. When we say God is one, we are referring to his *essence* or *being* or *nature* (these three words are synonymous). When we refer to God as three, however, we are referring to three *persons*, specifically the way the simple essence subsists (exists) in each person in a special manner. We do not mean that God's simple essence is *triple*—for then the essence would be multiplied by three and no longer simple at all. We mean instead that the God who is *simple* in essence is *triune* in persons. That is why the fathers "were accustomed to say . . . 'one essence, three subsistences.'"[14]

If this distinction between essence and persons is still foggy, perhaps a few analogies can help us by not helping us at all.

Fool's Gold: Augustine, Anselm, and Analogies

Sometimes Christians with the best intentions appeal to analogies as if they explain the Trinity. You've probably heard them all: The Trinity is like an egg; it is one egg, but it is made up of the shell, the white, and the yolk. Or the Trinity is like a shamrock; it is one shamrock but three leaflets. Or the Trinity is like water, which can be steam, liquid, or ice. Problem is, analogies are susceptible to heresies. The egg and the shamrock cannot avoid tritheism, and water changing into different forms sounds a lot like Sabellianism.

Apparently, analogies are as old as dirt (and in some cases just as useful as dirt). If you read the fathers, they too were accustomed to hearing analogies from well-meaning churchgoers. Augustine, for example, says the following analogies just won't work (so stop trying):

- three friends, common friendship
- three neighbors, common neighborhood
- three relatives, common family
- three statues, common gold
- three species, of one being
- three men, one manhood[15]

Take gold, for example. On the surface, the analogy is intriguing: three statues, each made out of the same mineral—gold.

But hold on, says Augustine, "We do not talk about three persons out of the same being, as though what being is were one thing and what person is another, as we can talk about three statues out of the same gold."

Augustine of Hippo

In my estimation, the North African theologian Augustine (354–430) was the greatest trinitarian theologian the church has ever seen. There are few rivals to his book *The Trinity*, perhaps the most faithful and mature articulation of Nicene orthodoxy. Augustine became disillusioned with the Manichean sect and converted to Christianity, which you can read about in his *Confessions*. He was made bishop of Hippo by force and spent most weeks preparing sermons and counseling church members still influenced by paganism. Augustine wrote books against the Manichees, the Pelagians, the Donatists, and the Arians of his day.

"But why not?" a fourth-century churchgoer in Hippo asks.

"In this case being gold is one thing, being statues another."

"But what if the statues look the same, even have the same weight in gold?"

"In equal statues, there is more gold in three together than in each one of them, and less gold in one than in two," Augustine responds.

"I see your point."

"But that is not how it is in God; Father and Son together are *not more being than Father alone or Son alone,* but those three substances or persons together, if that is what they must be called, are equal to each one singly, which *the sensual man does not perceive* (1 Cor 2:14)."

"Who you calling sensual?" the now irritated fourth-century churchgoer from Hippo asks.

The sensual man "can only think of masses and spaces, little or great, with images of bodies flitting around in his mind like ghosts."[16]

"And that's why analogies from our physical universe don't work when applied to God who has no body?"

"Exactly," says Augustine.

Augustine exposes major problems with the gold analogy (and most other analogies too). Gold is divisible, each statue being a mere percentage of the gold divided into different parts. If you put all the statues in a giant bowl of fire and melt them down, together they are more than they are apart. That's because each statue by itself is less than all three combined.

La casa de papel: The Most Unaugustinian Bank Heist There Ever Was

Not long ago, the simplicity of God's triunity hit me as I was watching the Spanish drama *La casa de papel* (*House of Paper*), also called *Money Heist*.[17] In part 3, the Professor (the brains of the operation) and his Italian thieves reorganize to rob the impenetrable Bank of Spain so that Europol has no choice but to return one of their members, Rio. But how will they get the gold out? The always creative Nairobi has an idea: melt all the gold into tiny little pebbles that can then be dispersed in their escape. As they do so, "*Bella ciao*," a song that captures their anti-fascist message, plays in the background. How genius, I thought while watching their strategy take form. But it occurred to me what a terrible illustration this would make for the Trinity; how *unaugustinian* those directors must be. For everyone knows that the gold is worth more together than when it's apart, each tiny pebble of gold worth far less by itself than all the pebbles combined.

God's essence does not work that way in the Trinity. God's one essence is indivisible; it has no parts. The divine essence does not break into three parts to form three persons. Introducing such a separation results in a God compounded of parts.[18] Rather, the three persons are one in essence, each a subsistence of the identical, self-same essence, wholly possessing that one essence, not merely a portion of it. Although we distinguish the persons from the essence, we dare not think the essence is some fourth thing that the persons divvy up to hold in common. That is no real unity; that preserves no true simplicity. Instead, as John Owen says, a "divine person is nothing but the divine essence . . . subsisting in an especial manner."[19]

Nor should we look at the persons and think that if we put two of them together, we have more "God" than if we only stick with one of them. That is to buy into the gold analogy all over again. No, says Augustine, the "Father and the Son together" are not "more truly than the Father alone or the Son alone." Both "together are not something greater than each one of them singly."[20] That treats the Trinity like a math problem involving addition. But as we said, each person is wholly God, a subsistence of the same divine essence as the other persons in the Godhead. The "trinity itself is as great as any one person in it."[21] That means that "all the relations are not something more than just one, nor are all the persons something more than just one"; rather, says Aquinas, "the whole fulness of divine nature is present in each of the persons."[22] Even when we say that the Son, for example, is God from God (Nicaea), we do not mean that he is "God from God as whole from part, or as part from whole, or as part from part." No, "If there is God from God, *the whole God is from the whole God.*" That is because "God has no parts."[23]

Paul, Andrew, and James? Away with Quaternity

Unlike the movies, not every priceless artifact has been stolen in a heist and sold on the black market. Sometimes the most precious artifacts are just destroyed. For centuries a medieval limestone sculpture stood tall on the Romanesque cathedral in Vic, a town just north of Barcelona, Spain. Eventually, the sculpture

The Dumb Ox

Thomas Aquinas (1224/25–1274) was made fun of in school and was nicknamed "the dumb ox" because of his figure. As it turns out, this dumb ox shook the Western world and to this day is considered one of the greatest theologians, philosophers, and biblical commentators the church has ever seen. He not only wrote an extensive apologetic for theology called the *Summa Contra Gentiles*, but an extensive (unfinished) guide to theology for students called the *Summa Theologiae*. Sadly, Protestants today, especially evangelicals, avoid Thomas like the plague, thinking he is Roman Catholic. That is a caricature that needs to die a sudden death. Yes, we should critique Thomas (like any theologian in history), but to hand him over to Rome is to miss out on his countless theological, apologetic, exegetical, and pastoral insights. As to the Trinity, you cannot improve on Thomas. It is orthodoxy with crystal clarity.

was destroyed, as was the cathedral that housed its beauty. Nevertheless, a fragment of the sculpture was saved and today is housed in the Nelson-Atkins Museum in Kansas City. This rock fragment exhibits three apostles: Paul, Andrew, and James. Since I live in Kansas City, I have seen this twelfth-century work of art with my own two eyes. The paint colors are long since worn away; yet every curve, every crease is still sharp. The apostles stand one right next to the other with their Gospels in hand and circular halos adorning their brows. In my opinion, it is one of the museum's greatest treasures.

As much as I cherish this sculpture, it too is a bad analogy for the Trinity. Paul, Andrew, and James are three persons, and they all have the same human nature.[24] We might say they all possess the nature we call humanity. But can we say they are one human? We cannot.[25] Paul, Andrew, and James all participate in what we call humanity, but they are not a single human being. They are, rather, three separate individuals, three separate beings. They are not only distinct but independent. They may have much in common, but three they remain, not one. The illustration buckles: what we call a human nature can be divided. Never can it be a single human essence and at the same time three humans. "The common humanity of the three human persons does not indicate, as it must in God, a numerical unity of essence, only a generic unity."[26] And a generic unity will not do when we are speaking of the triune God.

Paul, Andrew, and James can exist without one another; they do not need one another, nor is their identity dependent on one another. There is no genuine unity between the three. They are, in short, separable and divisible. Not so with Father, Son, and Spirit. The Father does not exist without his Son, the Son does not exist without his Father, and the Spirit does not exist without the Father and the Son, not if all three have the same divine essence.[27] Yes, they are distinguishable, but only in terms of their eternal relations of origin (personal properties), not in terms of their essence (nature).

The divine essence they hold in common. For the essence is communicable, while the personal properties are not (they are incommunicable).[28] "The Father and the Son are one in all things except what concerns their personal properties: the Son is all that the Father is, except that he is not Father and not without principle," says Emery. "In the Father, in the Son, and in the Holy Spirit, the divine nature therefore is identical and the same."[29]

In sum, the divine essence isn't one thing and the three persons another thing, as if we now have four things, creating a *quaternity* instead of a Trinity—this is the real danger of both analogies (gold and apostles). As much as we distinguish between the essence and the persons, we cannot forget that each person is a divine subsistence of the one, undivided, indivisible essence. If not, simplicity dissolves and the Trinity with it. As John of Damascus says, "Each of the three has a perfect subsistence, . . . not one compound perfect nature made up of three imperfect elements, but one simple essence, surpassing and preceding perfection, existing in three perfect subsistences."[30]

Can Simplicity Help Fight Trinitarian Heresy?

The failure of the Paul-Andrew-James analogy teaches us one vital truth: everything hinges on this distinction between essence and persons. It's that important. Without it we either stray toward radical oneness (Sabellianism) or radical threeness (tritheism). But simplicity keeps us from both. In other words, simplicity is not only consistent with a God who is triune, but *simplicity is the reason we can affirm a God who is triune*, ironic as that may sound. Not only that, but simplicity guards us from several major trinitarian heresies.

Sabellianism. According to Sabellianism (also called modalistic monarchianism), God is not three persons but one person who merely changes into three different forms. The one person we call God wears three different masks: sometimes he puts on his mask to become Father, but then he changes masks to become Son or Holy Spirit. The one God is not three distinct *persons* but transitions into three *impersonal* modes, as if we do not have a Trinity unless the one person of God engages with his creation in three different ways.

Simplicity, however, comes to our rescue. When we affirm that there are three modes of subsistence (paternity, filiation, spiration), we do not mean three *impersonal* modes of subsistence (Sabellianism) but three *personal* modes of subsistence. In other words, the one essence is not manifested in three different ways (this is impersonal). Rather, the one essence eternally and wholly subsists in three undivided yet distinct *persons*, each person being a subsistence of the one, undivided essence.[31]

Tritheism. Simplicity also has a way of avoiding tritheism. As both Aquinas and Anselm explain, just because "there are three having divinity" does not mean there are "three Gods."[32] The one, divine essence is not multiplied three times: that is *triplicity*.[33] Triplicity leads to tritheism, because "if God is composed of three things, either there is no simple substance, or there is another substance that surpasses the substance of God in something."[34] Three things, three parts, would compromise the one, simple essence of God.[35]

However, *triplicity* is not the same thing as *Trinity*. Triplicity divides the essence of God by making each person an individual agent. But the Great Tradition avoids this pitfall by stressing that the one, simple essence has *three modes of subsistence*. Rather than merely saying God is three persons, we can be more specific: the one, undivided essence wholly subsists in three persons, each person a subsistence of the same, simple essence. Listen to what John Gill says: "There is but one divine essence, undivided, and common to Father, Son, and Spirit, and in this sense but one God; since there is but one essence, *though there are different modes of subsisting* in it which are called persons; and these *possess the whole essence undivided.*"[36] While simplicity precludes parts, it

Is God Only One Person?

In the first three centuries of the church, Christians lived in a polytheistic culture that believed in more than one god. Christianity, by contrast, taught there is but one God, and this one God is ruler over all, Lord of heaven and earth. However, in an effort to preserve the rule of the one God, some went in a heretical direction: *modalistic monarchianism*. To make sense of the biblical names—Father, Son, Spirit—they claimed that the one monarch was merely being described in different ways. His one rule takes on three revelatory forms. In the third century, a man named Sabellius was excommunicated. We don't know much about Sabellius, but it appears an enhanced version of modalistic monarchianism was associated with him. The one person of God enters into three different roles, each one serving a unique purpose in salvation history. Sabellianism taught, as a result, *patripassianism*. When the Son suffered on the cross, the Father suffered on the cross, for they are the same person. Different church fathers responded to Sabellianism's various representatives. For example, Tertullian (c. 160–220) wrote a book called *Against Praxeas*. While the book gives the impression his target is Praxeas, the name in Greek means "busy body." Most likely, the real name of the person in question was Callistus. To protect the Trinity from heresy, Tertullian developed a trinitarian grammar in Latin:

trinitas = Trinity
persona = person
substantia = substance

Tertullian and Origen also argued that the Son is eternally begotten from the Father, thereby distinguishing him as a person. He is not another god but a *persona* who is from the same *substantia* as the Father who begot him.

Besides Tertullian and Origen, Hyppolytus also responded to Sabellianism.

does not preclude eternal relations or personal properties. For these relations do not undermine the oneness of God, but undergird such unity.

How so?

The eternal relations of origin—the Father unbegotten, the Son begotten, the Spirit spirated—not only distinguish the persons, but these relations also guarantee the persons are subsistences of the *same* divine essence. The divine essence is communicated from the Father to the Son and from the Father and the Son to the Spirit. For example, consider eternal generation. The Son is begotten from the Father's essence, or as the church fathers so often said, from the Father's *ousia*. Later theologians picked up on this point too. Francis Turretin wrote, "By generation the divine essence is communicated to the begotten, not that it may exist, but subsist."[37] So, whenever we stress the relations as that which alone distinguish the persons, we must not forget these same relations preserve the simplicity of the essence.

Does Social Trinitarianism Make God More or Less Personal?

If God is made up of parts, his parts would need to be actualized; God would have to reach his potential and become something more than he is. But simplicity teaches us that God is without parts and therefore is maximally alive. He is, as the Great Tradition liked to say, *pure act*; he need not become anything more than he is from eternity. That means he cannot become any more personal than he already is from eternity. Ironically, the social trinitarian who rejects simplicity makes God less (not more) personal. And by defining the Trinity as a society or community in which each person is his own center of consciousness and will, social trinitarians must explain why the persons need not *become* more personal in their interdependent relationships of love. To learn more about God as pure act, see chapter 6 and the glossary.

Social trinitarianism. If simplicity guards against tritheism, then so too does it protect us from social trinitarianism. If God is one in *essence*, then he is without a doubt one in *will*. "The Father, Son, and Spirit," says John Owen, "have not distinct wills. They are one God, and God's will is one, as being an essential property of his nature."[38] This is essential to orthodox trinitarianism, a key pillar that protects the Trinity from heresy as well as Trinity drift.

However, many forms of social trinitarianism reject this belief and instead teach that there are three centers of consciousness and therefore three wills in the Godhead. Social trinitarianism places emphasis on the persons as a community, as a society, each person having his own will that is not only distinct but different from the wills of the other persons (see chap. 3).

This is a mistake of colossal proportions. Despite protests to the contrary, social trinitarianism has all the ingredients for tritheism. For where there are three wills there are three separate centers of consciousness, and where there are three separate centers of consciousness there are three separate gods. In this view, God no longer *acts* as one because he *is* one (inseparable operations), but he acts as one because the three wills of the three persons merely cooperate with one another. We will revisit the one will of the Trinity in chapter 10, because only one will can explain how the external works of our triune God remain indivisible. For now, here is a teaser: "God is one, therefore the power and operation of all the Persons are one and undivided; and each Person is the immediate and perfect cause of the whole work."[39]

To conclude, true unity is not a mere *unity of will(s)* (this is what the Arians argued), but there must be a *unity in being* (the Great Tradition).[40] The persons act as one because they are one—one in essence and therefore one in will. "For there is one essence, one goodness, one power, one will, one energy, one authority, one and the same, I repeat, not three resembling each other," says John of Damascus. "But the three subsistences have one and the same movement. For each one of them is related closely to the other as to itself: that is to say that the Father, the Son, and the Holy Spirit are one in all respects, save those of not being begotten, of birth and of procession."[41]

What, then, distinguishes the persons if not different wills? As chapter 6 will explain, the persons are identical in all things except their eternal relations of origin (personal properties): paternity, filiation, spiration. These and these alone distinguish the persons. Anything more, anything else, and the unity of our triune God is divided; divine simplicity is compromised. God is no longer *simply* Trinity.

But that's not all. These relations don't just distinguish; they also unite.

Simplicity Matters for Equality: The Athanasian Creed

We've now seen that simplicity matters. It guards us from both Sabellianism and tritheism, as well as social trinitarianism. But simplicity also matters for another reason: *equality*. No simplicity, no equality. Or, to get your attention: simplicity protects us from the heresy of Arianism (and any shade of subordinationism).

If God is not made up of parts but the one divine essence wholly subsists in three persons, then it must also follow that each person is wholly God. Simplicity guards us from thinking that one person of the Trinity is superior to another, or that one person of the Trinity is inferior to another, either in essence, power, will, or authority.

But again, such coequality can only be affirmed if simplicity is true of God. Should he be divided by parts we call Father, Son, and Spirit, then those parts are either not wholly God—each only possessing part of God, tallying up to God when they are added together—or they are wholly divine because they are each their own God, resulting in tritheism. But if God is simple, then he is not made up of three parts, nor is he divisible by three centers of consciousness or three different wills. Instead, he is one, his

The Athanasian Creed

There was a time when some said this creed was written by Athanasius, but scholars now recognize that Athanasius did not write it. They believe the creed does not originate from the East but from the West, and dates to the late fifth or early sixth century. Nevertheless, the creed's language is indebted to both East and West, reliant as it is on the Nicene Creed and Augustine. Medieval fathers believed anyone preparing for ministry should know the Athanasian Creed. Some said it was just as important as the Nicene Creed. The Apostles' Creed, the Nicene Creed, and the Athanasian Creed formed the *Tria Symbola*. And the Reformers considered the Athanasian Creed just as monumental as the other two, believing it to teach the same faith. To find out more, read J. N. D. Kelly, *The Athanasian Creed*.

essence being without composition. Indivisible, his one essence cannot be divided up among three persons nor can it be dismantled into three separate agents of divinity. Rather, the one, indivisible essence wholly subsists in three persons, so that each person is a subsistence of the one, undivided divine essence.

That means, then, that whether we are talking about the Father or the Son or the Holy Spirit, each is to be considered true God, wholly divine. Not one of them, not even in the slightest, is less than another. "This is so," says Aquinas, "because the divine essence is not the Father's more than the Son's and accordingly even as the Son has the Father's greatness, i.e. is the Father's equal, so the Father has the Son's, i.e. is the Son's equal."[42] Inferiority cannot exist where each person is a subsistence of the same, identical divine nature. No one person is eternally subordinate to the next because no one person is less divine than the next. The simplicity of the divine essence is not the property of just one or two persons, but all three. When Moses confesses, "Hear, O Israel: The LORD our God, the LORD is one" (Deut. 6:4), the Son and Holy Spirit are included in that confession as much as the Father, as our friend Zipporah confirmed from John 10.[43]

The fathers understood the importance of simplicity for equality. Consider, for example, the Athanasian Creed.[44] It begins with doxology, confessing

> that we worship one God in Trinity, and Trinity in Unity,
> neither confusing the Persons
> nor dividing the *divine Being*.

For there to be a Trinity in unity, the Athanasian Creed says the Godhead (Father, Son, and Spirit) "is all one," and if all one, then there must be total equality: "their glory equal, their majesty co-eternal." Apart from the one thing that distinguishes them (i.e., eternal relations of origin: paternity, filiation, spiration), they wholly share all the properties of God's undivided essence. This is why the Athanasian Creed can begin with a long list describing Father, Son, and Holy Spirit alike as uncreated, infinite, eternal, almighty, and both God and Lord. Consider each:

Such as the Father is, such is the Son and such is the Holy Spirit:

> Uncreated:
> the Father uncreated, the Son uncreated
> and the Holy Spirit uncreated,
>
> Infinite:
> the Father infinite, the Son infinite
> and the Holy Spirit infinite,
>
> Eternal:
> the Father eternal, the Son eternal
> and the Holy Spirit eternal; . . .
>
> Almighty:
> In the same way, the Father is almighty, the Son almighty
> and the Holy Spirit almighty,

Notice, not even authority, which is synonymous with "almighty," can be withheld from all three. The Son is not subordinate to the Father, who is a greater almighty—that would make them two almighties, one less than the other.

If we attribute these attributes to all three, does that mean that there are three Uncreateds, Infinites, Eternals, and Almighties? No.

> . . . they are not three Eternals
> but one Eternal,
> just as they are not three Uncreateds, nor three Infinites,
> but one Uncreated and one Infinite.

> . . . they are not three Almighties
> but one Almighty.

Notice, the creed asserts the divine equality of each distinct person in the Godhead (each one being uncreated, infinite, eternal, and almighty) and at the same time avoids the heresy of tritheism by affirming that there are not three Infinites or three Eternals but one and only one. God's triunity is always but a whisper away from his simplicity. To affirm one is to affirm the other in the same breath. For when the creed addresses divinity itself we read:

> Thus, the Father is God, the Son is God
> and the Holy Spirit is God,
> and yet there are not three Gods
> but one God.
> Thus, the Father is the Lord, the Son is the Lord
> and the Holy Spirit is the Lord,
> and yet not three Lords
> but one Lord.

As we will see in the coming chapters, the creed does go on to spell out what distinguishes the three persons (paternity, filiation, and spiration). But even when it says, for example, that the "Son is from the Father" (eternal generation), it is quick to qualify that such a relation is *eternal*. Why? For if it is not eternal, then the Son is less than the Father, subordinate and inferior. But if coeternal, then all three persons are also coequal. We conclude, then, on this catchy tune:

> And in this Trinity there is no before or after,
> no greater or less,
> but all three Persons are co-eternal with each other
>   and co-equal.
> So that in all things, as has already been said,
> the Trinity in Unity, and the Unity in Trinity, is to be
>   worshipped.

Is the Son Begotten from the Father?

Paternity and Filiation, Part 1

He begets, therefore he is Father.

THOMAS AQUINAS,
SUMMA THEOLOGIAE

The Father bestows being on the Son
without any beginning in time.

AUGUSTINE, *THE TRINITY*

All the sound and orthodox writers have
unanimously declared for the eternal generation
and Sonship of Christ in all ages.

JOHN GILL,
THE ETERNAL SONSHIP OF CHRIST

Where we're going: The days when Jesus walked the earth. A (fictional) woman named Zipporah, who lived in the first century, will introduce us to Jesus, who will tell us where he came from before the incarnation.

Key point: The Father is unbegotten, the principle without principle in the Godhead. The Son is eternally begotten (generated) from the Father's essence. We must not fall prey to nine marks of an unhealthy generation, which threaten to compromise his eternal equality and personal distinction from the Father. Takeaway: only if he is the Son of the Father *by nature* can we boldly approach the throne of the Father *by grace*.

My Beloved Son

Sometimes I'm asked by others in my church, "Were you really there? Did you really see Jesus?"

"Yes, I was there," I respond reluctantly.

"You must have seen so much. Zipporah, will you share with us one of your memories?"

This may sound selfish, but I don't enjoy sharing my memories. I want others to know what Jesus did. I really do. But I fear my short stories do not present Jesus as he was, as I knew him. My words are like sketches of the sun. They portray the sky's source of light, but they cannot make you feel its heat. But I am a pessimist at heart, which is why my sister Naomi keeps looking at me with her darting eyebrows, as if to say, "Zipporah, must I remind you yet again that our Lord used words to convey who he is?"

"There was one time when I saw Jesus and I wasn't supposed to," I said. Those listening, who were barely old enough to marry and have children, gave me a look of suspense, which I fully intended to create.

"I was about your age," I said, pointing to a young woman with dark brown hair and a belly just starting to balloon. "Peter, who we now call an apostle, had become a friend. But back then, Peter was not all confidence like he is now. Peter had real doubts, real struggles. One time, he confessed Jesus to be the Christ, the Son of the living God. Yet when he heard Jesus foretell his own death, Peter rebuked Jesus.

156

Jesus's response cut Peter in half, 'Get behind me, Satan!'[1] Peter was like that—one minute fervent, the next in disarray. But on this day, Peter was full of faith and fortitude.

"'I have to go, Zipporah. Sorry, you can't come,' Peter said with assertiveness.

"'Why?' I asked.

"'I don't know, but Jesus said only James, John, and I can go with him. I'm sure it's nothing and we'll be back in a few hours, at the latest tomorrow.

"I didn't listen but followed Jesus and the three others at a distance as they hiked up a high mountain, thinking they were all alone. At the top, I saw something I wasn't supposed to see, something I can never unsee but don't wish to forget either."

"What was it?" one of the younger boys interrupted.

"I saw Jesus transfigured."

"Transfigured?"

"Yes. Climbing the mountain, he was just Jesus, as we always saw him. He looked much like the others. But at the top of the mountain, his face became radiant. It shimmered like the sun. You couldn't look him in the face—it burned. And his clothes too. They turned white with light."

"What about the others?" the young man interrupted again.

"No. Not them. Just Jesus. But then something else happened. Jesus was met by two others. I couldn't tell who they were, so I quietly crept up until I could see better. I stopped when I could make them out. To my disbelief, it was Moses and Elijah. They stood next to Jesus, talking to him as if they had done it before. But their conversation came off urgent, like something was about to happen and they needed to speak to Jesus about it."

"What were Peter, James, and John doing?" the girl with child asked.

"Nothing. They were as shocked as I was. Wait . . . I take that back. Peter did do something, he *said* something. Peter was nervous. Again, he wasn't the Peter you know now. Back then, Peter was, well, reactionary, saying whatever came to mind. He spoke up and asked Jesus if he could prepare tents to shelter Jesus, Moses, and Elijah. Classic Peter. He didn't know what to say, so he talked about tents. *Tents.* Anyway, Peter kept mumbling on, but he stopped when a luminous cloud overshadowed everyone. When I saw the cloud, I became all the more nervous. Think back to our forefathers: God appeared to our people in a cloud in the desert. Now the cloud hovered over *us*. Then came a voice from the cloud, 'This is my beloved Son, with whom I am well pleased; listen to him.'"

Naomi gave me another one of her looks, this time eyebrows raised, as if to say, "I told you so. Did you *listen*, Zipporah, to his *words*?"

"When Peter, James, and John heard this, they fell on their faces and were terrified. But Jesus comforted them, telling them to get up, not to be afraid. They looked around, expecting to see Moses and Elijah again, but they were gone. The cloud was gone. The blinding whiteness was gone. There was only Jesus."[2]

"Did Peter really say those stupid things?" one of the children asked, incredulous.

"I did," said Peter from the back of the room, and with a hint of disapproval at my secret now revealed. "Zipporah is right. It was as if heaven itself was speaking. We looked up but could see nothing but the cloud itself."[3]

"Whose voice was it?" asked one of the older men.

"The *Father's*," one the children said with a tinge of precociousness.

"Yes, the Father's. I heard his voice, and those same words, now that I think about it, were spoken at Jesus's baptism. But now, when Jesus was about to suffer, the words came again. More for our sake than his, I'd say. Wouldn't you agree, Peter?" I said, but without glancing at the back of the room.

"Yes," Peter said, darting an amicable stare back at me. "And I *have* listened ever since." The pregnant woman laughed, which made her belly jiggle up and down. The children saw and tried hard not to laugh.

"Jesus told us many times during his ministry that he was the Father's beloved one. Not because he was somehow adopted by the Father. He was the Father's beloved Son from all eternity. Never was there a time when he was not the Father's beloved Son. But now, for our sake, the

Father confirmed his Son's identity so that we would listen to him. *We all* needed to hear that, since *we all* struggled to understand why Jesus had to die. But now we know why," I said. Peter looked at me again, this time with gratitude.

"Now listen to me. All of you. God sent his beloved Son to speak his words, saving words, and if you listen to his words, if you receive his words, the same words Jesus passed down to Peter, then he will give you the Spirit without measure. And though you do not see Jesus as we did, you will know him. But more importantly, he will know you." ▪

Principle without Principle

Zipporah's memory of the transfiguration, which you can read about in Matthew 17, and Peter's recollection of that same event, which you can read about in 2 Peter 1, bring us face-to-face with Christ in his unveiled glory. But as much as we focus, like Zipporah's audience, on what Peter saw, the ultimate purpose was to move the disciples' faith beyond mere sight so that, in the end, they would listen to what Jesus had to say. But it took the Father himself speaking, confirming that Jesus is, indeed, his beloved Son. In doing so, the Father not only presupposed

Key Phrase: Eternal Relations of Origin

By "origin" we mean that which is "the source of another" and that which is "coming from another," says Aquinas. By "relation" we mean "personal properties," *personal* because these properties are what "set apart or constitute hypostases or persons" in the Trinity. "Eternal relations of origin," therefore, identifies from whom each person proceeds and what it is about each person that distinguishes that person from the others (*Summa* 1a.32.3). Eternal relations of origin alone can tell us why God is Trinity. "The aim," says Gregory of Nazianzus, "is to safeguard the distinctness of the three hypostases within the single nature and quality of the Godhead" (*On God and Christ* 4.31.9).

his Son's identity *as Son*, but he presupposed his identity *as Father* as well.

As Father, he is his Son's *eternal origin*, the source from whom the Son is begotten.[4] *Eternal relations of origin*—you may remember our discussion of that phrase from chapter 2. There we learned that the three persons who hold the one, simple essence in common are distinguished by eternal relations of origin: the Father is unbegotten, the Son is begotten, the Spirit is

> **Key Word** | **Innascibility**
>
> This is a fancy theological word that means the Father is from no one, the source without source, the principle without principle. While the Son is begotten, the Father is unbegotten. Terms like these, says John Webster, highlight the "identity of the Father in *relation to* the Son" but by no means connote "the Father's *elevation over* the Son as a superior principle from which the Son is a derivative emanation" (*God Without Measure*, 31).

spirated. These alone distinguish the persons. We discovered that the Great Tradition used other phrases to say the same: the one essence has three modes of subsistence (personal properties).[5]

In Matthew 17, the only reason the Father can refer to Jesus as his beloved Son is because the Son has his origin from the Father and from all eternity. Jesus is not beloved because he became incarnate; he became incarnate because he is beloved. As Zipporah said, never was there a time when he was not the Father's beloved Son. As Jesus said time after time, the Father loves him (John 3:35; 5:20). Begotten from the Father from all eternity, he was sent by the Father into history for us and our salvation.

But unlike human fatherhood, God the Father has no father. He is, in a word, *unbegotten*; no Father brought him into existence. The Great Tradition, our Dream Team, used the word "principle," which, according to Aquinas, "means simply that from which something proceeds." Since "the Father is one from whom another originates, it follows that the Father is principle" and the only one in the Trinity who is without principle, the principle who himself has no principle.[6] If he were not, then Christ would not have "taught us to direct our prayer to the Father through the Son."[7]

That said, what does it mean exactly for the Father to beget his Son?

What Is Eternal Generation?

As we learned in chapter 2, the word "generation" means "coming forth," and with reference to the Trinity it refers to the Son coming forth from the Father's essence.[8] The concept takes us to the very heart of what it means for the Son to be a *Son*. He is eternally from the Father, which is why he is called Son. To be more specific, in eternal generation the "Father from all eternity communicated his name, his perfections, and his glory, to the Son."[9] *From all eternity, the Father communicates the one, simple, undivided divine essence to the Son.* Or to use the vocabulary of John's Gospel, eternal generation means the Son is eternally *begotten* from the Father's essence (see chap. 7). If the Son is not begotten from the Father, the divine essence cannot subsist (exist) in the Son.[10]

At the risk of stating the obvious, a son is, by definition, one who is generated by his father, one who has his origin from his father. While we will point out dissimilarities between human and divine sonship soon enough, we cannot miss the one fundamental similarity: sonship means one is *generated* by a father. When the concept is applied to the Son of God—as it so often is by the authors of Scripture—it means in its most basic sense that he, as the eternal Son, is *from his Father.*

To clarify, to be *from* the Father does not refer to the incarnation, to Christ as Mediator; being sent by the Father to save may reflect eternal generation but in no way constitutes eternal generation. Instead, to be from the Father refers to the Son's origin in eternity, apart from creation. Generation is between Father and Son, an eternal act, and not between the Trinity and creation, as if it were a temporal act. As we will learn, generation is internal to the triune God, *ad intra* as we like to say in Latin, as opposed to external, *ad extra*.[11] The Father sending his Son into the world on mission for the world reflects his eternal origin from the Father (generation), but that mission in no way constitutes his eternal relation of origin. The Son is generated (begotten) by the Father before all ages apart from the world, irrespective of creation. He is Son whether or not he is ever sent into the world; he is the eternal Son from the Father whether or not he ever becomes incarnate.[12] It is the immanent Trinity that is in view, not the economic.

As we've seen, there is another term that conveys the concept of generation: *begotten*. Perhaps you've heard the word used when reading those long genealogies in the Bible: so-and-so begat so-and-so begat so-and-so. But as we will see in chapter 7, John applies this language to Jesus as well, referring to him as the *only begotten* Son of God (e.g., John 3:16). This begotten language, however, long predates the King James Bible. Way back in the fourth century, the church fathers who wrote the Nicene Creed used it as well. For example, the Nicene Creed says, "We believe in . . . one Lord Jesus Christ, the only-begotten Son of God, begotten from the Father before all time."

Since this is the one, undivided God we are talking about, for the Son to be begotten from the Father means that God is begotten from God, which is why the creed confesses the Son to be "true God from true God." To confess the Son as true God from true God is not an overstatement since he is, we dare not forget, consubstantial with the Father. Consubstantial means the Son is equal to the Father in every way, from the same essence or substance as the Father, no less divine than the Father. But we can only affirm such coequality if the Son is begotten from the Father's essence.

Furthermore, generation *alone* is what distinguishes the Son as Son. There is not some other concept or function or activity in the Trinity that distinguishes the person of the Son from the Father.

Generation alone can, for it alone conveys the nucleus of sonship. That is no small point, because without generation, not only is there no Son, but there is no Trinity. As John Gill warns, "Without his eternal generation no proof can be made of his being a distinct divine Person *in the Godhead.*"[13] Without generation, we fall head first into Sabellianism, for what previously distinguished Son from Father is dissolved, and as a result the persons are conflated until there is no plurality of persons at all.

With the basic idea of generation in place, we must qualify Sonship in the Trinity lest we interpret it in a literalistic fashion, with a one-to-one correspondence to creaturely sonship. There are significant differences between a divine generation and a human one. Understanding these differences—what eternal generation is *not*—aids us in better understanding what eternal generation *is*. It also avoids legions of heresies. Let's begin with this question: *when* is the Son generated by the Father?

When Is the Son Generated?

That's a trick question if there ever was one. There is no "when." Why? The short answer: our triune God is *eternal.* He is not bound by time but is timeless; he has no beginning. A succession of moments cannot apply to him. He just *is.* That means the following question is most relevant:

> Q: *If God is timelessly eternal, what does that mean for the Son and his generation from the Father?*

> A: *Unlike human generation, the Son's generation is eternal. There never was a time when the Son was not, nor ever a time when the Son was not from the Father.*

Or, as fathers like Gregory of Nyssa like to say, there is no "sometime" for the Son because he was not generated in time. "He exists by generation indeed, but nevertheless He never begins to exist."[14]

It's not as if God the Son did not exist but then came into existence at a point in time, created by the Father and therefore after the Father. That describes how generation works in our human existence, but it cannot depict the Son's generation. He is, says Nicaea, "begotten not created." He is, we cannot forget, the *eternal* Son from the Father (see chap. 7). If the divine essence subsists in him, then he too shares in the attributes of deity, eternity being one of them. He is no creature, and if not a creature, then his generation cannot be temporal. The generation of the Son "does not fall within time, any more than the creation was before time."[15]

If the Son's generation did fall within time, then not only is there a time when the Son was not, but there is a time when the Father was not *Father*. And if there was a time when the Father was not, then there was a time when the *Trinity* was not. As Athanasius points out, "If the Son is not proper offspring of the Father's essence, but of nothing has come to be, then of nothing the Triad consists, and once there was not a Triad, but a Monad."[16]

Furthermore, if he is Son because he is from the Father, then his sonship must be as eternal as the Father himself, at least if he is begotten from the same essence as the Father. That is why the Nicene Creed stresses that the Son is "begotten from the Father *before all time* . . . begotten not created . . . through Whom all things came into being." The generation within God is unlike any other; it is not susceptible to the limitations of time. The Son's filial identity has no duration or succession of moments; it is timeless. Everlasting in nature, there never was a time when the Son was not begotten from the Father.

That may sound like a contradiction—how can someone be generated and eternal? It only sounds like a contradiction because we only know generation within the experience of our own finitude. For the infinite, timelessly eternal deity, the confines of our finitude do not apply. Let's not forget that whatever words are used of God—even scriptural words and metaphors—this is *God* we have in view, infinite and eternal, immutable and everlasting.

Language is, by definition, analogical in every way. The metaphor must then be adapted to the incomprehensible One, not vice versa. So too with generation. As Augustine says, since the generation of the Son is eternal, "one exists not as *before* the other, but as *from* the other."[17] The Son is not generated *after* the Father, which would make him less than the Father, but the Son is generated *from* the Father and from all eternity.[18]

One more thing: we will learn in chapter 7 that Scripture refers to the Son's eternal origin from the Father with a variety of metaphors and titles, including radiance, image, wisdom, Word, and Ancient of Days. But one we can consider now is *truth*. As Jesus himself says, he is the truth (John 14:6). Was there ever a time when God the Father was without his Truth? The Arians said yes. With a look of terror on his face, Athanasius ponders this bizarre scenario: "For if the Son was not before His generation, Truth was not always in God." It is a sin to say such a thing, Athanasius concludes. That sin multiplies if we also say there was a time when the Image was not, for "God's Image is not delineated from without, but God Himself hath begotten it; in which seeing Himself, He has delight. . . . When then did the Father not see Himself in His own Image?"[19] Answer: never. The Father always and forever has seen himself in his own image. So yes, the Son is the image of the Father, but unlike images in our finite world, there has never been a time when the Son was not the image of the invisible God (Col. 1:15).[20]

How Is the Son Generated? Nine Marks of an Unhealthy Generation

So far, we've stressed that divine, eternal generation must be distinguished from human, temporal generation. We must rid our minds of anything "carnal and impure," says John Gill. What else might that include?

Gill lists nine marks of human generation that should *not* characterize divine generation. Actually, these are not original to Gill, but are voiced by the Great Tradition as well, as seen in someone like Gregory of Nyssa.[21] These are the nine marks of an unhealthy generation:

1. Division of nature
2. Multiplication of essence
3. Priority and posteriority
4. Motion
5. Mutation
6. Alteration
7. Corruption
8. Diminution [i.e., to lessen]
9. Cessation from operation[22]

We cannot touch on every one of these, but we can address a few that are especially dangerous, along with a few of our own, looking for help from teammates on our Dream Team.

John Gill

John Gill may be one of the most neglected trinitarians in church history. That is our loss because his *Body of Divinity* (a systematic theology) contains one of the most concise and accurate articulations of Nicene orthodoxy in theological literature. He was a Calvinistic Baptist pastor in London in the eighteenth century, when Unitarianism was gaining a strong hold on the church. Gill once led his church through church discipline, removing someone from membership for rejecting the eternal generation of the Son. He also wrote a book defending the doctrine, called *The Eternal Sonship of Christ*. Theologians debate whether Gill was a hyper-Calvinist, and that debate has scared many away from Gill (throwing the baby out with the bathwater). The irony is that Gill is far more orthodox than many Baptists today. Gill can help Baptists jettison their social trinitarianism and return to a Nicene orthodoxy.

No Multiplication, No Division

First, the Son's generation involves no multiplication or division of nature. No multiplication of the divine essence is involved in the generation of the Son. When the Father begets he communicates the one (simple) divine essence to his Son, but he does not multiply the divine essence.[23] If he did, there would no longer be one, simple essence, but two essences. Likewise, when we say the Son is begotten, we do not mean he receives from the Father the divine essence in part but in whole.[24]

Or think of it this way: God is "not triple (triplex) but trinitary (trinum)."[25] The Father does not give to his Son what he previously received from his own Father. Generation works that way among created, finite fathers, but God the Father has no beginning nor is he himself generated. He is fathered by no one. He alone is unbegotten, without origin. "Human parents transmit what they have received," but "God the Father alone gives to the Son and to the Holy Spirit what he has from no other person."[26] This does not involve a multiplication of the divine nature, which would result in three gods (tritheism). The Son is begotten of the Father by nature, so that the Son is a subsistence of that one divine nature, not the production of another, second nature.

Not only is the divine nature not multiplied, it is not divided as a result of the Son's generation either. In the fourth century, the Arians claimed it must be. They appealed to divine simplicity to argue against the Son's eternal generation from the Father and coequality with the Father. As Athanasius reports, the Arians "deny that the Son is the proper offspring of the Father's essence, on the ground that this must imply parts and divisions."[27] The Son cannot be from the Father's essence, for then the Father must part with a portion of the essence to generate a Son.

In human generation, the human nature is divisible. It can, says Turretin, "remain the same in species when propagated by generation, although it is not the same in number because it detaches a certain part of its substance, which passes over to the begotten."[28] That's because human generation is physical and material. The divine nature, however, is spiritual and therefore indivisible. God is spirit, so he remains one, simple, and undivided. That's why some call the generation of the Son *hyperphysical* to communicate that the Son's generation is not in time or space, nor does it result in divisible parts.[29]

As mentioned, the Son does not receive what the Father received from his father, since the Father has no father himself. It does not follow, however, that the Son is born out of nothing (*ex nihilo*) as the Arians insisted.[30] If he was, then he would be no different from the rest of creation, which was made by God out of nothing. But the Son is no creature; yes, he is begotten, but he is not made (Nicaea). Let's not confuse the two. Rather than the Son being "born out of nothing," says Aquinas, he is "born out of the substance of the Father."[31] Again, this should not be taken in the human sense. The "Son of God is born of the substance of the Father. Yet not in the same way as a human son. For a part of the substance of the human father passes into the substance of his offspring." That would *divide up* the substance or nature of God. By contrast, the divine substance "is above being divisible." "Necessarily, then, the Father in begetting the Son did not pass on *part* of his nature to the Son, but bestowed the *whole* nature upon him, with only the distinction based on origin remaining."[32] The divine nature belongs to the Son—not in part, but in whole—due to his origin from the Father, and if in whole then the divine nature has not been multiplied nor has it been divided.

Notice, divine simplicity plays a major factor at this point. Since God is not made up of parts, it's not as if eternal generation involves a portion of the divine essence being broken off and given to the Son by the Father. The Son, Hilary of Poitiers objects, is no "mutilated fragment of the Father."[33] Not only would that make God a composition of parts, but it would sacrifice the full deity of the Son, as if he were only part divinity. Nor would the

Trinity be *simply* Trinity. Rather, to be begotten from the Father is to wholly possess the one, undivided divine essence. "That birth, which brought Him into being, constituted Him divine, and His being reveals the consciousness of that divine nature. God the Son confesses God His Father, because He was born of Him; but also, because He was born, *He inherits the whole nature of God.*"[34] Each person is a subsistence of the one divine nature, that nature wholly subsisting in Father, Son, and Holy Spirit. "The Son is begotten of (*de*) the Father's essence," says Aquinas, "because the Father's essence, bestowed on the Son through generation, is subsisting in the Son."[35]

Since the Son is begotten of (*de*) the Father's essence, there is "no partition, or withdrawing, or lessening, or efflux, or extension, or suffering of change, but the birth of living nature from living nature"; eternal generation is "One from One," that is, "God going forth from God."[36] Or as the Nicene Creed says, the Son is "true God from true God." The Son's existence "did not take its beginning out of nothing, but went forth from the Eternal." It is appropriate to still call it a birth (that is the meaning of begetting), but "it would be false to call it a beginning."[37] *Birth, not beginning.* Unlike the creation of the universe *ex nihilo*, the "proceeding forth of God from God is a thing entirely different from the coming into existence of a new substance."[38] Hilary is right, the Son "has no

---

Hilary of Poitiers

Hilary (c. 300–367) has been nicknamed the Athanasius of the West. And for good reason, too: his tome on the Trinity is one of the most in-depth, precise, and lucid articulations of Nicene trinitarianism. What's all the more remarkable is that Hilary didn't even become a Christian until later in life. His episcopate started around AD 350, the same time opposition to the creed of Nicaea grew fierce. Hilary played an important role opposing Homoian creeds. Most forget that Hilary also wrote commentaries on the Bible, including one on Matthew.

origin external to God, and was not created out of nothing, but is the Son, born from God."[39]

One might object that it is a sheer impossibility for the Father to generate the Son without producing a fourth thing. How can the same essence be communicated by the Father to the Son without creating something or someone else? The answer is found in the triune God's *infinite* nature. As Turretin says, "The same numerical and singular essence can nevertheless be communicable to more than one (because infinite)."[40]

No Priority, No Posteriority, No Inferiority

Second, the Son's generation involves no priority or posteriority, and certainly no inferiority, but designates order alone. If it did involve priority or posteriority of any kind, then the Son would be inferior to the Father.

Previously, I emphasized that the Son is begotten by the Father, but unlike our human experience, the Son's generation is eternal (before all ages; timeless). And if eternal, then the generation of the Son is not the generation of a lesser being (made in time or before time) but the generation of a Son who is equal in deity to his Father. But the reason the Son is not inferior to the Father is because the one divine essence wholly subsists in the Son due to his generation from the Father's nature or substance. True God from true God, there can be "no diminution of the Begetter's substance" in the generation of the Son.[41] The Father begets his Son, and the two are, to return to that key word from Nicaea, *consubstantial*, meaning they are to be identified by the self-same divine essence. Priority or posteriority would undermine the Son as consubstantial, as one who is of the same nature as the Father.

As we saw earlier, the lack of priority or posteriority is due in part to the timeless nature of the Son's generation, which is eternal, not temporal. Gregory of Nazianzus was once asked why the Son and the Spirit are not co-unoriginate along with the Father if it is true that they are coeternal with the Father. His response: "Because they [Son and Spirit] are *from* him [Father], though not *after* him. 'Being unoriginate' necessarily implies 'being eternal,' but 'being eternal' does not entail 'being unoriginated,' so long as the Father is referred to as origin." To drive this point home, Gregory appeals to the illustration of the sun. "So because they [Son and Spirit] have a cause they are not unoriginated. But clearly a cause is not necessarily prior to its effect—the Sun is not prior to its light. Because time is not involved, they are to that extent *unoriginated*—even if you do scare simple souls with the bogey-word; for the sources of time are not subject to time."[42]

With a nudge from Gregory, consider the biblical imagery of light once more (John 1:4, 8–9). Nicaea says the Son's eternal generation from the Father can be compared to "light from light." The Cappadocian fathers also appealed to this imagery of light to counter the belief of subordinationists who said an effect is inferior to its cause, the Son subordinate to the Father. Consider the sun, they said in response. It is the cause of light, but by no means is light inferior to its source. In essence they are one and the same. How much more so with divinity? Is not the divine essence simple and inseparable, eternal and immutable?

We might also add, the Son cannot be less than his source (the Father), because there is no hierarchy in the Trinity. The Father is not greater than the Son—not in any way. In order to avoid misunderstanding, some may prefer the word "source" instead of "cause" (as I do) when talking about the Father, which better safeguards the Son's equality. But regardless, in the Great Tradition neither word means the Son has a beginning or is less than the Father because he is from the Father.

In sum, the Father is the principle in the Godhead—the principle who alone is without principle. Unbegotten. But that does not mean that the Father and Son are not coequals. Rather, the eternal relations reveal the personal origins of the persons. To read hierarchy of any kind into these origins is to abuse them, even manipulate them. The Father may be the principle without *principle*, but he is also the "principle without *priority*." Scott Swain clarifies, "The Father is the fontal source of the Son and the Spirit, and these relations manifest his distinct personal perfection. However, the Father's identity as fontal source of the Son and the Spirit is not (even logically) *prior* to the existence of the Son and the Spirit but is rather constituted *by* his eternal relations to the Son and the Spirit."[43] In other words, "we cannot ascribe any *priority* to the Father in relation to the Son and the Spirit in terms of either being or hierarchy."[44]

To conclude, whenever we or the Great Tradition use words like "source," the intention, for example, is only to identify the personal origin of the Son: the Father.[45] Hierarchy and priority are precluded by the very *nature, will, power, and glory* the three persons hold in common. As Gregory of Nazianzus says, "They do not have degrees of being God or degrees of priority over against one another. They are not sundered in will or divided in power. You cannot find there any of the properties inherent in things divisible." In short, "the Godhead exists undivided."[46]

If the Son's generation involves no priority or hierarchy, then is it also safe to conclude that it cannot involve any change (mutation) either?

No Change

Third, the Son's generation involves no change in the Trinity. In a sermon series on the Gospel of John, Augustine once said to his congregation, "Although changeable things are made through the Word, that Word is unchangeable."[47] God may create the changeable world through his Word, but remember, the Word himself does not change. For he is not created but begotten from the Father's nature from all eternity. The Son, says Athanasius, "being from the Father, and proper to His essence, is unchangeable and unalterable as the Father Himself."[48] Whereas a bodily begetting involves mutation, a begetting that is without a body (incorporeal) does not.[49]

Remember, says John of Damascus, eternal generation means that the Son is "from the Father's nature."[50] If he is from the Father's nature, a nature that is not only simple and eternal but immutable (unchanging), then no change can occur in generation. If it does, then either the Father's nature is not immutable or the Son is generated from another nature, external to God, and in that case could no longer be coequal to the Father in divinity.[51]

In Gill's nine marks of an unhealthy generation, you may have noticed that five of them—motion, mutation, alteration, corruption, diminution—have one thing in common: they are all the result of change. This is inevitable with human generation, for

What Does Eternal Generation Have to Do with Impassibility?

Not only does the Nicene tradition say the Father begets the Son immutably but impassibly as well. (Impassibility means God is not subject to emotional fluctuation; that is, he does not suffer.) The Arians charged that begetting involves change in the Son, and therefore passions. But, the Nicene fathers countered, that assumes generation is external to God, between the Father and a created being. But generation is internal, within the immanent Trinity. The Son is true God of true God from eternity. In *Against Eunomius*, Gregory of Nyssa writes, "How is it allowable to entertain the idea of passion in thinking of generation as it concerns the incorruptible Nature?" (4.4). Likewise, Gregory of Nazianzus says that the "Only-Begotten" Son is related to the Father, "identical with the Father in Essence," on account of his "passionless Generation" (*Theological Orations* 4.20). John Webster connects the dots: "Impassibility is not indifference, but the infinitely deep, unrestrictedly realized divine life from which Christ emerges as the presence of God to us. Begetting is not passion because the Son is intrinsic to the fullness of God, very God of very God. Begetting is a mode of God's perfection" (*God Without Measure*, 33).

where finite creatures are involved there is always change, and where there is change, we have the potential to change for the worse, which means corruption is a real possibility. But not so with the triune God, whose nature is not only eternal but immutable. If immutable, then the Father begets his Son without alteration to the divine nature. That is because there is *no potency* in God, meaning God has no unactualized potential he must reach, as if he is not true God until he reaches his full potential. Instead, he is the Perfect Being, self-existent, self-sufficient, always and forever his perfect self, maximally alive, without any need to somehow *become* more perfect than he is for all eternity—which is why the fathers call him *pure act*.[52] The Father does not beget his Son as if the Son must somehow reach his potential over time, as if he must grow and change and become more perfect than he was before. Remember, the Trinity is perfect, maximally alive, never in need to become something more or greater or better. That means eternal generation "is a perfect generating perfect act."[53] *Perfect generating perfect*—that sounds a lot like Nicaea's *true* God from *true* God.[54]

All that to say, if the Son's generation is eternal, so also must it be immutable.[55] Where there is a succession of moments (time), change will follow; indeed, it must. But in eternity, there is no successiveness, and therefore no mutation in God. The Father begets his Son not as a new moment in time but from eternity. To say, as the Nicene fathers did over against the Arians, that there never was a time when the Son was not is to also confess there never was a time when the Son was not immutable. If he was not begotten out of the eternal, immutable nature of the Father, then we would be right to ask whether something is lacking in God, whether God himself is incomplete and imperfect.

But we can rejoice with Aquinas, who says, "The Father's nature has been complete from all eternity; the action whereby the Father brings forth the Son is not successive, because then the Son of God would have been begotten in stages and his begetting would have been material and involved movement. All impossible consequences. What remains, then, is that whenever the Father was, the Son also was and so is co-eternal with the Father, as also is the Holy Spirit with them both."[56]

That leaves us with a final question:

> Q: *If the Son's generation is immutable, then must his generation also be immanent, internal to the Trinity?*

Not Transitive but Immanent

Fourth, the Son's generation from the Father is not transitive but immanent. This final point separates orthodoxy from heresy as well. While Nicaea believed the Son's generation to be an *immanent* action (occurring within God), heretical notions said generation is *transitive* (God generating a creature external to himself, not one who is God of God).[57] Athanasius believed this was a dividing line with the Arians of his day. The "Son is not attached to the Father, but co-exists with Him."[58] When the "Son says that God is His own Father, it follows that what is partaken is not external, but from the essence of the Father."[59]

What a scary thought: a generation that issues someone *external* to the begetter's nature.[60] In this scheme, the Father begets a Son, but this Son is not begotten from the same nature as the Father; he must be of a different nature, a lesser nature, than the Father. But the "nature with which God is born is necessarily the same as that of His Source," Hilary of Poitiers clarifies. The Son "cannot come into existence as other than God, since His origin is from none other than God. His nature is the same, not in the sense that the Begetter also was begotten—for then the Unbegotten, having been begotten, would not be Himself—but that the substance of the Begotten consists in all those elements which are summed up in the substance of the Begetter, Who is His only Origin."[61]

The Arians refused to accept the immanent generation Athanasius and Hilary describe. But the medieval fathers who followed embraced it without reservation. They even applied the same conviction to the Spirit. Take Anselm, for example: "When God [the Spirit] proceeds from God the Father and the Son, he does not proceed outside God"; the Spirit "abides in God from whom he proceeds" so that there are not different gods but "one God the Father and the Son and the Holy Spirit."[62] Our triune God's eternal nature supports such a claim: "Since God is eternity, as there is altogether nothing of eternity outside of eternity, so there is absolutely nothing of God outside of God, and as eternity upon eternity is only one eternity, so God in God is only one God."[63] *There is nothing of God outside of God*—that is but another way of applying Nicene language: true God of true God.

Abba! Father! Our Sonship in the Son

If Jesus is not the eternal, only begotten Son of the Father, then we have no hope, nor any right to call God our Father in the first place. Only if he is the Son of the Father *by nature* can we boldly approach the throne of the Father *by grace*. The Father, through his Son, has accomplished our redemption, and we, as a result, are the recipients of his Son's grace a thousand times over.[64]

Is this not what Paul assumes when he writes to the Galatians concerning their adoption? "In the same way we also, when we were children, were enslaved to the elementary principles of the world. But when the fullness of time had come, God sent forth his Son, born of woman, born under the law, to redeem those who were under the law, so that we might receive adoption as sons. And because you are sons, God has sent the Spirit of his Son into our hearts, crying, 'Abba! Father!'" (Gal. 4:3–6). We, as his adopted sons, have life in his eternal Son, and through him the Spirit communicates to us the Father's benevolence. As recipients of his everlasting grace, as benefactors of his unceasing mercy, we cry out to him, "Abba! Father!" with every confidence he will receive us as sons in his Son (Rom. 8:15). "So you are

Nature versus Grace

What's the difference between the Son's sonship and our sonship? His sonship is by nature, eternally begotten from the Father's essence, whereas our sonship is by grace (John 20:17). As Hilary of Poitiers says, "For He is God's true and own Son, by origin and not by adoption, not by name only but in truth, born and not created" (*On the Trinity* 3.11). The nature-grace distinction also affects how we define love: Is Christ the Son because the Father loves him, or does the Father love him because he is his Son? The latter must be true if he is the Son by nature, from eternity, rather than adopted as Son at some point in time by grace, only to be loved thereafter. He is not "the Son because beloved," says Turretin, "but beloved because he is the Son" (Turretin, *Institutes*, 301).

no longer a slave, but a son, and if a son, then an heir through God" (Gal. 4:7).

How central is eternal generation to the gospel? That question will consume us in the next chapter. But we can say this: it is only because Jesus is the eternally begotten Son that he is able and qualified to descend into the deep depths of this God-forsaken world, be born as a babe in a manger, and ascend back to his Father with a host of newborn sons in his wake. Unless he is born from the Father from all eternity, he cannot be sent by the Father to be born as a man in salvation history nor ensure that those who have trusted in him as the only begotten Son of God will be adopted as sons themselves. Apart from his eternal sonship, we have no hope that we might be adopted as sons and receive all the benefits of our union with the Son, Christ Jesus.

Is Eternal Generation Central to the Gospel?

Paternity and Filiation, Part 2

For as the Father has life in himself, so he has
granted the Son also to have life in himself.

JESUS, JOHN 5:26

The Son is ever the proper offspring of the Father's essence.

ATHANASIUS, *AGAINST THE ARIANS*

[Eternal generation] is the distinguishing criterion
of the Christian religion. . . . Without this the
doctrine of the Trinity can never be supported.

JOHN GILL, *BODY OF DIVINITY*

TO THE DELOREAN!

Where we're going: The days when Jesus walked the earth. With Zipporah we will listen to Jesus as he tells us where he came from before his incarnation.

Key point: The Son is eternally begotten (generated) from the Father's essence. The Son's name, who sent him into the world, and a mosaic of biblical images and titles like birth, radiance, image, wisdom, Word, and Ancient of Days are all scriptural attestations to the Son's eternal generation. Takeaway: if the Son is not eternally begotten from the Father, we have no confidence we can be born again in the Son.

A Doctrine to Die For

The Jews were ready to kill him. Jesus, that is. And not just ready; they were tracking Jesus down, looking for the right opportunity. I know because I was there; I saw them. Here's what happened.

I was walking home, and as usual I passed by the pool called Bethesda, the pool where the blind and paralyzed linger. They believe that if they can get into the pool when the water stirs, they might just be healed. I don't enjoy passing by this pool. It can be depressing, seeing so many crippled people with little hope. I know people who have been there since they were children. Nothing changes.

But one day something changed. Jesus walked up to the pool, turned, and made eye contact with a crippled man, a man I've seen at the pool for thirty-eight years now. With a word, Jesus commanded him to get up and walk. I laughed to myself. But to my shock, the man stood up and started walking. The woman to my left, who knew me from synagogue, shouted in disbelief, "Did you just see that, Zipporah? I know that man. He's been lying there for . . . well, forever. Look at him, he's walking!"

But when I turned to the man on my right, a rabbi in training, I discovered he was not in awe but outraged. Puzzled, I asked him why. He gave me a heated response: "Because it's the Sabbath. Don't you know the law? Jesus is breaking the Sabbath, telling this man to pick up his bed and walk." But, I thought to myself, doesn't that miss the whole point of the law?

Before I had time to think, everything took a turn for the worse. The man Jesus healed was escorted to a small gathering of Jewish leaders, and the man next to me joined them. I don't know what I was thinking—my sister would kill me—but I decided to follow closely behind. One thing led to another, and next thing I knew the Jews were confronting Jesus as well, condemning him for violating the Sabbath. Jesus's reply infuriated them: "My Father is working until now, and I am working."[1]

According to the religious leaders, not only was Jesus "breaking the Sabbath, but he was even calling God his own Father, making himself equal with God."[2] I paid enough attention to my father when he used to teach us the Torah as children to know that only God works on the Sabbath. He created the heavens and the earth and then rested on the seventh day. But since he is God, he alone can sustain the universe, and he alone has the right to do so on the Sabbath. That is his prerogative. So, when Jesus said that his Father is working until now *and so is he*, Jesus was making a divine claim. Personally, I thought the Jews misunderstood Jesus, as if he was claiming to be a second, rival God, discarding the monotheism of our fathers. But it sounded to me like he was claiming to be one with God the Father as he who is the Son of God himself.

Regardless, what Jesus said next revealed far more about who he claims to be: "Truly, truly, I say to you, whoever hears my word and believes him who sent me has eternal life."[3] Promising that a future

Read the Bible with the Church

What did Jesus mean when he said, "For as the Father has life in himself, so he has granted the Son also to have life in himself" (John 5:26)? Augustine has the answer: "He did not mean that the Father gave life to the Son already existing without life, but that he begot him timelessly in such a way that the life which the Father gave the Son by begetting him is co-eternal with the life of the Father who gave it" (*The Trinity* 15.47).

day is coming, one in which those who hear his voice—the voice of the Son of God himself—will live, Jesus then said something I am still trying to understand: "For as the Father has life in himself, so he has granted the Son also to have life in himself."[4]

Jesus then said his Father has given him authority to execute judgment, and Jesus even guaranteed that one day all those who hear his voice will rise from their tombs to the resurrection of life.[5] Jesus really believed he had the right and power to give life, whether now or in the future, because he has been given such life from his Father.

But Jesus's filial claim—"For as the Father has life in himself, so he has granted the Son also to have life in himself"—left me with more questions: Where is this Jesus from? What is his origin that he would make such a claim? It occurred to me that Jesus's words, as much as they were directed toward life here and now, were directed toward eternity. I don't think Jesus was claiming to be merely a man set apart by God or a man sent by God—that would have neither impressed nor offended the religious leaders. No, his claim was greater: he must be from God the Father himself. Jesus was saying something divine about his origin, as if he is from the Father from all eternity and for that reason he can offer life to mere mortals. In his original statement—the one that instigated a reaction—he identified himself with the Father's work of creation. Perhaps Jesus precedes creation itself, not born like the rest of us but born of God.

If I'm right, then by claiming equality with the Father, Jesus must be the Son who is *from* the Father. Otherwise, how could he claim to be granted such life, life which is eternal? Surely there is not a more ultimate claim than this, to say that just as the Father has life *in himself*, so too has he granted his Son to have life *in himself*. Any Jew knows the difference between Creator and creature. And Jesus's claim was in no way appropriate for a creature. If Jesus was calling himself the Son—the Son of the Father, to be exact—then he was claiming an eternal identity when he referred to the eternal Father, who alone has life in himself, granting him—the Son!—life "in himself." If not, then why was this religious leader next to me so bent out of shape, ready to kill Jesus? I believe God is my Father, but Jesus was calling God his Father in a way no creature should. ■

What's in a Name? Everything

What Zipporah heard—which you can read about in John 5—approaches the doctrine of *eternal generation*. As we have seen in previous chapters, ever since Jesus's encounter with these religious leaders, the church has drawn similar conclusions to Zipporah's. For example, Augustine, reflecting on John 5:26, says, "So this is the meaning . . . that he begot the Son to be unchangeable life, that is to say eternal life."[6]

Sometimes critics will object, "Eternal generation is the stuff of theologians, something imposed on the text. Name just one verse where eternal generation is taught." Such an objection misses something almost too simple to say: eternal generation is intrinsic to the very *names* Scripture reveals—Father and Son. Far more persuasive than a proof text are the biblical names by which God himself reveals his eternal relations of origin.

Let's recap. To be a son is to be generated from a father; this is the essence of sonship. It is the fundamental characteristic that distinguishes a son from a father. Generation communicates that a son shares the nature of his father and, at the same time, that he is distinct from his father. Otherwise a father need not be called a father, and a son need not be called a son. The titles would be meaningless.

The biblical names give away the persons' relations to one another. That is by design. The Father is only Father if he generates the Son, and the Son is only Son if he is generated by the Father. In that sense, it is impossible to choose between Son and begotten. The two define each other; one cannot be understood without the other. As Augustine says, "When we say begotten we mean the same as when we say 'son.' Being son is a consequence of being begotten, and being begotten is implied by being son."[7] While

Scripture may not spell out the doctrine of eternal generation in any one verse, the concept is assumed whenever Scripture refers to the Son *as Son* and the Father *as Father*.

Furthermore, eternal generation is inferred whenever the Son says he is *from* the Father. Whenever Jesus says he has been *sent* from the Father—and there is no shortage of such language in John's Gospel—he assumes he is *from* the Father before all ages as well. For that is the very basis of his mission, what makes his mission possible to begin with. As we saw in John 5, being sent by the Father in salvation history reflects the origin of the Son from the Father in eternity. The mission of the Son (being sent by the Father for our salvation) is designed by God himself to reveal the eternal relation of the Son (being begotten by the Father from all eternity).

Do We Approach the Bible Like Socinians?

Those who adopt a critical stance toward eternal generation sound a lot like Socinians in the seventeenth century. Listen to a Socinian statement like the Racovian Catechism:

> This generation out of the Father's essence involves a contradiction. For if Christ had been generated out of the essence of his Father, he must have taken either a part of it, or the whole. He could not have taken a part of it, because the divine essence is indivisible. Neither could he have taken the whole; for in this case the Father would have ceased to be the Father, and would have become the Son: and again, since the divine essence is numerically one, and therefore incommunicable, this could by no means have happened.

The Puritan John Owen responded, "This is the fruit of measuring spiritual things by carnal, infinite by finite, God by ourselves, the object of faith by corrupted rules of corrupted reason." But "what is impossible in finite, limited essences, may be possible and convenient to that which is infinite and unlimited, as is that whereof we speak" (*Vindiciae evangelicae*, in *Works*, 12:237).

The connection between being sent and being begotten is conspicuous in John 10:36, for example. When the Jews are ready to stone Jesus "because you, being a man, make yourself God" (10:33)—a hostility instigated by Jesus's claim "I and the Father are one" (10:30)—Jesus then asks why they are persecuting "him whom the Father *consecrated* and *sent* into the world," why they are ready to kill him for saying "I am the Son of God" (10:36). That word "consecrated" means something more than the Father sending his Son into the world. Like his self-attested title Son of God, the word "consecrated" takes the reader back to eternity, for there, as Jesus said already, we see not only that he is preexistent but also one with God the Father. Consecrated by God is another Johannine way of referring to the Son as only begotten, eternally generated by the Father. As the consecrated Son, it is appropriate for him to be sent into the world by God the Father. But couldn't this consecration merely refer to Jesus's anointing, say, at his own baptism? From Thomas Aquinas to John Calvin, those in the Great Tradition have answered no. "Christ's statement cannot refer to His consecration at His baptism, otherwise Christ would have spoken, first, of being sent into the world and then His subsequent consecration. Hence, Christ speaks of a pre-temporal, or eternal, consecration."[8]

Lost in Translation: The Only Begotten Son

One reason Bible-reading Christians today find this language of "begotten" so foreign and strange is because they, unlike all English readers of the Bible before them, have been fed new translations of the Bible that have removed the word "begotten" from the Gospel of John. No, I'm not a stubborn skeptic, always grumbling that they don't make translations like they used to. I am, for the most part, happy with many contemporary translations of the Bible. As a pastor and a professor, I use contemporary translations such as the ESV and NIV when preaching and lecturing.

However, when it comes to the Gospel of John, a misstep has been made, and it is no small one. Its theological consequences are serious. As I shared at the start of this book, when I was a young, eager student and was taught the doctrine of the Trinity by evangelical teachers at evangelical institutions, never had I ever heard a word about eternal generation. When it was mentioned, they swore it was nowhere in the Bible. But here's the problem: all the Bible translations I was given to read and memorize—NIV, ESV, RSV, HCSB, etc.—excised "only begotten" from John's Gospel, as well as from his first epistle. For over four centuries, those who translated the New Testament from Greek to English translated the word *monogenēs* as "only begotten." For example, consider that famous passage John 3:16, which reads in the King James Version, "For God so loved the world, that he gave his *only begotten* Son, that whosoever believeth in him should not perish, but have everlasting life." John says something similar in his first epistle: "In this was manifested the love of God toward us, because that God sent his *only begotten* Son into the world, that we might live through him" (1 John 4:9 KJV). "Only begotten" language is found throughout John's writings (e.g., John 1:14, 18; 3:18).

However, in the twentieth century, scholars erased "only begotten" from John's corpus and replaced this phrase with "only" or "unique" instead.[9] Starting with the Revised Standard Version, translators followed suit. God so loved the world, that he gave his *only* Son or his *unique* Son. Whether it was always intentional or not, generations of Christians were never introduced to the concept of eternal generation, nor could they see why the concept was so ingrained in Scripture's presentation of the *Son of God*, not even in a Gospel like John's. And, as we saw at the start of this book, even theologians like Wayne Grudem used to jump on board, concluding from new translations of the Bible that eternal generation was not a biblical concept but one imposed on the text.[10]

However, that consensus is now changing, and fast. In recent years, biblical scholars are now conceding that English translators for the past four hundred years were on to something when they translated *monogenēs* as "only begotten." And not just Bible scholars since the Reformation, but all the church fathers who believed the word conveyed the biological metaphor of begetting. For example, Charles Lee Irons warns against two extremes: those who force *monogenēs* to mean "only begotten" in every possible New Testament text versus those who deny that *monogenēs* can ever mean "only begotten" in any New Testament text.[11] The truth is somewhere in between: when the context is right, *monogenēs* does mean "only begotten." Irons surveys biblical and ancient literature and concludes that the "earliest meaning of *monogenēs* was *biological*, in reference to an only child."[12] Yes, later on other uses occurred as well (metaphorical and scientific). However, "the fundamental biological concept of 'begetting' is surely present in the word when used in literal or metaphorical familial contexts."[13]

That last word, "contexts," is key. We don't decide what meaning a word takes on by looking it up in a dictionary and flipping a coin to determine which definition we should use. For instance, the word "light" can refer to something that is radiant and bright (like light from the sun; daylight), or it can refer to something that is not very heavy (like a newborn baby or a purse with nothing inside). How do we know which meaning to use? Context. How the word is used in a sentence or in a paragraph. Likewise with *monogenēs*. The word may have different definitions, but its earliest history shows that the word was used to refer to something *biological*, something *familial*. And when we open the ancient Scriptures, the biblical authors use the word in a similar, biological manner, referring to the filial relations between the Father and the Son.

Consider John, for example. In the five times *monogenēs* appears (1:14, 18; 3:16, 18; 1 John 4:9), its context is familial and filial every single time. In other words, the context assumes a biological metaphor is applied to God: he is called *Father* and his offspring is called *Son*. Of course, the language is analogical, not literal (there is no mother!). Nevertheless, it is familial at its core.

Ask yourself: how does John begin his Gospel? Yes, the context of the latter half of John 1 is the incarnation. But in order to understand the incarnation, John takes us back to the beginning. "In the beginning was the Word, and the Word was with God, and the Word was God" (1:1 KJV). John intends his readers to know, from the start, that Jesus's divine existence didn't begin like every other man's existence; in fact, it never began. He is preexistent. His past is unlike our past, without a genesis, and is to be traced back to God himself in eternity. Never was there a time when God (the Father) was without his Word (John 1:1), and as John will soon reveal, this Word is none other than God's *Son*.

We know the context is filial and sonship is in view because in 1:14, 18, John refers both to "God" and "Father," treating the two as synonyms. The backstory of the incarnation is biological, analogically speaking. The eternal origin of the Word is none other than God the Father. Yet, unlike human sons, the Word (Son) has no point of generation; he is begotten from eternity. For not only was the Word with God, the Word was God.

When John turns to the miracle of the incarnation, he presupposes eternal sonship: "And the Word was made flesh, and dwelt among us, (and we beheld his glory, the glory as of the only begotten of the Father,) full of grace and truth" (1:14 KJV).[14] Glory reflects his familial origin: from the Father. He is the *glory* of God because he is none other than the *Son* of God, the very image and likeness of his Father. Begetting, therefore, must be in view. "The concept that the son bears the father's family likeness or image and reveals who the father is further reinforces the biological metaphor of begetting."[15] In all our efforts to translate *monogenēs* as "only" instead of "only begotten," we have failed to finish John's sentence: the Word's glory is the "glory as of the only begotten *of the Father*." Have we forgotten already where the Father came from and what his eternal origin then implies for his Son, the Word, the one in whom such glory radiates?

If we have forgotten, perhaps verse 18 will jog our memory: "No man hath seen God at any time, the only begotten Son, which is in the bosom of the Father, he hath declared him" (KJV). Or, as the verse reads in the NASB, "No one has seen God at any time; the only begotten God who is in the bosom of the Father, He has explained Him." Notice the context once more: the *monogenēs* is located where? In the bosom of the Father. The reason John can say the Word was sent by the Father to become flesh and dwell among us is because the Word is none other than the Son, whose origin is from the Father. Begotten by the Father in eternity, the Son can be sent by the Father to become incarnate in history.

That explains why he alone, as the Word, can reveal the Father. God as God is hidden from our finite gaze. But if he who is begotten, who is in the very bosom of the Father, becomes flesh and dwells among us, then this God is made known to us. As John moves back and forth between eternity and incarnation, the context in which he does so is filial. Irons says, "Thus, John 1:14 and 18 are of crucial importance for demonstrating that the Johannine *monogenēs* cannot be reduced to 'only of his kind' but must have a metaphorical biological meaning, 'only begotten.' John views Christ as the only begotten Son of God in the sense that he is the Father's only proper offspring deriving his divine being from the Father."[16]

In sum, there is a lesson here: sonship and begetting go hand in hand; they define each other. To put forward *monogenēs* as if it means "only" and has nothing to do with Jesus's preexistent, eternal, trinitarian origin from the Father is to rob the word of its meaning and treat the context of John 1 out of context altogether.

However, the doctrine of eternal generation does not merely depend on whether *monogenēs* is translated as "only begotten." That assumption has led translators and theologians to abandon the doctrine. But the concept is far more ingrained within the scriptural presentation of the Son to depend on one word. It is not only rooted in the meaning of the divine name itself (Son), as we've seen, but embedded within a diverse mosaic of scriptural imagery.

One Colorful Mosaic

Not only do the names Father and Son, along with John's language of "only begotten," lead us to drink from the well of eternal generation, but so do colorful images and metaphors planted across the Scriptures, forming a bright, brilliant mosaic in the end. The concept is organic, rooted in biblical language for the Son.

Hilary of Poitiers captures many of these biblical images and metaphors when he says the Son "is the Offspring of the Unbegotten, One from One, true from true, living from living, perfect from perfect; the Power of Power, the Wisdom of Wisdom, the Glory of Glory, the Likeness of the Invisible God, the Image of the Unbegotten Father."[17] We would need volumes (!) to explore each of these rich, biblical metaphors for eternal generation. But in this volume, we can at least tease out five: radiance, image, wisdom, Word, and Ancient of Days.

Radiance

Out of all the images and metaphors the author of Hebrews could have chosen to describe God the Son, he chose to open his letter with this one: *radiance*. The author of Hebrews first attests to the Son as the very revelation of God himself. Next, he makes the extraordinary claim that this Son is the one "through whom also he [God] created the world" (1:2). Which makes the reader wonder, who is this Son, that the cosmos should be created through him and for him? The answer arrives in verse 3: God can create the cosmos through his Son because, unlike everything in the created order, this Son's origin is from eternity. He is, in other words, "the radiance of the glory of God and the exact imprint of his nature," so it should not surprise us that the world was created through him and its ongoing governance is due to his sustaining power. For this Son "upholds the universe by the word of his power" (Heb. 1:3). How radiant this Son must be to be ascribed such works of divinity.

Light is a common image throughout Scripture, but it is used in Hebrews 1 in a way that is unique. For example, James also uses light to talk about God: "Every good gift and every perfect gift is from above, coming down from the Father of lights with whom there is no variation or shadow due to change" (James 1:17). But notice, James uses the imagery of light to differentiate between the immutable Creator and the mutable creation. The Father of lights, a phrase which describes him as Creator of the great lights in the sky, is unchanging in every way, without variation or shadow due to change, and therefore is the giver of all good gifts in our ever-changing created order. For all the biblical authors there is a clear, indisputable distinction between the immutable Creator and his mutable creation, a distinction we dare not violate.

Does the author of Hebrews locate God the Son with the Father of lights or with his changing creation? We saw in chapter 2 how Arius answered that question: the Son is to be identified with creation, the first of the created order. But not Hebrews: the Son shares in the same glory as God because he is the very radiance of God's glory, the exact imprint of God's nature. And lest we think otherwise, the author then identifies the Son with the Creator himself rather than the creation, naming the Son as the sustainer of the universe. He will do the same at the end of Hebrews 1 by appealing to Psalm 102, a passage that speaks of God as Creator, concluding that what the psalmist says should be said of the Son himself: "You, Lord, laid the foundation of the earth in the beginning, and the heavens are the work of your hands" (Heb. 1:10; cf. Ps. 102:25–27). One could hardly ask for a more direct affirmation of the Son's coeternality and coequality with the Father.

The Son, then, is not to be identified with the creation but with the Creator. The Father is not his Creator, like the creation in James 1:17. Instead, the Father is the Son's eternal source, his everlasting principle, which is why Hebrews 1:3 describes the Son as the radiance of the glory of God. The Father is not the Son's Creator, but he is the Son's *Father*. He did not create his Son but generated him from all eternity. Big difference. "Unlike the imagery of James 1:17, where clear lines of discontinuity are drawn between the immutable Father of lights and his mutable creaturely offspring, the imagery of Hebrews 1:3 suggests that the Father should be understood as the *natural principle* of the Son—as light naturally radiates its brightness, so too God naturally radiates his Son. 'Lights and its splendor are one.'"[18] *God naturally radiates his Son*—that captures the heart of eternal generation. The Son is the resplendent effulgence of the glory of God.[19]

Is this not how light works? I'll never forget the first time I traveled back to the States after my family moved to London. Tourists in July don't realize that most of the year the city is covered in a blanket of gray gloom, expunging incandescence wherever it can be found. But one year I was invited to speak at a conference in Houston, Texas. After a fourteen-hour flight over the Atlantic, the plane finally landed. I walked out of the airport and was met by the giddy smile of a prosperous blue sky, its glistening sunshine coating my Vitamin-D deficient face. And I felt as if I had been redeemed, brought back to planet earth after a dreary, dispirited exile. With a smile spreading from ear to ear, I would have kissed the green grass under my feet if the police officer standing next

Read the Bible with the Church

Gregory of Nyssa says Hebrews 1:3 highlights not only the deity of the Son but the Son's "ineffable mode of subsistence" as the "Only-begotten."

to me had not looked at me like I was an alien from another planet. On that happy day, I looked up and thanked the sun for its radiance.

But our finite, partial, and quite limited experience of radiance is nothing in comparison to the type of radiance Hebrews has in mind. Grasping for words to describe this eternal mystery called eternal generation, light seems entirely appropriate. The Son, Hebrews says, is the radiance of the glory of God, the resplendent, ever lucent, and beaming effulgence of God and his everlasting immensity. He is "the self-diffusive presence of the one who is himself unapproachable splendor. God's glory is God himself in the perfect majesty and beauty of his being. The glory is resplendent. Because God himself is light, he pours forth light."[20] So when Nicaea describes the Son's generation from the Father as "light from light," Nicaea is not speculating but echoing the biblical witness to describe the Son's eternal relation of origin: filiation. The Son is light because he is the eternal offspring of light.

Contrary to critics who object that such an idea makes the Son inferior, the idea of radiance, according to Hebrews, does not undermine but underlines the Son's equality with the Father. The reason the Son is coeternal and coequal with the Father is because he is the *radiance* of divine glory—light from light—and the *imprint* of the divine nature itself. Words like "radiance" and "imprint" not only distinguish the Son as Son, insinuating his divine origin, but affirm his identity with the divine nature itself. While we might distinguish light from light, radiance from glory, we do so knowing full well one is from the other, inseparable and indivisible, Father and Son alike holding the same nature in common. "The metaphor thus indicates the unbroken continuity of being between God's glory and its effulgence, light and its splendor are one."[21] But that can only be said if the Father is the source of such radiance and the Son his radiating light. And it must be in that order, too—the Son from the Father rather than the Father from the Son. For the Son, says Hebrews, is the radiance of the glory of God, not the other way around. As Gregory of Nyssa says, "The brightness [comes] from the glory, and not, reversely, the glory from the brightness."[22]

In similar fashion, Hebrews switches metaphors from "light" to "imprint," but only to convey the same point. Plus, Hebrews says the Son is the *exact* imprint of God's nature, once again confirming the coequality of the Son with the Father. Yet, as an imprint, he is not the same person as the Father. Same nature, yes, but distinguished as the Son who is from the Father, much like an imprint from its originating template or source. The concept of imprint does not undermine or distract from what we learned about radiance but complements it in every way. For if he is the exact imprint—"in the form of God" (Phil. 2:6)—then he is begotten from the Father's nature. "The metaphor of imprinting," says John Webster, "does not take us in a different direction from that of effulgence, but reinforces it by speaking of the Son as the exact representation of the divine essence."[23] Radiance of the glory of God, imprint of God's nature—both accentuate the Son's eternal origin from the Father's essence.

Are we imposing this concept of eternal generation onto Hebrews, reading it into the text (eisegesis) rather than from the text (exegesis)? Not at all. For if you keep reading, you will discover that the author transitions from the imagery of radiance and imprint to the vocabulary of begetting itself. In an effort to communicate the superiority of the Son to creation, in an attempt to set the Son apart from creation and position the Son in the Godhead, the author of Hebrews goes way back to the Old Testament: "For to which of the angels did God ever say, 'You are my Son, today I have begotten you'?" (Heb. 1:5).[24] The author is quoting Psalm 2:7.[25]

In Psalm 2, the nations rage against the Lord and also against his Anointed One (2:1–2). But they are no match: "He who sits in the heavens laughs; the Lord holds them in derision" (2:4). Their rage is futile, for as soon as the Lord speaks, his wrath will "terrify them in his fury" (2:5). These nations pose no real threat to the

Lord and his everlasting kingdom. "As for me, I have set my King on Zion, my holy hill" (2:6).

But lest we think this Anointed One, this King in Zion is but a mere mortal, the Lord takes us beyond our finite, temporal vision and opens our eyes to his decree, a decree that speaks of things eternal (2:7a).[26] The reason Zion's foundations will not be shaken is because its King is from of old, hailing from a divine origin as a Son from his Father. "You are my Son; today I have begotten you" (2:7b). Now here is something extraordinary: David is the speaker of Psalm 2, but the Spirit is speaking through the prophet David so that he takes on the very voice of the Father addressing his Son.[27] David is overhearing a divine conversation concerning the Son's origin *from eternity*.[28]

Some will object that the word "today" in Psalm 2:7 and Hebrews 1:5 must preclude the concept of *eternal* generation, and instead refers only to the Son being sent into the world or being appointed to his office as King. Not only does such an objection ignore the rest of Hebrews 1, which cites one psalm after another to demonstrate the Son's everlasting dominion (1:6–14), but it settles for a superficial understanding of the word "today." The Old Testament authors use the word at times to refer to God's everlasting existence and purview.[29] Because the context of Hebrews 1 concerns the eternal divinity of the Son, the author is pressed to compare Christ to the angels and conclude that Christ is far superior (1:5, 7, 13). Unlike these created angelic beings, Christ is a natural Son, not an adopted Son; a Son from all eternity, not a Son whose origin begins in time. As Augustine explains, "The word today denotes the actual present, and as in eternity nothing is past as if it had ceased to be, nor future as if it had not yet to come to pass, but all is simply present, since whatever is eternal is ever in being, the words, 'Today I have begotten you,' are to be understood of the divine generation. In this phrase, the orthodox catholic [i.e., universal] belief proclaims the eternal generation of the Power and Wisdom of God who is the only-begotten Son."[30]

David may be speaking, but as he takes on the very voice of the Father addressing his begotten Son, that divine conversation transcends time. Defying the limitations of time altogether, God is timelessly eternal in his generation of his Son.

Soon enough the author of Hebrews will describe the Son's entrance into the world (see Heb. 1:6), but before he does so, he first establishes the superiority of the Son *as Son*, something the angels cannot claim in the least because they, for all their luster, are not the radiance of the glory of God nor the exact imprint of his nature. If this begetting in Hebrews 1:5 is an eternal begetting, then perhaps it is right to paraphrase Psalm 2:7 as one scholar has: "You are my Son; *forever* I have begotten you."[31] After all, later chapters in Hebrews will refer to Jesus himself as the one who is the same yesterday, today, and forever (13:8; cf. 1:8–9; 7:3, 24).[32] Hebrews doesn't quote Psalm 2:7 to say Jesus climbs up the divinity ladder, as if he were a lesser glory and must arrive at a more exalted position. Hebrews quotes the psalmist to convey that the Son's origin has always been from the Father. *Never was there a time when the Son was not, because never was there a time when*

Eavesdropping on God

The quotation of Psalm 2:7 in Hebrews 1:5 is an example of prosopological interpretation (Greek: *prosōpon*, "person"). It sounds sophisticated, but you've seen it already. Remember our friend Zipporah? When she witnessed the religious leaders oppose Jesus (chap. 4), Jesus responded by quoting David in Psalm 110 ("The Lord said to my Lord"), letting us in on the Father's speech to his Son in eternity. The New Testament writers use a prosopological method so that we can eavesdrop on a divine conversation, helping us identify one divine person from another. Prosopological interpretation is not invented by the apostles but emerges from dialogue in the Old Testament itself, as we've seen in Psalm 2:7. For that reason, prosopological exegesis is a common practice in the Great Tradition, as it was in Bible times.

the Son was not begotten from his Father. A higher claim to divine equality does not exist. The author of Hebrews knows it, too, which is why he directs Psalm 2:7 at Christ himself.[33]

But what about Acts 13:33, which refers to Psalm 2:7 and seems to apply it to Christ's resurrection, not his eternal state? In the past, commentators felt obliged to choose one or the other. But if we understand how the New Testament uses the Old, there is no reason both cannot be in view. The reason is found in Psalm 2:7 itself. God says, "today I have begotten you" after he says, "You are my Son." Paul does not rip begotten language out of eternity in order to refer to the resurrection of Christ. Rather, it is because this is the *Son*, the *eternal* Son, begotten by the Father before all ages, that Paul can then apply begotten language to the resurrection of Christ as well. At the resurrection, God is announcing to the world not only what his Son has accomplished but who his Son is from eternity. Here's the bottom line: "The Messiah was God's Son before He was inaugurated as Zion's king."[34]

The surrounding context of Psalm 2 may have the Davidic king in mind, but David is but a type that points forward to a much greater king, the greater David to come: Jesus, the Messiah. The covenant God made with David (2 Sam. 7) is fulfilled in the Davidic son, the Lord Jesus, the type (David) culminating in the antitype (Christ). The resurrection of Jesus is proof such fulfillment has taken place. That's why in Acts 13:33, Paul can say that Psalm 2 is fulfilled. But Paul does not do so as if this Davidic, risen king has no eternal origin.[35] The reason he is a greater David in the first place, and the ultimate reason he is not still dead in the tomb like David (see Acts 2:29), is this: he predates David as the Son whose eternal origin is from the Father ("You are my Son").

In summary, the New Testament authors may apply Psalm 2 to the enthronement of the new Davidic king (Jesus) due to his achievement of salvation. But they also recognize, based on the intra-trinitarian conversation in Psalm 2, that this Davidic king who has been appointed from eternity to accomplish our salvation

(Heb. 1:2; Ps. 2:8) is none other than the Son who proceeds from the Father before all time.

Image

If the author of Hebrews uses the idea of radiance to capture the Son's eternal relation of origin, Paul conveys the same truth with the term *image*.

He begins his letter to the Colossians by praising God for delivering us "from the domain of darkness" and transferring us "to the kingdom of his beloved Son" (1:13). Already, that phrase "beloved Son" speaks volumes: this is *God's* beloved Son. What it means for the Son to be a Son is conveyed next: "He is the image of the invisible God, the firstborn of all creation. For by him all things were created, in heaven and on earth, visible and invisible, whether thrones or dominions or rulers or authorities—all things were created through him and for him. And he is before all things, and in him all things hold together" (1:15–17).

The Hands of John of Damascus

One Eastern church father who has been lost in the shadows is John of Damascus (675/76–749), who left the family business in government to enter the monastic life. One legend says John's obedience was tested when he was forbidden to write. When another monk's brother died, John wrote a letter to comfort him. As penance, John had to clean toilets with his bare hands. Another legend says John was set up when a letter in his name was forged, encouraging revolt. As punishment, John's hand was chopped off. But after he prayed, his hand was miraculously restored. Whether true or not, John did put his hands to good use when he wrote theology. If you want a concise summary of Nicene trinitarianism, you cannot beat John's *Exposition on the Orthodox Faith*. John draws on the Cappadocian fathers, and his summary of the Trinity is so profound that later on Thomas Aquinas would quote him often.

An image, by definition, is not to be separated from that which it images, but reflects, represents, and reveals that which it images. While an image may be distinct in important ways from that which it images, it is an image first and foremost because it shares something in common with that which it images, whatever that may be. Image language is found throughout Scripture. As soon as we open our Bibles, we read in the first chapter of Genesis that man and woman have been made in the image of God. While commentators have debated for centuries what the image of God is (something we are? something we do? both?), there is no debating that the *imago Dei* is fundamental to what it means to be human. Unlike many secularists, Christians are set apart by this basic belief.

But have you ever noticed that for all the image talk that pervades the opening chapters of the Bible, God never says to any one person in an absolute sense, "You and you alone are *the* image"? No one except for one: his Son. And he is not mentioned in the creation account because he is no creature. But when the apostle Paul reads his Old Testament and reflects on the person of the Son, he believes this prerogative belongs to the Son and the Son alone. He is "the image of the invisible God" (Col. 1:15). That is an unprecedented claim. You may remember that in the wilderness God made it extra clear to Israel that he has no form; he is not like the idols of the surrounding nations (Deut. 4:15). John opens his Gospel saying the same: "No man hath seen God at any time" (1:18a). But that's not all John says. "No man hath seen God" but (!) "the only begotten Son, which is in the bosom of the Father, he hath declared him" (KJV). Who is John referring to? None other than the Son, Christ Jesus our Lord. As the only begotten Son, begotten by the Father before all ages, he and he alone is the true image of the invisible God. By assuming our human nature to his person, he was then able to manifest and reveal God to us in the flesh. He alone could do so because he alone is "in the bosom of the Father."

Paul may not use John's "only begotten" vocabulary, but the same concept is implied when he says the Son is the image of the invisible God. Yes, we are said to be image bearers in Scripture. But we are created creatures, redeemed by the blood of the Son, and only on that basis are we said to be transformed more and more until we are finally conformed to the true image of the Son. In fact, it's only because the Son is the Image of the Father that we can be remade into the image of God. As Athanasius says, "The Word of God came in his own person, that, as he was the Image of the Father, he might be able to recreate man after the image."[36] But to be clear, he alone is *the* Image, because he alone is *the* Son. As Nicaea says, he alone is begotten, not made, and therefore he alone is said to be the image of the invisible God. Nicaea and the fathers do not mean—and neither do we—that the Son is merely a mirror of the Father, as if the Son only appears to be like the one he reflects. Rather, the Son is the image of God because he shares the very nature of God.[37] As Gregory of Nyssa says, the Son is said to be in the Father "as the beauty of the image is to be found in the form from which it has been outlined; and the Father in the Son, as that original beauty is to be found in the image of itself."[38] The implications for those found in Christ are extraordinary.

But wait, doesn't Paul say in his very next breath that the Son is the "firstborn of all creation"? How then is the Son begotten but not made? Arians conclude that "firstborn" (Greek: *prototokos*) means the Son is created. The difference between him and creation is not one of class or type, as if the Son is to be identified with the eternal Creator in distinction from everything else that is temporal and created. No, the Son also is part of the created order, but he's the firstborn, meaning he is the first one to be created, and in that sense holds supremacy over everything else. If Arianism is right, then what we just said about the Son being the image of the invisible God takes on a whole different meaning: the Son is created by the Father, and so he is an image bearer like we creatures are image bearers, although he is first. He cannot be the image of the invisible God because he is one with God, begotten from the Father's nature—not if he is a created being like us.

However, Arianism misrepresents Paul. When Paul says the Son is the firstborn of all creation, he is not referring to God creating his Son. No, Paul is referring to Christ in relation to creation. *Paul is not referring to God's supremacy over his Son but to Christ's supremacy over his creation.* That's why Paul says in the very next verse, "For by him [the Son] all things were created" (Col. 1:16a). The point is not to say the Son was the first created of the created order, but that the preexistent Son is preeminent to the created order, transcending it altogether as the one who created it in the first place, and therefore has full rights to rule and reign over it.[39] "He is before all things, and in him all things hold together" (1:17), not because he was made first but because that which was made (the cosmos) was made through him who is begotten not made.[40] But if the Son was created, then Paul overreaches in the worst way possible when he confesses, "For in him [the Son] all the fullness of God was pleased to dwell" (1:19) and "For in him the whole fullness of deity dwells bodily" (2:9).[41]

In brief, image does not mean the Son is inferior to that which he images, as if the Son were subordinate to the Father. Image conveys likeness.[42] The Son, says Gregory of Nazianzus, "is called 'Image' because he is consubstantial with the Father."[43]

Wisdom and Word

Christians today refer to Christ in many ways: the Way, the Truth, and the Life; the Light of the World; the Good Shepherd; the Alpha and the Omega. But never have I ever heard a Christian (or a pastor, for that matter) talk about Christ as the wisdom of God. Never. But this image—wisdom—is one that Scripture (both Old and New Testaments) applies to Christ. It goes to show that when we read Scripture, we are sometimes drawn only to those concepts that are familiar to us, overlooking others that are foreign to our

Christianese. As a result, our knowledge of Christ is stunted and we do not learn how to read the Bible as a whole, seeing Christ from beginning to end as God intended. The consequences can be serious: doctrines like eternal generation, which pervade Scripture's story line, are neglected or rejected altogether. Wisdom is a case in point.

But it was not always so. It's hard to read any church father, East or West, without hearing about the wisdom of God, by which they mean God the Son. Athanasius, the Cappadocians, Augustine, and so many more from our Dream Team not only refer to the Son as wisdom but spend chapter after chapter of their tomes unveiling this biblical name with robust exegesis.[44] Sometimes they even preached sermons on the Son as the wisdom of God. When was the last time you heard a sermon like that? They did so because they were convinced this title, across both Testaments, communicates the Son's eternal generation. Believing the canon to be a unity, they also believed Proverbs 8 points to he who is wisdom itself.

At the opening of Paul's first letter to the Corinthians, the cross of Christ is said to be foolishness to those who are perishing. It certainly appears that way to the unbelieving eye: What kind of king is crucified? What kind of God is nailed to a cross? But to the believing eye, what appears to be weakness is actually the power of God on display. For by Christ's death, we sinners are saved (1 Cor. 1:18). Paul quotes from the book of Isaiah and concludes that God has destroyed the wisdom of the wise; the wisdom of the world is made foolish by the cross (1 Cor. 1:19–20; cf. Isa. 29:14). "For since, in the wisdom of God, the world did not know God through wisdom, it pleased God through the folly of what we preach to save those who believe" (1 Cor. 1:21).

Next, Paul takes wisdom to a new level, no longer just referring to wisdom as a noun or a verb but as a person: "For Jews demand signs and Greeks seek wisdom, but we preach Christ crucified, a stumbling block to Jews and folly to Gentiles, but to those who are called, both Jews and Greeks, Christ the power of God and the wisdom of God" (1:22–24). Jews and Greeks alike look at Christ on the cross and they stumble, walking away from Calvary in disbelief. For the Jews, the crucifixion is a sign of defeat, not victory, and as they told Jesus during his ministry, they want miraculous signs, more and more and more until they are convinced that he is from God. As for the Greeks, they pride themselves on their physical, intellectual, and rhetorical sophistication. They look at the bloody death of Jesus and think it foolish, an embarrassment to be sure. But, says Paul, everything is not what it seems: what the world says is wise is foolishness to God, and the very "foolishness" of God—the cross of Christ—is, it turns out, wisdom. For it is not weakness as it seems but God's power to save. How appropriate, then, for Paul to conclude that this Christ is the power of God for salvation, and the wisdom of God on display to every nation. "And because of him you are in Christ Jesus, who became to us wisdom from God" (1 Cor. 1:30).

Question is, where did this wisdom originate from? It might appear that Paul is unique in calling Christ the wisdom from God, wisdom personified in the person of the Son. But Paul is anything but novel. Remember, as a rabbi who trained under the best of rabbis, Paul knew his Old Testament. And the Old Testament personifies wisdom in Proverbs 8. Coincidence? I doubt it. In Proverbs 8, Solomon portrays wisdom as a person calling in the streets, summoning any and all who will listen. For if they listen, they will live; if not, they will meet destruction in this life and the next.

> The LORD possessed me at the beginning of his work,
>   the first of his acts of old.
> Ages ago I was set up,
>   at the first, before the beginning of the earth.
> When there were no depths I was brought forth,
>   when there were no springs abounding with water.
> Before the mountains had been shaped,
>   before the hills, I was brought forth,

before he had made the earth with its fields,
    or the first of the dust of the world.
When he established the heavens, I was there;
    when he drew a circle on the face of the deep,
when he made firm the skies above,
    when he established the foundations of the deep,
when he assigned to the sea its limit,
    so that the waters might not transgress his command,
when he marked out the foundations of the earth,
    then I was beside him, like a master workman.
        (Prov. 8:22–30)

As wisdom calls in the streets, proclaiming its way of righteousness and its paths of justice (8:5–20), we then hear wisdom not only personified further but also self-conscious of its own origin. Wisdom is said to be from "of old" (8:22). We will explore this more when we look at the title Ancient of Days, an Old Testament name and title also attributed to Jesus. But here in Proverbs 8, "of old" says something: it says wisdom has an eternal origin. Not only that, but its origin from of old has a *source*: "Before the mountains had been shaped, before the hills, *I was brought forth*" (8:25). Brought forth from where? From whom? The answer is in verse 22, where the Lord himself is identified. It is the Lord who "possessed me at the beginning of his work," and this same Lord "brought forth" wisdom before "the mountains had been shaped" and before he made "the dust of the world."

Wisdom, in other words, was brought forth from the Lord and from all eternity. Perhaps you can now see why so many from the Great Tradition believed wisdom as personified in Proverbs 8 either directly or typologically refers to God the Son and his eternal generation from the Father. Even more so when we also consider, as we saw in 1 Corinthians, how the New Testament authors called Christ the wisdom of God (1 Cor. 1:24, 30). But to see the connection, we must read our Old Testament like Christians, that is, *christologically*, the way the New Testament authors read their

Old Testament. God has embedded his divine authorial intent throughout so that types and shadows in the Old Testament find their fulfillment and culmination in Christ Jesus (our New Testament). That said, so too should we read Proverbs 8 with 1 Corinthians 2 in view. Wisdom is personified in God the Son, brought forth from the Lord from of old, powerfully revealed to us as the wisdom of God in the most unforeseeable circumstances: the humiliation of the cross.

"But wait!" protested the Arians of the fourth century. Proverbs 8:22–23 says wisdom was "possessed" and "set up" at the "beginning," so eternal generation cannot be in view—impossible. This wisdom was created, not generated; it was made along with creation, not begotten by the Father from all eternity. Unlike Proverbs 8:25, which refers to wisdom's eternal origin from the Lord, verses 22–23 refer to wisdom's relation to the rest of creation (similar to Paul's use of "firstborn" language in Col. 1). In other words, he was "set up," so to speak, "before the beginning of the earth" (v. 23) because the cosmos was created through him and for him, a point the New Testament authors were all too eager to emphasize (cf. Col. 1; Heb. 1). While verse 25 refers to what occurs inside the Godhead (*ad intra*), verses 22–23 refer to what occurs external to the Godhead, toward the created order (*ad extra*).

To identify the eternal Son as the wisdom of God is most fitting in the eyes of the biblical authors. The resemblance is uncanny: Wisdom is born of God; the Son is born of God. Wisdom reflects divine glory; the Son reflects divine glory. Wisdom is from the beginning; the Son is from the beginning. Wisdom is the agent of creation; the Son is the agent of creation. Wisdom descended from heaven; the Son descended from heaven. Wisdom enlightens those in darkness; the Son enlightens those in darkness.[45] And, like wisdom, he is the *Word*. What we've learned about wisdom is encapsulated in John's title for Jesus: "In the beginning was the Word, and the Word was with God, and the Word was God. The same was in the beginning with God. All things were made by him; and without him was not any thing made that was made" (John 1:1–3 KJV).

The parallel between wisdom in Proverbs 8 and the Word in John 1 is nothing short of extraordinary. The *Logos*, a title which itself overlaps with wisdom, was not brought into existence sometime before creation but was with God from eternity. As the church fathers like to say, never was there a time when God was without his wisdom. Could we not also say, never was there a time when God was without his Word?

As John will reveal in the rest of his opening chapter, this Word is none other than the Son himself (1:14, 18). As such, John can make the most shocking claim of all: the Word was God (1:1). John could not more closely identify the Son with the Father. As Jesus will later say, "I and the Father are one" (John 10:30). His divinity is unquestionable because he is identified with God himself from eternity.

But there is more to be said about the title Word. Consider John 1:14, 18: "And the Word was made flesh, and dwelt among us, (and we beheld his glory, the glory as of the only begotten of the Father,) full of grace and truth. . . . No man hath seen God at any time, the only begotten Son, which is in the bosom of the Father, he hath declared him" (KJV). We often focus, as John does in verse 18, on how the Son reveals the Father to us. That is, in part, why John has chosen this title. The Father speaks to us a saving Word, and it is none other than his own Son. Yet there is something more fundamental about the title Word. Jesus is not just the Word because he reveals the Father to us; he is the Word first and foremost because he is from the Father before all ages as a Son. Which is why John can move, in the same breath, from the title "Word" to the filial title "Son." This Word, in other words, not only reveals the Father to us as the Son who is "in the bosom of the Father" (1:18), but he can reveal the Father to us because he is the Son born from the Father's essence (*ousia*). Otherwise, John has no right to call this Word, this Son, "only begotten." In sum, the Father can speak his creation into existence through his Word, only to speak a saving Word to make a fallen creation new, because there never was a time when God was without his Word. Worded by the Father from all eternity, the Word can then, at the proper time, become incarnate to reveal the Father to us in history. Now that is wisdom.

Ancient of Days

Unlike today, names meant something during biblical times; they had meaning, significance, and even communicated a message. One of my favorite names in the Old Testament is Ichabod. The name occurs in 1 Samuel 4, which is one of the most dismal chapters in all the Bible. Eli, the priest, has two sons who are leading the people of God into immorality and making a mockery of God's holiness. They are, in God's own words, wicked and worthless. So God lets the Philistines defeat the Israelites in a battle in which the two sons of Eli are killed and the ark of the covenant is captured. Forget his wicked sons; when Eli hears the ark has been taken, he falls over, and his weight breaks his own neck (Eli was not a slim man). When Eli's daughter-in-law hears the news, her labor pains begin and she gives birth to a son. She names him Ichabod, meaning "The glory has departed from Israel!" Can you imagine? Whenever someone said that boy's name, everyone was reminded that the presence of God was no longer in Israel. That is one hopeless name.

But not all names in the Old Testament were so tragic. The prophet Micah, for example, had a name that was filled with good news. Unlike Ichabod, Micah's name conveyed hope. His name meant "Who is like Yahweh?" who pardons the people's iniquity (7:18). But in Micah's day, the people of God had grown corrupt, and such corruption stemmed from their leaders. As a result, they deserved condemnation for their many perverse deeds. As much as the Lord pronounced judgment on his people through the prophet

Micah, it turns out that judgment was not the last word. Although they deserved destruction, Yahweh gave them forgiveness. Unlike his unfaithful people, Yahweh is a God who stays true to the covenant he has made, unwavering in his fidelity.

God's undeserved benevolence and pardon toward Israel reaches its pinnacle in a promise made in Micah 5:

> But you, O Bethlehem Ephrathah,
>> who are too little to be among the clans of Judah,
> from you shall come forth for me
>> one who is to be ruler in Israel,
> whose coming forth is from of old,
>> from ancient days. (5:2)

Ancient of Days—for some reason I've never associated that title with the book of Micah. Perhaps that's because I'm so used to hearing it in the book of Daniel, which repeatedly refers to one called the Ancient of Days (Dan. 7:9, 13, 22). But it's there in the book of Micah as well, standing tall and handsome. In the midst of warfare and calamity, the Lord speaks a word of promise and hope: a day is coming when Bethlehem, of all places, will sprout a new leader, a ruler, a shepherd. If that sounds familiar, it's most likely because every Christmas we hear Matthew 2:4–6 read at some point. When wise men from the east came to Jerusalem asking, "Where is he who has been born king of the Jews?" King Herod asked his chief priests and scribes where this Christ was to be born, to which they responded, "In Bethlehem of Judea" (Matt. 2:5). Apparently these counselors knew a thing or two about the Old Testament, identifying Micah 5:2 as the verse to tell them not only that a king would be born but where this king would be born.[46]

Why is this king, this prophesied shepherd, so unique? Look again at Micah 5:2. Yes, he will come from a little town called Bethlehem. But what should jump out at you is this: Bethlehem is not this king's ultimate place of origin. His origin predates

Bethlehem. "[His] coming forth is from of old." How old? "From ancient days." This language is used throughout the Old Testament to refer to Yahweh's eternal origin. But if Israel's God is from everlasting to everlasting, having no beginning and no end, how can this ruler, king, and shepherd be Jesus when we know where Jesus was born?

As we've seen already, the birth of Jesus was no ordinary human birth, despite its humble appearances. The irony is explicit: this babe, born among animals and laid within the trough from which they feed, is none other than the eternal Son, begotten from the Father before all ages. His birth in Bethlehem may be the start of his incarnation, but the identity of this babe points us back to eternity, where the origins of his Sonship are located with the Father. His coming forth is from of old because this newborn king is none other than the Ancient of Days himself.

For Matthew to attribute Micah 5:2 with Jesus is to say nothing less. Matthew puts this quotation in his Gospel not merely because Jesus is the ultimate fulfilment of the king and son God promised would sit on David's throne. He is that, but he is so much more. This shepherd from the line of David can come and establish his kingdom because his *divine, trinitarian* identity does not begin in Bethlehem but originates in eternity.[47] The Ancient of Days originates from ancient days. As John Owen says, "He that was in the fulness of time born at Bethlehem, had his goings forth from the Father from eternity."[48]

Rise and Be Reborn!

Is eternal generation a doctrine without biblical warrant? Only if one adopts a narrow, crude biblicism. But if one reads Scripture how God intended—as an integrated whole rather than disparate parts, and with the *triune* God himself as its one, divine author who has revealed himself across the whole sweep of redemptive history—then eternal generation is seen for what it really is: the warp and woof of the Bible, the doctrine on which the entire story depends.

If we (1) consider history's redemptive structure (the Father sending the Son), (2) pay attention to what the names Father and Son intrinsically mean, (3) mind the Johannine context of *monogenēs* to confirm Jesus as the only begotten Son, and (4) observe the many diverse metaphors and titles attributed to Jesus (radiance, image, wisdom, Word, Ancient of Days), what we discover is that eternal generation is implied and inferred in legions of ways. Strip the Scriptures of this concept and it is impossible to understand what it means for Jesus to be called Son, at least in its trinitarian, biblical, and, yes, distinctively *Christian* sense. Remove this pillar of orthodoxy and we no longer can understand what distinguishes the Son from the Father, nor why the Father would send his Son to redeem a fallen humanity.

But eternal generation is also essential for understanding salvation. For if the Son is not the only begotten Son, then there is no basis on which the Father can send his Son into the world to save sinners like you and me. Only one who is God himself, begotten from the very essence of the Father, is qualified let alone capable of saving a fallen humanity. If he is not eternally generated, what hope do we have that we will be regenerated? Unless he is born from the Father from all eternity, we have little confidence we will be born again and enter the kingdom of the Son (John 3:3, 16). Perhaps we should revisit the verse that opened this chapter, the one our friend Zipporah heard from Jesus's own lips: "For as the Father has life in himself, so he has granted the Son also to have life in himself" (John 5:26). Only he who has life in himself can give life to those who so desperately need it.

That should empower our evangelism: we do not hold out to the world a Savior who hopes and wishes he can turn this world around; we hold out to a world lost in the depths of darkness a Savior who can raise the dead to new life. For that reason, Augustine boldly summoned unbelievers everywhere to look to none other than the only begotten Son: "What about you, soul? You were dead, you had lost life; listen to the Father through the Son. Arise, receive life, in order that the life which you do not have in yourself you may receive in the one who does have life in himself."[49]

If Augustine's words sound strange, perhaps a more familiar tune will sound familiar, a tune you sing every Christmas season: "Hark! The Herald Angels Sing." The third stanza of Charles Wesley's timeless hymn says,

> Hail the heav'n-born Prince of Peace!
> Hail the Sun of righteousness!
> Light and life to all He brings,
> Ris'n with healing in His wings:
> Mild He lays His glory by,
> Born that man no more may die;
> Born to raise the sons of earth;
> Born to give them second birth.

Apart from the only begotten Son, begotten from the Father from all eternity, we have no confidence, no assurance that we can or will be reborn. *The sons of earth only receive their second birth if this Prince of Peace is heav'n-born.*

Is the Son Eternally Subordinate to the Father?

A Son Worthy of Worship

The Father is almighty, the Son almighty
and the Holy Spirit almighty,
. . . they are not three Almighties
but one Almighty.

THE ATHANASIAN CREED

In the light of the Jesus who insists that proper stances of rule
are characterized less by authoritative rights and more by
self-sacrificing service for the good of those ruled, in a way
that leads directly to the cross (Matt. 20:20–28), to discuss the
relationships among the persons of the Godhead in terms of
authority structures (as we have been taught by our culture to
think of authority structures) might be hugely misleading.

D. A. CARSON

Interpretation is the cheerful acceptance of the
text's offer of more than lies on its surface.

OLIVER O'DONAVAN, *FINDING AND SEEKING*

TO THE DELOREAN!

Where we're going: Evangelicalism

Key point: A novel view has emerged within evangelicalism called EFS, claiming the Son is subordinate to the Father in authority *within the immanent Trinity*. EFS is not biblical, comes dangerously close to three heresies, and threatens a Christian view of salvation and worship. EFS is also a version of social trinitarianism, which is a departure from biblical and Nicene orthodoxy.

A Ford Mustang and Texas Creepy Crawlers

Seminary can be an exciting time. I know it was for me. My wife, Elizabeth, and I had just married in Malibu, California. We were young and free to take off and plant ourselves wherever God might call us. My college professors had encouraged me to go to seminary. So, off we went.

That's when I made a decision that I am still recovering from to this day: we sold my midnight-black Ford Mustang convertible. We needed the money. But we kept Elizabeth's boxy, faded-silver 1990 Volvo—an indestructible tank—and packed up what little we had for a cross-country drive.

Our new home was Louisville, Kentucky, the Bluegrass State, home to the Kentucky Derby and the finest bourbon east of the Mississippi River. But to get there we had to drive through Texas in the middle of July. As they say in Texas, it was as hot as the hinges of hell. And our Swedish steel tank felt it, too; its air-conditioner gave up just when we crossed the border. Knowing we'd roast alive if we drove during the day, we decided to drive at night. It barely helped. Windows rolled down, we drove and drove with nothing but dirt on each side of the road, praying to God our car would not overheat. But we'd failed to take into consideration another Texas phenomenon: in the middle of the night, a car with four windows rolled down and beaming headlights was the equivalent of an open ecological invitation, welcoming the biggest and nastiest bugs in all of Texas to join two newlyweds on their ill-planned road trip. I don't know who first said everything is bigger in Texas, but they were right. I had just noticed that not even the truck drivers were on the road, when a bug that had eaten a cow for dinner darted its way into my driver's seat. So I did what any man in Texas would do: I screamed.

Somehow we survived and made it to Louisville just in time to start classes. I took classes in every subject, but I could hear a heartbeat inside my theological soul whenever I took a class in systematic theology. I couldn't get enough. That eagerness gave me a front-row seat to teaching from outstanding theologians, many of whom drew from Nicene orthodoxy. With practice, I was learning to sing the tune of the Trinity.

Since I couldn't get enough theology, I asked around, trying to find out who else I should take classes with. Many said, "Take Bruce Ware. He'll teach you an evangelical view of the Trinity." Ware stood out for his combination of theological conviction and personal piety. It was obvious Ware was a godly man committed to teaching the Bible. Furthermore, his devotion to scriptural fidelity was contagious. And, as a leading evangelical, he taught his students to guard the faith from unsound doctrine. Also, I have always admired his personal investment in his students and have no doubt benefited in many ways.

But as Ware sang the praises of the Trinity, he would sometimes say things that sounded off-key: the Father is "supreme over" the Son; the Father "stands above the Son"; the Father alone deserves "ultimate glory," even over the Son, who only deserves "penultimate" glory; and the Father alone should receive "ultimate praise."[1] These were discordant notes that manipulated the Nicene song I was learning to sing.[2]

What could they mean? It took time and a whole lot of serious study, but I finally got to the bottom of it.

A New Kind of Biblicism

For almost seven years, I heard Bruce Ware articulate his doctrine of the Trinity. This was just after his book *Father, Son, and Holy Spirit: Relationships, Roles, and Relevance* was released.[3] Ware and Wayne Grudem spoke at churches, colleges, and seminaries teaching a view known as the eternal functional submission or subordination (EFS) of the Son to the Father.[4] EFSers told an entire generation that the immanent Trinity—God in himself, apart from the economy of salvation—is defined by eternal relationships of authority and submission (ERAS).[5]

Ware, for example, presented his doctrine of the Trinity as a formula:

1. List Bible verses that teach God is one (monotheism).
2. List verses that support the deity of each person: Father, Son, and Spirit.
3. Appeal to *homoousios* to argue that each person has the same divine nature.
4. List verses where two or three persons are mentioned.
5. Conclusion: God is one essence, three persons.[6]

With strong conviction, Ware simply listed text after text apart from context, focusing only on select words in each text and concluding with much enthusiasm, "I just believe the Bible!"

You may have also noticed that eternal generation and eternal spiration are missing. At that time, eternal relations of origin did not factor into the EFS formula. Not at all. Nor did they factor into an EFS presentation of history. When EFSers talked about the Son, they presented Nicaea and then moved to Augustine, but only with a focus on the word *homoousios*, abstracting that word from its creedal context (eternal generation).[7]

Only after Ware had put forward his Trinity formula did he identify *what* distinguishes the persons.[8] It was *not* the eternal generation and spiration we see in Scripture and in the Nicene Creed. Rather, one thing alone distinguished the persons: "roles" or "relationships."[9] Ware presented the Trinity with a strong *social* emphasis, defining the Trinity as "triune persons in *relational community.*"[10] "Eternal relationality calls for and calls forth a created community of persons."[11] As a society itself, the Trinity is the model for human society. Sometimes Ware even looked to human society to define the Trinity.[12]

But then came the million-dollar question: What kind of "roles" and "relationships" distinguish the persons? What kind of "society" is the Trinity, and should this divine society become the prototype for human society?

EFS's answer: a society of authority and submission. A relational community of hierarchy *inside God.*

A Society of Hierarchy

For EFS, the position of supremacy within the Trinity belongs to the Father alone, not to the Son, and definitely not to the Spirit, who has the least authority of all. The Father alone is "supreme among the persons of the Godhead."[13] He alone has "ultimate supremacy," and he alone is "supreme in the Trinity."[14] The Father "stands above the Son," and the "Father has *absolute* and *uncontested supremacy*, including authority over the Son and Spirit."[15] The Father "stands above the Son" and is "supreme within the Godhead."[16]

EFSers were adamant that these indications of supremacy and subordination tell us who the persons are apart from creation and salvation. They are even person-defining. Just as subordination distinguishes the Son *as Son*, so too does supremacy distinguish the Father *as Father* within the Trinity. Apart from these roles there is no Trinity, a point Grudem also stressed repeatedly.[17]

At one point, EFSers even placed the Son alongside creation since both are subordinate to the Father. "The Father is supreme over all [creation], and in particular, he is supreme within the Godhead as the highest in authority and the one deserving of ultimate praise"[18] and "ultimate honor and glory."[19] That last phrase is super important: the Father alone is the "one deserving of ultimate praise" and "glory," not the Son. To the Son belongs a lesser praise. His is a lesser glory.

EFSers often cited 1 Corinthians 15:28, which Ware paraphrased as follows: "At the completion of history, when all things finally and fully are subjected to Jesus Christ the Son, then the Son himself will also be subjected to his own Father, who is the very one who put all things in subjection under his Son, so that God the Father, who is not subjected to anyone—not even to his own Son—may be shown to be supreme and over all that is." Then came a most significant statement: "The Father *stands above the Son*, and the Son gladly acknowledges this fact."[20]

The subjugation of the Son is not just an *economic* reality either, limited to salvation or the incarnation. The subordination of the Son is ingrained within the very DNA of the Trinity apart from creation, within the *immanent* Trinity itself (which EFSers assume is synonymous with what they label eternity past and future).[21] There is a split-level hierarchy of authority and subordination *inside the Trinity*.

Does the Father Really Need the Son or Spirit? Jealousy . . . in the Trinity?

The EFS position swelled with implications whenever they described the Father's supremacy over the Son as "comprehensive, all-inclusive, and absolute."[22] Because the Father alone has such authority by virtue of his paternity, the Father could, if he wanted, act all by himself. *Alone.* The Son and Spirit could be, hypothetically at least, "sidelined" since the Father is "supreme"; nevertheless, the Father "chooses not to work in such a way."[23] Well, most of the time. Grudem said that sometimes the Father does do without the Son; for example, when the Father plans salvation he acts alone.[24]

Ware went so far as to compare the Son to creation: "In many ways, what we see here of the Father choosing not to work unilaterally but to accomplish his work through the Son, or through the Spirit, *extends into his relationship to us.* Does God need us to do his work?"[25] The answer is no, but for EFSers the reason why stems from the Trinity: the Son's involvement is optional. The Son is not involved, because he is the Son. He is only involved because the Father chooses to include him. The Father could have asked the Son to stand aside and watch him do all the work. Likewise with the work of creation.

At times, EFSers put this point in raw form: "For, although the Father is supreme, though he has in the trinitarian order the place of highest authority, the place of highest honor, *yet he chooses* to do his work in many cases through the Son and through the Spirit *rather than unilaterally.*"[26] Ware imitated the voice of the Father in conversation with the Son and Spirit: "Rather than saying to the Son and Holy Spirit, 'Just stand aside and watch me as I do all the work,' it is as if the Father, instead, says to us, 'I want you to see my work accomplished through my Son.'" But lest anyone think the Son is the reason why the Father makes this choice, think again; it's ultimately about the Father: "Look at my Son! Notice my Son! Look at the marvelous obedience he has *given to me.*"[27] It is even an act of generosity for the Father to include the Son in the first place. "The Father does his work through the Son and through the Spirit, and that *generosity in sharing* his work with others spills over into how he relates to us."[28]

Generosity is key to the EFS view. Otherwise, the Son might be ungrateful, buck his place of submission, and attempt to exalt himself to the Father's position of authority within the Trinity. But EFSers say the Son won't do that because he "accepts his role" and minds his place below the Father.[29] There is, then, "neither jealousy nor pride"; rather, each person "works together with the others for one unified, common purpose."[30] They don't let their "diversity" and "differentiation"—that is, hierarchy and subordination—"lead to discord."[31]

Jealousy, pride, discord? Why would EFSers feel the need to preclude these *within* the eternal, immanent Trinity?

Against Orthodoxy

Back in the day, Ware's presentation was taken to a whole new level in more advanced lectures on the Trinity, where he openly rejected the orthodox creeds and the Great Tradition, and did so with confidence. Consider two examples.

First, on a number of occasions Ware, following the lead of Grudem, criticized and rejected eternal generation as speculative and unbiblical (there's no chapter and verse); the doctrine itself just doesn't make sense (generation cannot be eternal). When students asked about the Nicene Creed, which affirms eternal generation and does so to defend the deity of Christ, Ware would shake his head and say with a laugh, "Well, I guess I'm a heretic!"[32]

Second, roles and relationships of hierarchy *within* the immanent Trinity were so essential, defining and differentiating the persons, that Ware asserted, even insisted, on multiple wills in the Trinity over against orthodox creeds that say there is but one will in the Trinity. If the Father "stands above the Son" and is "supreme within the Godhead," then the Father must exercise his own will over the Son, and the Son must submit his own will to the Father's.[33] Ware had already implied this much when he said the Father can act "unilaterally" without the rest of the Trinity.[34] He doesn't need the Son or Spirit, but can act by his own will. He could say to his Son, "Just stand aside and watch me as I do all the work," operating out of his own will, but instead, he includes the Son: "Look at the marvelous obedience he has given to me."[35]

Do multiple wills forfeit unity? Ware dismissed the question because, he said, the persons cooperate like a society: "Each divine

Person accepts his role, each in proper relation to the others, and each works together with the others for one unified, common purpose."[36] Ware denied a singularity of will; singularity of purpose was sufficient.[37] Nevertheless, Ware reassured others he was no tritheist, since the persons hold the essence in common. But this sounded peculiar because Ware, on no few occasions, criticized and rejected divine simplicity for the same reasons he rejected eternal generation (extra-scriptural and illogical). "Scholasticism! Metaphysics!" he protested.

Social Trinity Is the Prototype for Society . . . Especially Gender Roles

In chapter 3, we saw just how hard social trinitarians labored to make the Trinity relevant again. By redefining the Trinity as a society of relationships, the Trinity became the prototype for human society. So, too, with EFS. If the Trinity is a "society of Persons" who are "socially related" by authority and submission, then the Trinity "provides one of the most important and neglected *patterns* for how human life and human relations are to be conducted."[38] But Ware went further, not just calling the Trinity a "pattern" but the "paradigm" and "prototype."[39] For what exactly? Everything: the workplace, ministry, and the home.[40] Grudem said the same.[41] This was their way of saying what many social trinitarians before them had already said: *the Trinity is our social program.*

To be specific, the Trinity is the paradigm for *gender roles* in the workplace, ministry, and the home. In fervent opposition to evangelical egalitarianism, which sees male and female as equals in authority, EFS argues for complementarianism, which sees the husband as the head of his wife, and the wife's "role" as one of submission to her husband. But the "paradigm" and "prototype" for such authority-submission is the Trinity. Just as the Son submits to the Father, so also wives are to submit to their husbands.

These roles are even intrinsic to their identity. Just as the Son cannot be Son if not subordinate, so the wife cannot be wife if not subordinate.[42] "[The] most marked characteristic of the trinitarian relationships is the presence of an eternal and inherent expression of authority and submission."[43] Likewise with gender roles.[44] EFS's proof text was 1 Corinthians 11:3: "The head of every man is Christ, the head of a wife is her husband, and the head of Christ is God." EFSers were always quick to reiterate, however, that no inequality was present. Like the Son, the wife's submission is functional, not ontological; it is submission in role, not essence.[45]

Something New . . . and Far More Radical Than Before

EFSers taught their view for decades. But recently, a massive debate over their view heated up and erupted like a volcano.[46] Liam Goligher, pastor of Tenth Presbyterian Church in Philadelphia, sounded the alarm. He writes, "I am an unashamed biblical complementarian," but "to use the intra-Trinitarian relations as a social model is neither biblical nor orthodox. God is not a *collection of people*, but we are [a collection of people]. . . . The inner life of the Triune God does not support hierarchy, patriarchy, or egalitarianism."[47] The Trinity is not our "social program." Also,

Charge: Semi-Arian

Other complementarians such as Carl Trueman also sounded the alarm, calling on the New Calvinist movement in particular to hold its own accountable. Egalitarians such as Michael Bird agreed. Bird has labelled EFSers "Homoian Complementarians." "Bruce Ware and Wayne Grudem are not Arians . . . but they are perilously close to Homoianism, which is semi-Arianism, or in the very least, they are non-Nicenes. . . . Homoianism is a more subtle and therefore more dangerous sub-variety of Arianism." See Trueman, "Fahrenheit 381," and Bird, "The Coming War."

EFSers are not transparent: "They are building their case by re-inventing the doctrine of God, and are doing so without telling the Christian public what they are up to."[48] Goligher called on evangelicals everywhere to "weigh what is at stake" before they "jettison the classical, catholic, orthodox and Reformed understanding of God."[49]

After these initial blasts of the cannon, thousands of responses followed, a majority against EFS. Representatives of EFS also responded.[50] Did they change their view? Yes but no. In one sense, their view became even more radical, even more unorthodox.[51] They now affirm eternal generation, for which we should be thankful.[52] But in what sense do they affirm eternal generation? And to what end?

In chapter 2 we learned that the Nicene fathers did not just affirm eternal relations of origin (Father is unbegotten, Son is begotten, Spirit is spirated), but they said eternal relations of origin *alone* distinguish the persons. Ware disagrees. There are two categories of "distinctiveness": (1) eternal relations of origin, and (2) eternal functional relations or roles of hierarchy. These two are not unrelated, but eternal functional relations/roles (authority/submission) "flow from" and are found "within" eternal relations of origin.[53] That is strategic, giving EFSers an opportunity to insert subordination within the eternal Godhead. Does EFS's newfound affirmation of eternal relations of origin undermine their inclusion of authority and submission in the Godhead? "Absolutely not! It only strengthens the view," claims Ware.[54] In order to avoid the charge of heresy (Arianism), EFS says the eternal relations of origin are "ontological," while roles of authority/submission are "functional."[55] EFS denies that the Son is *ontologically* subordinate; the Son is only *functionally* subordinate. And yet, the functional flows out of the ontological. Despite the fact that EFS claims "ontological" belongs to the eternal relations of origin and has nothing to do with functional roles, nevertheless, after asserting the Father's "primacy," "priority," and "ultimate authority" over the Son, Ware says that the Father does have "onto-logical primacy" in the eternal Trinity.[56] EFSers do not explain how they resolve this apparent contradiction.

At first, Ware promises he is orthodox and Nicene, but the more he elaborates, the more noticeable it becomes that he is dissatisfied with the way the Nicene fathers and the Great Tradition have articulated the Trinity. For example, the orthodox "appeal to divine appropriations falls short of expressing fully what Scripture indicates regarding the functional relations." "Yes, the order of operations *ad extra* is expressive of the order of relations *ad intra*, but saying only this excludes a significant portion of scriptural indications." What exactly is excluded and "missing"? Authority. Hierarchy. *Inside the Trinity.* Without authority-submission within the *immanent Trinity*, Ware believes the Father sending the Son is but a "mechanical" and "impersonal outworking of the relations of origin." He does not explain why exactly. But if the Son is subjected to the Father within the immanent Trinity, then appropriations becomes personal. In the end, pro-Nicene appropriations "falls short" if they do not stem from authority-submission within the immanent Trinity.[57] For that reason, when Ware does articulate appropriations, his language is not pro-Nicene but goes social instead, speaking of the persons as if they are their own separate agents. That is not surprising, since Ware has added a social category like "roles" within the immanent Godhead.

> **Key Word** **Appropriations**
>
> According to the Nicene fathers, since the Trinity is one in essence (simplicity), the three persons always work inseparably in the economy. Nevertheless, since the one essence has three modes of subsistence (eternal relations of origin), a particular work may be "appropriated" by a particular person, but always in a way that is consistent with that person's mode of subsistence. For example, the Son is sent by the Father to become incarnate, which corresponds to his mode of subsistence (eternal relation): begotten.

In sum, although EFSers appear to have reformed their position by accepting eternal relations of origin, critics conclude that EFSers have actually radicalized their position, embedding subordination deeper within the eternal, immanent identity of God. The result: EFSers claim to be orthodox but simultaneously say a "pro-Nicene" Trinity "falls short." EFSers are aware their view is "different than, *even contrary to*" the "pro-Nicene tradition" (or at least, in their mind, "some" of that orthodox tradition); but they are convinced they have "the Bible while others do not."[58]

How Then Should We Respond?

In churches, colleges, and seminaries, evangelicals continue to drink in EFS. Perhaps you can relate to my story: you've been told EFS is just Bible. But it's time to sober up: EFS undermines biblical orthodoxy and threatens to sink evangelicalism in the swamp of social trinitarianism. In a word, EFS is *novel*. While EFS claims fidelity to Nicene orthodoxy, it is a clear departure, and one that comes dangerously close to resurrecting heresies the church has long buried. Let's consider some of the reasons why.[59]

Social Redux

The Trinity "is by very nature a unity of Being while also existing eternally as a *society* of Persons. God's tri-Personal reality is intrinsic to his existence as the one God who alone is God. He is a *socially related* being within himself."[60]

Who said this?

If you've read chapter 3, you might think it's one of the social trinitarians we covered. Jürgen Moltmann perhaps? But it's actually Bruce Ware. It sounds so familiar because EFSers define the Trinity just like every other social trinitarian in the last century. In chapter 3 we identified several key marks of a social Trinity.

Now that you've seen the EFS view, notice how so many of these marks are an exact match:

- Starting point (and emphasis) is not simplicity but the three persons—some reject simplicity altogether
- Trinity redefined as society and community, analogous to human society
- Persons redefined as three centers of consciousness and will
- Persons redefined according to their relationships and roles
- Large overlap (sometimes collapse) of immanent and economic Trinity
- Social Trinity is paradigm for social theory (ecclesiology, politics, gender, etc.)

EFS lines up with each of these marks, which makes EFS a species of social trinitarianism. As we saw in chapters 2 and 3, social trinitarianism is a departure from biblical orthodoxy. The main difference between EFS and previous social trinitarians is this: while modern theologians reenvisioned the Trinity in social categories as a prototype for equality in society, EFS takes that same social view but instead concludes it is defined by an "authority-submission structure," one that is also a prototype for society.[61] The EFS view of personhood differs little from that of a social trinitarian like Leonardo Boff, who said, "The modern notion of person is basically that of being-in-relationship; a person is a subject existing as a centre of autonomy, gifted with consciousness and freedom."[62] Except, for EFS the persons are not just societal subjects, but the Son and Spirit are *subject*, that is, *subjected to* the Father who alone has "supreme authority" and alone "deserves ultimate praise."[63]

As much as EFSers say they are just teaching the Bible, they are operating with a view of the Trinity that is social through and through. But does a social approach betray orthodox, biblical fidelity, especially one that treats the Son as a lesser authority and glory? As it turns out, EFS, albeit unintentionally, flirts with three heresies: tritheism, Sabellianism, and subordinationism.

Has EFS Forfeited Unity in the Trinity? The Danger of Tritheism

In chapter 2 we learned that to be pro-Nicene one must affirm *inseparable operations*. Inseparable operations means more than just a cooperation or involvement of all three persons. The persons are not three centers of consciousness and will, as if they merely work together, share the same desires, and agree to the same plan. Inseparable operations means every act of God is the *single act* of the triune God. There are not different acts by different agents, but one act according to one divine agency. Singularity in will, singularity in operation. We will say more in chapter 10.

But EFS language betrays this basic premise of biblical orthodoxy when EFSers refer to the persons as if they are their own agents, or when they use words like "roles" and "functions" to define the persons. Ware now says he holds to one will in the Trinity, whereas previously he taught three wills. But when he describes the persons of the Trinity, especially the gradations of authority between them, it is unlikely Ware's view (the EFS view) can legitimately hold to inseparable operations as he claims, let alone divine simplicity. Grudem even criticizes inseparable operations.[64]

All the more so when EFSers use language that has historically entailed multiple wills. For example, EFSers not only say the Father begetting the Son means the Father has "ontological primacy," but the Father sending his begotten Son into the world out of love for the world reveals the "motive of the Father," "which must be *exclusively* the Father's even if his motive is in concert with or united with the motives of the Son and Spirit."[65] Multiple motives? Exclusive motives? That's a recipe for tritheism.

EFS also attributes to the Father a "distinct purpose," and one exclusive to him. There is a "paternal authority" that is essential to the "Father's distinct motive and the Father's distinct purpose," at least if he is to send his Son.[66] Ware goes so far as to say the Father is his own "distinct agent." [67] Multiple purposes? Distinct agents? Again, more ingredients for tritheism.

On the surface, such language might seem harmless. But if one considers how EFS has introduced a new, novel category of functional relations of authority-submission into the immanent Trinity, suddenly this language is very alarming. Especially talk of an authority *exclusive* to the Father and a subordination *exclusive* to the Son. It screams, "Multiple wills!" Here is EFS's social trinitarianism—distinct centers of consciousness—coming through thick and heavy. Point is, EFS segregates the persons of the Trinity from one another, even sets them over against one another. Fragmentation is the result.

In contrast, the persons are not "quasi-independent agents," warns John Webster. "In the economy the Trinity acts indivisibly, and the works of the Trinity are to be attributed 'absolutely' to the one divine essence." So, "it is insufficient to speak of the 'mutual roles' enacted by the persons in the economy; inseparable or coinherent action is not simply conjoint operation. . . . Common activity is not indistinguishable activity."[68] *Mutual roles*—that is precisely the language EFS uses. Problem is, it assumes "insepa-

On Purpose

EFSers look at how the triune God acts toward creation and assume that Father-to-Son is synonymous with authority-to-submission. But Father-to-Son is not the equivalent of power-to-instrument or superior-to-inferior, says John Webster (*God Without Measure,* 72). As we talk about the one, simple but triune God in reference to creation and the economy of salvation, it is only appropriate to speak of purpose-to-enactment.

rable operations" is merely a joint operation. But a shared activity is not the same thing as a singular activity.

John Owen says that the persons are "undivided in their operations, acting all by the same will, the same wisdom, *the same power*. Every person, therefore, is the author of every work of God, because each person is God, and the divine nature is the same undivided principle of all divine operations; and this ariseth from the unity of the person in the same essence."[69] Notice, Owen does not exclude *power*. One in will, the persons act by the same power. Just as the Son is not a lesser glory, so too the Son is not a lesser power. That is something EFS cannot say.

Furthermore, the three persons cannot perform a *single* action if one or more persons are, by definition of their personhood, inferior in authority to another person. As soon as you insert gradations of authority within the *immanent* Trinity, gradations that are person-defining and therefore *essential* for the Trinity to be a Trinity, you forfeit *one will* in God.[70] *You forfeit the Trinity's one, simple essence. Our God is simply Trinity . . . no more.*

Additionally, the minute someone projects authority and subordination into the inner life of God (immanent Trinity), the burden of proof is on them to explain how there is not now three wills in the Trinity (tritheism) rather than one will (simplicity). "Where there is one simple will, there can necessarily be no authority and submission." Why is that? Answer: "authority and submission require diversity of volitional faculties"—in other words, multiple wills in God.[71] For this very reason, social trinitarianism has been accused of tritheism.

EFSers deny the heresy of tritheism, but it is uncertain how they can avoid it when they introduce a novel, functional category into the immanent Godhead. Granted, nobody claims to be a tritheist, but tritheism can sneak in, and in ways we don't realize. This happens in one of two ways: "One form would use a modern concept of 'person' that overemphasizes individuality for each of the three. Another form would overemphasize distinctive traits for each divine person, rather than rooting person distinctions in the relations of origin that underlie their missions."[72] That is exactly what EFS has done: overemphasizing individuality, over-emphasizing distinctive traits, distinguishing persons according to functional roles of hierarchy rather than relations of origin alone. "Modern 'social' forms of trinitarianism regularly face this accusation."[73]

EFS is one such modern social form.

Functional Overload: The Danger of Sabellianism

So far, we've seen EFS's tendencies toward tritheism. But what about Sabellianism? As mentioned above, it's all about emphasis. *Over*emphasis is fatal. Not only does EFS overemphasize the persons as distinct agents, but it also overemphasizes *function.* Again and again, EFSers stress (in order to avoid accusations of Arianism) that subordination in the Trinity is not ontological but functional. But as we've seen, they read functionality—authority and submission, in particular—back into the *immanent* Trinity.

Remember, Nicene orthodoxy argues that one thing alone defines the persons: eternal relations of origin. That judgment is right on target: as we just saw in chapter 7, Scripture says eternal generation alone explains the Son's eternal origin. Not only is "begotten" language applied to the Son (e.g., John 3:16), not only

---

What about the Spirit?

EFSers claim the biblical names for the persons convey authority/submission by definition. But isn't it curious that EFSers struggle to explain how the name "Holy Spirit" conveys submission and subordination? It seems it must if they are to be consistent. They insist *Son* not only means begotten but subordinate in function. But they cannot apply that same narrow approach to Spirit. The word is not even familial vocabulary.

---

does the title Son itself convey the metaphor of birth, but both testaments convey the same when they use words like radiance (Heb. 1:3, 5), image (Col. 1:15–17, 19), wisdom (Prov. 8; 1 Cor. 1:22–24, 30), Word (John 1:1, 14, 18), and Ancient of Days (Mic. 5:2; Matt. 2:5). Likewise, in chapter 9 we will witness the Spirit's origin. The Spirit's origin is conveyed not only by the meaning of spiration itself but also by means of the many other titles Scripture attributes to him, including Breath (Gen. 1:2; Job 33:4; Ps. 33:6; John 3:8; 20:22; 2 Tim. 3:16), Gift (John 3:14; 4:10; 7:38–39; 15:26; Acts 2:38; 5:32; 8:20; 10:45), and Love (Rom. 5:4–5; Gal. 5:22; 1 John 4:7–16).

But EFS adds another category, one that Scripture *never* places within the *immanent* Trinity: functional relations of hierarchy (authority/submission). They say these functions are not accidental but essential, not optional but necessary. And notice, such functional relations are *social* at the core. The persons of the Trinity are no longer defined by ontological relations alone, but they are now defined by social relationships of hierarchy. With such emphasis on functionality within the immanent Godhead, how can EFS avoid the persons becoming mere societal activities of hierarchy? When what the persons *do* (exhibit power over another, submit to the power of another) defines who the persons *are* (Father, Son, Spirit), Sabellianism is not far away. Who the Trinity is has been conflated with what the Trinity does.

Traces of Sabellianism also appear like invisible ink held under fluorescent light when EFS says that the Father doesn't need the Son and the Spirit to act in creation and salvation. He can act unilaterally; nevertheless, he is generous enough to include them. Not only is this a blatant violation of simplicity and a flagrant dissolution of God's one will, but this is something very close to Sabellianism. In the ancient world, Sabellianism took variegated forms.[74] One type said there is but one divine person who appears and reveals himself in three ways (Father, Son, Spirit). A second type said there is but one divine person who changes sequentially.

EFS slides somewhere in between the two. For if God the Father has the right to act by himself, unilaterally, without the Son and Spirit, one wonders if the Son and Spirit must wait their turn until the Father decides they are eligible for action. This is not a Trinity that works indivisibly.

Also, the way EFS speaks of the Son's lesser glory only furthers suspicions of Sabellianism, as if, in the end, the Son steps aside in his subordination so that the Father gets "ultimate praise"; after all, says EFS, the Father alone "deserves" it.[75] The very fact that Ware must reassure the reader that there is no jealousy or envy or discord within the immanent Trinity due to the Father's greater authority and glory only opens the door that much further to welcome in Sabellianism.

The Achilles' Heel: The Danger of Subordinationism

Throughout this book we keep repeating that basic principle of Nicene orthodoxy: eternal relations of origin *alone* distinguish the persons in the immanent Trinity. But EFS adds a novel category: eternal roles of authority and submission. Nevertheless, EFSers insist eternal relations of origin are ontological while eternal functional relations/roles of authority/submission are functional.

First of all, it is fallacious to say there is something ontological as opposed to something functional within the immanent Trinity. This is a strange dichotomy, one that is not just novel in every way but antithetical to biblical, Nicene orthodoxy. In all their exegesis of Scripture, the pro-Nicene fathers would never have recognized such categories. The Nicene Creed never refers to "roles" of hierarchy within the immanent Trinity. To speak of the *immanent* Trinity was always to speak of ontology. This is the triune *God* we are talking about. All that is in God is ontological, otherwise it would not be *God*. What distinguishes plurality in the simple God is not something functional but personal, *hypostaseis* to be exact. Even then, each person is a subsistence of the one essence.

The essence has three modes of *subsistence*. It doesn't get more ontological than that. But by projecting societal roles into the immanent Trinity, the persons are no longer *subsistences* alone but distinct agents cooperating to form a community, in this case a community of hierarchy. That may fit with a social Trinity, but it is anything but biblical, Nicene orthodoxy.

Second, EFS's insistence that subordination is functional, not ontological, fails to understand the connection between person and essence. EFSers have created a divide between the two, and they must if they are to safeguard the Son's ontological equality in essence from his functional subordination as a person.[76] Despite the Son's subjection in authority and lesser glory, EFS assures us that the "Son is equal to the Father precisely because he possesses the identically same nature as the Father possesses."[77] But why? *Why* does the Son possess the identically same nature as the Father? Ware never answers that question.

But the answer to that question reveals the Achilles' heel of EFS. Remember from chapter 2, eternal relations—like the Son's generation—not only distinguish the persons, but Nicaea put eternal generation forward to claim, over against Arianism, that the Son is equal to the Father. For the Son is eternally begotten from

Houston, We Have a Problem

We cannot implant hierarchy within the eternal relations of origin, making hierarchy *intrinsic* to the immanent Trinity, without also implanting hierarchy within the divine essence itself. To say we can is a failure to understand what the eternal relations of origin are to begin with: *the persons are subsistences of the divine essence itself*. The eruption of controversy may have pushed Grudem and Ware to publicly reconsider and adopt eternal relations of origin, but it quickly became clear they did so by also inserting functional hierarchy within the immanent Trinity. Attaching subordination to eternal relations of origin is a manipulation of biblical, Nicene categories.

the Father's essence (*ousia*). As Athanasius said against the Arians, "The Son is ever the proper offspring of the *Father's essence*."[78] And as Gregory of Nyssa said, the "Only-begotten [Son] . . . is in the Father, and so, *from His nature*."[79] Those in the West agreed. In eternal generation, said Augustine, "the Father bestows being on the Son without any beginning in time, without any changeableness of nature."[80] Anselm wrote that the Father "has his essence from nothing but himself," but "[the] Son, on the other hand, has his essence from the Father, as well as having the same essence as the Father."[81] Aquinas said the same: "[The] divine essence is the source by which the Father begets."[82] The Great Tradition that followed continued this line well into the post-Reformation era. Turretin is an example: "Essence is communicated by generation or spiration."[83] John Owen saw the connection as well: "[A] divine

Don't Miss Your Connection

It may sound neat and tidy to say there is something ontological (essence) and something functional (hierarchal roles) in the immanent Trinity, and one need not affect the other. But that bifurcation divorces essence and person and misunderstands what a divine person is and how each person relates to the essence. The persons don't have an ontological side to them and a functional side (let alone one of hierarchy). As subsistences *of the essence*, the persons are ontological through and through. EFS doesn't recognize this because it has added a novel category, a *social* category (roles of authority/submission) that does not fit with Nicene language. We would be wise to listen to the Great Tradition, which does not miss the connection between essence and person: "For to God it is not one thing to be and another to be a person, but it is altogether the same thing," says Augustine. "Just as for him to be is to be God, . . . thus also for him to be is to be personal" (*The Trinity* 7.6). Or as Bavinck explains, in "each of the three persons . . . the divine being is completely coextensive with being Father, Son, and Spirit" (*Reformed Dogmatics* 2:304, 305).

person is nothing but the divine essence, upon the account of an especial property, subsisting in an especial manner."[84]

But EFSers fail to see the connection. They treat *homoousios*—the Son is one in essence with the Father—as if it is but a box to check on the orthodoxy card, so that they can simultaneously say that the Son is equal in essence but subordinate in role. But they have removed *homoousios* from its organic, biblical context. The reason the pro-Nicene tradition could claim the Son is *homoousios* with the Father is only because the Son is begotten from the Father's essence.[85] Hence, the Great Tradition said repeatedly that the one essence has three modes of subsistence, each person a subsistence of that one, simple, undivided essence. How does the Son subsist in the same essence as the Father? He is eternally begotten from the Father's essence. This is Nicene Orthodoxy 101.

It is also basic to preserving the equality of the persons in Scripture. Notice, any and every time Scripture reflects on the *immanent* Trinity—and those times are rare, considering the focus most of the time is on salvation and the humility of the incarnation—Scripture always emphasizes the Son's equality with the Father without any qualification. And when I say always, I mean *always*. "The Word was with God, and the Word was God" (John 1:1)—no qualification added. "He is the image of the invisible God" (Col. 1:15)—no nuance needed. The Son of God is "the radiance of the glory of God" (Heb. 1:3)—no lesser glory or authority mentioned. He is the "exact imprint of his nature" (Heb. 1:3)—no exception clause around the word "exact." If he were a lesser power, Hebrews could not say he "upholds the universe by the word of his power" (1:3). "Christ [is] the power of God" (1 Cor. 1:24) no less than the Father. How else could he say, "Whoever has seen me has seen the Father" (John 14:9)? He is not some god lower on the Trinity totem pole of divine authority. Do we dare (!) correct Jesus when he says, "I and the Father are one" (John 10:30), and interrupt, *"Except in power and authority*—don't forget that part, Jesus"?

Even the Pharisees, who did not believe in Jesus, understand that he is claiming to be the Son of God; even his most vicious opponents comprehend that he is claiming *total* equality with the Father (John 5:18). If Jesus had merely qualified himself—as he should have if EFS is correct—to explain that he did not mean equal in authority, the Pharisees never would have put this so-called blasphemer to death.

So, I ask again, why is it that subordination is never mentioned in any of these scriptural reflections on the immanent Trinity? The answer is very simple: subordination would absolutely throw into question the divine equality attributed to the Son. And should EFSers object that they only mean the Son is inferior in authority (person), not essence (divinity), let's not forget that the Son *is* a subsistence of the divine essence. Begotten from the Father's essence from all eternity (see chaps. 6–7), the Son can be nothing less than equal with the Father in every way. For the divine essence cannot be severed, wrenched away, or divorced from divine power, authority, and glory, each of which subsists in the three persons equally. Again, the Pharisees get this. Notice their accusation: "[They] were seeking all the more to kill him, because . . . he was even calling God his own Father, making himself equal with God" (John 5:18). Jesus's Sonship (person) is directly tied to divinity, and divine authority with it.

Furthermore, EFS insists that roles of hierarchy are person-defining. You cannot have a Trinity without hierarchy is a point Grudem belabors again and again.[86] To ensure their necessity, EFS now says roles of hierarchy flow from the eternal relations of origin.[87] But wait: *if the persons are subsistences of the essence, what is to keep subordination from the essence?* If the essence has three modes of subsistence, and if subordination flows out of the Son's mode of subsistence itself (eternal generation), what is to keep hierarchy from divinity? Inventing a division between ontological and functional is a farce. The essence subsists in the Son by means of his mode of subsistence (eternal generation), and that mode of subsistence, according to EFS, is littered with subordination.

Third, EFS has robbed the divine essence of power and authority and segregated power and authority to the persons, but the Father above all, violating the simplicity of the Trinity. Nicene orthodoxy was very careful in its affirmation of simplicity: essence and attributes are not different things; attributes are not parts of God's essence. Rather, God's essence *is* his attributes and his attributes his essence. As subsistences of the same divine essence, no one person possesses one attribute more or less than another—God's power and authority included. As the Athanasian Creed says,

> the Father is almighty, the Son almighty
> and the Holy Spirit almighty,
> and yet they are not three Almighties
> but one Almighty.

The Father, then, is not a greater almighty than the Son. That would divide the simple essence of God and create an inferior Son. Coequal in power and authority, there is but one Almighty.[88]

By contrast, EFS does affirm a greater almighty in the Father, and not just a greater almighty but a greater glory. As we saw, EFS even says the Father alone deserves ultimate glory within the immanent Trinity, and not just in the economy but by nature of his paternity in eternity. The Son is a lesser glory than the Father.[89] Must EFSers not also conclude, if they are to be consistent, that the Father is to receive more, greater worship than the Son?

Not only does this contradict the Athanasian Creed, but it dispenses with biblical simplicity altogether. "The exchange of glory given and received" in the Trinity, says Hilary of Poitiers, "proclaims the *unity of power* in the Father and in the Son."[90] By claiming that the Son is a lesser power and glory, EFS takes what belongs to the essence of God, and therefore what belongs *equally, wholly* to all three persons who subsist in that same essence, and gives it to the Father over and above the Son and Spirit, dividing the Trinity. Stripping the essence of such authority and giving it to the Father above all creates a lesser Son.[91]

Whose Rules Do We Play By? Ruled by Scripture

Now that we've identified the Achilles' heel of EFS, we might also identify its central fault line: hermeneutics (biblical interpretation). One reason EFS sounds so intuitive is because EFSers get you to play by their rules of the game. Consider even the label itself: eternal functional subordination. EFSers want you to think (as they do) that the disputed question is this: Is the functional

---

Wrong Eternity

In chapter 4, we distinguished between God in himself (immanent) and God toward the world (economic). The big mistake EFSers make comes down to an assumption: they assume something that is *eternal* must also be immanent. They then look at a text like 1 Corinthians 15 and conclude that if Paul speaks of the *future*, then submission must define the Son within the immanent Trinity. However, EFS has failed to recognize that the economic can be eternal too. Election, for example, occurs before the foundation of the world. It is, however, optional; God doesn't have to elect. Just because election is eternal doesn't mean it is necessary for God to be God (immanent Trinity). Here's the lesson: don't confuse the economy of salvation, even in eternity, with the immanent, inner, and necessary life of God in eternity. In 1 Corinthians 15, Paul is teaching "that the last act of God's saving work will be the Son's handing over the Kingdom to the Father might appear to speak of an act of submission or subordination in eternity, but again it is, if the language may be allowed, the wrong eternity: it is the consummation of the divine work, not an aspect of the divine life" (Stephen Holmes, "Classical Trinitarianism and Eternal Functional Subordination," 97).

subordination of the Son *eternal*? If EFS can produce enough proof texts saying it is *eternal*, then they conclude that they win. That sounds simple, but it is exegetically *simplistic*, and, as we are starting to see, it takes texts out of their contexts.

But EFS is asking the wrong question. The right question is this: Is submission *ad intra* or *ad extra*; is it intrinsic to the *immanent* Trinity, or is it something that occurs in the *economy* (in the context of salvation history)? Biblical Christian orthodoxy has always acknowledged that the economy of salvation involves the incarnate Son submitting to the mission his Father has given to him for the purpose of salvation. It has also acknowledged that this mission does not originate the moment the Son assumes flesh. In eternity the Son is appointed by the Father and at the proper time is sent on his mission of redemption.[92] To say, then, that we must determine whether the Son's submission is eternal is an odd category mistake, like showing up to prom in your Halloween costume. Of course the Father planned redemption from eternity. Of course the Son is sent by the Father in eternity. No one disputes that. But that does not prove that something like subordination is *intrinsic* to who the triune God is in and of himself, *apart from the economy of salvation*. Even if we were to grant the EFS belief that submission is present in eternity—which is a misreading of Scripture, but let's just say it is so for the sake of argument—EFS still has not demonstrated that there is hierarchy within the immanent Trinity; they have only demonstrated that submission is appropriate in the economy of salvation.

I suggest we play the game by a different set of rules that do justice to the diversity of biblical texts. In chapter 4 we learned about Rahner's Rule, which led to a conflation of immanent and economic, but now we meet Augustine's rules, which avoid conflation and preserve proper distinctions between who God is and what God does. Always the exegete, Augustine pays keen attention to the nuances within the biblical text and pinpoints three different ways Scripture describes the Son in relation to the Father:

1. *Form of God*: Some texts say the Son is one with the Father (John 10:30) and is in the very form of God (Phil. 2:6). These texts describe the Father and the Son's "unity and equality of substance."

2. *Form of a Servant*: Other texts say the Father is greater than the Son (John 14:28; cf. 5:27). These texts do not mean that the Son is an inferior deity to the Father; the Son is "lesser" only in the sense that he has taken on the form of a servant (Phil. 2:7), "that is because of the created and changeable human substance he took." According to his manhood, he humbles himself and obeys the Father for the purpose of fulfilling his mission of salvation.

3. *Sent from the Father*: Still other texts say the Father gave to the Son life in himself (John 5:26) and the Son only does what he sees the Father doing (John 5:19). These texts do not refer to the Son being "equal" or "less" but instead reveal that the Son is *from* the Father. "This then is the rule which governs many scriptural texts, intended to show not that one person is less than the other, but only that one is from the other."[93]

These rules are not unique to Augustine; these are basic to good Bible interpretation. They are nothing less than Scripture's rules.

Sometimes multiple rules are in view in the same passage, as with Philippians 2. On the one hand, Christ is in the "form of

Projection?

"[Do] not conceive the eternal procession[s] . . . by a *projection* of the economy into the inner life of the Trinity, but rather it holds that the mission *reflects* the origin."—Gilles Emery, *The Trinity*

Social Trinitarianism versus Biblical Orthodoxy

Social Trinitarianism

1. Modern Theology

| Economic | → | *constitutes* | → | Immanent |

2. EFS/ERAS

| Economic (hierarchy) | → | *projected onto* | → | Immanent |

Biblical, Orthodox Trinitarianism

| Missions | → | *reveal / reflect* | → | Eternal Relations of Origin *alone* |

God." On the other hand, he humbles himself and takes on the "form of a servant," born in the likeness of men.[94] Whenever Scripture speaks of our salvation, it is in the habit of distinguishing between both: "In the form of God, the Word *through whom all things were made* (John 1:3); in the form of a servant, one *made of woman, made under the law, to redeem those who were under the law* (Gal. 4:4). Accordingly, in the form of God he made man, in the form of a servant he was made man."[95] Such a distinction affects the way we understand Christ's mediatorial work on our behalf: "It is as less than the Father that he begs for us, but as his equal he hearkens to us with the Father."[96]

However, EFSers confuse these rules, mixing and meshing all three. They look at "sent" language in the Gospels or language that says the Son is dependent on his Father in some way and conclude that authority-subordination reaches back into eternity, even into the immanent Trinity. That is a category mistake. "The life of the

Son is unchanging like the Father's, and yet is from the Father," says Augustine; "[the] work of Father and Son is indivisible, and yet the Son's working is from the Father just as he himself is from the Father."[97] Or think of it this way: "The working of the Father and of the Son is equal and indivisible and yet the Son's working comes from the Father."[98]

Augustine grows frustrated with those who are reckless with the biblical text and confuse one set of passages (or one rule) with another. "This has misled people who are careless about examining or keeping in view the whole range of the scriptures, and they have tried to transfer what is said of Christ Jesus as man to that substance of his which was everlasting before the incarnation and is everlasting still."[99] How prophetic of Augustine, for this is exactly what EFS does. EFS fails to keep "in view the whole range of the scripture." EFSers take "what is said of Christ Jesus as man" (i.e., submission to the Father) and they "transfer" that concept "to that substance of his which was everlasting before the incarnation and is everlasting still." They will deny it, but EFSers read humanity back onto divinity, *projecting* the form of a servant in history back onto the form of God in eternity. EFS laments that Christology no longer informs the Trinity, but EFS has swung the pendulum so far that Christology now swallows up the Trinity.

Let's consider an example.

Context, Context, Context: 1 Corinthians 15 and the Second Adam

Is it a coincidence that the silver-bullet proof text in the EFS argument is 1 Corinthians 15:24–28, the same proof text Homoians appealed to in the fourth century to argue against orthodoxy?[100] The Homoians looked to Paul to say that the Father is a greater authority than the Son, but the Homoians took the next step and concluded the Son must not be consubstantial in deity as a result. EFSers don't take that next step, but their argument applies the same logic.

What is Paul saying in this text? In the form of God, the Son is consubstantial with the Father. Paul affirms this much throughout his letters (e.g., 1 Cor. 8:6). However, in 1 Corinthians 15 his attention is not on the Son in the form of God but *in the form of a servant* (Augustine's Rule #2). The context is not the *immanent* Trinity but the *economy*, the redemptive mission of the incarnate Son.[101]

The entire chapter is about the resurrection of Christ, something EFSers rarely mention. Paul goes to great lengths to outline Christ's death, burial, and resurrection to substantiate the believer's own resurrection from the dead one day. Furthermore, Paul compares and contrasts Christ to Adam: "For as by a man [Adam] came death, by a man [Christ] has come also the resurrection of the dead. For as in Adam all die, so also in Christ shall all be made alive" (15:21–22). Paul has a habit of contrasting Adam and Christ; he also does so in Romans 5. Here is the contrast: Adam failed, but the second Adam succeeded.

But don't overlook the *context*: Paul's focus is on *history*, specifically redemptive history, exhibiting the second Adam as the one who counters the curse by rising from the grave. Paul's focus is on Christ as the Adamic mediator and redeemer of God's people. Victorious over death, Christ has fulfilled his mission from the Father. And a day is coming when those in Christ will rise, and "then comes the end, when he [Christ] delivers the kingdom to God the Father after destroying every rule and every authority and power" (15:24).

By handing over the kingdom, Christ completes his mission by ushering his sheep into the hands of his Father. Don't miss this: *as their Adamic mediator* (vv. 20–22), Christ is subjected to the Father, who himself put all things in subjection to his crucified and risen Son (15:28), which concludes the mission the Father had given to him. Eternal obedience or subordination within the immanent Trinity is nowhere in view, but rather *incarnational, Adamic* obedience as mankind's *mediator*. EFSers violate the distinction between form of God and form of a servant when they assume—ignoring the context—that such a subjection must be true of the Son in eternity, *within the immanent Trinity*, as if the Son is Son because he is subject to the Father, subordinate in role. That assumption could not be more foreign to Paul. His focus, by contrast, is on the Son's servanthood as the last Adam in the economy of salvation, and in 1 Corinthians 15 we see that economy at its pinnacle, the Mediator submitting his mission to the Father who sent him. This is the Son saying, "Redemption is complete. It is finished!" *To superimpose a subjection that continues in the immanent Trinity is to undermine Christ's finished work of salvation.*

That is apparent in Psalm 8:6, the Old Testament passage Paul quotes. Unlike other psalms that do speak of eternity, in Psalm 8 David focuses on creation, on what God has made, including man himself. David's use of the phrase "son of man" is central (v. 4), for the son of man is said to be "a little lower than the heavenly beings" but nonetheless crowned with honor. The son of man is given "dominion over the works of your hands" (v. 6). Is this not the same language God used of Adam in Genesis 1:26? It is. Almost verbatim. When Paul uses this language from Genesis 1:26 and Psalm 8:6, he intends this Adamic language to be applied to Christ, the last Adam. That's why he says in 1 Corinthians 15:22, "For as in Adam all die, so also in Christ shall all be made alive."

Christ, as the second Adam, is not original to Paul, but can be traced back to the Gospels.[102] The Gospels present Jesus as the covenant-obedient son both Adam and Israel failed to be (Deut. 1:30–31; 8:5–6; 32:6–7, 18, 23–25). The contrast is striking: Adam and Israel failed to obey the covenant, but Jesus succeeds in obeying the covenant, not for his own sake but for their sake. Using the sonship language first applied to Adam and Israel, God announces at Jesus's birth, "Out of Egypt I called my son" (Matt. 2:15). But notice, this quotation from Hosea 11:1 referred to Israel, but Matthew now applies it to the new Israel, Jesus the Christ. Once summoned, this Christ, this Messiah, then obeys the law Israel transgressed and establishes a new covenant by fulfilling all righteousness (Matt. 3:13–17), living by every word from the mouth of God (Matt. 4:1–11). Luke's Gospel even traces Jesus back to Adam himself (Luke 3:38). Luke portrays Jesus's wilderness temptation as a recapitulation of the garden of Eden (Luke 4:1–13) and concludes his Gospel with paradise reopened thanks to Jesus's obedience to the point of death (Luke 23:43). In Mark's Gospel, the Son of Man surrenders himself to the cross as an act of fidelity to the Scriptures (Mark 8:31–32; 9:30–31; 10:33–34). Notice Jesus's mindset: "Whoever would be great among you must be your servant, and whoever would be first among you must be slave of all. For even the Son of Man came not to be served but to serve, and to give his life as a ransom for many" (10:43–45). As the suffering servant Isaiah promised (Isa. 53), Jesus announces he has come to obey God's covenant where Adam and Israel, God's firstborn son, failed. This is at the heart of the gospel. His obedience then becomes our righteousness upon faith.

Jesus's disciples, and most certainly his opponents, struggled to understand that the Messiah had not come to save with the sword but to redeem by his righteous obedience and sacrificial death. The true enemy was not Rome but sin. To correct their misconceptions of the Messiah, Jesus stressed again and again that he would save God's people by suffering for God's people. To get that message across, Jesus emphasized his adherence to the Father's plan of redemption: he only does what the Father is doing, he does the will of the Father who sent him, and he does not act on his own authority alone but on the authority of his Father (John 5:19, 30; 6:38; 8:28–29; 12:49–50; 14:28, 31; 15:10; 17:2). Jesus is lighting off fireworks in the sky that spell out the words, "I am the true Adam, the faithful Israel, the obedient son you never were. I've humbled myself that low just to save you!"

Notice, each and every one of these passages occurs within the context of redemption, within the economy of salvation, within the shadow of the cross (John 8:28–29). Christ obeys *as our covenant Mediator.* That's the whole point of his obedience. As God's firstborn son, Adam (and then Israel) disobeyed and plunged the world into sin. Not Jesus. By his perfect record of obedience, we are declared righteous. But EFS extracts this Adamic obedience out of its covenantal context entirely and superimposes this incarnational obedience into the immanent Trinity, undermining the Son's equality. Again, it may sound simple, but it proves simplistic, ignoring context altogether.

To summarize, in the form of God, "together with the Father he [the Son] is one God." But in the form of a servant, as the one who has assumed our humanity and can therefore be our Mediator, our true Adam, Christ hands the kingdom over to the Father. In doing so, says Augustine, we are brought into "direct contemplation of God and the Father."[103]

Missing the Point of the Incarnation: Obedience Is Scandalous

EFS looks at the obedience of Christ in the economy of salvation and assumes that subordination must be what defines the Son *as Son*; his personal property is intrinsically inseparable from his subjection. But that is to miss the whole purpose of the incarnation; it is to misconstrue why God became man at all, confusing and conflating the Son in the form of God with the Son in the form of a servant.

Consider Philippians 2. Paul is very careful to first confess Christ as the eternal Son: he was in the "form of God" (2:6). Nevertheless, in order to die on the cross, the eternal Son of God took on the "form of a servant" (2:7). How so? By "being born in the likeness of men" (2:7). What will this servanthood entail? Humility and obedience. "And being found in human form, he humbled himself by becoming obedient to the point of death, even death on a cross" (2:8).

Don't miss this: obedience was not something the Son did prior to the incarnation, in the "form of God" as the eternal Son of God.

No, the Son had to humble himself first (become incarnate and suffer) to become obedient. EFS misses this point, assuming obedience is, at least in part, what makes the Son a Son in eternity, assuming obedience to the Father defines his personal property within the immanent Godhead. EFSers turn incarnate obedience into nothing more than a continuation of obedience within the immanent Trinity.

But that is to undermine the flow of Paul's logic: obedience is not the defining quality of the Son *as Son* to the Father in the immanent Trinity, but something the Son *learns* by virtue of his incarnation; obedient is something the Son *becomes* by virtue of his humanity.[104] And he does so only when he *humbles* himself, taking on "human form." Otherwise Paul could not say Christ humbled himself "by becoming" obedient.

Furthermore, notice the context of such obedience: it is not eternity or the immanent Trinity (the form of God) but the cross. He *became* obedient for the purpose of dying on a cross, which is why Paul applies to this obedient suffering the phrase "form of a servant" rather than "form of God." It's not that the suffering Son ceases to be God; please don't misunderstand or misconstrue what Paul means by "emptied himself." Paul's emphasis falls on the Son in the form of a servant because it is as a servant that he suffers *as a man* so that salvation is accomplished. That is what Paul means by "emptied himself" (2:7). The Son did not empty himself of his divinity or divine attributes; instead, he emptied himself "by taking the form of a servant" (2:7). To project obedience, submission, and subordination into the immanent Trinity, making it an essential and additional component to the Son's personal property, is to relinquish the Son's motive to "empty" himself (become incarnate). He did not empty himself and take the form of a servant because he is intrinsically subordinate to the Father; he emptied himself and took the form of a servant in order to become obedient on a cross.[105] Otherwise Paul could not juxtapose the Son's "equality with God" with his obedience "to the point of death," let alone boast that Christ refused to grasp the former at the expense of the latter.

Is this not what the author of Hebrews says? "Although he was a son, he *learned* obedience through what he suffered" (5:8). Or as Jesus himself says, "I have come down from heaven, not to do my own will but the will of him who sent me" (John 6:38). Coming down from heaven and becoming a man was necessary for Jesus to obey and suffer. To reverse that order is to miss the whole point of the incarnation. If the Son was already obedient as the Son *ad intra* (within the immanent Trinity), then Hebrews could not set up a contrast and say "although" he was a son, he "learned" obedience through what he suffered. Nor could Paul set up the same contrast in Philippians 2:8 and say that the Son "humbled" himself by becoming obedient to the point of death, even death on a cross. Why was he obedient? Because he *humbled* himself (something he had not done before). How did he do that? By *becoming* obedient to death (also something he had not done before).

For that reason, obedience is not intrinsic to the immanent Trinity but occurs within the context of the economy, the Son becoming a suffering servant to accomplish our salvation, just as the prophet Isaiah said. That is not something he is by virtue of his immanent Sonship in the Trinity but something he must become, through humility, by virtue of his humanity in the economy. Project obedience from the economy back into the immanent Trinity, and suddenly the incarnate Son is not the servant Scripture says he is. The humility of suffering and death is not that amazing anymore. The gospel is that much less extraordinary. Incarnate, humiliating obedience is scandalous because it is *not* something the Son of God does in glory as the Second Person of the Godhead.

Why Is Grace So Amazing, Really?

I just emphasized that if we project obedience from the economy back into the immanent Trinity, then the incarnate Son is not the servant Scripture says he is. But that would mean the incarnate Son cannot be the *Savior* Scripture says he is.

According to Isaiah, Christ "was pierced *for our transgressions*; he was crushed *for our iniquities*" (53:5). "In this is love," says John, "not that we have loved God but that he loved us and sent his Son to be the propitiation *for our sins*" (1 John 4:10; cf. 3:16; Mark 10:44; Rom. 5:8; 1 Cor. 7:23; 15:1–3; 1 Pet. 1:18–19; 2:21).

But EFS muddies this purely benevolent, altruistic divine motive. Not only did the Son live and die for us, *but for himself.* His obedience was not an obedience for our sake only, *but for his own sake as well.* Remember, EFS teaches that subordination is what makes the Son a Son before the world was ever created or a sinner ever sinned; he cannot be Son otherwise. In eternity, within the immanent Trinity, the Son *must* be obedient . . . or else. Or else what? As EFSers say time after time: or else he is no longer Son. That logic transfers into history as well. For EFS, the incarnation is but a *continuation* of an eternal subordination, yet notice what is lost. Obedience to the point of death, then, cannot be all that altruistic in the end. *The Son has to obey anyway*, otherwise the very meaning of his Sonship is relinquished. EFSers won't admit this, but the Son obeys and dies not only for us but to ensure he continues and does not forfeit his Sonship.

However, Jesus did not go to the cross for himself; he went to the cross *for us* and for us *alone.* Obedience was only necessary for the sake of sinners, not for the sake of the Son continuing his subordinate Sonship. The latter is affirmed nowhere in Scripture. What *is* affirmed in Scripture is this: the motive of the incarnation and the cross is God's sacrificial love for us. The most basic question of the Christian gospel is this: *Why did God become man?* John 3:16 answers, "For God so loved the world, that he gave his only begotten Son." Why? "That whosoever believeth in him should not perish, but have everlasting life" (KJV). If Jesus obeys the Father on earth merely as a continuation of his obedience to the Father in heaven, then grace is not all that amazing in the end. *It's what the Son had to do anyway.* The very thought empties the cross of sacrificial, self-giving love. His incarnate obedience was a mere perpetuation of heaven; his subjugation to suffering was a mere continuation of eternity.

Perhaps it's time, then, that we change our vocabulary. We evangelicals have a bad habit of using words like "submission" and "subordination." Not only do these words never appear in Scripture with reference to the eternal Son of God, but they imply a lesser Son, an inferior Son. It is much wiser if we use the language of the New Testament: *humiliation* (Phil. 2). That biblical word conveys what we should be after: the Son's self-humiliation, not frozen subordination.

In the end, the stakes are high: if we follow EFS into the valley of its low Christology, we should not be surprised when our soteriology suffers too.[106]

Since When Did the Trinity Get Sexual?

EFSers have exerted no little effort to present their position as the complementarian view, even though complementarians and egalitarians alike have criticized EFS. In doing so, they are convinced that they have the model, the paradigm for gender roles: the woman's submission is intrinsic to what it means to be a wife just as the Son's submission is intrinsic to what it means to be a Son.

EFSers often don't realize it, but this is an old move, one tried by social trinitarians for the last century (see chap. 3). We just learned that EFSers project submission in the economy of salvation back into the immanent Trinity, but they project their gender agenda back onto the immanent Trinity as well. "This is no accident: it is not just that as it happens social theories of the Trinity often project our ideals onto God," says Kilby. "Rather it is built into the kind of project that most social theorists are involved in that they *have to be* projectionist."[107]

Let me put my cards on the table: I am a committed, convictional complementarian. I believe there are strong scriptural reasons for restricting the office of pastor to qualified males. I also believe the husband is the head of his wife and the wife is to submit to her husband. But I agree with other complementarians that EFS smells like manipulation, the modern flavor we saw in chapter 3 that sought to redefine the Trinity for the sake of its many social programs. For all our disagreement, we complementarians and egalitarians can agree on this: *the Trinity is not our social program.*

EFSers appeal to two texts in particular: 1 Corinthians 11:3 and Ephesians 5:22–32. But as we've seen, exegesis is a lot like real estate. While the agent says, "Location, location, location," the exegete says, "Context, context, context." To begin with, it is a stretch, to say the least, to think that Paul has discussions of the immanent Trinity, *ad intra*, in view when he is talking about head coverings in 1 Corinthians 11 and husband-to-wife relationships in Ephesians 5. "A text without a context is a pretext for a proof text," says Carson.[108] Well, these are just those sorts of proof texts in the hands of EFS. Why is that?

When we do look at the context, we discover that Paul has no intention to make a beeline from metaphysical discussions about the immanent Trinity to gender roles. Instead, Paul has the *economy* in view, specifically Christ's *incarnate* mission to be our Mediator before God our Father—his very name (Christ/Messiah) gives this away. First Corinthians 11 begins with a command from Paul: "Be imitators of me, as I am of Christ" (v. 1). Paul just finished telling the Corinthians to be mindful of the consciences of others who might struggle with eating food offered to idols (10:23–33). He says the believer has the right to eat, but to abstain if it's not "helpful." "Let no one seek his own good, but the good of his neighbor" (10:24). In that self-giving, sacrificial spirit, which Christ himself exemplified in his own incarnate sufferings, Paul says to imitate him as he imitates Christ. Christians are to emulate the cross, their lives a replication of their Savior's sacrificial love.[109] Christ's selfless death for others—that is the proper context for what Paul says next. The Corinthians were being selfish, thinking of their own rights rather than the good of the whole community.[110] But now they are to model their lives on the cruciform model of their Savior, imitating his same selflessness.

So, when Paul says the "head of a wife is her husband, and the head of Christ is God" (11:3), he has in view the *incarnate, suffering servant*, who fulfilled his mission by means of his obedient life, death, and resurrection as the Messiah (Christ). There is absolutely nothing in the immediate or wider context that says anything at all about the Son apart from creation and salvation within the immanent Trinity. To infuse and impose discussions of immanent Trinity on this text is a failure to treat the context with integrity. Paul has in view the salvific lordship of the anointed One, the Messiah.

What, then, does Paul mean by calling God the head of Christ? Christ does submit to God the Father, but he does so *as the incarnate Redeemer* fulfilling his mission of salvation. Yes, there is submission between the Father and the Son, but the text never indicates this submission is within the *immanent* Trinity but always within the context of the economy. For *salvation* is the very point of this submission, not hierarchy within the very being of God. As we saw in Philippians 2:5–7, the Son must *become* obedient. Appealing to 1 Corinthians 11 to inject subordination within the immanent Godhead is a classic case of manipulating a text until it says far more than it can bear, stretching it like a bungee cord until it snaps.

It's ironic that EFSers appeal to Ephesians 5 to further their case from 1 Corinthians 11, because Ephesians 5 could not be more grounded in the *economic* context of the incarnation. The mystery of the gospel now manifested not just for Jews but for Gentiles (Eph. 3) drives Paul's letter from start to finish. So much so that he begins by discussing election (Eph. 1), then justification (Eph. 2), and finally our walk with God or sanctification (4:17–5:21). When he transitions to address what life in the church should look like, Paul again operates within the context of the gospel. "Wives, submit to your own husbands, as to the Lord. For the husband is the head of the wife even as Christ is the head of the church, his body, and is himself its Savior" (5:22–23). Notice, God the Father isn't mentioned at all. The comparison isn't husbands over wives like Father over Son. No, the comparison is husband as head of the wife like Christ is head *of the church*. The subordination of the Son is nowhere in view, only the subordination of the church. Even then, the Christ Paul refers to is the *Savior*, reminding us yet again that the immanent Trinity is not in view, only the incarnate Mediator. We know that because Paul goes on to tell husbands to sacrifice for their wives as Christ gave himself up on the cross for his bride, the church (5:25–27).

One last point while we're on the topic of the Trinity and gender: to claim that the Trinity, specifically subordination within the immanent Trinity, is a model for gender roles is about as novel as it gets. Two thousand years of church history have gone by, yet until EFSers arrived on the scene nobody thought to appeal to subordination in the immanent Trinity as the model for female submission. I find that not just amazing but telling, for they also labored to properly interpret the Bible. It's all the more telling because for most of history, societies were patriarchal. Yet these patriarchal societies never thought to use the Trinity to establish female subordination.

Putting Out a Forest Fire

So far, we've been digging around, looking at one tree at a time. But it's time we took a step back and considered the forest as a whole. Unfortunately, EFS has set the forest on fire, and its flames are licking up three trees that we cannot afford to lose: Bible, history, and worship. Let's consider each.

It's Time to Fly First Class, Not Economy: How (Not) to Read the Bible

There is a popular television series named for its star Los Angeles police detective, *Bosch*. When someone is murdered, all the other police officers rush to the scene and look at whatever's on the surface—the open window, the stolen wallet, the jealous husband. Confident and uncorrectable, they quickly conclude, "Case closed." But not Bosch. "A nice, neat little bow," he keeps patiently observing, studying the context in which the evidence was so conveniently placed. "I feel like we're being played, brother." Likewise with EFS. Sure, its treatment of the text appears simple on the surface, but take a longer look: it's exegetically simplistic. Like Bosch, we must move beyond the flurry of assumptions and pay close attention to the context of Scripture. Consider a few examples.

First, for all EFS's talk about just believing the Bible, isn't it puzzling that there is not one—not even one—text that says there is subordination *within the immanent Trinity*? The only text that can, on the surface, appear to come close is 1 Corinthians 15, but as we've seen, the context is the economy of salvation, not the immanent Trinity. As it turns out, EFS lacks hard evidence. Without scriptural support, it rides on the back of speculation.

Second, evangelicals have been taught to read their Bibles in a literalistic fashion, zeroing in on specific words, regardless of context or genre. We read the Bible as if finite, human speech is to be taken in the most literalistic way possible, forgetting that we are describing the indescribable: the infinite, incomprehensible God. Our language is not univocal, as if there is a one-to-one, direct correspondence between our words and the God we are describing. Can you imagine? We would read the psalms and conclude God has a body with big ears, eyeballs, and wings like a bird.

For instance, evangelicals today have been bred on a Christian culture that emphasizes the gospel—in and of itself that's a good thing. *Amen!* But let's not forget that conflation can be smuggled in through the gospel as well. Although the incarnation of Christ may be the culmination of God's special revelation, the human experience of Christ (suffering, submission) is not to be the take-off zone for our doctrine-of-God aircraft. If we make the human sufferings of Christ on the cross our launching pad, we then project suffering into the immanent Trinity, as if God suffers in his deity. Likewise, if we start with submission in the incarnation of Christ, we project submission into the immanent Trinity, making hierarchy a personal property of the triune God.

What's happened? We've read creaturely characteristics like subordination back into the divine names, assuming that the human relationships we experience *in society* are the same for the Trinity, even stem from the Trinity. I am reminded of that one person—there's always one—who gets on the plane with a suitcase five times too big to fit in the overhead compartment. They hold up the entire line of passengers, convinced, determined even, to make . . . it . . . *fit*. Let's not treat the Bible the same way. Not everything that occurs in the economy is meant to fit within the immanent Trinity. It's time for a first-class approach instead.

Raising the Bar: The Humility of History

EFSers were (and still are) shocked, even outraged, that their view was accused of heresy. "We're not Arians!" they protested. True, EFS is not the exact same view as Arianism; for that we should be thankful. However, as scholars have pointed out, EFS's approach to Scripture (hermeneutics) is remarkably similar, and at times the EFS view does overlap with the Homoian view, which was also condemned by the Nicene Creed (see chap. 2). For this reason, some label EFS semi-Arian.[111]

Aside from whether EFS is heresy or not, the incredulous response to such charges demonstrates that EFSers do not understand why heresy charges were lobbed in the first place. One might affirm the Son's equality, but the *logic* of one's inner argument can very well undermine what one affirms. That is how theology works: formal confession is a start, but the path to confessional fidelity is just as revealing and must also be held to account. Even if EFS is not an exact match with a historical heresy, we've seen that the *logic* of its position as well as its substitution of orthodox categories for social ones brings EFSers, albeit inadvertently, dangerously close to three heresies: subordinationism, tritheism, and Sabellianism. This should go without saying, but three heresies is, well, three too many. For Christians who believe in the importance of creedal fidelity, "it's not technically heresy" is a bar way too low. The Nicene fathers set the bar much higher. After all, this is the Trinity, the defining belief of Christianity.

Furthermore, such dismissiveness toward heresy charges also reveals a lack of historical sensitivity by EFSers. Even if EFS has no exact historical parallel or direct association, that does not qualify it as orthodoxy or excuse it from confessional accountability. That only means its nuanced subordinationism is far more subtle, far more difficult to detect due to its novelty. For example, take another topic, like open theism (the denial of God's foreknowledge), which has made inroads within evangelicalism in years past. Open theism was never addressed by the ecumenical creeds. In many ways, open theism is unprecedented until the modern era. But evangelical theologians have argued that open theism is clearly out of bounds, not only contradicting Scripture but violating confessional fidelity. In other words, the creeds and confessions of the church are not

Don't Try This at Home

EFSers deny that their position is novel. If they see the word "subordination" used by past theologians, they assume EFS must be in view. Not only is this anachronistic, but it fails to pay attention to how Nicene vocabulary works. When the word is used it merely refers to the order within the Godhead (Father, Son, Spirit) due to the eternal relations of origin. *Suborder is not the same as subordination.* Processions, not authority, are in view. Lesson is, we should not force our modern, social categories (like hierarchy), which are novel, on past theologians who never considered describing the Trinity in anything but Nicene categories.

a dead tradition but a *living* tradition. In that light, EFS's novelty is a fatal strike against it. The living democracy of the dead does not rule in its favor.

In contrast, how should we approach the Trinity? With historical humility. After two thousand years of robust creedal accountability, we *should* feel uneasy and suspicious whenever someone advocates a position on the Trinity that is novel. The burden of proof is on them, not us, to show otherwise. Even if I'm a novice in biblical interpretation, it is wise of me to trust the time-tested Bible hermeneutics of my fathers. Not only is it wise, but it displays hermeneutical humility, the kind we want our churchgoers to imitate, the kind that says, "Let's read our Bible . . . with the church."

Bottom Line: Worship

Again and again, EFS says the Son is a lesser authority, a lesser glory than the Father, for the Father *alone* deserves ultimate praise and worship.[112] Which raises a question: *does EFS manufacture a subordinate Son who cannot be worshiped?*

In the Gospel of Matthew, immediately after Jesus fed five thousand people with just five loaves and two fish, he made his disciples get into a boat and sail ahead of him so that he could stay behind and pray (14:22–23). But the boat was caught in a vicious, merciless storm. Can you imagine how terrified the disciples must have been? As the waves beat down on their boat, they must have thought they were about to die. But then, when all seemed lost, they looked up and saw a figure walking toward them *on the water*. Matthew says the disciples were "terrified" (14:26). Nature had turned into a demon—first the waves, now a ghost. They started wailing, crying out in fear. And then Jesus spoke: "Take heart; it is I. Do not be afraid" (14:27).

Do you know what happened next? The unthinkable. Jesus got into the boat and the text says—I am not making this up—that the disciples "worshiped" Jesus and confessed him to be the "Son of God" (14:33). *They worshiped him.*

But wait! Shouldn't Jesus have stopped them and said, "No, no, no. Ultimate praise and glory is not mine. I am a lesser authority than the Father. Worship him. Give your praise to him." He must say that if EFS has its way. But he didn't. Instead, he stood there and received their worship in full. *In full.* No restriction. No correction. No hesitation.

When Arianism swept the church in the fourth century, Athanasius knew the bottom line was worship. If Arius was right, then on Sunday mornings churchgoers could not worship the Son, at least not like they worshiped the Father. Despite its nuances, EFS finds itself in a similar boat: can they fall to the ground with the disciples in the boat and worship *Jesus?* He is, after all, a lesser glory.

I don't know about you, but the Jesus I read about in the Bible is a Jesus who declares, without qualification or reservation, that he is one with the Father (John 10:30). Never does he ever—not even once—tell his disciples to stop worshiping him as they worship Yahweh himself. Yet others do, for they refuse to believe he is equal with the Father. But never Jesus. He claims that right (John 5:17–18; 8:58–59) and the worship that comes with it (Matt. 28:9, 17; John 9:38). He even claims he should receive the same honor as his Father: "For the Father judges no one, but has given all judgment to the Son, that all may honor the Son, *just as they honor the Father.* Whoever does not honor the Son does not honor the Father who sent him" (John 5:22–23).

Here is the bottom line: if Jesus is not equal to the Father *in every way*, Christianity itself is no more. We might as well stay home on Sunday morning, for we cannot sing with the angels on the last day,

> Worthy is the Lamb who was slain,
> to receive power and wealth and wisdom and might
> and honor and glory and blessing! (Rev. 5:12)

We cannot join that chorus across the earth and say,

> To him who sits on the throne *and to the Lamb*
> be blessing and honor and glory and might forever and
> ever! (5:13)

Glory to the Father, *and to the Son*, and to the Holy Ghost! As it was in the beginning, is now, and ever shall be, world without end.[113]

Is the Spirit Spirated?

Spiration

We have not even heard that there is a Holy Spirit.

THE EPHESIANS, ACTS 19:2

For the Spirit searches everything, even the depths of God.

1 CORINTHIANS 2:10

[The Spirit] is the gift of God insofar as he is given to those he is given to. But in himself he is God even if he is not given to anyone, because he was God, co-eternal with the Father and the Son, even before he was given to anyone. Nor is he less than they because they give and he is given. He is given as God's gift in such a way that as God he also gives himself.

AUGUSTINE, *THE TRINITY*

TO THE DELOREAN!

Where we're going: The Holy Spirit

Key point: The Spirit is spirated from the Father and the Son, so he holds the one, simple essence in common. The Bible puts a spotlight on spiration in many colorful ways: the Spirit's name, the Spirit's origin, and the titles applied to the Spirit, such as Breath, Gift, and Love. Takeaway: if the Spirit does not spirate from the Father and the Son, then there is no Spirit to indwell us, sanctify us, and bring us into communion with the Trinity.

In Rome: *My Brilliant Friend*

Several summers ago, I delivered lectures to a group of Protestants nestled in the heart of Rome. After each day's lecture, it was up to me to find my way back to my flat. One afternoon the walk back was scorching hot, so at the halfway point I took shelter under a bridge that arched across the Tiber River. Just then, two dozen tents threw open their white flaps. I couldn't see inside the tents, but there was no need to; the aroma of roulade and manicotti floated down the Tiber, intoxicating hungry tourists like myself. Summoned, who was I to resist? So began my journey, poking my head in one tent after another to find out where this irresistible aroma originated.

Some tents entertained their diners with the *chitarra battente*, the strumming guitar. But one restaurant caught my eye for the way it nestled novels along the side of each table. I don't speak Italian, but I recognized the books right away by their distinguishable baby-blue spines and whitewashed covers. They were the Neapolitan Quartet by Elena Ferrante, who is popular not only in Italy but America as well.[1] These four books are a saga about the competitive but enduring friendship of two girls, Lenù and Lila, who become women during the 1950s. Yet unlike America in the '50s, Italy suffered in poverty due to the aftermath of World War II.

In the first book, *My Brilliant Friend*, Lenù and Lila's friendship turns a disappointing corner when Lila is swept off her feet by Stefano and the unbreakable friendship the two girls once shared begins to fracture. Courted with jewelry and wooed by her charming fiancé, Lila's interests change. Previously, Lila and Lenù talked about intellectual matters, matters of the mind. But now, with Stefano in the picture, all Lila cares about are her lover's gifts and the image those gifts project to her friends.

Lenù convinces herself that her academic success is just as valuable as Lila's gifts. The black-covered Bible she won is all the evidence she needs, a trophy confirming her brilliance in the classroom—not to mention her recent report cards, which display her high marks, including one in theology. When Lenù talks to Lila that summer, Lenù tells her about school and poses a theological conundrum, hoping their conversation will be like old times and their friendship will be rekindled. But Lenù is met with a cold rebuke.

"I told her about my theology course and said, to impress her with the questions that tormented me, that I didn't know what to think about the Holy Spirit, its function wasn't clear to me. 'Is it,' I argued aloud, 'a subordinate entity, in the service of both God and Jesus, like a messenger? Or an emanation of the first two, their miraculous essence?" With no response from Lila yet, Lenù answers her own questions:

> But in the first case how can an entity who acts as a messenger possibly be one with God and his son? Wouldn't it be like saying that my father who is a porter at the city hall is the same as the mayor . . .? And, if you look at the second case, well, essence, sweat, voice are part of the person from whom they emanate: how can it make sense, then, to consider the Holy Spirit separate from God and Jesus? Or is the Holy Spirit the most important person and the other two his mode of being, or I don't understand what his function is.

At last, Lila responds, revealing just how much the two girls' friendship has changed: "You still waste time with those things,

Lenù? . . . And what are you doing? A theology course in which you struggle to understand what the Holy Spirit is? Forget it, it was the Devil who invented the world, not the Father, the Son, and the Holy Spirit. Do you want to see the string of pearls that Stefano gave me?"[2]

Bewildered, Lenù leaves the conversation dejected. She didn't bring up the "Very Holy Trinity" because theology was on her mind—not really. The Trinity was an excuse to somehow save a friendship now slipping through her fingers. Nevertheless, Lenù's confusion over the Holy Spirit is one shared by many today, Christian and non-Christian alike. And Lila's attitude is more pervasive still: *stop wasting your time!*

Lenù's Trinity

I can't fix Lenù and Lila's friendship—we'll let Elena Ferrante do that. But this mess about the Spirit and the Trinity? Now that I can help with, if only you will trust me that this is anything but a waste of time. The reason Lenù is perplexed is because she wavers between subordinationism and (a weird form of) Sabellianism. Did you spot each?

First, Lenù wonders if the Spirit is subordinate to the Father and the Son. If the Spirit is a messenger, then it must be inferior. Her father, a mere porter, is not the mayor's equal; Lenù knows that much. Neither can this messenger Spirit be "one with God and his son." Lenù is flirting with subordinationism. Back in the fourth century, some shared Lenù's evaluation. They were called Spirit-fighters; they did not believe the Spirit was coequal with the Father and the Son, because they did not believe the Spirit proceeded from the same essence (see chap. 2).

Second, if the Spirit is an emanation of the Father and the Son and their "miraculous essence," says Lenù, then is there any real difference between the Spirit and the Father and the Son? It seems not. This, as we know, is the error of Sabellianism. Lenù conflates the persons—which are mere emanations—until God is but one person who merely wears different names, the Spirit being one of them. Or, in Lenù's conceptual world, essence, sweat, and voice are but parts or phases of one divine person.

Third, Lenù is curious whether the Spirit is the superior one in the Trinity. Maybe the Father and Son are the Spirit's mode of being. I confess, no one has ever said to me, "I think the Spirit is it. The Spirit is where it's at, not the Father and the Son." But in some circles—radical Pentecostalism being one of them—the Spirit is sometimes treated this way.

If you are as bewildered as Lenù or as disenchanted as Lila, this chapter will help. With the assistance of Scripture and biblical interpreters from the Great Tradition, we will clarify just who the Spirit is and who the Spirit is not, avoiding some of the pitfalls Lenù has fallen into.[3]

We Believe in the Holy Spirit . . . Right?

"We believe in the Holy Spirit." At least that's what the Nicene Creed says. But it has good reason for saying so. In Scripture, the Spirit is not presented as subordinate to the Father and the Son as a lesser deity, nor is the Spirit to be confused with the Father and the Son, indistinguishable as a person.

The Spirit is, first and foremost, coeternal and coequal with the Father and the Son. "We believe in the Holy Spirit," says the creed, because the Spirit is "the Lord, the giver of life." Notice, the creed turns to the *works* of the Spirit—observing that these are none other than *divine* works—to identify the Spirit as the Lord himself. That is a move Scripture itself makes, attributing to the Spirit the work of not only creation but salvation. From regeneration (John 3:5–8) to conversion (1 Cor. 12:3) to adoption (Gal. 4:6) to sanctification (1 Thess. 5:23) to glorification (Rom. 8:9–11), it is the Spirit who is at work in us from start to finish. Nor should we forget the Spirit's work of revelation and inspiration. It was the

Spirit who "spoke through the prophets," says the creed. That is what Peter says too: "For no prophecy was ever produced by the will of man, but men spoke from God as they were carried along by the Holy Spirit" (2 Pet. 1:21).

We could go on—the works of the Spirit are innumerable. And these works attributed to the Spirit are ones that God alone can perform. The Creed concludes that the Spirit is to be "worshiped and glorified" along "with the Father and the Son." For the Spirit is just as divine as the Father and the Son, wholly sharing in the one divine essence, will, power, authority, and glory. Otherwise Paul could not say, "Now the Lord is the Spirit, and where the Spirit of the Lord is, there is freedom" (2 Cor. 3:17). But Paul can only say that because the Spirit proceeds in eternity from the Father and the Son's same essence. The Spirit, too, is "true God with the Father and the Son, the third person of the holy trinity, consubstantial and coeternal with the Father and the Son, omnipotent, and the creator of all things," says that theologian of the Holy Spirit, John Calvin.[4]

But not only is the Spirit coequal with the Father and the Son, the Spirit is not to be confused with the Father and the Son, as Lenù is so tempted to do. The Spirit is no mere force or impersonal emanation, nor is the Spirit a divine attribute.[5] No, the Spirit is a distinct person of the Godhead, the Third Person to be precise: one with the Father and the Son in essence, yet distinct from the Father and the Son in subsistence. Or, to be more precise yet, the Spirit is a personal subsistence of the one, simple essence.

How then does the divine essence subsist in the Third Person of the Godhead, the very one we call Spirit?

What Distinguishes the Spirit from the Father and Son?

We've seen with Lenù that conflating the persons of the Trinity is a real problem, and it has a long history thanks to Sabellianism. But if we are to distinguish the Spirit as a person, what exactly does the distinguishing? As chapter 2 taught us, the three persons are distinct according to their eternal relations of origin (personal properties). That means the Spirit also has a unique (incommunicable) relation.

Q: What is it that distinguishes the Holy Spirit as a person?

A: The Holy Spirit eternally proceeds (or spirates) from the Father and the Son.

That answer is found in the Nicene Creed as well.

Our English word "procession" is how we translate the Greek word *ekporeusis*. We see this language in John 15. In context, Jesus is explaining to his disciples that the world hates him just as the prophets foretold. If they hate Jesus, then they will hate his disciples as well. But fear not, Jesus promises he will not leave his disciples as orphans, helpless and powerless in the world. The Helper himself will come, the Holy Spirit. But who will send this Helper, and from whom does this Helper originate? "But when the Helper comes, whom I will send to you from the Father, the Spirit of truth, who proceeds [*ekporeuetai*] from the Father, he will bear witness about me" (John 15:26).

This is not the first time Jesus has promised that he and the Father will send the Spirit. In John 14, Jesus announces that he will return to the Father. But again, fear not, for he will not leave his disciples as flotsam, like useless wreckage from a dismembered ship, drifting farther and farther out to sea. Instead, his presence will continue with his disciples. How is that possible? Christ will ascend to his Father, but the Spirit of Christ will journey with his disciples and instruct them in the way they should go. "The Helper, the Holy Spirit, whom the Father will send in my name, he will teach you all things and bring to your remembrance all that I have said to you" (John 14:26).

Jump ahead to John 16. By now Jesus has mentioned several times that he is leaving his disciples. His departure is starting to sink in, and the disciples are filled with sorrow at the thought that

Jesus will leave them. But again, Jesus tells his disciples not to fear. Counterintuitive as it may seem, it is better for them that Jesus leaves. How can Jesus say this? What could be better than Jesus himself? Jesus can say this and mean it because when he goes, the Spirit will come. "It is to your advantage that I go away, for if I do not go away, the Helper will not come to you. But if I go, I will send him to you" (John 16:7).

Holy Toledo!

Does the Spirit proceed from the Father *and the Son*? That last phrase in Greek is *filioque*. In the West, the church inserted the word *filioque* into the Nicene Creed at the Council of Toledo (AD 589), but the East objected. In a messy cascade of politics that lasted centuries, East and West eventually split during the Great Schism (AD 1054).

Should we affirm the *filioque*? The East said no because they believed it created two sources or principles in the Trinity (Father/Son) rather than just one (Father). But the response of the West is more convincing. Anselm wrote *On the Procession of the Holy Spirit* and gave several reasons why:

1. The *filioque* preserves unity and equality between all three persons.
2. Without the *filioque* the Spirit would not be given by the Son, but the Son would be given by the Spirit.
3. Whenever Scripture speaks of the Spirit as the Spirit of Christ, it is assumed that the Spirit proceeds from the Son as well as the Father (John 14:25; 15:26; 16:6–7).

The Spirit proceeds from the Father and the Son as from *one, single source or principle* (not two), since the Father and Son are both subsistences of the same, simple essence. Others pointed out that the *filioque* not only guarantees that the Spirit proceeds with the same divine nature as the Father and Son but ensures we can be united to Christ, a union impossible if the Spirit does not proceed from the Son.

In the moment, it was hard for the disciples to grasp what Jesus was saying; their sorrow clouded their trinitarian vision. But after Jesus ascended and the Spirit descended, they experienced the Spirit's indwelling firsthand. They could tell their listeners, as did the apostle Paul, that if they believe in the crucified and risen Jesus, then they too will be adopted as sons. "And because you are sons, God has sent the Spirit of his Son into our hearts, crying 'Abba! Father!'" (Gal. 4:6). It is because the Spirit proceeds from the Father and the Son that the Spirit of the Son can lead us to the Father.

All these mentions of the Spirit in John's Gospel should warn us against segregating the Spirit from the Father and the Son. The Spirit is just as much the Spirit of the Son as he is the Spirit of the Father; together the three of them hold the one divine essence in common, each a subsistence of the same divine nature. That

What Does Spiration Have to Do with Generation?

The spiration of the Spirit is distinct from the generation of the Son. But one should not assume that the spiration of the Spirit has nothing to do with paternity and filiation. The reason the Spirit is spirated from the Father *and the Son* is because it is in eternal generation that the Son is empowered to spirate the Spirit. Gilles Emery says, "[The] Father, in begetting his Son, gives to his Son the power to 'breathe forth' or to 'spirate' the Holy Spirit." What does this look like for each person of the Trinity? "The Father as *Father* gives to the Son the power to spirate with him the Holy Spirit, and the Son as *Son* receives from the Father the power (the active power) of spirating with him the Holy Spirit." Or think of it this way, "The power of spirating the Holy Spirit is *included* in the generation of the Son: by his generation, the Son receives from the Father to be with him the principle of the Holy Spirit." What does that entail for the Spirit? The "procession of the Holy Spirit is inscribed in the mutual relation of the Father and the Son. This means that the process of the Holy Spirit is connected *in itself* to the generation of the Son by the Father" (*The Trinity*, 116).

means the Spirit proceeds not only from the Father in eternity but from the Son as well. The Spirit proceeds from the Father and the Son, yet he does not do so separately but from both as from one source. From all eternity, the Father and the Son communicate the one, simple, undivided divine essence to the Spirit. Likewise, when the Spirit descends at Pentecost and indwells God's people, he is not sent by the Father alone but, as we heard Jesus say, by the Father *and the Son*. But again, he is sent not from two separate sources but from one source. Anselm paraphrases Jesus to mean, "I shall send as if the Father should send, so that my sending of the Spirit and the Father's sending of the Spirit are one and the same."[6] *In summary, the gift of the Spirit in history reflects and reveals (but by no means constitutes) the procession of the Spirit in eternity, and in both cases the Spirit is sent from one source: the Father and the Son.*

Objection!

Some will object that Jesus does not refer to eternity but to the Father and the Son sending the Spirit at Pentecost; Jesus is not talking about processions within the Trinity but the Spirit's descent in creation for the purpose of salvation. But as we've learned, this objection is shortsighted, a type of narrow, crude biblicism that fails to read Jesus's words in view of the whole Bible—that is, God's redemptive plan across all of history—or in light of who the triune God is in eternity. Such a disconnect between temporal missions and eternal relations is foreign to Jesus, as seen in John 15:26 when he grounds his sending of the Spirit in the procession of the Spirit from the Father. Yes, there is a difference between eternal relations within the Trinity and temporal missions in creation; we dare not confuse the two. But it is a step too far to restrict the temporal missions from revealing the eternal relations. While we should not *project* everything in the mission of the Son or the Spirit onto the eternal Trinity (see chap. 8), nevertheless, it would be extreme to conclude that such missions do not *mirror* eternal relations in one specific way: the only reason the Spirit can be sent by the Father and the Son to save a lost humanity is because he proceeds from the Father and the Son from all eternity.

We've seen this to be true of the Son (see chaps. 6 and 7), but it's no less true with the Spirit. The Spirit "is poured out by the Father and the Son," which is "the *expression* of what the Holy Spirit is from all eternity." "Just as the Holy Spirit proceeds from the Father and the Son in eternity, he comes forth from the Father and the Son in the economy." Whether we are referring to the Son or the Spirit, the "economy of divine persons in time is conformed to the eternal order of origin of these persons."[7] It is not arbitrary then that the Father and Son *send* the Spirit. That order follows from his eternal relation: the Spirit proceeds from the Father and the Son in eternity, and therefore is called the Third Person of the Trinity (not third in time, not third in rank, but third in order).

I realize "procession" may sound strange. Why not say the Spirit is generated, as we did with the Son? But remember, these eternal relations of origin are what *distinguish* the persons one from another. If we say the Spirit is generated, then we have not distinguished the Spirit from the Son in relation to the Father. If we say the Spirit is generated, then the Spirit might replace the Son and lose its distinct personhood altogether. If we say that the Spirit is generated, we might also turn the Spirit into a second Son, which would make the Spirit a brother to the Son.

But the Spirit is not from the Father in the same way that the Son is from the Father. The Spirit is not the Son's twin brother.[8] "For the Son is from his Father, that is, from God who is his Father, while the Holy Spirit is not from God as his Father but only from God who is Father," says Anselm.[9] The Son is generated from the Father, which is why he is called Son, but the Spirit is not called Son, because he is not generated but spirated, proceeding from the Father and the Son *as Spirit*.[10]

271

Spiration is another way to talk about procession. It stems from the biblical name itself. While the names Father and Son convey *generation*, the name Spirit conveys *spiration*. The word "Spirit" in Scripture can also be translated as "breath." Applied theologically, the Spirit is the one breathed out by the Father and the Son in eternity, which explains why the Spirit is the one sent from the Father and the Son in history.[11] The Spirit's mission then reflects the Spirit's eternal relation of origin.[12]

Catch a Wave and You're Sitting on Top of the World

In the 1960s, rock and roll took on a life of its own. The 1950s were its younger years, with the rise of Buddy Holly, Ritchie Valens, and the Big Bopper. But the '50s ended with the tragic plane crash that killed all three of those musicians. However, the road they pioneered was not in vain. In 1960, John Lennon, Paul McCartney, George Harrison, and Ringo Starr formed a band in Liverpool called the Beatles and took rock and roll into a whole new world with their psychedelic sound. One year later, on the opposite side of the world, another band was born: the Beach Boys. Two brothers and their friends in California started the band in a garage. But unlike the Beatles, the Beach Boys sang about California culture: surfer girls, good vibrations, and cruising down the coast in a little deuce coupe. One of my favorite songs by the Beach Boys is "Catch a Wave." "Catch a wave and you're sitting on top of the world," begins this hit song in which the Beach Boys make their apologetic for surfing.

If you've ever been surfing, then you know how hard it is to catch just the right wave. Surfers are known to get up at an ungodly hour of the morning, all to catch that wave and ride it in to shore. Hard as it is to balance yourself on that waxy board, once you do you'll be amped, bros shouting out, "Dude!" as you perform that perfect 10. If you can rip a wave, you'll be stoked, especially if you can glide through the tube before it crashes on your head and you wipe out. Pure bliss.

I doubt he ever surfed, but the medieval theologian Richard of Saint Victor had something to say about waves and the Trinity. Grasping for words to describe the "fullness of supreme love" between the three persons of the Trinity, Richard says it's like a "wave of divinity."[13] Richard may not be a beach bum, but I must admit, when Richard can get up on his board, the dude's got rip.[14] This is Richard's way of describing the simplicity the three persons hold in common: "One being . . . one, single will!" "In the Trinity, all have one, single truth, one, single charity, and one, single goodness, with no differences." The same can be said of the love they hold in common: "There will be one, single, and same love in all persons."[15]

Nevertheless, as Richard rides this wave, he does not fail to distinguish between the three persons according to their personal properties. Yes, there is "one, single, and the same love in all persons," but this love "will be beautifully distinct in each of them, on the basis of the different properties." The three hold the one essence in common, but they are distinguished by their eternal relations of origin, which manifest themselves to us in Scripture in all kinds of ways—or shall we say *waves*? That said, let's catch a couple of these waves as they relate to the Spirit in particular. Perhaps we will understand the Spirit's personal property— spiration—better in the end and can hang loose as beach bums, telling the stories of how we caught that wave of divinity once upon a time.

Wave #1: Breath

One title that conveys the concept of spiration is hidden within the very name Scripture uses for the Spirit: *pneuma*. The word is translated as "spirit" or "wind" or "breath."[16] But in context, one or more of these meanings may overlap to refer to the person and work of the Holy Spirit. For example, when Jesus tells Nicodemus he must be born again by the Spirit (*pneumatos*) to enter the kingdom of God (John 3:6), it is anything but accidental that Jesus then says, "The *wind* [*pneuma*] blows where it wishes, and you hear its sound, but you do not know where it comes from or where it goes. So it is with everyone who is born of the *Spirit* [*pneumatos*]" (3:8). Jesus uses the same word for wind and Spirit, and then compares the Spirit to the wind to convey the sovereignty of the Spirit to bring about our new birth. How fitting, since the Old Testament speaks interchangeably of Spirit, breath, and wind (e.g., Gen. 1:2; Job. 33:4; Ps. 33:6).

In other cases, the Spirit may not be mentioned but presupposed in a concept. For example, consider how Paul says to Timothy that "all Scripture is breathed out by God" (2 Tim. 3:16). But how does God breathe out the Scriptures? Peter gives us the answer: "Men spoke from God as they were carried along by the Holy Spirit" (2 Pet. 1:21). While Paul may not refer to the Spirit in his affirmation of Scripture's inspiration, we know (and no doubt Paul did too) that the breath of God that produces these Scriptures is none other than the Third Person of the Trinity. The Father breathes out his Word through his Spirit.

The connection between Spirit and breath transitions from black-and-white to vivid color when Jesus appears to his disciples in his resurrected body. It was a perilous moment for the disciples; they were in hiding behind locked doors, fearing that the Jews might find them and kill them like they had killed their rabbi. Suddenly, Jesus stood in their midst, bypassing the laws of physics altogether and announcing peace to their fearful souls. Then Jesus showed them his hands and his side, proving to them that the rumors were true: he is risen indeed. Now that he has risen, however, the disciples have a job to do: they must go into all the world and announce this good news. "As the Father has sent me, even so I am sending you" (John 20:21). But how exactly is Jesus going to send them? "And when he had said this, he breathed on them and said to them, 'Receive the Holy Spirit'" (20:22).

Breathing on the disciples? That seems odd to us today, perhaps even awkward. But the breath of Jesus is none other than the Spirit. Not literally, as if the Spirit is now material. Breath is symbolic, exhaled by Jesus to assure the disciples their Savior is with them to the end of the age (Matt. 28:20).[17] "Not that the physical breath that came from his body and was physically felt was the substance of the Holy Spirit," explains Augustine, "but it was a convenient symbolic demonstration that the Holy Spirit proceeds from the Son as well as from the Father." [18] Not only is there a procession of the Spirit in redemptive history—the Father and the Son sending the Spirit to indwell and lead the disciples—but such a procession in history reflects the procession in eternity: the Spirit proceeds from the Father and the Son before all ages; he is the spirated Spirit.

Jesus can breathe the Spirit on his disciples—inaugurating the Spirit's mission now that Christ is risen—because this same Spirit proceeds from the Father and the Son from all eternity. In real time, the disciples receive the Spirit, and his mission becomes as palpable to them as Jesus's breath on their faces.[19] But that mission reveals the Spirit's eternal origin: spiration. As the Spirit that proceeds

Anselm

Anselm of Canterbury (1033/34–1109) is a personal favorite of mine. His portrayal of God as the perfect being gets at the very essence of a classical doctrine of God, demonstrating that certain perfect-making attributes must follow, from simplicity to immutability (see his *Monologion* and *Proslogion*). But we also see his doctrine of the Trinity shine in his books *On the Incarnation of the Word*, *Why God Became Man*, and *On the Procession of the Holy Spirit*. Readers today may be surprised how much they enjoy Anselm when they discover he writes in the form of a dialogue and with profound devotional fervor. Most importantly, Anselm believes in a faith that seeks understanding (not vice versa), which is the humble posture one must have when approaching the mystery of the Trinity.

from the Father and the Son in eternity, it is fitting that the Father and the Son should send the Spirit in history. The Father breathes out his Spirit through his Son. As a result, the Spirit gives us new hearts to hear and embrace the gospel of God's only begotten Son so that we are adopted as sons by the Father into the family of God. "Now we have received not the spirit of the world, but the Spirit who is from God, that we might understand the things freely given us by God" (1 Cor. 2:12).

Wave #2: Gift

Not only is the Spirit described as breath, but he is also said to be the gift the Father and the Son give. And again, it is Jesus himself who says so: "For he whom God has sent utters the words of God, for he gives the Spirit without measure" (John 3:34).

In John 7, hatred for Jesus is heating up. But that does not stop Jesus from showing up for the Feast of Booths. At last, Jesus gets everyone's attention, standing up and crying out, "If anyone thirsts, let him come to me and drink. Whoever believes in me, as the Scripture has said, 'Out of his heart will flow rivers of living water'" (John 7:37–38). What is Jesus referring to when he talks about water? Better question, *who* is Jesus referring to when he talks about water? John tells us, "Now this he said about the Spirit, whom those who believed in him were to receive, for as yet the Spirit had not been given, because Jesus was not yet glorified" (7:39).

In the Old Testament, water was a sign of life, and not just physical life but also spiritual life, which is why prophets like Ezekiel used the imagery of water to refer to the new life of the Spirit, a life that wells up and washes away sin (Ezek. 36:25). Jesus uses this same water imagery, applying it to the Spirit whom he will send. But notice, for our purposes, that John says the Spirit is given by Jesus to be received. He is, in other words, a *gift*. And what a gift he is to us needy sinners. Sent by the Father and the Son, the Spirit is a gift of life for all those dying of thirst. Is this not what Jesus says to the Samaritan woman at Jacob's well? "If you knew the gift of God, and who it is that is saying to you, 'Give me a drink,' you would have asked him, and he would have given you living water" (John 4:10). The gift Jesus extends is nothing less than eternal life (cf. 3:14–16; 1 John 3:23–24), but eternal life comes only through the Spirit. How appropriate it is then to title him Gift.

Jesus is not the only one who refers to the Spirit as a gift. In the book of Acts, right after Jesus ascends into the heavens, this language appears once more. Remember, Jesus promised to send the Spirit, a promise fulfilled at Pentecost when the Spirit descended on the disciples like tongues of fire. Such a miraculous mystery invokes a speech from Peter, who explains that the advent of Jesus and the descent of the Spirit were both promised by God through the prophets, promises now fulfilled in their very midst. When the crowd hears this good news, they are "cut to the heart" and ask what to do next, to which Peter responds, "Repent and be baptized every one of you in the name of Jesus Christ for the forgiveness of your sins, and *you will receive the gift of the Holy Spirit*" (Acts 2:38). The *gift* of the Holy Spirit—that is Peter's go-to label for the Spirit as this new covenant community gathers for the first time. And he will return to it again when the Gentiles receive this same gift (10:45).

Later, Peter will say something similar, calling the Spirit not only a gift but a *witness*. When pressured not to speak out about Jesus, Peter says he cannot stay quiet. They may have crucified Jesus, but the "God of our fathers raised Jesus" and "exalted him at his right hand as Leader and Savior, to give repentance to Israel and forgiveness of sins" (5:30–31). But Peter doesn't stop there. Just like in Acts 2, he transitions from Christ to the Spirit: "And we are witnesses to these things, and so is the Holy Spirit, whom God has given to those who obey him" (5:32). In a sense, Acts 5 elaborates on Acts 2. What Jesus has accomplished the Spirit has born witness to, but not merely in some external sense. The

Witness has born witness to the gospel by uniting the believer to Christ, and all those whom the Spirit has united to Christ have been *given* the Spirit of Christ. Just how generous is this gift? So generous that when Luke describes how the Spirit "fell" on the Gentiles, he says, "the *gift* of the Holy Spirit was *poured out* even on the Gentiles" (Acts 10:45). Luke returns to the imagery of water (poured out) to describe what it must have been like for these Gentiles to receive this gift.

Or perhaps you will remember that story in the book of Acts where Simon the Magician tries to buy rights to the Holy Spirit so that he can impress everyone by giving this Spirit to others? Working his magic, Simon tells the apostle Peter, "Give me this power also, so that anyone on whom I lay my hands may receive the Holy Spirit" (Acts 8:19). But Peter responds with a harsh and well-deserved rebuke: "May your silver perish with you, because you thought you could obtain *the gift of God* with money!" (8:20). What did Simon do wrong? He failed to understand that the Spirit is a *gift*. He is not for sale.

The reason we, like Jesus and the apostles, can call the Spirit a gift is because the Father and the Son (the givers) not only give to us sinners the Spirit for the sake of our salvation, but such a giving is consistent with and reflects the giving nature of the Father and the Son in eternity.[20] It is because the Spirit is given in eternity—spirated by the Father and the Son—that he can then be given to us in redemptive history. As Gift he can give gifts to the people of God.[21] But he only gives gifts because he proceeds from eternity. What does it mean for the Spirit to be given by the Father and the Son in eternity (spiration)? It means, says Augustine, that "the Holy Spirit is a kind of inexpressible communion or fellowship of Father and Son."[22]

One qualification is needed before we move on. To call the Spirit a gift is not the same thing as calling the Spirit a donation.[23] The Spirit, says Augustine, "is everlastingly gift [*donum*], but donation [*donatum*] only from a point of time."[24] What Augustine is trying to say is this: the Spirit is gift in eternity whether or not he is ever given to us in history.[25] Just as the sending of the Son in history does not constitute the Son's generation in eternity, so too the Spirit's sending or giving in history does not constitute the Spirit's spiration or procession in eternity. It's the other way around. As we learned in chapter 4, relations constitute missions; missions do not constitute relations. If the latter, then God does not become a Trinity *until* he acts in history. If the latter, God is not triune until he acts to save us.

As to the Spirit, the distinction between gift and donation matters, lest we assume that to be given is to be inferior to the one who gives—as if the Spirit only becomes a gift if he is then given to us by the Father and the Son. But the Spirit is Spirit from all eternity, proceeding from the Father and the Son, regardless of whether he is ever donated or sent to us in history. For that reason, he is consubstantial with the Father and the Son; being given only reflects that order, but it by no means makes the Spirit inferior.

Wave #3: Love

In our affirmation of simplicity (chap. 5) we learned that no one attribute of God can be kept from any one person of the Trinity. He is, after all, *simply* Trinity. As long as each person is a subsistence of the same divine nature, all three persons holding the same divine nature in common, and as long as God's nature or essence is identical with all that is within him (attributes), then whatever attribute we have in mind, it must be true of each person of the Trinity. That is the case with love. To confess God is love is to confess that the *triune* God is love.

Yet we cannot forget that the persons of the Trinity are distinct according to their personal properties: paternity, filiation, and spiration. There is a sense in which certain works and attributes can be *appropriated* by specific persons of the Godhead in a special way that is consistent with each person's eternal relation of origin.

(The nuances of "appropriations" must be carefully articulated to avoid confusion and heresy, and such nuances will occupy our attention in chapter 10.) A certain person of the Godhead may appropriate a specific work or attribute in a way that only serves to highlight that person's relation of origin.

For example, while love is attributed to all three persons—for God is love—there is also a sense in which the Third Person is called love in a way that captures his personal property of spiration. Augustine says it best: "While in that supremely simple nature substance is not one thing and charity another, but substance is charity and charity is substance, whether in the Father or in the Son or in the Holy Spirit, yet all the same the Holy Spirit is distinctively named charity."[26] Or, as he says elsewhere, "If therefore any of these three can be distinctively named charity, which could it more suitably be than the Holy Spirit? What is meant is that while in that supremely simple nature substance is not one thing and charity another, but substance is charity and charity is substance, whether in the Father or in the Son or in the Holy Spirit, yet all the same the Holy Spirit is distinctively named charity."[27] And if the Holy Spirit is called charity, then the Spirit must be "the sweetness of the begetter and the begotten, who showers us with an immeasurable generosity and richness."[28]

Identifying love with the Spirit is a common scriptural maneuver. For example, consider Paul's letter to the Romans. Paul rejoices that we have been justified by faith and have "peace with God through our Lord Jesus Christ" (Rom. 5:1). But then Paul says something crazy and seemingly absurd: "Not only that, but we rejoice in our sufferings" (5:3). Rejoice in our sufferings? Suffering is hard, agonizing, and tortuous, so why would anyone rejoice in their pain? Because, says Paul, our "suffering produces endurance, and endurance produces character, and character produces hope, and hope does not put us to shame, because God's love has been poured into our hearts through the Holy Spirit who has been given to us" (5:4–5). The pouring out of love within us is the work of the Holy Spirit. By pouring out the love of God, the Spirit himself is poured into our hearts as well, indwelling us to make us holy.

So closely is the Spirit associated with love that elsewhere in Scripture we are taught that those who possess the Spirit, those indwelt with the Spirit, those who walk by the Spirit are those characterized by love. As Paul says, the fruit of the Spirit is love (Gal. 5:22). The Spirit is manifested whenever we love God and neighbor. Paul doesn't sound all that different from Luke. As we just saw, when Luke describes the Spirit falling on the Gentiles, he says the "gift" of the Spirit was "poured out" on them (Acts 10:45). Paul, too, loves the aquatic language of *pouring*: "God's love has been poured into our hearts through the Holy Spirit who has been given to us" (Rom. 5:5). Apparently, the Spirit as Gift and the Spirit as Love are not at all disconnected but are two ways of describing the Third Person of the Godhead. After all, *love is a gift*, and in the spirit of giving, this gift is one to be *received* (1 Cor. 2:12–16; 5:5; 1 Thess. 4:8).

But no one has more to say about love than the apostle John; it's a theme that permeates not only his Gospel but his first epistle. John issues a command to the church, one that sits at the core of Christianity: "Beloved, let us love one another, for love is from God, and whoever loves has been born of God and knows God." Then comes a warning: "Anyone who does not love does not know

All You Need Is Love?

Many social trinitarians appeal to love to push their redefinition of the Trinity as a society of relationships, each person his own center of consciousness and will. Love becomes an additional distinction, and no longer do eternal relations alone distinguish the persons. In the Great Tradition, however, love is appealed to as one among other scriptural metaphors to describe the eternal relations of origin. The fathers do not speak of love as another societal distinction but as further proof for subsisting relations.

God, because God is love" (1 John 4:7–8). Then John tells us the gospel story: the love of God was manifested when he sent his beloved Son to die and absorb the wrath that was ours (4:9–12). How then can we not love one another if we have been shown such sacrificial love (4:11)? While we cannot see God, in a sense we do see God whenever someone loves like God loves. For "if we love one another, God abides in us and his love is perfected in us. . . . God is love, and whoever abides in love abides in God, and God abides in him" (4:12, 16).

But how do we know, John, that we abide in him? Jesus's beloved disciple knows the answer from personal experience: "By this we know that we abide in him and he in us, because he has *given us of his Spirit*" (4:13). Like Paul, John is quick to tie love and gift together. Notice John's logic:

1. God is love.
2. Whoever abides in love abides in God.
3. We know we abide in him (in his love) because the Spirit abides in us and has been given to us.

In Johannine terms, how then can we not call the Spirit love? To abide in God's love is to abide in the Spirit, and to abide in the Spirit is to abide in God's love. As Augustine remarks, "It is God the Holy Spirit proceeding from God who fires man to the love of God and neighbor when he has been given to him, and he himself is love."[29]

The sending of the Spirit by the Father and the Son is the gift of love to us even when we were quite unlovely. Yet such love in the economy of salvation mirrors the infinite love within the Godhead. The Son is the only begotten Son, the one whom the Father loves, which means the Father is the Lover and the Son is his Beloved. The title itself is assumed when the Father speaks at Jesus's baptism, addressing his Son as his Beloved (Matt. 3:17; cf. 17:5). But as the only spirated person in the Godhead, the Spirit proceeds from the

Father and the Son as Love itself proceeds from the Lover and the Beloved. Augustine explains the analogy: "For I do not love love unless I love it loving something, because there is no love where nothing is being loved. So then there are three, the lover, and what is being loved, and love."[30] The analogy serves to accentuate the eternal procession of the Spirit from the Father and the Son.

Some would object that speaking of the Spirit or the entire Trinity in terms of love succumbs to Sabellianism, but that objection forgets what Sabellianism teaches. Sabellianism cannot describe the triune God in terms of love, because there is not a plurality of persons to love. For the Sabellian, Love has no Beloved, it has no Lover. Reducing persons to *roles* makes it impossible for the Sabellian to speak of love in a personal way, that is, by way of subsistence. Only orthodox trinitarianism can do justice to love as an analogy because it operates within an orthodox context that refuses to redefine the Trinity as a society or community, but instead insists that the Beloved, Lover, and Love are subsistences of the same divine essence, each subsistence having a unique personal property. What we have, then, is not Sabellianism, which strips the persons of their personhood, but one essence that subsists in three *personal* modes of existence or being. One biblical metaphor, among others, to capture those modes of existence is love.

The danger in referring to the Spirit as Love is to risk misunderstanding, as if the Love between the Lover and the Beloved is a mere quality, not a person (*hypostasis*). Augustine himself recognized this error, a point too often overlooked by his critics.[31] At the risk of stating the obvious, we speak by way of *analogy* when we call the Spirit Love, just as we did with Breath and Gift. We don't derive our doctrine of the Trinity from love, but the analogy of love is helpful as far as the triune God himself reveals his triunity in charity.[32] As far as the analogy is designed to go, it conveys eternal procession, and for that reason, the Spirit has been called the bond of love between the Lover and the Beloved.[33] "According to the holy scriptures," says Augustine, "this Holy Spirit is not just the Father's alone nor the Son's alone, but the Spirit of them both, and thus he suggests to us the common charity by which the Father and the Son love each other."[34]

Trading Cards While Hell Burns?

Unlike our friend Zipporah, whose faith in the Trinity seeks understanding the more she encounters Jesus, Lenù is a woman whose objections to the Holy Spirit, and the Trinity as a whole, are not pacified by the time Elena Ferrante finishes her novel *My Brilliant Friend*. When her religion professor criticizes the Communists for their nonreligious outlook on history and on life, Lenù will have none of it. With all the confidence of one who has finished a correspondence course in theology, Lenù raises her hand and protests: "The human condition was so obviously exposed to the blind fury of chance that to trust in a God, a Jesus, the Holy Spirit—this last a completely superfluous entity, it was there only to make up a trinity, notoriously nobler than the mere binomial father-son—was the same thing as collecting trading cards while the city burns in the fires of hell."[35]

Collecting trading cards while the city burns in the fires of hell—is that what theological discussions over the Spirit have become? Perhaps for some. But for others they are the very source of life itself. Without them, and without the eternal procession of the Spirit, the Trinity itself dissolves and we might as well join Lenù. As Anselm once lamented, if the Spirit's spiration "is not true, the Christian faith is destroyed."[36]

Is Anselm being extreme? Not in Lenù's estimation. And not in ours. For if the Spirit does not proceed, if he is not spirated from the Father and the Son's divine nature, then how can he give to us poor, needy, and helpless sinners all the benefits of salvation the Father has in store for us, all the riches of redemption the Son has purchased for us? As Herman Bavinck says, "If he is a creature he cannot in fact and in truth communicate to us the Father and the

Son with all their benefits; he cannot be the principle of the new life either in the individual Christian or in the church as a whole." The consequence of this sad reality is too heavy to bear, too devastating for the Christian life: "In that case, there is no genuine communion between God and humans; God remains above and outside of us and does not dwell in humanity as in his temple. . . . He who gives us God himself must himself be truly God."[37]

What Bavinck is trying to say is this: if the Spirit does not spirate from the Father and the Son's divine essence from all eternity, if he is not Breath, Gift, and Love, then the Father and the Son have no Spirit to give us, no Spirit to indwell us, no Spirit to sanctify us, and no Spirit to bring us into communion with the one who is simply Trinity.

Do Father, Son, and Spirit Work Inseparably?

Communion with the Indivisible Trinity

The Father does all things through
the Word in the Holy Spirit.

ATHANASIUS,
LETTER TO SERAPION

As we say that the operation of the Father, and of the Son,
and the Holy Spirit is one, so we say that the Godhead is one.

GREGORY OF NYSSA, *ON THE HOLY TRINITY*

As the Father and Son and Holy Spirit are
inseparable, so do they work inseparably.

AUGUSTINE, *THE TRINITY*

TO THE DELOREAN!

Where we're going: Inseparable operations

Key point: The Trinity performs a single operation because the persons subsist from a single essence and will. The external works of the Trinity are indivisible. Yet, a particular work may be appropriated by a person of the Trinity in a way that corresponds to that person's eternal relations of origin. Takeaway: Christians can, therefore, have communion with all three persons of the Trinity.

What Does Grace Have to Do with the Trinity?

Do you remember the first time you heard the doctrines of grace (aka, the five points of Calvinism)? Many meet the doctrines of grace like Jacob met God in Genesis 32, wrestling with each point until the sun rises. I understand why: these points are a shock to our default theological instinct, which is to hold on to human autonomy for dear life. Plus, we've been told that these points are the enemy; when we meet them, we are ready for a fight. For some, the doctrines of grace win in the end, and they have the limp to prove it.

My introduction to the doctrines of grace was different. Growing up, I never heard a word about the doctrines of grace. It was either not on my pastor's radar, or he was exceptional at keeping these doctrines off the radar. Regardless, he did one thing well: he preached through the whole Bible. Year after year, Sunday after Sunday, I was taught to wrestle with the text until it gave up its blessing. The outcome was ironic: when I met the doctrines of grace for the first time, I embraced these old doctrines like a long-lost brother, much like Esau hugging Jacob after years apart. The reason is simple, really: by taking my pastor seriously, reading the Bible cover to cover, I knew the doctrines of grace long before we were formally introduced. Meeting them in person only gave me a label to slap on what I had already learned from the Scriptures for so many years.

One passage of Scripture that proved instrumental was Ephesians 1. Paul has much to say about the sheer gratuity of predestination, but what influenced me just as much was Paul's sweeping view of the whole Christian life. God does not plan salvation and leave it up to us, hoping we will believe and persevere to the end. No, God's grace gives us every assurance that what he planned he will accomplish in us. He is that sovereign.

But as I read and reread Ephesians 1, I noticed something else, something I've never forgotten since: the sovereignty of God's grace in our salvation is *trinitarian* from start to finish. On further reflection, the Trinity is the reason grace is sovereign to begin with. So inseparable are Trinity and grace that Paul cannot describe our salvation without referring to all three persons of the Trinity. When I read Ephesians 1 in the past, it was the sovereignty of God's saving plan that stuck out. But when I reread Paul's words, Father, Son, and Holy Spirit popped out with prominent repetition.

For example, Paul says it is "God the Father" who has "blessed us in Christ" and "chose us in him [Christ]" before the world was created (1:3–4). We are elected by the Father and chosen in his Son. Next, Paul grounds our adoption in time and space in our eternal predestination. But he does not do so apart from the Trinity: God the Father "predestined us for adoption to himself as sons through Jesus Christ" (1:5). Yet not only does God the Father elect us in his Son from all eternity, he then sends his Son to die for his elect

The Christian Life: Incurably Trinitarian

Paul was incurably trinitarian whenever he wrote about our salvation or the Christian life. For example, he says to the Thessalonians, "But we ought always to give thanks to God for you, brothers beloved by the Lord, because God chose you as the firstfruits to be saved, through sanctification by the Spirit and belief in the truth. To this he called you through our gospel, so that you may obtain the glory of our Lord Jesus Christ" (2 Thess. 2:13–14).

in history. That's why Paul says in the verses that follow that it is "in him" [Christ] that "we have redemption through his blood, the forgiveness of our trespasses" (1:7). Far from ad hoc, the Trinity planned Christ's death from the beginning.

What about the Spirit? Has the Third Person of the Trinity been left out? Not on Paul's watch. What the Father planned and the Son accomplished, the Spirit has applied. Think of the moment you first heard about Christ. Was it not the Spirit who sealed you? "In him you also, when you heard the word of truth, the gospel of your salvation, and believed in him, were sealed with the promised Holy Spirit, who is the guarantee of our inheritance until we acquire possession of it, to the praise of his glory" (1:13–14). The Spirit is our assurance, the down payment until we secure in full that inheritance predestined for us from eternity.

When my eyes were opened to the trinitarian DNA of the doctrines of grace, I wondered, does the work of salvation say something important about the unity and plurality within the Trinity? Or perhaps we might ask the question this way,

> Q: Does the nature of redemption reflect the one who is simply Trinity?

The answer brings our study full circle.

Does God Act as One or as Three? Inseparable Operations

The correlation between who God is and what God does raises a difficult question: *Does God act as one or as three?* At first glance it might seem as if Father, Son, and Spirit act as three separate, independent persons. Some have said as much, assuming that each person in the Trinity must have his own will, totaling three separate wills in the Godhead. But as we saw in chapters 3 and 8, this is a move with catastrophic consequences. No longer is there one God who is three persons, each person being a subsistence of the one, undivided essence. Now there are three separate centers of consciousness and three separate wills, and the simple essence of God is divided as a result. This is the fallout of social trinitarianism, and we've witnessed its collateral damage for over a century now.

In contrast, chapter 5 argued that will is not tied to *person* but to *essence* (nature). Since God has one essence, he has one will. He must if he has any hope of remaining undivided and unified in his own being. His one essence and will subsists in three persons; those three persons remain undivided due to the one, single essence and will they have in common. That is why we call our God *simply* Trinity, protecting both simplicity in substance and Trinity in subsistence. Triunity is what we're after.

The unity we just highlighted has real implications for how God acts. It is because our triune God is one that he acts as one. Or better said, his action *is* one. His internal simplicity is exhibited in all the triune God's external actions toward the world. There is a famous Latin phrase that captures this priceless trinitarian point: *opera Trinitatis ad extra indivisa sunt.* What does it mean? It means that the external works of the Trinity are undivided. Now why is that?

The three persons are undivided in their *external* works because they are undivided in their *internal* nature. As Augustine said, "The Father, and the Son, and the Holy Ghost are inseparably united in themselves" since "this Trinity is one God," and therefore "all the works of the one God are the works of the Father, of the Son, and of the Holy Ghost."[1] So, whenever we refer to the triune God's action toward the world, we must recognize that it is an indivisible, singular action, as indivisible as the one, single essence the persons share in common. Likewise, whenever we refer to the triune God's essence, we recognize that it is an indivisible essence, as indivisible as the one, singular action the three persons perform.[2]

To clarify, the unity between Father, Son, and Spirit is *not merely a cooperation* between three separate persons. Again, that assumes each person has his own, individual will (three wills in God). That type of cooperation may give the appearance of unity, but it is not the unity of a triune God who is one in *essence*; mere cooperation does not result in a God who is *simply* Trinity. Instead, we are left with three gods who get along with one another, each deciding he will cooperate with the other two. In this view, there are three actions, all different but nonetheless synchronized with one another. The Trinity is like a society or community. There may be a unity of wills but not a unity of being (which would require one will). But defining the Trinity in social categories cannot avoid tritheism, and it certainly is vulnerable to subordinationism, one person's will being the superior will in the Godhead. All that to say, mere compliance is not enough.

Nor is this unity accomplished by a division of labor, as if there is one work to accomplish and that one work is divvied up among the three persons. In this scheme, distribution and allocation result in unity once the work is successfully finished. The triune God never acts as one because Father, Son, and Spirit perform *one single act*. Instead, works are divvied up among the Godhead or a single work is portioned out among the persons. In this scheme, says Augustine, the Trinity "does not work inseparably, but the Father does some things, the Son others and the Holy Spirit yet others." But "if they do some things together and some without each other," then the Trinity "is no longer inseparable."[3]

Both of these options—mere cooperation or division of labor—are insufficient and riddled with heretical tendencies. When we talk about the unity or simplicity of God—the one who is *simple* or *simply* Trinity—we mean something far more intrinsic to the very being of our triune God himself. When we say God acts as one, we assume he *is* one. Since his very nature or essence is one, he *acts* as one, not merely cooperating but performing a single act that accords with the triune God's single will. Yes, there are three persons, but since it is the same divine essence subsisting in each, these three persons always perform the same act. "The three persons act together not by the juxtaposition or the superimposition of three different actions, but *in one same action*, because the three persons act by the same power and in virtue of their *one divine nature.*"[4]

I cannot emphasize this enough: *one and the same action, one and the same divine nature.* The three act as one because they are one; they act "in virtue" of the one nature they hold in common. In theology, this unity-in-act is called inseparable operations. The three persons are without separation or division in their external operations toward the world, whether they be creation, providence, or redemption. Every operation is *from* the Father, *through* the Son, *in* the Spirit.[5]

Few captured this triunity better than the Cappadocian father Gregory of Nyssa. "We are not to think of the Father as ever parted from the Son, nor to look for the Son as separate from the Holy Spirit. As it is impossible to mount to the Father, unless our thoughts are exalted thither through the Son, so it is impossible also to say that Jesus is Lord except by the Holy Spirit." Gregory concludes, "Therefore, Father, Son, and Holy Spirit are to be known only in a perfect Trinity, in closest consequence and union with each other, before all creation, before all the ages, before anything whatever of which we can form an idea. The Father is always Father, and in Him the Son, and with the Son the Holy Spirit." In short, "these Persons . . . are inseparate from each other."[6] If the persons are inseparable, a perfect Trinity, each person in union with each other person and from all eternity, then it is no wonder we cannot think of the three without contemplating their unity nor contemplate their unity without thinking of the three. As another Cappadocian, Gregory of Nazianzus, said, "No sooner do I conceive of the One than I am illumined by the Splendour of the Three; no sooner do I distinguish Them than I am carried back to the One."[7]

Consider two examples of this triunity in action: the incarnation and Pentecost.

No Lone Ranger Trinity

Our triune God is indivisible in the incarnation of the Son. That may sound counterintuitive. It is the Son, after all, who is incarnate, not the Father or the Spirit. True. But notice, the incarnation is not the Son gone solo. The incarnation may be the incarnation of the Son, but the miracle of the incarnation is wrought by Father, Son, and Spirit alike. As Augustine explains, "Let him therefore understand the incarnation and the virgin birth in the same way, as *indivisibly wrought* by one and the same working of Father and Son, not leaving out, of course, the Holy Spirit, of whom it is said in so many words that *she was found to be with child of the Holy Spirit* (Mt 1:18)."[8]

Is this not what we witness in John 5? As we saw in chapter 7, our good friend Zipporah witnessed the religious leaders question Jesus after he healed a man on the Sabbath. Jesus's reply was so infuriating that they wanted to kill him: "My Father is working until now, and I am working" (5:17). Only God has the prerogative to keep working on the Sabbath. As Creator of the cosmos, he alone can "work" or sustain the cosmos on the seventh day. But here Jesus claims that same right. He can do so only if he is one with the Father. Inseparable and indivisible, he and the Father are at work together to sustain and renew the created order on the Sabbath, which is exactly what Jesus is doing by healing a lame man.

Aware that the Jews want to kill him for "calling God his own Father, making himself equal with God" (5:18), Jesus then adds,

Truly, truly I say to you, the Son can do nothing of his own accord, but only what he sees the Father doing. For whatever the Father does, that the Son does likewise. For the Father loves the Son and shows him all that he himself is doing. . . . For as the Father raises the dead and gives them life, so also the Son gives life to whom he will. For the Father judges no one, but has given all judgment to the Son, that all may honor the Son, just as they honor the Father.

Whoever does not honor the Son does not honor the Father who sent him. (5:19–23)

Whatever the Father does . . . the Son does likewise. Whatever the Father creates, the Son creates; whatever the Father sustains, the Son sustains; whatever the Father heals, the Son heals; whoever the Father raises to life, the Son raises to life. Even when we respond to the Father and the Son, such an inseparability is seen. To honor the Father is to honor the Son, and to honor the Son is to honor the Father. Jesus even says he is to be honored "just as they honor the Father" (5:23). This is why the Father has given all judgment over to him (5:22).

Only if Jesus is inseparable from the Father, indivisible in essence with the Father, can he make such a claim. That inseparability is not undermined by eternal generation but is all the more buttressed. For only if the Son is eternally begotten from the Father's essence, the Father granting the Son life in himself (John 5:26), can Jesus claim that he is one with God, that the actions his Father is doing he also is doing, and that the honor his Father is receiving he also is receiving.

Not only is our triune God indivisible in the incarnation, but our triune God is indivisible in the descent of the Holy Spirit as well. Whenever we witness the Spirit in Scripture, whether he is descending on the disciples at Pentecost or indwelling the assembly of believers in the book of Acts, it is not as if the Spirit has gone solo, nor as if the Spirit is merely cooperating with the Father and the Son. Whatever the Spirit does or accomplishes, the triune God does or accomplishes.

For example, consider our sanctification. Paul can say that Christ himself is our sanctification (1 Cor. 1:2, 30) and pray that the "God of peace himself sanctify you completely" (1 Thess. 5:23), and Peter can rejoice that God's elect are secure "in the sanctification of the Spirit" (1 Pet. 1:2).[9] "In all things," says Basil of Caesarea, "the Holy Spirit is inseparable and wholly incapable of being parted from the Father and the Son. . . . In every operation the Spirit is closely conjoined with, and inseparable from, the Father and the Son."[10] *Conjoined with. Inseparable from.* This is the language we are after, for phrases like these protect the simplicity of our triune God, guarding us from tritheism and subordinationism alike. They ensure that our triune God acts as one because he is, by nature, one. He is simply Trinity.

Furthermore, apart from inseparable operations, we risk the heresy of inequality, and that is a risk too big to take. For example, inseparable operations assume not only that the triune God is one in nature and will but that each person of the Godhead is equal to every other person in the Godhead. For there to be an inseparable operation there cannot be inferiority in deity, power, or honor.

But it's not just subordinationism that is precluded; tritheism is as well, the other hurdle social trinitarianism struggles to overcome. For if the Trinity works inseparably, then there can only be one will in God. If there are three wills in God, then the three persons no longer hold the one essence in common, each a subsistence of the selfsame divine nature. Instead, each person's will is separate from the others, creating three centers of consciousness. As a result, no longer is there one, undivided, simple essence in which the three persons subsist. But if the Trinity acts inseparably because the persons are inseparable by nature, then we have not three gods merely cooperating with one another but one God who performs one and the same action as Father, Son, and Spirit.

But what about Sabellianism? Some assume that an inseparable operation succumbs to Sabellianism: if the three persons act as one by virtue of their common nature and common will, then they can no longer be three distinct persons. However, such an accusation fails to consider that an inseparable operation may be distinctly *appropriated* by Father, Son, and Spirit alike, yet in a way that is consistent with their personal properties or eternal relations of origin. "On the one hand, the work of the Father, Son and Holy Spirit is inseparably the work of the three *ad extra*. On the other hand, in this single act, the divine persons work according to their personal properties *ad intra*."[11]

Let's consider how divine appropriation works according to each person's personal properties.

Divine Appropriations

The word "appropriation" can be traced back to the Latin: *ad* and *proprium*, meaning "to draw toward the proper" and "to put nearer to the proper."[12] The word "appropriation" has been used by theologians to explain how the Scriptures can speak of a particular person of the Trinity whenever an act of the triune God is in focus. Appropriation "attributes an action or an effect to a divine person in a *special way*, without excluding the two others."[13] That qualification—"without excluding the two others"—is important lest we divide up the Trinity and compromise its singularity, its unity, its simplicity. For as we learned, the external works of the Trinity are always undivided. Appropriation does not undermine inseparability but reinforces it in every way.

The purpose of appropriation is to mimic Scripture, which can shine its spotlight on one person in a "special" way, though never to the exclusion of the other two.[14] Think of it this way: while every act of God in creation, providence, and redemption is the *single* act of the *triune* God, nevertheless, certain acts may terminate on certain persons, or be "appropriated" by one particular person of the Trinity in a special manner. While it is always the one, undivided God acting according to his one, undivided will, attention may be given to a certain person of the Godhead, but always in accordance with each person's eternal relation: the Father unbegotten, the Son begotten, and the Spirit spirated. "All things," says Herman Bavinck, "proceed from the Father, are accomplished by the Son, and are completed in the Holy Spirit."[15]

To reiterate, no single person of the Godhead goes off on his own, solo. To say so is to tempt tritheism, as if each person is out doing his own thing as his own agent. Nor are we saying that one person acts *more* than the others, as if the others are more passive while one person is more active; the Trinity is not mathematics, adding and subtracting one person to make more of another person.[16] To say so is to tempt Sabellianism, as if only one person can act at a time, or subordinationism, as if one person must become less so that another person can be greater (e.g., EFS). Rather, we are merely recognizing that in any single act of the triune God toward his creation, each person receives attention in a way that *corresponds* to each person's distinct, incommunicable, and eternal relation of origin: unbegotten Father, begotten Son, spirated Spirit.[17] That which is appropriated to each person is consistent with the personal properties: paternity, filiation, and spiration.

What we are saying is anything but novel. Both a patristic like Gregory of Nyssa and a reformer like John Calvin exemplify such a biblical nuance, as the following chart visualizes:

How Appropriate: Gregory of Nyssa and John Calvin

Person	Appropriation	Corresponding eternal relation
Father	"Beginning of activity"; "fountain and wellspring of all things" (Calvin)	Because the Father is unbegotten in eternity
	Every work has its "beginning from the Father" (Gregory)	
Son	Father's "wisdom, counsel, and the ordered disposition of all things" (Calvin)	Because the Son is begotten by the Father in eternity
	Every work is "advancing through the Son" (Gregory)	
Holy Spirit	Father and Son's "power and efficacy" (Calvin)	Because the Spirit is spirated by the Father and Son in eternity
	Every work is "completed in the Holy Spirit" (Gregory)	

For example, according to Gregory of Nyssa, when we look at creation we must recognize that it has its "beginning from the Father, advancing through the Son" and is "completed in the Holy Spirit."[18] Then comes one of Gregory's most priceless statements: "Every operation which extends from God to the Creation . . . has its origin from the Father, and proceeds through the Son, and is perfected in the Holy Spirit."[19]

As the unbegotten one, the principle without a principle in the Godhead, the Father is the "beginning" and "fountain" of all operations. As the only begotten, the Son is the Father's "wisdom," the one through whom all things are ordered. As the one who is spirated, the Spirit is the Father and the Son's power to accomplish all things, the very efficacy of the Father and Son to bring to fruition that which was planned. Spirated—or breathed out—by the Father and the Son, it only makes sense that it is the Spirit who is the "immediate agent of divine works" and the one "through whom the Father and Son immediately influence the hearts of the elect."[20]

Whenever the triune God acts, he acts as one, for he is one in essence, each person a subsistence of the same divine essence. For "just as there is a single divine essence, there is a single *ad extra* divine work."[21] Or, as Gregory of Nyssa says with such eloquence, if "the operation of the Father, the Son, and the Holy Spirit is one," then the "oneness of their nature" must be "inferred from the identity of their operation."[22] At the same time, we can make distinctions in the works of God that match the persons of God, and all because we can distinguish between personal properties in God. "Just as there are three persons or modes of subsistence in the Godhead, each distinguished by personal properties and a specific operation, there are also three modes of working in the single *ad extra* divine work."[23] How God acts toward the world (*ad extra*) mirrors who he is in himself (*ad intra*), and that rule of thumb applies not only to his united essence but his distinct ordering in personhood.[24] The order of operations in history reflects the order of relations in eternity. Or, as Turretin says, "The order of operating follows the order of subsisting."[25]

This order (e.g., Father begins, Son executes, Spirit perfects) does not introduce time into the essence of God, as if there is a before and after for God. If it did, then one person would be superior to another. For that reason, it is best to avoid the term "degree," which might communicate that one person is inferior to another. By contrast, the word "order" communicates how the persons are distinguished by their eternal relations of origin, all the while being coequal and coeternal.[26] And this order is then extended in the triune God's operations toward the world. "[The] Father is thought of as first, then from him the Son, and finally from both the Spirit," says Calvin. That order is far from "meaningless or superfluous," but reflects who the triune God is in and of himself.[27]

To see this order with a clearer lens, we need to consider what divine appropriations look like from ten thousand feet, like a helicopter flying over the Amazon, and from the vantage point of the pilgrim on the ground, taking photos of one exotic tree at a time.

Triune Appropriations from Ten Thousand Feet: The Forest

Creation

Creation is one act of the triune God. It's not as if only the Father creates while the Son and Spirit are left aside. Father, Son, and Spirit together will to create the cosmos, and they do so as the one, undivided God of the cosmos. For example, Scripture says God created the heavens and the earth (Gen. 1:1), and the Spirit of God hovered over the waters (1:2). The Creator Spirit appears on the lips of the psalmist as well: "By the word of the Lord the heavens were made, and by the breath of his mouth all their host" (Ps. 33:6). But notice, the psalmist also mentions the word of the Lord. That word, it turns out, is not just letters but

Creation: Basil of Caesarea

Original cause	Father
Creative cause	Son
Perfecting cause	Holy Spirit

the Son of God himself. Describing this Word, John says, "He was in the beginning with God. All things were made through him, and without him was not any thing made that was made" (John 1:2–3; cf. Col. 1:15–16).

Yet, consistent with their personal properties, we can also distinguish between the three persons as we observe creation's cause. As Basil says, it is the Father who is the "original cause," the Son who is the "creative cause," and the Spirit who is the "perfecting cause." Creation is brought into existence "by the will of the Father" and "by the operation of the Son" and is "perfected by the presence of the Spirit."[28]

The triune God creates the world, yet creation occurs according to each person in kind. Reflecting on Psalm 33:6, Basil clarifies that the Word is not a mere "impression on the air, borne by the organs of speech." John 1:1 teaches us that the "Word is He who 'was with God in the beginning' and 'was God.'" Nor "is the Spirit of His mouth a vapour, emitted by the organs of respiration." John 15:26 instructs us that the Spirit of his mouth is "the Spirit of truth which proceedeth from the Father."[29]

But Basil specifies further that each work of the Godhead is appropriated in distinct ways. For not only are Bible readers meant to "perceive three," but we do so recognizing that it is "the Lord who gives the order, the Word who creates, and the Spirit who confirms."[30] *Gives, creates, confirms*—here is Basil's way of appropriating creation to each person of the Trinity and at the same time recognizing that creation is the single act of the triune God.[31]

Does that order mean the persons are not equal with one another? That reminds me of a church service in the fourth century.

Basil's offensive prayer in church. One Sunday, Basil was tasked with saying the prayers. And so he did, giving glory "to the Father *with* [*meta*] the Son *together with* [*syn*] the Holy Spirit." The next Sunday he came back to church and was tasked with praying again. And so he did, this time giving glory "to the Father *through* [*dia*] the Son *in* [*en*] the Holy Spirit."[32]

"Aha!" the Arians protested when they heard Basil pray that second Sunday. "We knew it. You are one of us after all. You assume inequality in your prayers when you order the three persons, beginning with the Father, then the Son, then the Spirit." How did Basil respond?

Basil gave a confident smile (or at least I like to think he did) and said: "You foolish Arians. Have you forgotten your grammar lessons from elementary school? The 'inequality' of the *prepositions* does not prove the inequality of the *persons* but . . . points to a specific order in their existence and activity. The Father is 'the initiating cause'; the Son 'the operating cause'; the Spirit 'the perfecting cause.'"[33] The Arians had assumed that the appropriations—Father initiates, Son operates, Spirit perfects—presupposed the inferiority of the Son and Spirit to the Father. But in reality, these appropriations only underline what alone distinguishes the persons in eternity: eternal relations of origin, the Father unbegotten, the Son begotten, the Spirit spirated.

The Father's two hands. Basil was not the only one with such insight. The second-century father Irenaeus of Lyons, in his book *Against Heresies*, says that the Son and the Spirit are the two hands of the Father in creation. Countering the claim that God needed angels to help him create the world, Irenaeus says, "For God did not stand in need of these beings . . . as if he did not possess his own hands. For with him were always present the Word and Wisdom, the Son and the Spirit by whom and in whom, freely, he made all things."[34] Irenaeus believes these "hands" are insinuated when the plural is used in the creation account, for God says, "Let *us* make man after *our* image and likeness" (Gen. 1:26).[35]

Irenaeus in no way intends to sacrifice the unity or the equality of the three persons, as if being one of the Father's hands results in inferiority. That assumption misses Irenaeus's point. Irenaeus intends not to undermine but to underline the unity of the Trinity in the work of creation. Let's be sure to read Irenaeus in context: "Irenaeus rejects the gnostic idea according to which the corporeal world came forth from a reality inferior to God."[36] To Irenaeus's point, God does not depend on angels or lesser deities, because all three persons of the Trinity are indivisible in the work of creation. Otherwise Irenaeus could not refer to the Son and the Spirit as the hands of the Father. Like Basil's creative cause (Son) and perfecting cause (Spirit), Irenaeus's "two hands" confirms unity and equality in the Trinity as well as the personal distinctions that reveal themselves in a work like creation.[37] Can something similar be said about salvation?

Cross-pollination and the new creation. Many of the fathers and Reformed thinkers cross-pollinate between creation and salvation, appropriating creation to the Father, redemption to the Son, and sanctification to the Spirit. The layout of the Nicene Creed is a case in point, beginning with its affirmation of God the Father, the "creator of heaven and earth, of all things visible and invisible." Then it transitions to the only begotten Son who "for us men and because of our salvation came down from heaven, and was incarnate by the Holy Spirit and the Virgin Mary and became human." The uncreated but only begotton and eternal Son was born in a manger to redeem creation so that the Spirit, the one who eternally "proceeds from the Father [and the Son]," might descend as the "Lord and life-giver," breathing new life into those still in the throes of death. By the Spirit we become a new creation, remade and reborn into the image of the Son.

That cross-pollination between creation and salvation might seem odd at first. Yet, if we understand salvation in its broadest

Re-creation: Nicene Creed to the Reformation	
Creation	Father
Redemption (creation redeemed)	Son
Sanctification (re-creation)[38]	Holy Spirit

sense as *re-creation*, then our focus is not so much on two different domains (creation and salvation) but on a single domain: creation and re-creation. As Bavinck says, "Although it is true that all the external works of God [*opera Dei ad extra*] are undivided and inseparable, in creation and re-creation one can nevertheless observe an economy that gives us the right to speak of the Father and our creation, the Son and our redemption, the Spirit and our sanctification."[39] If not, the gospel and our union with Christ— even Christianity itself—is left unfinished. "The essence of the Christian religion consists in this, that the creation of the Father, ruined by sin, is restored in the death of the Son of God, and re-created by the grace of the Holy Spirit into a kingdom of God."[40] On the one hand, creation, redemption, and sanctification are the single work of the whole Trinity. On the other hand, each of these works may be appropriated to distinct persons, corresponding to their eternal relations of origin.[41]

To see these appropriations in full color, not just black and white, let's not keep moving back and forth between creation and re-creation but focus on salvation in particular.

Salvation

If Basil (and let's not forget Irenaeus) tutored us in creation, Augustine is our professor in salvation. He was, after all, called the Doctor of Grace. Looking to Scripture, Augustine says the Father is the *author* of salvation (predestination), the Son its *redeemer* (atonement), and the Spirit its *sanctifier* (sanctification).[42]

Or we could say the Father is the *Source* of our salvation, the Son the *Redeemer* of our salvation, and the Spirit the *Comforter*

Salvation: Augustine	
Author/Architect of our salvation	Father
Redeemer of our salvation	Son
Sanctifier of our salvation	Holy Spirit

of our salvation. We saw this much in Ephesians 1, where Paul says redemption is accomplished by the Son and applied by the Spirit, both of which correspond to the Son and Spirit's eternal relations of origin. This is a habit of Paul that keeps resurfacing throughout his epistles. For example, consider how Paul interweaves all three persons of the Godhead in his second letter to the Thessalonians: "But we ought always to give thanks to God for you, brothers beloved by the Lord, because *God [Author] chose you* as the first-fruits to be saved, through *sanctification by the Spirit [Sanctifier]* and belief in the truth. To this he called you through our *gospel*, so that you may obtain the glory of our *Lord Jesus Christ [Redeemer]*" (2 Thess. 2:13–14). We would be wise to imitate this Pauline habit as we move from relations to appropriations.[43]

When Paul, in Ephesians 1 and 2 Thessalonians 2, takes us back to eternity to reassure believers that their salvation was predestined in eternity by none other than the triune God himself, he assumes what theologians have called *the covenant of redemption* or the *pactum salutis*. Unlike many other covenants in the Bible that are between God and his people (Abraham, Moses, etc.), the covenant of redemption is between the persons of the Trinity. In other words, it is intratrinitarian, and since our triune God is timelessly eternal, so too must be the covenant of redemption.

What occurs in this intratrinitarian covenant? The Son enters into a covenant with the Father to be Mediator of God's people. The Son brings the covenant to fruition by means of his incarnation. Hence it is the covenant of *redemption*, the Son, our covenant surety, fulfilling the covenant by redeeming sinners by his own blood (Eph. 1:7). Far from some cold contract, the Son voluntarily accepts the stipulations of the covenant out of his love for the Father. John Owen says the covenant of redemption is that "compact, covenant, convention, or agreement, that was between the Father and the Son, for the accomplishment of the work of our redemption by the mediation of Christ, to the praise of the glorious grace of God." The Son is appointed to be the "head, husband, deliver[er], and redeemer of his elect, his church, his people, whom he did foreknow," the Son "freely undertaking that work and all that was required thereunto."[44]

Theologians have found support for this covenant across both testaments (Ps. 2:7; 110:1; Zech. 6:13), and it is insinuated whenever the New Testament refers to our election in Christ from all eternity (Eph. 1; 2 Tim. 1:9–10).[45] But it is most conspicuous in the words of Jesus whenever he says he has left the glory he had with the Father in heaven and has been sent by the Father to fulfill the mission the Father has given to him before the creation of the cosmos (Mark 12:1–12; Luke 22:29; John 4:34; 5:30, 43; 6:38–40; 17:4–23).[46] Other New Testament authors also assume this covenant of redemption when they go back into eternity to say that the Father has sent his Son to become incarnate for the sake of our redemption (Gal. 4:4; Heb. 10:5–10; 1 Pet. 1:20). While there has never been a time when

What Is the Covenant of Redemption?

The covenant of redemption is a fundamental pillar of Reformed orthodoxy. As Richard Muller explains, it is a "pretemporal, intra-trinitarian agreement of the Father and the Son concerning the covenant of grace and its ratification in and through the work of the Son incarnate. In the unity of the Godhead, the Son covenants with the Father to be the temporal sponsor of the Father's *testamentum* in and through the work of the Mediator" (Muller, *Dictionary*, 252, s.v. "pactum salutis"). For a robust explanation, read one of the players on our Dream Team, such as Francis Turretin, especially vol. 1 of his *Institutes of Elenctic Theology*.

the Son was not Son, he becomes our Savior in history because he was appointed to be our Redeemer from eternity. Such an appointment did not originate in the cradle nor was it prolonged until the cross, but it was established in the crown of heaven as the Father commissioned his Son by means of a covenant. Appointed to be our Messiah, he became our prophet (Acts 3:22–26), priest (Heb. 5:5–6), and king (Acts 2:34–36), just as the Father intended from the beginning.[47] As our Mediator, it is his blood that cuts the new covenant, bringing to fulfillment the covenant he made with the Father from all eternity (Matt. 26:28). Yet the one who spills his blood to ratify the covenant is not just anyone, but our eternal high priest, whose priesthood was sealed with an oath. By means of his immutable character, God himself swears to his begotten Son, "You are a priest forever" (Heb. 7:21; cf. Ps. 110:4).

The covenant of redemption is spectacular because it puts our redemption within its organic, trinitarian context. But it's also informative because it accentuates divine appropriations: the Father being the *Source* of our salvation, the Son the *Redeemer* of our salvation, and the Spirit the *Comforter* of our salvation. That's right, the Spirit too. For not only does the Son covenant with the Father to be our Mediator, our surety, but so too does the Spirit covenant in eternity to apply that which the Son purchases (our eternal salvation) to those whom the Father predestined (again, see Eph. 1:4–5, 11). For that reason, the Spirit is called the seal of our redemption (Eph. 1:13), for he is sent by the Father and the Son to perfect our redemption, the guarantee in the here and now that one day we will receive this great inheritance our triune God has secured and saved for us (Eph. 1:14; cf. John 14:25; 15:26; 16:7).

Some, however, object to the covenant of redemption: an intratrinitarian covenant must involve multiple wills in the Godhead, which violates divine simplicity.[48] Funny thing is, whenever the Reformed tradition, drawing on the Great Tradition, put forward the covenant of redemption, they never believed it violated the one will or essence of our triune God.[49] Why is that? Appropriations.

Way back in the seventeenth century, the puritan John Owen anticipated this objection. On the one hand, there is but one single action by the triune God consistent with the one, undivided will of the triune God. He is, after all, *simply* Trinity; every act occurs in accordance with his simple essence. No matter which person we are referring to, they all have the one will in common just as they all have the one essence in common. After all, the will is, as Owen says, "an essential property of his nature."[50] Owen is following the Nicene fathers. As Basil of Caesarea said, will is "concurrent with substance," and "is not only similar and equal, but also identical" in all three persons.[51]

On the other hand, the one, inseparable essence and will has three modes of subsistence: the Father as unbegotten, the Son as begotten, and the Spirit as spirated. As we saw in chapter 5, the

The Prince of Puritans

The seventeenth century theologian John Owen, whom many call the Prince of Puritans, is remembered today for his colossal intellect. And for good reason too. Few theologians, even during the age of the Puritans (seventeenth century), could compare to Owen's theological acumen. But did you know that this larger-than-life theologian was first a pastor? As a young man, Owen went to work, laboring to prepare sermons for the sheep God had entrusted to his care. But then he noticed something troubling: few in his congregation knew the gospel. As a remedy, Owen wrote a catechism for adults and another one for children, both of which taught his people about the person and work of Christ. Owen went on to write some of the most important books in Christian history. *Communion with God* is one of them. Not only does Owen retrieve a biblical, orthodox doctrine of the Trinity, but he encourages the Christian to enjoy fellowship with each person of the Trinity. Rather than manipulating the Trinity to somehow make the Trinity relevant, Owen says the Christian life is designed to contemplate the Trinity in all its mystery.

divine essence has three modes of subsistence, each person a subsistence of the one, simple essence. And each person subsists in a way that is distinct and incommunicable: the Father alone is unbegotten, the Son alone is begotten, and the Spirit alone is spirated.

Corresponding with these three modes of subsistence or eternal relations of origin, every work of redemption is simultaneously the single, one work of the Trinity and yet may be *appropriated* in a way that is consistent with each person's eternal relation. That is not to create three wills where there is but one will. Rather, to borrow Owen's vocabulary, there are "distinct application[s] of the same will," and these distinct applications correspond to the "distinct acts in the persons." Gilles Emery, one of today's best trinitarian theologians, says it this way: "Just as each divine person is characterized by a distinct mode of existence, each person possesses likewise a distinct mode of action."[52]

To create the covenant of redemption, the persons do not need separate wills—that would undermine not only divine simplicity but the unity intrinsic to the covenant itself. To enter into this eternal covenant, the persons appropriate their distinct application of the one same will in a way consistent with their personal mode of subsistence. By doing so, they only covenant in a way that corresponds to their eternal relations. The Father is unbegotten, so it is fitting that the Father be the one to appoint the Son as our covenant surety. The Son is begotten by the Father, so it is fitting that the Son be the Mediator, the Redeemer, of our salvation. The Spirit is spirated by the Father and the Son, so it is appropriate that the Spirit covenants to perfect that which the Father has predestined and the Son has accomplished. But again, they do not need three wills to do so, but one and the same will with distinct appropriations corresponding to each person's personal property.

Owen advises, then, that when we zero in on a specific person in the covenant of redemption, we not assume there is another will. Rather, we are witnessing distinct appropriations of the one will, or as Owen says, a "new habitude" that the person has "freely taken on" for the sake of our redemption.[53] In short, there is one will in the Trinity, and yet, when we travel through the land of the economy with divine appropriations as our guide, there is a "threefold execution" of that one will that matches each person's eternal relation of origin.[54]

Granted, the mystery remains. As it should. But notice, this mystery must be fenced by orthodoxy. The covenant of redemption is not an intruder in the camp of orthodoxy but a historic, even biblical, citizen. Properly understood, the covenant of redemption does not violate the one, simple will of our triune God, but shows us how the eternal relations of origin, which alone distinguish the persons, extend themselves, corresponding to each person's appropriation of that one will in the many layers of redemption. For each person acts not only "*in virtue of the common nature,*" but "*according to the mode of his personal property.*"[55] The covenant of redemption is but one example among many that displays how the personal properties manifest themselves in the mystery of the gospel.

Triune Appropriations on the Ground: The Trees

Not just the grand notions of creation and salvation but specific acts of God, acts that are attributed to the entire Godhead, can also be appropriated to specific persons. But to see this, we will need to ask our helicopter pilot to descend real low and drop a ladder so we can walk among the trees of the forest.

For example, consider a specific aspect of our salvation, such as our spiritual *adoption* into the family of God. On the one hand, adoption is credited to all three persons of the Trinity. It's not as if the Father adopts but the Son and Spirit do not. No, adoption is the one (singular) divine act of our triune God. We are adopted by the Father, through the Son, by the Holy Spirit. Adoption is "common to the whole Trinity," says Aquinas.[56]

Adoption: Thomas Aquinas

Author of adoption	Father
Model of adoption	Son
Imprint of adoption	Holy Spirit

At the same time, adoption may be appropriated to specific persons. Adoption, says Aquinas, is (1) "appropriated to the Father as its *Author*," (2) "to the Son, as its *Model*," and (3) "to the Holy Spirit as *imprinting in us the likeness of this Model*."[57]

That last one is a bit verbose—this is Aquinas we're quoting after all. Perhaps we could put it this way: while the Father is the *author* of our adoption, and the Son its *model*, it is the Holy Spirit who is its *imprint*.

Yet each appropriation is also consistent with each person's eternal relation of origin. Whether it's the Father, the Son, or the Holy Spirit, each corresponds to their distinct personal properties.[58] So consider adoption again. As the unbegotten person of the Godhead, the Father is the author and architect, the one who predestined us for adoption to himself as sons (Eph. 1:5) and who declares us to be his children upon faith in his Son. As John says, "All who did receive him [Christ], who believed in his name, he gave the right to become children of God" (John 1:12).

Since adoption is filial, a family metaphor, the only begotten Son himself, to use the wording of Aquinas, becomes the Model as to what our filiation looks like.[59] After all, it is the Son, not the Father or the Spirit, who is begotten, even though his generation is eternal and ours is temporal (a difference that guards us from the heresy of adoptionism).[60] United to Christ, we enjoy all the benefits that come with being children of God, including sonship, which is why Calvin says, "It would be the folly and madness of presumption, to call God our Father, except on the ground that, through our union to the body of Christ, we are acknowledged as his children."[61] Reformed confessions and catechisms reiterate Calvin's point. For example, the Heidelberg Catechism asks,

> Why is He called God's "only begotten Son," since we also are the children of God?

> Because Christ alone is the eternal, natural Son of God (John 1:14, 18), but we are children of God by adoption, through grace, for His sake (Rom. 8:15–17; Eph. 1:5–6).[62]

Our sonship is not identical with the Son of God's Sonship; he is a Son *by nature* and we are sons *by grace* (see chap. 7). While we were given the right to become sons of God (John 1:12), there never was a time when the Son of God himself became the Son (John 1:1).[63]

Despite this discontinuity, there is some continuity between our sonship and his Sonship. Although the Son's begottenness is *natural* and *eternal*, the image of begottenness itself becomes the metaphor and model of our own *spiritual* and *temporal* begottenness (analogical as it may be). The "God and Father of our Lord Jesus Christ," says Paul, "predestined us for *adoption* to himself *as sons through Jesus Christ*" (Eph. 1:3, 5). As sons, we are then conformed more and more to the image of *the* Son (Rom. 8:29), who is himself the true image of the invisible God (Col. 1:15). We can only be conformed to the image of the Son if he, the Son himself, is the true image of God, the "radiance of the glory of God and the exact imprint of his nature" (Heb. 1:3). This Son humbled himself to the point of death, suffering the curse of the law on a tree in order "to redeem those who were under the law, so that we might receive adoption as sons" (Gal. 4:5). By virtue of his humiliation, our predestination for adoption in eternity became a reality in history, sealed by the blood of the Son. Which is why Paul can say to the Romans, we are "heirs of God and fellow heirs with Christ" (Rom. 8:17).

With all this emphasis on the Father and the Son in our adoption, is the Spirit left out? Not at all. If the Father is the author of our adoption and the Son is the model of our adoption, then the Spirit is the *imprint* of our adoption, eagerly awaiting its final consummation (Rom. 8:23). Thanks to the Spirit, we can approach God as our Father. As Paul says, we have "received the Spirit of adoption as sons, by whom we cry, 'Abba! Father!'" (Rom. 8:15).

Furthermore, as the gift from the Father and the Son, the Spirit indwells us so that he might conform us into the image of the Son. The Spirit is sent by the Father and the Son to perfect the work of the Father and the Son *in us*.[64] As Paul tells the Galatians, not only did God send his Son to redeem us "so that we might receive adoption as sons" (Gal. 4:4–5), but because we are sons, "God has sent the Spirit of his Son into our hearts, crying 'Abba! Father!'" (4:6). We can pray to the Father thanks to the Spirit of his Son, a Spirit not out there somewhere, but a Spirit who dwells within our own hearts.

In sum, there is but one action by the triune God that we call adoption, and yet each person makes us a child of God in a way that matches each person's eternal relation of origin in eternity.[65] As Augustine says, "Some things are even said about the persons singly by name [like adoption]; however, they must not be understood in the sense of excluding the other persons, because this same three is also one, and there is one substance and godhead of Father and Son and Holy Spirit."[66]

Communion with the Trinity and the Christian Life

If divine appropriations give us a license to speak of the persons in ways that correspond to their eternal relations of origin, is it appropriate to believe that we, as adopted children of our triune God, can have communion (fellowship) with each of these persons? Not only is the answer yes, but John Owen believes the Christian who does not have communion with all three persons is missing out. Communion with each person, says Owen, is what makes the Christian life so . . . *Christian*. Apart from communion, all the riches we have in Christ are neglected, like unopened presents on Christmas morning.

On the one hand, we have communion with the whole Trinity any time we enjoy communion at all. "By what act soever we hold communion with any person, there is an *influence* from every person to the putting forth of that act."[67] Indivisible in essence, inseparable in operation. To enjoy fellowship with one person is to come under the *influence* of all three. Owen no doubt agreed with Gregory of Nazianzus, who said, "No sooner do I conceive of the One than I am illumined by the Splendour of the Three; no sooner do I distinguish Them than I am carried back to the One."[68]

On the other hand, Owen believes we can know each person in a distinct way that corresponds to each person's eternal relation of origin. As the unbegotten Father, from whom the Son is begotten and the Spirit is spirated, the Father is the source and principle of the Godhead. So, too, is he the source of our communion. From him flows an everlasting fountain of love, like sweet nectar from a flower. What distinguishes our communion with the Father is his "free, undeserved, and eternal love."[69] Out of his everlasting love for us, he sent his only begotten Son to die for us. United to his Son, we are the recipients of the Father's benevolence toward us, for he has redeemed his elect through his Son by his Spirit.

If the Father's love is the nectar in the flower, our communion with the Son by grace is the fruit of the flower. Bought with his blood, we enjoy his righteousness. Once we have tasted the fruit of his righteousness, our soul "melteth in longing after him."[70] Sin loses all its appeal; we want nothing more than Christ, who becomes our soul's one passion, our everlasting delight. "Upon discovery of the excellency and sweetness of Christ in the banqueting-house, the soul is instantly overpowered, and cries out to be made partaker of the fullness of it." Christ, however, is not only the reservoir of our everlasting delight, but the bedrock of our eternal fortress; we possess "great spiritual safety" through our "communion with him."[71]

Nevertheless, the daily cultivation of communion with Christ is impossible apart from the consolation of the Holy Spirit. As the Spirit who proceeds from the Father and the Son, the Spirit is the one who can bring us into communion with the Father and the Son. The love the Father shows to us through the grace of his Son is communicated by the Spirit of his Son.[72] The Spirit pledges the Father's love to us by comforting us, consoling us with all the promises that are ours in Christ Jesus. Hence he is called the Comforter or the Helper in Scripture. He is our consolation, our ever-present solace. Even in our worst moments of suffering, the Spirit is there to dispense the Father's love to us in Christ. As Athanasius says, "When we participate in the Spirit, we have the grace of the Word and, in the Word, the love of the Father."[73] Of course, Athanasius is only echoing the benediction of Paul to the Corinthians, "The grace of the Lord Jesus Christ and the love of God and the fellowship of the Holy Spirit be with you all" (2 Cor. 13:14).

If our communion with the Father is by his love, if our communion with the Son is by his grace, and if our communion with the Spirit is by his consolation and comfort, how then shall we respond? With joy and gladness in our hearts, we call out "Abba! Father!" knowing with full assurance from the Spirit that our Father will embrace us as his very own children, redeemed by the blood of his only begotten Son.

Conclusion

I have always wanted to travel to Lebanon and touch one of its ancient cedars. These cedars are so old that monks used to call them the Cedars of God. When Solomon built his temple, he told his architect to cut down the cedars of Lebanon (1 Kings 5:6). Solomon wanted a temple with a foundation he knew could last. The painter Vincent van Gogh felt the same way about the olive tree. As he prepared to paint his masterpieces, van Gogh liked to walk in the olive groves and just listen. What did he hear? "The murmur of an olive grove has something very intimate, immensely old about it," he said.

Something very intimate, immensely old—unfortunately, modern man has promised something immensely new instead. A Trinity liberated from the heavy shackles of old creeds and inspired texts, a Trinity that is relevant to the changing winds and whims of society. A Trinity that can be molded, even manipulated, until it at last acquiesces to the social agenda of our liking.

I can say from my own experience that we evangelicals have needed very little persuading or coaxing. When I was a young student, I was taught again and again to be suspicious toward the orthodox doctrine of the Trinity. In the name of the Bible, the creeds of the Christian faith—creeds that the church has trusted for almost two thousand years—were thrown into question. In the name of biblicism, time-tested doctrines like simplicity and eternal generation were castigated. *"Speculation!"* was the usual scorn.

But when I started lecturing on the Scriptures, when I started requiring my students to read the creeds, when I started revisiting the biblical insights of the church fathers, I came away with a different point of view. The Trinity I was taught, the Trinity I was told was pure Bible, the Trinity everyone else was soaking in, that Trinity was as novel as it was modern. But it was not biblical orthodoxy. It only appeared to be so.

C. S. Lewis once lamented that "a great many of the ideas about God which are trotted out as novelties today are simply the ones which real Theologians tried centuries ago and rejected."[1] Today, that trotting continues. It is now up to you to decide whether or not the church going forward will continue that trotting or recover the scriptural, orthodox doctrine of the Trinity. If our future is to look any different from our recent past, we must listen to the living voices of the dead. If we do, we might just rediscover something intimate, immensely old: a God who is simply Trinity. Unadulterated. Uncorrupted. *Unmanipulated.*

Glory to the Father, and to the Son, and to the Holy Ghost! As it was in the beginning, is now, and ever shall be, world without end.

Glossary

ad extra God's external operations toward the created order.
Compare to AD INTRA.

ad intra God's internal operations in and of himself, apart from the
created order; they are eternal and immutable. *See also* AD EXTRA.

analogical Likeness between one thing and another. God is infinite
and incomprehensible; therefore, the finite creature's language
for God says something true about God but is not to be taken
in an exhaustive or literalistic way. *Contrast with* UNIVOCAL and
EQUIVOCAL.

anthropomorphic When a human feature (e.g., hands, regret) is used
of God. This language is not meant to be taken in a literalistic
way but is figurative. *See* ANALOGICAL.

appropriation(s) Since God is one in essence (simple), every
operation is the one, singular, indivisible work of the Trinity. Yet
a particular work in creation or salvation may be appropriated
by a person of the Trinity in a special way that is consistent with
that person's eternal relation of origin. Appropriations draw our
attention to each person's distinctiveness. For example, the Father
is Creator, which conveys he is the origin in the Trinity.

aseity (*a se*) God is life in and of himself. He is independent of the
created order, self-sufficient and self-existent.

begotten   To come forth, to proceed. The Son is eternally begotten from the Father's essence. Only the Son is begotten. Other terms: eternal generation; filiation. *See* ETERNAL RELATIONS OF ORIGIN.

classical theism   The majority position of the church from the first through seventeenth centuries. Classical theism embodies trinitarian orthodoxy as represented by the Nicene Creed and the Great Tradition, but has been jettisoned by modern thinkers.

consubstantial, consubstantiality   From the same substance. The divine essence subsists in each person; therefore, they are consubstantial. In eternal generation, the Father communicates the one, simple essence to his Son; in eternal spiration, the Father and the Son communicate the one, simple essence to the Spirit. *See* ESSENCE.

compound   Made up of parts; composite. Unlike the finite creature, God is simple, uncompounded, and without parts. *Contrast with* SIMPLICITY.

economy   God's operations toward the created order (creation, providence, or redemption). God reveals his triune identity by means of the economy, but is not constituted by the economy. Other related terms: economic Trinity; *oikonomia* (God for us); *ad extra. Contrast with* IMMANENT TRINITY; *THEOLOGIA.*

essence   The being of God; his whatness. In scriptural language: God's "goodness," a word that encapsulates his attributes. God's essence is incomprehensible and simple. God's essence is not one thing and his existence and attributes another thing; they are one and the same. God is one essence, three persons. Each person is a subsistence (or subsisting relation) of the one, simple, divine essence. If the persons are one in essence, they are one in will, glory, power, and authority as well. Other terms for essence: substance, being, nature.

eternal   Timeless. The Trinity has no succession of moments. The relations of origin (generation, spiration) are timelessly eternal.

eternal generation   *See* BEGOTTEN; ETERNAL RELATIONS OF ORIGIN.

eternal relations of origin   Distinguishes how each person is related to another, identifying the everlasting provenance (principle/

origin/source) from which each person proceeds. Paternity: the Father is unbegotten (without origin), and therefore the eternal origin of the Son. Filiation: the Son's origin is the Father, begotten (generated) from the Father's essence from all eternity. Spiration: the Father and Son are the origin of the Spirit, spirating the Spirit from all eternity. These relations *alone* distinguish the persons, identifying each person's *personal property*. Another phrase, *modes of subsistence*, refers to the distinct way the one, simple essence of God eternally subsists in each person. Hence, persons are subsisting relations. *See* PERSON.

equivocal   No similarity. If applied to knowledge of God, we would know nothing true of God. *Contrast with* ANALOGICAL; UNIVOCAL.

filiation   The Son's personal property. He is eternally begotten from the Father. *See* BEGOTTEN; ETERNAL RELATIONS OF ORIGIN.

filioque   The (Western, not Eastern) belief that the Spirit proceeds (is spirated) from the Father *and the Son* as from one source.

heteroousios   From a different essence.

homoiousios   From a similar essence.

homoousios   From the same essence.

hypostasis   A Greek word used to distinguish Father, Son, and Spirit as persons. *See* SUBSISTENCE.

immanent Trinity   The Trinity in and of itself, apart from creation and salvation. Another term: *theologia* (Greek: "theology"). *Contrast with* ECONOMIC TRINITY.

immutability   God does not change in any way.

impassibility   God is without passions; he is not a victim of emotional change in any way; he does not suffer. The Son's generation and the Spirit's spiration are impassible. *See* IMMUTABILITY.

infinitude   God is without measure; his being is boundless.

innascible   *See* UNBEGOTTEN.

inseparable operations   Since the persons of the Trinity are indivisible in essence, they are also indivisible in their external operations. Having the one, simple will in common, they perform a singular act in any external operation. *Contrast with* APPROPRIATION(S).

metaphysics   The nature of reality. With reference to God, the nature of God. This book uses metaphysics and ontology as synonyms.

mission   Refers to the Son and Spirit being sent into the world. Each person's mission reflects each person's eternal relation of origin, although missions do not constitute eternal relations, nor should everything in the missions (e.g., incarnate suffering or submission) be projected back into the immanent Trinity. *See* ECONOMY.

modalism / modalistic monarchianism   *See* SABELLIANISM.

mode of subsistence (existence)   Refers to the unique (incommunicable) way the divine essence subsists (exists) in each person. For example, eternal generation is the Son's mode of subsistence. "Mode" is not to be confused with modalism (i.e., *Sabellianism*), a heresy that denies there are three distinct persons in the Trinity. *See* ETERNAL RELATIONS OF ORIGIN.

mutable   To change. God is not mutable. *Contrast with* IMMUTABILITY.

nature   *See* ESSENCE.

Nicaea, Council of   An official, ecumenical church council that met in AD 325 and condemned Arianism. The Nicene Creed teaches that the Son is eternally begotten (not made) by the Father and therefore is consubstantial with the Father, from the same essence as the Father. In AD 381, the creed was expanded and affirmed the Spirit's spiration/procession.

ontology   *See* METAPHYSICS.

order   The way the one essence subsists in three persons. Order does not involve hierarchy or subordination of any kind in the immanent Trinity, nor anything temporal. *See* ETERNAL RELATIONS OF ORIGIN.

passible   Emotional change; susceptible to suffering. God is not passible. *Contrast with* IMPASSIBLE.

passive potency   Must be activated and fulfilled to reach its potential and perfection. God has no passive potency. *Contrast with* PURE ACT.

paternity   The Father's *personal property*. He has no eternal origin (*unbegotten*); he is the eternal origin of his Son whom he begets from eternity. *See* ETERNAL RELATIONS OF ORIGIN.

perfect being   God is someone than who no one greater can be conceived (Anselm). *See* CLASSICAL THEISM.

perichoresis   Father, Son, and Spirit mutually indwell or interpenetrate one another. The West used the Latin word *circumincessio*. Contrary to *social trinitarianism*, perichoresis is not a substitute for *simplicity*. We can only affirm mutual life between the persons because each person is a subsistence of the simple essence.

person   A person is a subsisting relation, distinguished from another person by his *eternal relations of origin* alone (paternity, filiation, spiration). A divine person "is nothing but the divine essence . . . subsisting in an especial manner" (John Owen). *See* HYPOSTASIS; MODE OF SUBSISTENCE.

personal property   That property that distinguishes each person. Paternity: Father is unbegotten; he is the principle/origin of the Son. Filiation: Son is begotten from his Father. Spiration: Spirit is spirated from Father and Son. The persons have everything in common except their personal properties, which are expressions of the *eternal relations of origin*. *See* ETERNAL RELATIONS OF ORIGIN.

principle   The source/origin from which a person proceeds. Example: the Father is the principle of the Son because he begets his Son, but the Father alone is the principle who is without principle; he is *unbegotten*.

procession   Two uses: (1) the term broadly refers to *eternal relations of origin*; (2) the term narrowly refers to the Spirit's origin (Greek: *exporeusis*; Latin: *processio*). *See* SPIRATION; ETERNAL RELATIONS OF ORIGIN.

prosopological   When an author of Scripture helps readers identify and distinguish between one divine speaker/person (*prosōpon*) and another divine speaker/person (e.g., Ps. 2:7 and Heb. 1:5; Ps. 110:1 and Luke 20:41–43). The Great Tradition imitated the prosopological methods of Jesus and the biblical authors.

pure act (*actus purus*) / pure actuality (*purus actua*)   There is nothing in the simple, eternal, and infinite God to be activated as if he must reach his potential. As the perfect being, he is maximally alive, fully

actualized, absolute life in and of himself, incapable of change/
improvement. While God is able to affect and change others, he has
no *passive potency*, as if he could be affected and changed by others.

relation *See* ETERNAL RELATIONS OF ORIGIN.

Sabellianism A heresy that denies there is more than one person in
the Godhead. Persons are mere *functions*, as if what makes God
Father, Son, and Spirit are the forms he takes when he creates or
saves. Equivalent viewpoint: modalistic monarchianism, unitarian
monarchianism, or modalism (not to be confused with *modes of
subsistence*).

scholasticism Can refer to medieval scholasticism (e.g. Aquinas)
or Reformed scholasticism (e.g., John Owen). Scholastics
retrieved Nicene orthodoxy and the Great Tradition within a
systematic presentation of doctrine. Unfortunately, today the
word "scholasticism" is misused in a pejorative sense by narrow
biblicists to refer to anything they think is speculative.

simplicity God is not made up of parts; he is not composite or
a *compounded* being. He *is* his attributes. His essence is his
attributes and his attributes his essence; all that is in God simply is
God. Each person of the Trinity is a subsistence of the one, simple
divine essence. The persons, therefore, are not parts in/of God.

social trinitarianism Social trinitarianism is a diverse movement,
which makes it difficult to define. But in its fully developed form,
it's starting point (or at least emphasis) is not simplicity—some
reject simplicity—but the three persons. The Trinity is not
defined primarily by *eternal relations of origin*. ST redefines
the Trinity as a society and community analogous to a human
society, redefines the persons as three centers of consciousness/
will, redefines persons according to their relation*ships* (focus on
mutuality, societal interaction), and redefines unity as interpersonal
relationships of love between persons (redefinition of perichoresis).
ST collapses immanent and economic Trinity, sets East against
West, and treats social Trinity as a paradigm for social theory
(ecclesiology, politics, gender). ST has been adopted by modern
theologians but is an abandonment/revision of Nicene orthodoxy.

spiration Reflects the name "Spirit." The Spirit is spirated, eternally breathed out by the Father and Son. Since the Spirit is not another Son, he is not begotten but spirated. To be technical, *active* spiration refers to the Father and Son as the ones who breathe out the Spirit, while *passive* spiration (a *personal property*) refers to the Spirit as the one who proceeds or is spirated by the Father and Son. *See* ETERNAL RELATIONS OF ORIGIN.

subsistence Another way of referring to a divine *person*. The one, simple divine essence subsists or exists in three persons. Each person is a subsisting relation of the divine essence. The divine essence has three modes of subsistence (Latin: *subsistentia*; Greek: *hypostasis*): paternity, filiation, spiration. *See* ETERNAL RELATIONS OF ORDER.

substance *See* ESSENCE.

theologia Greek for theology; the inner life of the Trinity apart from the world. *See* IMMANENT TRINITY.

tritheism Belief in three gods. No one claims to be a tritheist, but one can fall prey to tritheism by virtue of an overemphasis on the persons or a redefinition of person in modern categories. *Social trinitarianism* has been accused of tritheism because it says there are three centers of consciousness and will in God (the ingredients for tritheism). Social trinitarians deny that their position leads to tritheism.

unbegotten Not begotten. The Father begets his Son from all eternity, but the Father alone is unbegotten from eternity, the principle without principle. Other words: innascible, innascibility. Unbegotten is not to be confused with uncreated: all three persons are uncreated, but only the Father is unbegotten. As the unbegotten Father, *paternity* is his *personal property*. To be precise, since the Father is unbegotten, he has no *eternal relation of origin* from another divine person.

univocal Same, identical meaning as something else. If applied to knowledge of God, we can know God as he is in himself, in his essence. Classical theism rejects univocal knowledge of an infinite, incomprehensible God. *Compare with* ANALOGICAL; EQUIVOCAL.

Notes

Chapter 1 Trinity Drift

1. Consult chapter 8, and also see Grudem, *Systematic Theology* (1994), 245, 251; (2000) appendix 6 (cf. chapter 14); Erickson, *Systematic Theology*, 308 (in the second edition eternal generation is totally absent!); Erickson, *Who's Tampering with the Trinity?*, 179–84, 251; Erickson, *God in Three Persons*, 309–10; Feinberg, *No One Like Him*, 112–14; 490–91, 498; Reymond, *New Systematic Theology*, 325–26, 335; Craig and Moreland, *Philosophical Foundations*, 593. Also see popular treatments like Mark Driscoll and Gerry Breshears, *Doctrine: What Christians Should Believe* (Wheaton: Crossway, 2010), 27–28. Others, like John Frame, accept the doctrine but not uncritically, suspicious that we are just playing with words. See Frame's *Doctrine of God*, 707–14.

2. After working through my collection, I read Keith Johnson's *Rethinking the Trinity and Religious Pluralism*, only to discover he had chronicled what I was experiencing. I am not the only one on this quest! See Johnson for survey of sources.

3. Holmes, *Listening to the Past*, 13.

4. This phrase "believe simply" is from Bonaventure, *The Tree of Life*, in *Bonaventure*, 126 (1); as quoted in Swain, *Retrieving Eternal Generation*, 42.

Chapter 2 Can We Trust the God of Our Fathers?

1. For what follows, consult Arius, "Arius's Letter to Eusebius of Nicomedia," in William G. Rusch, ed., *The Trinitarian Controversy*, 29–30; Arius, "Arius's Letter to Alexander of Alexandria," 31–32; Arius, "Arius's Letter to the Emperor Constantine," 61; Arius, *Thalia*, in John Behr, *Formation of Christian Theology*, 2.1:140–41. Cf. Athanasius, *Defence of the Nicene Definition* 3.6 (NPNF² 4:154). On how the debate evolved, see Hanson, *The Search for the Christian Doctrine of God*, 134–35; Williams, *Arius*, 48–61; Ayres, *Nicaea*, 15–20, 55.

2. Dünz, *Trinity in the Early Church*, 42.

3. It is common to trace Arius's conclusions back to Origen. But Ayres gives theological and historical reasons why that is "implausible" (*Nicaea and Its Legacy*, 21).

4. Dünz, *Trinity in the Early Church*, 43.

5. See Anatolios, *Retrieving Nicaea*, 17. For the Nicene fathers, affirming a unity in nature does not mean generation is against the will of God, as if the Father begets his Son even though he does not want to. Rather, affirming generation as an act of divine nature precludes the Arian belief that it is a product of mere will, as if the Son is a creature, external to the will of the Father and only an effect. "The Father's act of generation is a work of his *nature,* and only in a rather carefully specified sense can it be called a work of his *will*. Creation is a work of the will of God, in that it is not intrinsic to God's essence to be creator. Generation, on the other hand, is intrinsic to the personal properties and relations which constitute God's essence. . . . One way of saying this is to say that generation takes place 'necessarily'; but 'necessarily' does not contradict 'voluntarily' but specifies the operation of the divine will as not 'liberty of indifference' but 'spontaneity,' action in accordance with nature but not thereby lacking in freedom" (Webster, *God Without Measure*, 34; cf. 89).

6. Supporters included Eusebius of Nicomedia, Eusebius of Caesarea, and Asterius; they became known as the Eusebians.

7. "The Creed of Nicaea (325)," in John H. Leith, ed., *Creeds of the Churches*, 28–30. I have not retained all of Leith's bracketed Greek words for the sake of accessibility.

8. See Ayres, *Nicaea and Its Legacy*, 90; Anatolios, *Retrieving Nicaea*, 15–31.

9. Basil of Caesarea, *Against Eunomius* 2.25.

10. Barnes, "The Fourth Century as Trinitarian Canon," 51–62, explains that Arius was not the main focus after Nicaea.

11. For an overview of all four views, see Fairbairn and Reeves, *The Story of Creeds*, 67; Dünz, *Trinity in the Early Church*, 87–115; Smith, "The Trinity in the Fourth-Century Fathers," 109–22.

12. They said the Son is altogether "dissimilar" (*anhomoios*) in essence, which is why this group was sometimes called *Anhomoeans*; they were also called Heterousians. Representatives: Aetius and Eunomius; sometimes they were called Eunomians. Dünz, *Trinity in the Early Church*, 89; Ayres, *Nicaea and Its Legacy*, 144–49, 198.

13. Greek: *Homoios kat' energeian*.

14. Dünz, *Trinity in the Early Church*, 90–91; Ayres, *Nicaea and Its Legacy*, 149–53.

15. Greek: *Homoios kat' ousian*. Representatives: Basil of Ancyra; George of Laodicea.

16. Contra revisionist readings of simplicity; e.g., Frame, *The Doctrine of God*, 229.

17. Holmes, *The Quest for the Trinity*, 95.

18. Athanasius, *Defence of the Nicene Definition* 5.11 (NPNF[2] 4:157). For Athanasius's definition of simplicity, see 5.22 (NPNF[2] 4:165).

19. Athanasius, *Defence of the Nicene Definition* 5.11 (NPNF[2] 4:157).

20. Athanasius, *Defence of the Nicene Definition* 5.19 (NPNF[2] 4:163).

21. Athanasius, *Defence of the Nicene Definition* 5.23 (NPNF[2] 4:166). Athanasius also appeals to simplicity in his *Letters to Serapion on the Holy Spirit* 1.2.4; 1.16.4–7; 1.17.4; 1.20.4; 1.28.2; 1.30.3; 1.32.1–6.

22. Basil of Caesarea, *Against Eunomius* 2.30.

23. E.g., Plantinga, *Does God Have a Nature?*; Feinberg, *No One Like Him*, 326–27; Moreland and Craig, *Philosophical Foundations for a Christian Worldview*, 524. For a critique, see Dolezal, *All That Is in God*.

24. Gregory of Nazianzus, *Theological Orations* 4.12 (*NPNF*² 7:314).

25. Gregory of Nazianzus, *Theological Orations* 4.12 (*NPNF*² 7:314).

26. Gregory of Nazianzus, *Theological Orations* 5.14; 5.16 (*NPNF*² 7:322–33). And Basil of Caesarea: the persons are equal because there is an "identity of power" among them; "power and substance are the same" (*Against Eunomius* 2.32; 2.23).

27. Ayres, *Nicaea and Its Legacy*, 296–97, 358.

28. Gregory of Nyssa, *On the Holy Trinity*; Gregory of Nazianzus, *Theological Orations*; Basil of Caesarea, *Against Eunomius* 2.34; cf. Ayres, *Nicaea and Its Legacy*, 245, 280.

29. Ayres, *Nicaea and Its Legacy*, 245, 280.

30. See the report of Sozomen just after Nicaea in Ayres, *Nicaea and Its Legacy*, 101. After Nicaea, much controversy turned on Marcellus of Ancra and accusations of Sabellianism; Constantinople chose language that set itself apart from Marcellus. See Barnes, "The Fourth Century as Trinitarian Canon," 50–53.

31. Some decided to write their own creeds. Examples include the Dedication Creed (341), the creed of Sardica (343), and the Macrostich/Long-Line Creed (344). See Fairbairn and Reeves, *The Story of Creeds*, 64, who qualify that the creed of Sardica was not a substitute for Nicaea but merely an exposition.

32. Turretin says, "Thus the person may be said to differ from the essence not really (*realiter*), i.e., essentially (*essentialiter*) as thing and thing, but modally (*modaliter*)—as a mode from the thing (*modus a re*)" (*Institutes*, 1:278). "A 'mode of subsistence' or 'mode of existence' . . . 'is a relation inhering in the existence of God'" (Muller, *PRRD*, 4:184). For this reason, the distinctions between persons are "modal distinctions" (4:190–91). There can be "no real distinction between the three persons and the divine essence, as if the essence were one thing (*res*) and the three persons each another thing, for God is a simple or noncomposite being. Rather the persons are rationally or conceptually (*ratione*) distinct, not merely in the mind of the finite knower but *in ipsa re*, that is, in the Godhead or divine essence itself" (4:191). One qualification: by "modal" we do not mean the heresy of Sabellianism. With orthodoxy "modal" refers to God *ad intra*, whereas with Sabellianism it refers to God *ad extra*, what Muller calls "modes of self-presentation." "As the Reformed orthodox note, the Sabellians did not argue a modal distinction between the persons in the Godhead but rather a purely rational distinction of persons in their outward manifestation or role coupled with an insistence that the persons were not distinct *ad intra*" (Muller, *PRRD*, 4:194). Also see Webster, *God Without Measure*, 87–88; Dolezal, "Trinity, Simplicity and the Status of God's Personal Relations," 79–98.

33. Sometimes the Great Tradition will also refer to "relations of opposition."

34. To be technical, personal properties are an expression of eternal relations of origin; see Aquinas, *Summa* 1a.40.2.

35. Gregory of Nyssa, *On "Not Three Gods"* (*NPNF*² 5:336).

36. Gregory of Nyssa, *On the Faith to Simplicius* (*NPNF*² 5:339). Cf. Gregory of Nyssa, *Against Eunomius* 1.22 (*NPNF*² 5:94).

37. Athanasius, *Against the Arians* 1.9.29 (NPNF² 4:324), emphasis added. Cf. Athanasius, *Defence of the Nicene Definition* 5.19 (NPNF² 4:162–63); *Letters to Serapion on the Holy Spirit* 2.5.2; 2.6.1.
38. Athanasius, *Against the Arians* 3.62 (NPNF² 4:427).
39. Gregory of Nyssa, *Against Eunomius* 1.39 (NPNF² 5:94).
40. Augustine, *The Trinity* 15.47. See also Hilary, *On the Trinity* 11.25 (NPNF² 9:224); cf. 9:27 (NPNF² 9:164). Hilary calls the Father the "source of His [the Son's] being."
41. Anselm, *Monologion* 45, in *Works*, 58; Aquinas, *Summa Theologiae* 1a.41.5; Turretin, *Institutes* 1:272 (cf. 1:292–93).
42. To be clear, it's not the essence that generates, as if the essence is a fourth person. Rather, the Father generates his Son, but he does so from his divine essence, ensuring the Son is a subsistence from the same divine essence as him. Aquinas, *Summa* 1a.41.3–5; Hilary, *On the Trinity* 7.28, 7.31 (NPNF² 9:131); van Mastricht, *Theoretical-Practical Theology*, 2:503, 533–34.
43. Dünz, *Trinity in the Early Church*, 107.
44. Gregory of Nazianzus, *On God and Christ* 4.31.28 (p. 139).
45. Phrases like "from the *ousia* of the Father" and "God from God" are absent. Did the fathers change their mind about these phrases? No. The same concepts are still present in the creed in 381 when it says the Son is *true* God from *true* God, Light from Light, and *homoousios* with the Father due to his eternal generation from the Father. So why drop them? Without minutes from the meeting it is hard to identify the exact reason, but some historians think the fathers wanted to shorten the creed so that it was more amicable for liturgy and worship in the church. Pragmatics, not theology, was most likely the motive. Others believe the phrase was dropped since *homoousios* communicated the same idea anyway. See Fairbairn and Reeves, *The Story of Creeds*, 63, 75. Regardless, in countless ways the Nicene fathers reiterated the concept, from the *ousia* of the Father, throughout their works, as did the Great Tradition that followed. See Hanson, *The Search*, 817; Ayres, *Nicaea and Its Legacy*, 256–57.

Chapter 3 Since When Did the Trinity Get Social?

1. Charles Dickens, *A Christmas Carol* (London: Arcturus, 2018), 34–35.
2. Ayres, *Nicaea and Its Legacy*, 7, emphasis added.
3. G. E. Lessing, "On the Proof of the Spirit and Power," in *Lessing's Theological Writings*, 55.
4. E.g., Søren Kierkegaard (1813–1855). See his *Concluding Unscientific Postscript*.
5. Schleiermacher, *The Christian Faith*, 745. Cf. *On Religion: Speeches to Its Cultured Despisers*.
6. Schleiermacher, *The Christian Faith*, 738.
7. Schleiermacher, *The Christian Faith*, 738.
8. Schleiermacher, *The Christian Faith*, 739.
9. Schleiermacher, *The Christian Faith*, 741.
10. Schleiermacher, *The Christian Faith*, 741.
11. Schleiermacher, *The Christian Faith*, 743.

12. Schleiermacher, *The Christian Faith*, 750.
13. Schleiermacher, *The Christian Faith*, 749.
14. Albrecht Ritschl, *The Christian Doctrine of Justification and Reconciliation*. For a more extensive overview of Ritschl and Rauschenbusch, consult Olson and Hall, *The Trinity*, 93–96.
15. Walter Rauschenbusch, *A Theology for the Social Gospel*.
16. Rahner, *The Trinity*, 17.
17. Rahner, *The Trinity*, 18.
18. Rahner, *The Trinity*, 69.
19. Rahner, *The Trinity*, 22. Emphasis removed.
20. Proponents with a strict identity between immanent and economic include Catherine LaCugna, Jürgen Moltmann, Robert Jenson, Eberhard Jüngel, and Wolfhart Pannenberg. Others only willing to say economic is immanent (not vice versa) include Paul Molnar, Walter Kasper, Thomas Weinandy, Thomas Torrance, David Coffey, and Hans Urs von Balthasar. See Johnson, *Rethinking the Trinity and Religious Pluralism*, 66 n.3; Sanders, *The Image of the Immanent Trinity*; Sanders, *The Triune God*, 152; Jowers, *Karl Rahner's Trinitarian Axiom*.
21. Rahner, *The Trinity*, 24 (cf. 120).
22. LaCugna, *God for Us*, 6.
23. LaCugna, *God for Us*, 354. See response in Webster, *God Without Measure*, 40.
24. Moltmann, *The Trinity and the Kingdom*, 21–60, 160; Moltmann, *The Crucified God*. I've responded to Moltmann in *None Greater*.
25. Moltmann, *The Trinity and the Kingdom*, 139.
26. Moltmann, *The Trinity and the Kingdom*, viii.
27. Moltmann, *The Trinity and the Kingdom*, 144; for his critique of Rahner, see 144–48.
28. Moltmann, *The Trinity and the Kingdom*, 149.
29. Moltmann, *The Trinity and the Kingdom*, 16; cf. 77–79. Moltmann appeals to the East; others follow his lead: Jenson, Gunton, Pannenberg, LaCugna, McClendon, Brown, Placher, Coffey. But see Ayres's critique, *Nicaea and Its Legacy*, chap. 16.
30. Moltmann, *The Trinity and the Kingdom*, 18.
31. Moltmann, *The Trinity and the Kingdom*, viii, emphasis in original.
32. Moltmann, *The Trinity and the Kingdom*, 197.
33. Moltmann, *The Trinity and the Kingdom*, viii. On the church, see 202.
34. Moltmann, *The Trinity and the Kingdom*, viii and 193 (cf. 164). Also see Boff, *Trinity and Society*, 170ff.
35. Moltmann, *The Trinity and the Kingdom*, 108.
36. Moltmann, *The Trinity and the Kingdom*, 198 (cf. 217). Moltmann then appeals to *zimzum*, a panentheistic concept, to say his social Trinity is "open" to the world, a concept ultimately fulfilled in the incarnation (19, 64, 90, 99, 106–21).
37. See Volf, "The Trinity Is Our Social Program," 403–23. Also consult Volf, *Exclusion and Embrace*, 25ff; Volf, "Being as God Is: Trinity and Generosity," in Volf and Welker, eds., *God's Life in Trinity*, 3–12.
38. Volf, *After Our Likeness*, 191.
39. Zizioulas, *Being as Communion*.

40. Boff, *Trinity and Society*, 229.

41. Boff, *Trinity and Society*, 115, emphasis added. To be accurate, Boff is being descriptive of the "modern notion of person." Later he says he is proposing a "new starting-point." Nevertheless, Boff still operates within this modern revision of "person," however "new" his own view may be.

42. Boff, *Trinity and Society*, 115.

43. Boff, *Trinity and Society*, 117.

44. Boff, *Trinity and Society*, 119.

45. Boff, *Trinity and Society*, 119.

46. Boff, *Trinity and Society*, 119 (indebted to Moltmann).

47. Boff, *Trinity and Society*, 120 (cf. 130).

48. Boff, *Trinity and Society*, 133 (cf. his social perichoresis, 134ff).

49. Boff, *Trinity and Society*, 139.

50. Boff, *Trinity and Society*, 145.

51. Boff, *Trinity and Society*, 149.

52. Boff, *Trinity and Society*, 150.

53. Boff, *Trinity and Society*, 150.

54. Boff, *Trinity and Society*, 151.

55. Boff, *Trinity and Society*, 159.

56. Boff, *Trinity and Society*, 163.

57. Boff, *Trinity and Society*, 163. Boff also meshes eternal generation with the world's liberation from oppression (225).

58. Boff, *Holy Trinity, Perfect Communion*, xv.

59. Also known as postliberal theology. The following represents Frei, *The Identity of Jesus Christ*; Frei, *The Eclipse of Biblical Narrative*.

60. I am painting in very broad strokes. For more background, consult John Webster and George P. Schner, eds., *Theology After Liberalism*. Also consult diverse representatives, such as George A. Lindbeck and William C. Placher.

61. Jenson, *The Triune Identity*, 22.

62. Jenson, *ST*, 1:212.

63. Jenson, *ST*, 1:64.

64. Jenson, *The Triune Identity*, 126.

65. Jenson, *ST*, 2:99.

66. Swain, *The God of the Gospel*, 85.

67. See Jenson, *The Triune Identity*, 125. Besides Jenson, Bruce L. McCormack denies that there is a "metaphysical gap" between immanent and economic ("Grace and Being," in John Webster, ed., *The Cambridge Companion to Karl Barth*, 92–100). For a response, see Duby, *God in Himself*, 48–57.

68. E.g., Richard Swinburne, Stephen Davis, Edward Wierenga, and Peter van Inwagen. Other philosophers oppose social trinitarianism: Sarah Coakley, Michael Rae, Brian Leftow, Jeffrey Brower, Daniel Howard-Snyder, Keith Yandell.

69. Plantinga, "Social Trinity and Tritheism," 22. Cf. Thompson and Plantinga, "Trinity and Kenosis," in Stephen Evans, ed., *Exploring Kenotic Christology*, 179.

70. Plantinga, "Social Trinity and Tritheism," 27.

71. Plantinga, "Social Trinity and Tritheism," 43.

72. Any modest affirmation must be a "sub-theory." Plantinga, "Social Trinity and Tritheism," 22.

73. Moreland and Craig, *Philosophical Foundations for a Christian Worldview*, 583.

74. Craig, "Trinity Monotheism Once More," 101. Cf. Craig, "Toward a Tenable Social Trinitarianism," 89–99.

75. Moreland and Craig, *Philosophical Foundations for a Christian Worldview*, 592–93.

76. For what follows, see Grenz, *Theology for the Community of God*, chaps. 2, 3, and 13. Also see Grenz, *The Named God and the Question of Being*; Grenz, *The Social God and the Relational Self*.

77. Before Grenz's unexpected death, he softened his social trinitarianism, even backed away from other social trinitarians, but nevertheless maintained a relational view of the Trinity. Grenz appeared disenchanted with Colin Gunton and criticized John Zizioulas. Sexton believes it is better to categorize Grenz as a "trinitarian innovator" than a social trinitarian for this reason. See Sexton, "Beyond Social Trinitarianism," 473–86.

78. E.g., Johnson, *She Who Is*; Wilson-Kastner, *Faith, Feminism and the Christ*; LaCugna, *God for Us*. For a critique, see Coakley, "'Persons' in the 'Social' Doctrine of the Trinity," 123–44; Tanner, "Social Trinitarianism and Its Critics," 368–86.

79. Levering, *Scripture and Metaphysics*, 236.

80. Kilby, "Perichoresis and Projection," 444. Levering, however, questions whether Kilby's solution escapes her own criticism.

81. Holmes, *The Quest for the Trinity*, xv, xvi.

82. Holmes, *The Quest for the Trinity*, 2.

Chapter 4 How Does God Reveal Himself as Trinity?

1. Isaiah 40:3.
2. John 1:29–30, 34.
3. Matthew 3:14.
4. Matthew 3:15.
5. Matthew 3:16–17.
6. Deuteronomy 6:4.
7. Luke 20:41–43.
8. Ps. 109:3 LXX; Bates, *The Birth of the Trinity*, 53 (cf. 62).
9. 2 Samuel 7.
10. Isaiah 53.
11. John 19:30.
12. John 16:7–13.
13. Acts 2:14–36.
14. Acts 2:34–35; cf. Ps. 110:1.
15. Acts 2:38.
16. Matthew 28:19–20.
17. Warfield, "The Biblical Doctrine of the Trinity," in *Biblical and Theological Studies*, 33.

18. Kevin Vanhoozer, *The Drama of Doctrine*, 43–44. Others say the same: Johnson, *Rethinking Trinity*, 216; Sanders, *The Deep Things of God*, 9–10; Emery, *The Trinity*, ix.

19. Sanders, *The Deep Things of God*, 14. Against a proof-texting, compilation approach, see 33–36, 43. Also see 38 on the pietistic and rationalistic approaches.

20. Basil of Caesarea, *Letter* 26.3, quoted in Emery, 11. Also see Irenaeus of Lyons, *On the Apostolic Preaching* 7, trans. John Behr (Crestwood, NY: St. Vladimir's Seminary Press, 1997), 44.

21. "[The] mode of operating imitates the manner of subsisting" (Peter van Mastricht, *Theoretical-Practical Theology*, 2:505).

22. Warfield, "The Biblical Doctrine of the Trinity," in *Biblical and Theological Studies*, 33.

23. Bavinck, *Reformed Dogmatics*, 2:261.

24. John 15:26; 2 Cor 13:14; 1 John 5:1–12. Bavinck, *Reformed Dogmatics*, 2:269.

25. Barrett, *Canon, Covenant, and Christology*.

26. Barrett, *God's Word Alone*; Barrett, *Canon, Covenant, and Christology*.

27. Warfield, "The Biblical Doctrine of the Trinity," 142.

28. The Reformed Scholastics made this point, especially John Owen. See Muller, *PRRD*, 4:216.

29. On the Trinity and general revelation, see Aquinas, *Summa* 1a.32.1; 1a.39.7; Turretin, *Institutes*, 1:266; Muller, *PRRD*, 4:165; Swain, "Divine Trinity," 82.

30. Rahner, *The Trinity*, 24.

31. Rahner, *Theological Investigations*, 4:98.

32. The following critique is indebted to Emery, *The Trinity*, 177, though my points do not parallel his points exactly and at times focus more on revelation.

33. Giles, *The Eternal Generation of the Son*, 224, makes this point over against Feinberg, *No One Like Him*, 448–98; Erickson, *God in Three Persons*, 309–10; Erickson, *Who's Tampering with the Trinity?*, 179–84. A similar point is made by Marshall, "The Unity of the Triune God: Reviving an Ancient Question," 14–15.

34. Emery, *The Trinity*, 177.

35. Older theologians used the terms *theology* and *economy*, *processions* and *missions*.

36. Gill, *Body of Divinity*, 141.

37. Gill, *Body of Divinity*, 142.

38. Augustine, *The Trinity* 4.29, 174. Cf. Johnson, *Rethinking the Trinity*, 75.

39. Augustine, *The Trinity* 4.29, 175. Cf. Johnson, *Rethinking the Trinity*, 75.

40. Johnson, *Rethinking the Trinity*, 75–76.

41. Basil of Caesarea, *Against Eunomius*, 2.14–15.

Chapter 5 Why Must God Be One to Be Three?

1. The following quotations are from John 10:22–42.

2. Augustine, *The Trinity* 1.3.18.

3. For a classical view of perichoresis, see Hilary, *The Trinity* 3.4 (*NPNF²* 9:62–63); Aquinas (who quotes Hilary), *Summa* 1a.42.6; John of Damascus, *The Orthodox Faith* 8 (*NPNF²* 9:10).

4. Aquinas, *Summa* 1a.30.4.

5. Tertullian, *Against Praxeas* 25 (*ANF* 3:621).

6. Emery, *The Trinity*, 7.

7. Gregory of Nyssa, *Against Eunomius* 1.26 (*NPNF²* 5:71). Cf. Gregory of Nyssa, *On the Holy Spirit*, 5:324.

8. R. Kendall Soulen, "*Generatio, Processio Verbi, Donum Nominis*," 135.

9. Also consult John 20:28.

10. Hilary, *On the Trinity* 9.61 (*NPNF²* 9:176).

11. Richard of Saint Victor, *On the Trinity* 1.25.

12. The patristic and medieval fathers called him *pure act* for this reason.

13. Gregory of Nazianzus, *On God and Christ* 3.29.2 (p. 70).

14. *Mian ousian, treis hypostaseis* (Turretin, *Institutes*, 254).

15. Augustine, *The Trinity* 7.3.11.

16. Augustine, *The Trinity* 7.3.11 (cf. 7.4.12).

17. This show is rated mature, so please use discretion.

18. John of Damascus, *Exposition of the Orthodox Faith* 8 (*NPNF²* 9:10).

19. Owen, *Brief Vindication*, in *Works* 2:407. Also Dolezal, "Trinity, Simplicity and the Status of God's Personal Relations," 94.

20. Augustine, *The Trinity* 78.1.2.

21. Augustine, *The Trinity* 78.1.2.

22. Aquinas, *Summa* 1a.42.4. Also Dolezal: "The Father is wholly divine yet divinity is not wholly the Father, and so forth for the Son and Spirit" ("Trinity, Simplicity and the Status of God's Personal Relations," 95).

23. Anselm, *On the Procession of the Holy Spirit*, 396.

24. Gregory of Nyssa, *On "Not Three Gods"* (*NPNF²* 5:331–32).

25. Muller, *PRRD*, 4:211.

26. Muller, *PRRD*, 4:211.

27. Leigh, *Treatise* 2.16 (p. 128); quoted in Muller, *PRRD*, 4:212.

28. Ursinus, *Commentary*, 130; Muller, *PRRD*, 4:326.

29. Emery, *The Trinity*, 126.

30. John of Damascus, *Exposition of the Orthodox Faith* 8 (*NPNF²* 9:10).

31. Duby, *Divine Simplicity*, 214–15.

32. Aquinas, *Summa* 1a.39.3 (p. 111).

33. Aquinas, *Summa* 1a.31.1; Turretin, *Institutes*, 255.

34. Anselm, *On the Incarnation of the Word* 4 (*The Major Works*).

35. Gill, *Body of Divinity*, 128.

36. Gill, *Body of Divinity*, 128.

37. Turretin, *Institutes*, 301.

38. Owen, *Works* 19:87 (cf. 9:87–88; 12:497). Also Swain, *The God of the Gospel*, 159.

39. Witsius, *Exercitationes*, 6.2; quoted in Muller, *PRRD*, 4:258.

40. E.g., Basil of Caesarea, *Against Eunomius*, 2.14.

41. John of Damascus, *Exposition of the Orthodox Faith* 8 (*NPNF²* 9:10).

42. Aquinas, *Summa* 1a.42.1.

43. Gill, *Body of Divinity*, 129.
44. Translation by Bray, *Creeds, Councils and Christ*, 209–11.

Chapter 6 Is the Son Begotten from the Father?

1. Matthew 16:13–23.
2. Zipporah is describing Matthew 17:1–8.
3. 2 Peter 1:16–21.
4. Basil of Caesarea, *Against Eunomius* 1.15–16.
5. Aquinas, *Summa* 1a.29.4 (cf. 1a.40.1–3). Cf. Gregory of Nyssa, *Against Eunomius* 2.9 (*NPNF*² 5:114); 10.3 (*NPNF*² 5:224); Anselm, *On the Procession of the Holy Spirit*, 434: John of Damascus, *Exposition of the Orthodox Faith* 2 (*NPNF*² 9:2); 8 (*NPNF*² 9:8); Turretin, *Institutes*, 1:266 (cf. 270–71).
6. Why does Thomas not use "cause"? "The Greek authors use 'principle' and 'cause' interchangeably in referring to divinity; the Latins, however, do not use 'cause,' but only 'principle.' The explanation is that 'principle' is a broader term than 'cause'" (Aquinas, *Summa* 1a.33.1). Emery observes that "cause" or *aitia* was used in the East, but "Latin theologians prefer to use the term 'Principle' (*principium*) because . . . the word 'cause' connotes a dependence and an inferiority of the effect in relation to its cause, while the word 'principle' is clearer" (*The Trinity*, 112). Nevertheless, Emery gives reason for retaining the word. "However, given the usage of the Greek Fathers, the Catholic Church welcomes both words: *cause* or *principle*. Paternity does not imply the priority of the Father or a hierarchy in the Trinity, but only the relation according to which he is the principle of the Son" (*The Trinity*, 114). To see how "cause" can be used in a way that does not imply inferiority, see Hilary, *On the Trinity* 4.21 (*NPNF*² 9:77). But Hilary has limits: Hilary describes causation as an impossibility if by causation one infers a type of creation. The Son's eternal birth cannot be associated with creation for this reason; see 12.42 (*NPNF*² 9:229).
7. Thomas Aquinas, *Commentary on the Sentences*, Bk. IV, dist. 15, q. 4, a. 5, quaestiuncula 3; quoted in Emery, *The Trinity*, 118 n.9. Cf. Aquinas, *Summa* 1a.39.5.
8. Aquinas, *Summa* 1a.40.4. Elsewhere Aquinas defines generation as "the coming forth of a divine person into the divine nature" (1a.43.2).
9. Benedict Pictet, *Theologia Christiana* 2.17.2; quoted in Muller, *PRRD*, 4:287.
10. Eternal generation is the "personal and eternal act of God the Father whereby he is the origin of the personal subsistence of God the Son, so communicating to the Son the one undivided divine essence" (Webster, *God Without Measure*, 30). Mark Makin outlines three types of generation: causal, grounding, and essential dependence; see Makin, "Philosophical Models of Eternal Generation," in Sanders and Swain, eds., *Retrieving Eternal Generation*, 243–59.
11. Webster, *God Without Measure*, 31.
12. Webster, *God Without Measure*, 67.
13. Gill, *Body of Divinity*, 144.
14. Gregory of Nyssa, *Against Eunomius* 1.39 (*NPNF*² 5:94).
15. Gregory of Nyssa, *Against Eunomius* 1.26 (*NPNF*² 5:71).

16. Athanasius, *Against the Arians* 1.6.17 (NPNF² 4:316).
17. Augustine, *Contra Maximinum* 2.14, as quoted in Aquinas, *Summa* 1a.42.3, emphasis added. Also Richard of Saint Victor, *On the Trinity* 5.7.
18. Webster, *God Without Measure*, 36.
19. Athanasius, *Against the Arians* 1.6.20 (NPNF² 4:318).
20. Athanasius, *Against the Arians* 1.6.21 (NPNF² 4:319).
21. Gregory of Nyssa, *On the Holy Spirit* (NPNF² 5:317). Also Turretin, *Institutes*, 1:293.
22. Gill, *Body of Divinity*, 146.
23. Basil of Caesarea, *Against Eunomius* 1.11.
24. Leigh, *Treatise*, 2.16 (pp. 128–29); quoted in Muller, *PRRD*, 4:186.
25. Forbes, *Instructiones hist.* 1.33.1, 3; quoted in Muller, *PRRD*, 4:170.
26. Emery, *The Trinity*, 120.
27. Athanasius, *Against the Arians* 1.5.15 (NPNF² 4:315).
28. Turretin, *Institutes*, 1:256.
29. Turretin, *Institutes*, 1:300–302.
30. Athanasius, *Against the Arians* 1.5.15 (NPNF² 4:315); Aquinas, *Summa* 1a.41.3.
31. Aquinas, *Summa* 1a.41.3. Cf. Hilary, *On the Trinity* 6.13 (NPNF² 9:102).
32. Aquinas, *Summa* 1a.41.3, emphasis added. For a similar point, see Hilary, *On the Trinity* 6.12 (NPNF² 9:103).
33. Hilary, *On the Trinity* 3.23 (NPNF² 9:69); cf. 4.4 (NPNF² 9:72).
34. Hilary, *On the Trinity* 11.12 (NPNF² 9:207), emphasis added.
35. Aquinas, *Summa* 1a.41.3.
36. Hilary, *On the Trinity* 6.35 (NPNF² 9:111).
37. Hilary, *On the Trinity* 6.35 (NPNF² 9:111).
38. Hilary, *On the Trinity* 6.35 (NPNF² 9:111).
39. Hilary, *On the Trinity* 7.2 (NPNF² 9:118); cf. 9.30 (NPNF² 9:165). Also see Aquinas, *Summa* 1a.41.3.
40. Turretin, *Institutes*, 1:301.
41. Hilary, *On the Trinity* 5.37 (NPNF² 9:96).
42. Gregory of Nazianzus, *On God and Christ* 3.29.3 (p. 71). Later, Gregory will qualify that the illustration fails if pressed too far because with a sunbeam there is motion and with motion change. See 4.31.32–33 (p. 142). Also Gregory of Nyssa, *Against Eunomius* 8.1 (NPNF² 5:202); Aquinas, *Summa* 1a.27.1.
43. Swain, "Divine Trinity," 99, emphasis added in first quote.
44. Swain, "Divine Trinity," 100. Cf. Emmanuel Durand, "A Theology of God the Father," in Emery and Levering, eds., *Oxford Handbook of the Trinity*, 382.
45. If the tradition uses the word "priority" at all, it is meant only in terms of *order*, not time or superiority. See Gill, *Body of Divinity*, 145.
46. Gregory of Nazianzus, *On God and Christ* 4.31.14 (p. 127). Francis Turretin adds: "Nor do the properties by which they are mutually distinguished constitute unequal degrees (although they may designate their order as diverse modes of subsisting). By this neither is the essence divided in the persons nor are the persons separated from the essence, but they are only so distinguished that the one cannot be the other." Turretin, *Institutes*, 1:266.

47. Augustine, *Homilies on the Gospel of John 1–40*, 1.12. Cf. Basil of Caesarea, *Against Eunomius*, 1.8.

48. Athanasius, *Against the Arians* 1.10.36 (NPNF² 4:327). Cf. Athanasius, *Defence of the Nicene Definition* 3.13 (NPNF² 158).

49. Gregory of Nazianzus, *On God and Christ* 3.29.4 (p. 72).

50. The implications for the Father would be disastrous too: see John of Damascus, *Exposition of the Orthodox Faith* 8 (NPNF² 9:7).

51. John of Damascus, *Exposition of the Orthodox Faith* 8 (NPNF² 9:7).

52. John of Damascus, *Exposition of the Orthodox Faith* 8 (NPNF² 9:7).

53. The "generation of the Word is not an act that actualizes a potency, but rather is a perfect generating perfect act" (Levering, *Scripture and Metaphysics*, 156).

54. On the impassible nature of generation, see Athanasius, *Against the Arians* 1.8.28 (NPNF² 4:322); Athanasius, *Defence of the Nicene Definition* 3.11 (NPNF² 4:157); Basil of Caesarea, *Against Eunomius*, 2.5, 2.22–24; Gregory of Nazianzus, *Oration on Holy Baptism* 42 (NPNF² 7:375); John of Damascus, *Exposition of the Orthodox Faith* 8 (NPNF² 9:7); Turretin, *Institutes*, 1:293; Ambrose, *On the Christian Faith* I.x.67.

55. Aquinas, *Summa* 1a.42.2.

56. Yet the "Father does not beget the Son by will, but by nature." Aquinas, *Summa* 1a.42.2.

57. Aquinas, *Summa* 1a.27.1; 1a.34.2; Gregory of Nazianzus, *On God and Christ* 4.30.2 (p. 94).

58. Athanasius, *Against the Arians* 4.5 (NPNF² 4:435).

59. Athanasius, *Against the Arians* 1.5.15 (NPNF² 4:315).

60. Athanasius, *Against the Arians* 1.5.15 (NPNF² 4:315).

61. Hilary, *On the Trinity* 5.37 (NPNF² 9:96). Cf. John of Damascus, *Exposition of the Orthodox Faith* 7 (NPNF² 9:5).

62. Anselm, *On the Incarnation of the Word* 15, in *Works*, 258. Cf. *On the Procession of the Holy Spirit*, in *Works*, 433.

63. Anselm, *On the Procession of the Holy Spirit*, in *Works*, 433 (cf. 429).

64. He does not become our Father to somehow bring his eternal Fatherhood to its full potential. He is the Father of his begotten Son from eternity, and such paternity is as perfect as it is immutable, as impeccable as it is natural. It is because he is a Father apart from us that he can voluntarily become a Father to us.

Chapter 7 Is Eternal Generation Central to the Gospel?

1. John 5:17.

2. John 5:18.

3. John 5:24.

4. John 5:26.

5. John 5:27–29.

6. Augustine, *The Trinity* 1.4.26.

7. Augustine, *The Trinity* 1.15.16. Also see Samuel Miller, *Letters on the Eternal Sonship of Christ*, 38. Some contemporaries use the language of "corollary"

instead of "consequence": see Giles, *The Eternal Generation of the Son*, 77; Macleod, *The Person of Christ*, 131.

8. Fesko, *The Trinity and the Covenant of Redemption*, 170. Cf. Aquinas, *Commentary on the Gospel of John*, 2:216; Calvin, *John 1–10*, 276.

9. They argue that *monogenēs* is associated with *genos*, which refers to a special class, rather than to *gennaō*, which means to beget. Westcott, *The Epistle of St. John*, 169–72; Westcott, *The Gospel According to St. John*, 1:23, 28; Moody, "The Translation of John 3:16 in the Revised Standard Version," 213–19; Longenecker, "The One and Only Son," 119–26; Grudem, "Appendix 6," in *Systematic Theology*, 1233–34; Reymond, *New Systematic Theology*, 325. For a summary of the literature, see Giles, *The Eternal Generation of the Son*, 64.

10. At the 2016 meeting of the Evangelical Theological Society, Grudem said that he has now changed his mind about *monogenēs*.

11. Irons, "Lexical Defense," 105.

12. Irons, "Lexical Defense," 105.

13. Irons, "Lexical Defense," 112.

14. As to John 1:14, see Irons's critique of the NIV and ESV in "Lexical Defense," 114–15.

15. Irons, "Lexical Defense," 113. Cf. Lindars, *John*, 96.

16. Irons, "Lexical Defense," 115.

17. Hilary, *On the Trinity* 2.8 (NPNF[2] 9:54).

18. Swain, *Retrieving Eternal Generation*, 41, quoting Webster, "One Who Is Son," in *The Epistle to the Hebrews and Christian Theology*, 85.

19. Gregory of Nyssa, *Against Eunomius* 2.9 (NPNF[2] 5:114). Cf. Basil of Caesarea, *Against Eunomius* 2.17, 32.

20. Webster, *God Without Measure*, 73.

21. Webster, *God Without Measure*, 73.

22. Gregory of Nyssa, *Against Eunomius* 1.39 (NPNF[2] 5:94).

23. Webster, *God Without Measure*, 75.

24. The rest of the verse reads: "Or again, 'I will be to him a father, and he shall be to me a son'?" (cf. 2 Sam. 7:14).

25. Psalm 2:7 is picked up by other NT authors as well: cf. Acts 13:33.

26. Fesko believes "*decree* is a synonym for *covenant*" (*The Trinity and the Covenant of Redemption*, 173).

27. Peter attributes Psalm 2 to David's authorship (Acts 4:25).

28. Bates, *The Birth of the Trinity*, 70.

29. Depending on the Old Testament, the author of Hebrews uses the word "today" in a way that spans vast periods or even eternity itself: Heb. 3:7, 13, 15; 4:7.

30. Augustine, as quoted in Pierce, "Hebrews 1 and the Son Begotten 'Today,'" in Sanders and Swain, eds., *Retrieving Eternal Generation*, 129.

31. Pierce, "Hebrews 1 and the Son Begotten 'Today,'" 130.

32. Pierce, "Hebrews 1 and the Son Begotten 'Today,'" 130.

33. Pierce, "Hebrews 1 and the Son Begotten 'Today,'" 131.

34. The grammar gives the connection away: "Yahweh's declaration of the Messiah's sonship, 'You are my son,' is a *nominal* clause that expresses a condition or state. In contrast, the phrase, 'Today I have begotten you,' is a *verbal* clause,

which expresses an action." Fesko, *The Trinity and the Covenant of Redemption*, 172, emphasis added.

35. "Psalm 2:7 is quoted as evidence that the promise made to the fathers concerning the provision of a Davidic offspring has truly been fulfilled, not in support of the adoption of Jesus as messiah at the time of the resurrection or the enthronement." Bates, *The Birth of the Trinity*, 73–74.

36. Athanasius, *On the Incarnation of the Word* 3.13.7 (NPNF² 4:43); cf. Emery, *The Trinity*, 133.

37. Ayres, *Nicaea and Its Legacy*, 42.

38. Gregory of Nyssa, *Against Eunomius* 1.39 (NPNF² 5:94).

39. Paul will use firstborn language in v. 18 (this time concerning the resurrection) in a way that is consistent with the interpretation we've given of v. 15, namely, Christ in relation to creation (as preeminent), not Christ in relation to God the Father. He will also use firstborn language in Romans 8:29, but this time for the purpose of soteriology. Notice, this is one of those few passages where Paul uses both "image" and "firstborn" in the same context.

40. Bavinck, *Reformed Dogmatics*, 2:276. Also see Webster, *God Without Measure*, 33.

41. See Athanasius, *Defence of the Nicene Definition* 7.30 (NPNF² 4:171), who connects Word with Image.

42. Aquinas, *Summa* 1a.35.1. Also see Hilary, *On the Trinity* 10.6 (NPNF² 9:183).

43. Gregory of Nazianzus makes this statement through *Theological Orations* 3.1–4.21 (NPNF² 7:301–17).

44. See Athanasius, *Defence of the Nicene Definition* 3.6–14 (NPNF² 4:153–59); *Against the Arians* 2.16–22 (NPNF² 4:357–93); Gregory of Nyssa, *Against Eunomius* 2.10 (NPNF² 5:117–18). My exegesis will follow Gregory.

45. Giles, *The Eternal Generation of the Son*, 80 (cf. 83). Cf. Raymond E. Brown, *The Epistles of John* (New York: Doubleday, 1982), 620; Leon Morris, *Gospel According to John* (Grand Rapids: Eerdmans, 1971), 771. Also see John 5:18; 18:37.

46. Also see John 7:42.

47. Gignilliat, "Eternal Generation and the Old Testament," 74.

48. John Owen, *Defense of the Gospel*, in *Works*, 12:236–47.

49. Augustine, *Homilies on the Gospel of John 1–40*, 19.13 (cf. 1.12).

Chapter 8 Is the Son Eternally Subordinate to the Father?

1. I heard and documented this teaching firsthand; the following quotations are also recorded in Ware, *Father, Son, and Holy Spirit*, 46, 49, 50, 51, 154.

2. Credit goes to Fred Sanders for wording my thoughts in a musical key!

3. Crossway no longer publishes Ware's book.

4. It was not uncommon at the time to attend evangelical conferences or institutions where Nicene categories were neglected or criticized.

5. The view is also called ESS: eternal submission/subordination of the Son.

6. Consult chapter 2 of Ware, *Father, Son, and Holy Spirit*. Ware's view is plain elsewhere too: "Does Affirming an Eternal Authority-Submission Relationship in the Trinity Entail a Denial of *Homoousios*?," 237–48; "Equal in Essence, Distinct in Role," 13–38.

7. Ware devoted an entire chapter to history in *Father, Son, and Holy Spirit*, and eternal relations of origin were missing from start to finish. Ware's presentation of the Spirit fared no better. He talked about Constantinople and the Cappadocians but without any mention of eternal spiration or procession. See chap. 2 of *Father, Son, and Holy Spirit*.

8. Ware, *Father, Son, and Holy Spirit*, 41.

9. Ware, *Father, Son, and Holy Spirit*, 43, 45.

10. Emphasis added. This phrase is used throughout chapter 6 of Ware, *Father, Son, and Holy Spirit*.

11. Ware, *Father, Son, and Holy Spirit*, 133; cf. 134.

12. Ware, *Father, Son, and Holy Spirit*, 134.

13. Ware, *Father, Son, and Holy Spirit*, 46–51.

14. Ware, *Father, Son, and Holy Spirit*, 65.

15. Ware, *Father, Son, and Holy Spirit*, 49, 153, emphasis added.

16. Ware, *Father, Son, and Holy Spirit*, 51.

17. Grudem, *Systematic Theology*, 251. Cf. Grudem, *Evangelical Feminism*, 47, 433; Grudem, *Recovering Biblical Manhood and Womanhood*, 457, 540.

18. Ware, *Father, Son, and Holy Spirit*, 51.

19. Ware, *Father, Son, and Holy Spirit*, 67.

20. Ware, *Father, Son, and Holy Spirit*, 49.

21. Ware, *Father, Son, and Holy Spirit*, 21; cf. chapter 4 for full treatment. As for Ware's method, his argument relied on specific texts that he said supported submission in eternity past and future (e.g., 1 Cor. 11:3; 15:24–28). Ware argued that his case was further supported by any text in the Gospels that insinuated submission in the incarnation, as if the incarnation is a continuation of the Son's subordination in eternity. Ware also argued that authority and submission are what the divine names themselves mean. They refer not to eternal relations of origin (i.e., generation) but societal "roles" of hierarchy. The Son is named Son because it is his role to "submit." The Father is named Father because he "stands above the Son" and is "supreme within the Godhead" (49, 51; cf. 82). Even the *order* conveys supremacy and subordination: the Father first, the Son second. Ware thinks this was what "church theologians" meant by "order" or "*taxis*" in the Trinity (72).

22. Ware, *Father, Son, and Holy Spirit*, 75.

23. Ware, *Father, Son, and Holy Spirit*, 56.

24. Grudem, "Doctrinal Deviations," 39.

25. Ware, *Father, Son, and Holy Spirit*, 57.

26. Ware, *Father, Son, and Holy Spirit*, 55, emphasis added.

27. Ware, *Father, Son, and Holy Spirit*, 55, emphasis added.

28. Ware, *Father, Son, and Holy Spirit*, 58.

29. Ware, *Father, Son, and Holy Spirit*, 20.

30. Ware, *Father, Son, and Holy Spirit*, 20.

31. Ware, *Father, Son, and Holy Spirit*, 20. Cf. 157 where Ware mentions "no competition" or "bitterness" or "hubris" or "oppression" as well.

32. To be clear, Ware was not saying this as a liberal but out of a spirit of biblicism.

33. Ware, *Father, Son, and Holy Spirit*, 49, 51.

34. Ware, *Father, Son, and Holy Spirit*, 55.

35. Ware, *Father, Son, and Holy Spirit*, 55.

36. Ware, *Father, Son, and Holy Spirit*, 20.
37. Ware took such an approach not only to the Trinity but also to the attributes of God and Christology. He modified divine immutability in a way not all that different from his approach to the Trinity: God is immutable *in essence* but mutable in his *relations* with the world. He took this approach to a slew of attributes: omnipresence, omniscience, impassibility, etc. As to the person of Christ, Ware taught monothelitism (one will in the incarnate Christ) and rejected the orthodox, creedal position established by the Third Council of Constantinople in 680–81. This council was the sixth ecumenical council, and it confessed *two wills* (dyothelitism) in Christ, corresponding to his *two natures*, one divine and one human; otherwise he cannot be true man and truly able to act as our redeemer. The council condemned monothelitism as heretical because it not only leads to tritheism (if there are three wills in the Trinity, how can there not be three gods?) but cannot do justice to both natures (divine and human) in the person of Christ (see the creed of Chalcedon). At the time, Ware taught one will in Christ to be consistent with his belief that there are three wills in the Trinity (a key tenet of social trinitarianism). Ware ties will to person in *Father, Son, and Holy Spirit*, 18; *The Man Christ Jesus*, 20, 75–76, 84, 88; "Equal in Essence, Distinct in Roles," 36.
38. Ware, *Father, Son, and Holy Spirit*, 21.
39. Ware, *Father, Son, and Holy Spirit*, 58.
40. Ware, *Father, Son, and Holy Spirit*, 59–67.
41. Grudem, *Systematic Theology*, 459–60.
42. Ware, *Father, Son, and Holy Spirit*, 139.
43. Ware, *Father, Son, and Holy Spirit*, 137.
44. Ware, *Father, Son, and Holy Spirit*, 150. Grudem can be the most aggressive: see *Evangelical Feminism*, 207–14; *Evangelical Feminism and Biblical Truth*, 45–48, 403–42; *Systematic Theology*, 459.
45. Ware, *Father, Son, and Holy Spirit*, 139.
46. Controversy erupted in 2016. Bruce Ware and John Starke published a book called *One God in Three Persons*, with contributions from EFSers like Wayne Grudem. I learned of the book after landing on the other side of the pond, only to discover that Mike Ovey, my new colleague and principal, had contributed a chapter and used words like "subordination" to describe the Son's subjection to the Father within the immanent Trinity. When controversy over the Trinity erupted, Mike was surprised to learn that in the past Grudem and Ware had questioned eternal generation, among other tenets of classical Christianity. Mike discovered that there was more to the version of EFS Grudem and Ware maintained than he was willing to affirm. Nevertheless, Mike stayed committed to the word "subordination" despite the Arian and semi-Arian baggage it carried (or how it played into the hands of his opponents who already accused him of Arianism). One day, perhaps, I'll write a review of Mike's book *Your Will Be Done: Exploring Eternal Subordination, Divine Monarchy and Divine Humility*. Until then, here are a few criticisms that need more fleshing out: (1) Rather than giving an extensive treatment of Nicaea, Mike focuses on creeds that are outliers and carry little to no creedal authority today; some of his interpretations are debatable as well. (2) Influenced by Colin Gunton, Mike is sympathetic with a relational view of the Trinity, a version of social trinitarianism. Mike, like Gunton, is skeptical of

Augustine. (3) Mike misreads the historical sources, assuming (like Grudem and Ware) that whenever subordination/submission is referenced the Trinity *ad intra* is in view, whereas a contextual reading demonstrates that Hilary, for example, was referring to the economy of salvation. (4) Mike does give far more attention to John's Gospel than Grudem and Ware, but again, he assumes subordination refers to the Trinity *ad intra*, when context shows John has the economy in view; in other Johannine passages Mike reads his subordinationism into the text when it is just not there. (5) Although Mike tries to assert one will in the Trinity, he is inconsistent and at times uses language that directly and indirectly teaches multiple wills in the Trinity; in doing so Mike not only succumbs to a social definition of the Trinity but compromises the simplicity of the divine essence that subsists in each person. In short, the way Mike wields the term "will(s)" does not preserve a clear distinction between essence and person, especially when he discusses the incarnation. (6) At strategic points in Mike's book, he reveals how motivated he is by gender debates, which leaves the reader curious to what extent Mike's advocacy for subordination is colored by a social agenda.

47. Goligher, "Is It Okay to Teach a Complementarianism Based on Eternal Subordination?"

48. Goligher, "Is It Okay?"

49. Goligher, "Reinventing God."

50. His official publication and response: Ware, "Unity and Distinction of the Trinitarian Persons," 17–62.

51. Ware applies the same method, literally listing text after text with little context. Ware, "Unity and Distinction of the Trinitarian Persons," 26–34. For his listing method, see 32–33.

52. While Ware says this is a "change in my position," he then claims, "I never in the past said that the doctrine of eternal generation is wrong, but I have questioned whether Scripture teaches it, and frankly I've puzzled over just what it means." However, Ware not only questioned and puzzled over it, he outright criticized and denied it, and encouraged others to do the same. Ware did so believing Scripture did not teach eternal generation, yet he was much more against it than he implies (Ware, "Unity and Distinction of the Trinitarian Persons," 50 and n.24.)

53. Ware, "Unity and Distinction of the Trinitarian Persons," 23, 25–26.

54. Ware, "Unity and Distinction of the Trinitarian Persons," 51.

55. Ware, "Unity and Distinction of the Trinitarian Persons," 20, 21.

56. Ware, "Unity and Distinction of the Trinitarian Persons," 34–36, esp. 36.

57. Ware, "Unity and Distinction of the Trinitarian Persons," 24–25.

58. Ware, "Unity and Distinction of the Trinitarian Persons," 27, emphasis added.

59. Others who have opposed EFS include Holmes, Jowers, Butner, Swain, Bird, Emerson and Stamps, Bray, and Johnson (see bibliography).

60. Ware, *Father, Son, and Holy Spirit*, 21.

61. Ware, *Father, Son, and Holy Spirit*, 21.

62. Boff, *Trinity and Society*, 115.

63. Ware, *Father, Son, and Holy Spirit*, 21, 51.

64. Grudem is incorrect to assume inseparable operations means indistinguishable operations. See Grudem, "Biblical Evidence," 258.

65. Ware, "Unity and Distinction of the Trinitarian Persons," 34–36 (esp. 36), emphasis added. Cf. Grudem, "Doctrinal Deviations," 39.

66. Ware, "Unity and Distinction of the Trinitarian Persons," 37.

67. Ware, "Unity and Distinction of the Trinitarian Persons," 38.

68. Webster, *God Without Measure*, 94.

69. John Owen, *Pneumatologia, or a Discourse Concerning the Holy Spirit*, in *Works* 3:93, emphasis added. Cf. Webster, *God Without Measure*, 95.

70. Giles, *The Eternal Generation of the Son*, 232.

71. Holmes, "Classical Trinitarianism and Eternal Functional Subordination," 104.

72. Treier, *Introducing Evangelical Theology*, 84.

73. Treier, *Introducing Evangelical Theology*, 84.

74. Brown, *Heresies*, 101.

75. Ware, *Father, Son, and Holy Spirit*, 21, 51.

76. Not to mention, such a divide creates a quaternity in God.

77. Ware, "Unity and Distinction of the Trinitarian Persons," 19.

78. Athanasius, *Against the Arians* 1.9.29 (NPNF[2] 4:324), emphasis added. Cf. Athanasius, *Defence of the Nicene Definition* 5.19 (NPNF[2] 4:162–63).

79. Gregory of Nyssa, *Against Eunomius* 1.39 (NPNF[2] 5:94), emphasis added.

80. Augustine, *The Trinity* 15.47.

81. Anselm, *Monologion*, 45, in *Works*, 58.

82. Aquinas, *Summa* 1a.41.5.

83. Turretin, *Institutes* 1:272. Cf. 1:292–93.

84. John Owen, *A Brief Declaration and Vindication of the Doctrine of the Holy Trinity*, in *Works*, 2:407. Webster, *God Without Measure*, 87, elaborates on this inseparability between essence and persons.

85. Ayres, *Nicaea and Its Legacy*, 93–96, 140; Hanson, *Christian Doctrine of God*, 673, 693.

86. Grudem, *Systematic Theology*, 251. Cf. Grudem, *Evangelical Feminism*, 47, 433.

87. Ware, "Unity and Distinction of the Trinitarian Persons," 23, 25–26.

88. The Evangelical Theological Society's statement of faith says all three persons are "one in essence, equal in power and glory." It is unclear how Ware and Grudem can affirm this statement without qualification.

89. Ware, *Father, Son, and Holy Spirit*, 51. EFSers also appeal to Jesus's ascension to the "right hand" of the Father (Heb. 1:3). Ware, "Unity and Distinction of the Trinitarian Persons," 44; Grudem, *Recovering Biblical Manhood and Womanhood*, 457. This, again, is a failure to pay attention to context. The context of Heb. 1:3 is the "purification for sins." The economy of salvation is in view. "Right hand" refers to the Son *as Mediator and intercessor* for sinners, not some intrinsic hierarchy within the Trinity *ad intra*, apart from the economy. And in Matthew's Gospel, the ascension signals Jesus's coronation as the risen king, not subordination within the immanent Godhead. Also, what are Ware and Grudem to do with the book of Revelation (3:21; 7:17; 12:5; 22:3), where Jesus sits at the *center* of the throne for all eternity? Or Acts 2:25, where David (Ps. 16:8) speaks in the persona of the Son, the Son who says the Lord (the Father) sits at *his* right hand? EFSers also claim that "glory" in Scripture is attributed to the Father because the

Son is a subordinate authority. Several problems: (1) When texts like Phil. 2:11 say "to the glory of God the Father," the context is the economy of salvation. The verses that precede are all about the humility Christ has chosen for the sake of salvation. (2) In the economy of salvation, the Father sends the Son, and the Father and Son send the Spirit, an order that corresponds to each person's eternal relations of origin. When the incarnate Son finishes his work of redemption, of course glory moves in the reverse direction. But it does so to match the order of the missions (from the Father through the Son by the Spirit), not to communicate primacy and hierarchy within the immanent Godhead itself. (3) Many passages, like Phil. 2, *also* assume or even state the Son's total equality with the Father, precluding subordination within the immanent Trinity. Funny, Paul never stops to say, "Oh, I mean equal in essence, but not in hypostatic authority." That bifurcation is foreign to Paul. (4) EFSers ignore texts where there is mutual glorification. They love to quote John 5:19 but forget to keep reading: "For the Father judges no one, but has given all judgment to the Son, *that all may honor the Son, just as they honor the Father*" (5:22–23). Like I've said, EFS has a bad habit of ignoring context, a product of their narrow biblicism.

    90. Hilary, *On the Trinity* 3:12 (NPNF² 9:65).

    91. Ware tries to avoid the charge of semi-Arianism by saying authority is *not* a nature-property, so it's not as if the *essence* of God involves hierarchy. Instead, it's a person-property. But the burden of proof is on Ware to prove this claim. For authority has everything to do with divine power, and omnipotence is a divine attribute, synonymous with the essence of God (simplicity). Also, Ware redefines authority in the category of a relation*ship*; just as humans can have differing authority relationships and be equal as persons, so too God. But this is univocal reasoning, applying creaturely and social characteristics to the divine, where the persons are alike in all things (simplicity) except their modes of subsistence.

    92. We will unpack the covenant of redemption in chapter 10. But for now, one issue must be addressed: some EFSers try to inject hierarchy and subordination into the covenant of redemption as a way of establishing hierarchy within the immanent Trinity, the persons *a se*. That is a misuse—even an abuse—of the covenant of redemption for many reasons. Consider four:

    (1) Even if (for the sake of argument) subordination were to be located in the covenant of redemption, we are still speaking of the economy. "The pactum salutis is eternal in that it is pre-temporal, but it is not eternal in the sense that it belongs to the perfect life of God" (Holmes, "Classical Trinitarianism and Eternal Functional Subordination," 87). EFSers think that if they can prove subordination exists in eternity, not just in the incarnation, then there must be functional hierarchy intrinsic to the immanent Trinity. That assumption conflates "eternity" with "immanent" Trinity; but the former is a far broader category, also including the economic. The economy refers to the triune God's outward, external acts toward the world, which begin in eternity, as seen with the covenant of redemption. The immanent Trinity, however, is internal, referring to God in himself (*a se*), to his ontological unity (simplicity) and personal properties (relations). We should not assume that if something is eternal it then defines the immanent Trinity. To do so is to risk pantheism or panentheism, as if what occurs in the economic (even

in eternity) must be true and necessary for the immanent. After defining the covenant of redemption, Turretin describes the obedience of the Son, but notice how he frames such obedience within the economy: "For thus the Scriptures represent to us the Father in the economy of salvation as stipulating the obedience of the Son even unto death, and for it promising in return a name above every name that he might be the head of the elect in glory; the Son as offering himself to do the Father's will, promising a faithful and constant performance of the duty required of him and restipulating the kingdom and glory promised to him" (Turretin, *Institutes* 12.2.13).

(2) It is illegitimate to read subordination back into the covenant of redemption. EFSers like to read their definition of subordination into Reformed *pactum* language. Not only is that terribly anachronistic, manipulating Reformed categories for a novel agenda like EFS, but it fails to see what is occurring in the covenant itself. The Reformed are adamant that when the Son covenants with the Father to be Mediator, he does so voluntarily and temporarily, becoming incarnate at the appointed time to be Israel's Redeemer. In other words, the Son's agreement to the covenant does not stem from some intrinsic subordination between the Father and the Son, but the Son accepts the covenant for the specific purpose of accomplishing redemption. The covenant is *economic* and therefore *optional*. If the Father and Son never entered into a covenant, nothing within the Trinity would change.

(3) EFS projects Christology, the economy in particular, back onto its doctrine of God. By appealing to the covenant of redemption to substantiate subordination, EFS allows the submission of the Son to the Father in the economy to define and determine the immanent Trinity. This is entirely backward. Fesko's evaluation of Barth could just as easily apply to EFS: "Christ's mission ends up defining the Trinity rather than revealing it" (Fesko, *The Trinity and the Covenant of Redemption*, 190). Furthermore, the EFS method invites Christology to be the all-revealing starting point when approaching the Trinity. Countering the Socinians in his own day, John Owen warned against this tendency when he said, "Christ is the immediate object of faith, but God in his all-sufficiency is the ultimate object of faith" (Owen, "God the Saints' Rock," in *Works* 9:250; cf. Duby, *God In Himself*). By contrast, we distinguish between the form of a servant and the form of God (Augustine). Taking on the form of a servant, and in that state becoming subservient to the mission the Father had given to him, is something the Son does for the sake of our salvation, not because he is *as the eternal Son* subordinate to the Father. His obedience brings the covenant of redemption to fulfillment, but we dare not conclude that this *economic* accomplishment (obedience) is what defines the personal property of the Son (eternal generation) within the immanent Trinity, a personal property that not only distinguishes him *as Son* but ensures he is coequal in essence, power, and authority with the Father, begotten as he is from the Father's *ousia*. To project obedience back into the immanent Trinity as that which defines the Son *as Son* is to create an inferior Son, undermining biblical, Nicene orthodoxy.

(4) EFSers will argue that if the Son can covenant with the Father without violating the one will of God, then the Son can eternally submit to the Father without violating the one will of God. After all, that charge is often thrown at EFS:

hierarchy, even in function, undermines the unity of the divine will. In response, EFSers have not thought through their own view. For they do not merely claim there is obedience in the *pactum*; no, they are claiming far more. Submission is what defines the Son *as Son*. This is apparent in Grudem and Ware. Even when Ware more recently stopped rejecting eternal generation, he continues to use eternal generation to import submission within the immanent Trinity. For EFS, submission is a defining quality for the Son, and all the more so when it becomes intrinsic to the Son's personal property (filiation), his mode of subsistence (eternal generation). As such, it now threatens the unity and coequality of the persons. Submission is not merely an economic appropriation for EFS; it is intrinsic to the immanent identity of the Son. For the Reformed, the Son's obedience in the covenant of redemption is optional, an economic deliberation that is not necessary for God to be triune. For EFS, the Son's obedience in the covenant of redemption is necessary, an extension of the submission that defines him as a person within the immanent Trinity, necessary for the Son to be *Son* and therefore necessary for the Trinity to be triune.

Commendable treatments of "obedience" in reference to the Trinity, each avoiding the pitfalls of EFS, include Fesko, *The Trinity and the Covenant of Redemption*, 181–93; White, "Intra-Trinitarian Obedience," 377–402; Swain and Allen, "The Obedience of the Eternal Son," 114–34; Swain, "The Covenant of Redemption," 107–25.

93. Augustine, *The Trinity* 2.1.3 (cf. 1.3.14). This method of interpretation, which does not originate with Augustine, is called *partitive exegesis*. Cf. Hilary, *On the Trinity* 8.45 (*NPNF²* 9:150); 10.21–22 (*NPNF²* 9:187).

94. Christ so humbled himself that, according to Rule 2 (Form of a Servant), Augustine can even say there is a sense in which the Son is "less" (servant) than himself. See Augustine, *The Trinity* 1.3.14.

95. The incarnation did not involve a change or mixture of the two natures of Christ: Augustine counsels us to use the language of "taking on" instead of "taking over." *The Trinity* 1.3.14 (cf. 2.2.9; 4.5.30).

96. Augustine, *The Trinity* 1.3.21. Cf. Gregory of Nazianzus, *On God And Christ* 3.29.20 (p. 87); 4.30.6 (p. 97).

97. Augustine, *The Trinity* 2.1.3.

98. Augustine, *The Trinity* 2.1.3.

99. Augustine, *The Trinity* 1.3.14.

100. See Ayres, *Nicaea and Its Legacy*, 133–66.

101. Even if the immanent Trinity were in focus, the Son *in the form of God* must be on the receiving end of the kingdom: see Augustine, *The Trinity* 1.3.15.

102. Crowe, *Death in Adam, Life in Christ.*

103. Augustine, *The Trinity* 1.3.17.

104. "Becomes" does not mean the Son is no longer immutable. He does not empty his divine nature and its attributes. His divinity is not circumscribed by his humanity (*extra Calvinisticum*). See Weinandy, *Does God Change?*

105. Maximus, *Opusculum* 6.4, in Maximus, *Cosmic Mystery*, 176.

106. Bilezikian, "Hermeneutical Bungee-Jumping," 66.

107. Karen Kilby, "Perichoresis and Projection."

108. See D. A. Carson, *Exegetical Fallacies.*

109. Schreiner, *1 Corinthians*, 219.
110. Schreiner, *1 Corinthians*, 219.
111. Bird, "Preface: Theologians of a Lesser Son," in Bird and Harrower, eds., *Trinity Without Hierarchy*, 10. To compare EFS and Homoians, see Smith, "The Trinity in the Fourth-Century Fathers," 113, 115.
112. Ware, *Father, Son, and Holy Spirit*, 46ff, 50–51, 57–58, 154.
113. Glory be.

Chapter 9 Is the Spirit Spirated?

1. These include *My Brilliant Friend, The Story of a New Name, Those Who Leave and Those Who Stay*, and *The Story of the Lost Child*, translated by Ann Goldstein, published between 2012 and 2015 by Europa.
2. Elena Ferrante, *My Brilliant Friend* (New York: Europa Editions, 2012), 261–62.
3. "Spirit" can be used in three ways in Scripture: essential, personal, and metonymical. Witsius, *Exercitationes* 23.3; cf. Muller, *PRRD*, 4:341.
4. Calvin, *Institutio* (1536), ii (p. 135), as quoted in Muller, *PRRD*, 4:333. See also Gregory of Nyssa, *On the Holy Spirit* (NPNF² 5:315).
5. E.g., Socinianism.
6. Anselm, *On the Procession of the Holy Spirit*, in *Works*, 406.
7. Emery, *The Trinity*, 143.
8. On this point, see Augustine, *The Trinity* 15, epilogue.
9. Anselm, *On the Procession of the Holy Spirit*, in *Works*, 391. Cf. John of Damascus, *Exposition of the Orthodox Faith* 1.8 (NPNF² 9:9); Turretin, *Institutes*, 1:309.
10. Anselm, *On the Procession of the Holy Spirit*, in *Works*, 393.
11. On spiration, see Oration 5 in Gregory of Nazianzus, *Theological Orations* 5.1–33 (NPNF² 7:318–28); Augustine, *On the Trinity* 1.5.8; 2.3.5; 5.14.15; 15.25.45; 15.26.47; 15.27.48; 15.27.50. Others define spiration as "the procession of subsisting Love." See, for example, Aquinas, *Summa* 1a.43.2.
12. Bavinck, *Reformed Dogmatics*, 2:311, explains why spiration is not as conspicuous as generation.
13. Richard of Saint Victor, *On the Trinity* 5.23.
14. He doesn't always get up on his board. Sometimes he wipes out with his logical persistence, and at times he sounds a bit like a social trinitarian. But that may be a premature criticism since Richard lived long before the modern era.
15. Richard of Saint Victor, *On the Trinity* 5.23.
16. Bavinck, *Reformed Dogmatics*, 2:277.
17. By breathing on them, Jesus gives them the Spirit he promised prior to his death (John 14:26; 15:26; 16:7).
18. Augustine, *The Trinity* 4.5.29 (cf. 4.20.29).
19. Peter seems to understand this by Pentecost (Acts 2:33).
20. Another text where the Spirit is associated with "gift" is Hebrews 6:4.
21. Basil of Caesarea, *On the Trinity* 16.37 (NPNF² 8:23).
22. Augustine, *The Trinity* 5.3.12.

23. He is "*given* by both [Father and Son], not as *born* from both (*ut datus, non ut natus*)" (Bavinck, *Reformed Dogmatics*, 2:313).

24. Augustine, *The Trinity* 5.17, quoted in Johnson, *Rethinking the Trinity*, 76.

25. The Spirit "can be a gift even before it is given, but it cannot be called in any way a donation unless it has been given" (Bavinck, *Reformed Dogmatics*, 2:321).

26. Augustine, *The Trinity* 15.5.29. Aquinas takes a similar line, calling the Spirit not only love but joy (Gal. 5:22). See Aquinas, *Summa* 1a.39.8.

27. Augustine, *The Trinity* 15.5.27.

28. Augustine, *The Trinity* 6.10; *PL* 42, 931, as quoted in Aquinas, *Summa* 1a.39.8.

29. Augustine, *The Trinity* 15.5.32.

30. Augustine, *The Trinity* 9.1.2.

31. Following Augustine, so too did the Reformers: Calvin, *Institutes* 1.13.4; Bullinger, *Decades* 4.3 (3:156). Cf. Muller, *PRRD*, 4:202.

32. Bavinck, *Reformed Dogmatics*, 2:331.

33. Just as the person of the Spirit appropriates attributes like "holy" without losing his personal distinction (see the Nicene Creed), so too can the person of the Spirit appropriate "love" without losing his personal distinction. See Augustine, *The Trinity* 15.5.37.

34. Augustine, *The Trinity*, 15.5.27. Aquinas also says the Spirit "proceeds from them as the Love uniting the two" (*Summa* 1a.36.4; cf. 1a.38.2).

35. Ferrante, *My Brilliant Friend*, 296.

36. Anselm, *On the Procession of the Holy Spirit*, in *Works*, 429.

37. Bavinck, *Reformed Dogmatics*, 2:312.

Chapter 10 Do Father, Son, and Spirit Work Inseparably?

1. Augustine, *Homilies on the Gospel of John* 20.13 (NPNF[1] 7:137). Cf. Beeke and Smalley, *Systematic Theology*, 1:895.

2. Johnson, *Rethinking the Trinity and Religious Pluralism*, 119.

3. Augustine, *The Trinity* 1.3.8.

4. Emery, *The Trinity*, 162, emphasis added.

5. John 1:1–3; Rom. 11:36; 1 Cor. 8:6; Eph. 1:3–14.

6. Gregory of Nyssa, *On the Holy Spirit* (NPNF[2] 5:319).

7. Gregory of Nazianzus, *Oration on Holy Baptism* 41 (NPNF[2] 7:375).

8. Augustine, *The Trinity* 2.2.9, emphasis added.

9. Paul may not be using "sanctify" or "sanctification" in the same way in every instance. Much of the time he has a definitive past in mind, but sometimes an ongoing process. Context is key.

10. Basil of Caesarea, *On the Spirit* 16.37 (NPNF[2] 8:23).

11. Johnson, *Rethinking the Trinity and Religious Pluralism*, 119.

12. Emery, *The Trinity*, 165. These translations are Emery's, and he attributes the language to the twelfth and thirteenth centuries.

13. Emery, *The Trinity*, 165. Cf. Ayres, *Nicaea and Its Legacy*, 297–98.

14. Bavinck speaks of a "special task" (*Reformed Dogmatics*, 2:319).

15. Bavinck, *Reformed Dogmatics*, 2:319.

16. On these two dangers, see Emery, *The Trinity*, 164.

17. Swain, "Divine Trinity," 104.
18. Gregory of Nyssa, *On the Holy Spirit* (NPNF² 8:320). Cf. Calvin, *Institutes* 3.13.18; Muller, *PRRD*, 4:200.
19. Gregory of Nyssa, *On "Not Three Gods"* (NPNF² 5:334). Likewise, the Reformed: Venema, *Inst. Theol.*, x (p. 222); Owen, *Pneumatologia* 3.1, in *Works*, 3:209; Mastricht, *Theoretical-Practical Theology* 2.27.11; Muller, *PRRD*, 4:265 (cf. 269); 4:380.
20. Ursinus, *Commentary*, 271; cf. Muller, *PRRD*, 4:341.
21. Muller, *PRRD*, 4:268 (cf. 4:378).
22. Gregory of Nyssa, *On the Holy Trinity* (NPNF² 5:328).
23. Muller, *PRRD*, 4:268 (cf. 4:378).
24. "[The] order of the persons *ad intra* in the *opera personalia* is mirrored *ad extra* in the *opera appropriate*" (Muller, *PRRD*, 4:200).
25. Turretin, *Institutes*, 1:281–82.
26. William Perkins is especially helpful; see Muller, *PRRD*, 4:208.
27. Calvin, *Institutes* 3.13.18; cf. Muller, *PRRD*, 4:200.
28. Basil of Caesarea, *On the Spirit* 16.38 (NPNF² 8:23).
29. Basil of Caesarea, *On the Spirit* 16.38 (NPNF² 8:24). Also note John Owen, *Pneumatologia*, in *Works*, 3:94.
30. Basil of Caesarea, *On the Spirit* 16.38 (NPNF² 8:24).
31. Leigh will even appropriate creation and salvation to different persons: *Treatise*, II.xvi (pp. 139); cf. Muller, *PRRD*, 4:189.
32. Basil of Caesarea, *On the Spirit* 1.3 (NPNF² 8:3); Bavinck, *Reformed Dogmatics*, 2:319.
33. Bavinck, *Reformed Dogmatics*, 319; quoting Basil of Caesarea, *On the Spirit*, 21, 22, 38 (NPNF² 8:14, 15, 23).
34. Irenaeus, *Against Heresies* 4.20.1; cf. Emery, *The Trinity*, 169.
35. Translation is Irenaeus's; emphasis added.
36. Emery, *The Trinity*, 169.
37. "The divine action is one, and its modality is essentially Trinitarian." Emery, *The Trinity*, 169.
38. Not just the narrow sense (internal renewal of believer) but in the broad sense (entire order of salvation).
39. Bavinck, *Reformed Dogmatics*, 3:570.
40. Bavinck, *Reformed Dogmatics*, 1:112.
41. Muller, *PRRD*, 4:259, describing Wollebius, *Compenndium* 1.4, canons A.1.
42. Bavinck is even so bold to say the persons can be assigned to eras of redemptive history, the Father in the OT, the Son with the incarnation, and the Spirit at Pentecost. Elsewhere Bavinck warns against turning the persons into revelatory modes as Sabellianism does. Has Bavinck contradicted himself? No, there is a difference between divine appropriations and dissolving the persons altogether in the guise of revelatory epochs. We know Bavinck avoids the latter: Bavinck, *Reformed Dogmatics*, 2:320. Also see van Mastricht, *Theoretical-Practical Theology*, 2:505.
43. Augustine highlights divine appropriations via incarnation and Pentecost. See *The Trinity* 1.2.7. Also Muller, *PRRD*, 4:274.

44. John Owen, *The Mystery of the Gospel*, in *Works*, 12:497. Owen appeals to Hebrews 10:7 and Psalm 40:7–8. Cf. *An Exposition of the Epistle to the Hebrews*, in *Works*, 18:87–88. In *Death of Death* (*Works*, 10:170) he also appeals to Isaiah 49:6–12.

45. To be technical, election and the covenant of redemption are not synonymous, though they no doubt relate. Berkhof, *Systematic Theology*, 268; Swain, "The Covenant of Redemption," 110–16.

46. Berkhof, *Systematic Theology*, 270.

47. See Swain, "The Covenant of Redemption," 119; Bavinck, *Our Reasonable Faith*, 333–34.

48. Critics are diverse: Barth, *Church Dogmatics* IV.1, 65, 177, 192–93, 199; J. B. Torrance, "Covenant or Contract?," *Scottish Journal of Theology* 23 (1970): 51–76; T. F. Torrance, *Scottish Theology* (London: T&T Clark, 2000), 1–4, 107; O. Palmer Robertson, *The Christ of the Covenants* (Phillipsburg, NJ: P&R, 1987), 54; Robert Letham, *The Westminster Assembly* (Phillipsburg, NJ: P&R, 2009), 235–37; Letham, *The Work of Christ* (Downers Grove, IL: InterVarsity, 1993), 52–53, 254. Although Letham has qualified his criticism more recently in *Systematic Theology* (Wheaton: Crossway, 2019), 431–39.

49. Anselm, *On the Procession of the Holy Spirit*, in *Works*, 393; Aquinas, *Summa*, 1a.34.1; Aquinas, *Gospel of John*, 1:294–95.

50. Owen, *Hebrews*, in *Works*, 18:87.

51. Basil of Caesarea, *On the Holy Spirit*, 8.21 (NPNF[2] 8:14).

52. Emery, *The Trinity*, 163.

53. Owen, *Hebrews*, in *Works*, 18:87–88.

54. Fesko, *The Trinity and the Covenant of Redemption*, 173–90. Fesko also uses the term "pluriform." Dolezal, "Trinity, Simplicity and the Status of God's Personal Relations," 94, uses the phrase "threefold manner."

55. Emery, *The Trinity*, 164 (cf. 122–23).

56. Aquinas, *Summa* 3.23.2.3.

57. Aquinas, *Summa* 3.23.2.3, as presented in Emery, *The Trinity*, 167. Swain says something similar: *The God of the Gospel*, 160.

58. Emery, *The Trinity*, 167.

59. Here I am following the lead of Emery, *The Trinity*, 167, but I am giving my own take on it (which sounds more Protestant than Roman Catholic).

60. Adoptionism was an early heresy that claimed Jesus is not the eternal Son but was adopted as God's Son at a specific point at the start of his ministry (e.g., baptism). Aquinas is not teaching adoptionism.

61. Calvin, *Harmony of the Evangelists*, Matt. 6:9 in loc.; quoted in Muller, *PRRD*, 4:247.

62. Question and answer 33 in "The Heidelberg Catechism (1563)," in Dennison, ed., *16th and 17th Century Reformed Confessions*, 2:775.

63. Augustine, *The Trinity* 5.4.17.

64. Swain, "Divine Trinity," 104.

65. Emery, *The Trinity*, 168.

66. Augustine, *The Trinity* 1.3.19 (cf. 5.3.14).

67. Owen, *Of Communion with God*, in *Works*, 2:18.

68. Gregory of Nazianzus, *Oration on Holy Baptism* 41 (NPNF[2] 7:375).

69. Owen, *Of Communion with God*, in *Works*, 2:19.
70. Owen, *Of Communion with God*, in *Works*, 2:44.
71. Owen, *Of Communion with God*, in *Works*, 2:45.
72. Owen, *Of Communion with God*, in *Works*, 2:262.
73. Athanasius, Letters to Serapion on the Holy Spirit 2.15.1.

Conclusion

1. C. S. Lewis, *Mere Christianity* (New York: HarperSanFrancisco, 1980), 155.

Bibliography

For a full bibliography of Trinity resources, go to www.credomag
.com/simplytrinity.

Primary Sources

Anselm of Canterbury. *The Major Works*. Oxford: Oxford University Press, 1998.

Aquinas, Thomas. *Commentary on the Gospel of John*. Translated by Fabian Larcher and James A. Weisheipl. 3 vols. Washington, DC: Catholic University of America Press, 2010.

————. *Summa Theologiae*. Vol. 6, *The Trinity*. Edited by Ceslaus Velecky. Cambridge: Cambridge University Press, 2006.

————. *Summa Theologiae*. Vol. 7, *Father, Son, and Holy Ghost*. Edited by T. C. O'Brien. Cambridge: Cambridge University Press, 2006.

Arius. *Letter to Alexander of Alexandria*. In *The Trinitarian Controversy*, edited and translated by William G. Rusch, 31–32. Louisville: Westminster John Knox, 1980.

————. *Letter to Eusebius of Nicomedia*. In *The Trinitarian Controversy*, edited and translated by William G. Rusch, 29–31. Louisville: Westminster John Knox, 1980.

————. *Letter to the Emperor Constantine*. In *The Trinitarian Controversy*, edited and translated by William G. Rusch, 61–62. Louisville: Westminster John Knox, 1980.

Athanasius. *Against the Arians*. In *Nicene and Post-Nicene Fathers*, second series, edited by Philip Schaff and Henry Wace, 4:303–447. Peabody, MA: Hendrickson, 2012.

———. *Defence of the Nicene Council*. In *Nicene and Post-Nicene Fathers*, second series, edited by Philip Schaff and Henry Wace, 4:149–172. Peabody, MA: Hendrickson, 2012.

———. *Letters to Serapion on the Holy Spirit*. In Athanasius and Didymus the Blind, *Works on the Spirit*. Popular Patristics Series 43. Yonkers, NY: St Vladimir's Seminary Press, 2011.

———. *On the Incarnation*. In *Nicene and Post-Nicene Fathers*, second series, edited by Philip Schaff and Henry Wace, 4:31–67. Peabody, MA: Hendrickson, 2012.

Augustine. *Homilies on the Gospel of John*. In *Nicene and Post-Nicene Fathers*, first series, edited by Philip Schaff, 7:7–458. Peabody, MA: Hendrickson, 2012.

———. *Homilies on the Gospel of John 1–40*. Edited by Allan D. Fitzgerald. Translated by Edmund Hill. Hyde Park, NY: New City Press, 2009.

———. *The Trinity*. Edited by John E. Rotelle. Translated by Edmund Hill. The Works of Saint Augustine 5. Hyde Park, NY: New City Press, 1991.

Basil of Caesarea. *Against Eunomius*. Fathers of the Church Patristic Series. Washington, DC: Catholic University of America Press, 2011.

———. *On the Spirit; De Spiritu Sanctu*. In *Nicene and Post-Nicene Fathers*, second series, edited by Philip Schaff and Henry Wace, 8:1–50. Peabody, MA: Hendrickson, 2012.

Boethius. *A Treatise against Eutyches and Nestorius*. Loeb Classical Library 74. Cambridge: Harvard University Press, 1973.

———. *The Trinity Is One God Not Three Gods*. In *The Theological Tractates: The Consolation of Philosophy*, translated by H. F. Stewart, E. K. Rand, and S. J. Tester. Cambridge, MA: Harvard University Press, 1968.

Bonaventure. *Breviloquium*. Vol. 9, *Works of St. Bonaventure*. New York: The Franciscan Institute, 2005.

———. *St. Bonaventure's Disputed Questions on the Mystery of the Trinity*. Vol. 3, *Works of St. Bonaventure*. New York: The Franciscan Institute, 2005.

———. *The Tree of Life*. In *Bonaventure: The Soul's Journey into God, the Tree of Life, The Life of St. Francis*. Translated by Ewert Cousins. New York: Paulist, 1978.

Bullinger, Heinrich. *The Decades of Henry Bullinger.* Edited by Thomas Harding. Translated by H. I. 4 vols. Cambridge: Cambridge University Press, 1849–52.

Calvin, John. *Commentary on the Holy Gospel of Jesus Christ According to John.* Translated by William Pringle. Vol. 17 of *Calvin's Commentaries.* Reprint, Grand Rapids: Baker Books, 2005.

———. *Institutes of the Christian Religion.* Edited by John T. McNeill. Translated by Ford Lewis Battles. 2 vols. The Library of Christian Classics. 1960. Reprint, Louisville: Westminster John Knox, 2006.

Dennison Jr., James T., ed. *Reformed Confessions of the 16th and 17th Centuries in English Translation: Volume 2, 1552–1566.* Grand Rapids: Reformation Heritage Books, 2010.

Gill, John. *A Complete Body of Doctrinal and Practical Divinity.* Atlanta: Turner Lassetter, 1957.

Gregory of Nazianzus. *On God and Christ: The Five Theological Orations and Two Letters to Cledonius.* Popular Patristics Series 23. Crestwood, NY: St Vladimir's Seminary Press, 2002.

———. *Select Orations.* In *Nicene and Post-Nicene Fathers,* second series, edited by Philip Schaff and Henry Wace, 7:203–436. Peabody, MA: Hendrickson, 2012.

Gregory of Nyssa. *Against Eunomius.* In *Nicene and Post-Nicene Fathers,* second series, edited by Philip Schaff and Henry Wace, 5:33–314. Peabody, MA: Hendrickson, 2012.

———. *On "Not Three Gods."* In *Nicene and Post-Nicene Fathers,* second series, edited by Philip Schaff and Henry Wace, 5:331–36. Peabody, MA: Hendrickson, 2012.

———. *On the Holy Spirit against Macedonius.* In *Nicene and Post-Nicene Fathers,* second series, edited by Philip Schaff and Henry Wace, 5:315–25. Peabody, MA: Hendrickson, 2012.

———. *On the Holy Trinity.* In *Nicene and Post-Nicene Fathers,* second series, edited by Philip Schaff and Henry Wace, 5:326–30. Peabody, MA: Hendrickson, 2012.

Hilary of Poitiers. *On the Trinity.* In *Nicene and Post-Nicene Fathers,* second series, edited by Philip Schaff and Henry Wace, 9:40–234. Peabody, MA: Hendrickson, 2012.

Irenaeus of Lyons. *Against Heresies.* In *Ante-Nicene Fathers,* edited by Alexander Roberts and James Donaldson, 1:309–567. Peabody, MA: Hendrickson, 2012.

John of Damascus. *An Exact Exposition of the Orthodox Faith*. In *Nicene and Post-Nicene Fathers*, second series, edited by Philip Schaff and Henry Wace, 9:1–101. Peabody, MA: Hendrickson, 2012.

———. *Orthodox Faith*. In *Saint John of Damascus: Writings*, translated by Frederic H. Chase Jr., 1.14:165–406. The Fathers of the Church 37. Washington, DC: The Catholic University of America Press, 1958.

Leith, John H., ed. *Creeds of the Churches*. 3rd edition. Louisville: Westminster John Knox, 1982.

Mastricht, Petrus van. *Theoretical-Practical Theology: Faith in the Triune God*. Vol. 2. Edited by Joel R. Beeke. Translated by Todd M. Rester. Grand Rapids: Reformation Heritage Books, 2019.

Maximus the Confessor. *On the Cosmic Mystery of Jesus Christ*. Popular Patristics Series 25. Crestwood, NY: St Vladimir's Press, 1993.

Miller, Samuel. *Letters on the Eternal Sonship of Christ: Addressed to the Rev. Stuart, of Andover*. Philadelphia: W. W. Woodward, 1823.

Origen. *On First Principles*. Translated by John Behr. Oxford: Oxford University Press, 2019.

Owen, John. *An Exposition of the Epistle to the Hebrews with Preliminary Exercitations*. Vol. 2. Edited by W. H. Goold. Edinburgh: Banner of Truth, 1991.

———. *The Glory of Christ*. Vol. 1, *The Works of John Owen*. Edited by William H. Goold. Edinburgh: Banner of Truth Trust, 2009.

———. *The Gospel Defended*. Vol. 12, *The Works of John Owen*. Edited by William H. Goold. Edinburgh: Banner of Truth Trust, 2009.

———. *Of Communion with God the Father, Son, and Holy Ghost*. Vol. 2, *The Works of John Owen*. Edited by William H. Goold. Edinburgh: Banner of Truth Trust, 2009.

Richard of St. Victor. *Richard of Saint Victor, On the Trinity*. Edited and translated by Ruben Angelici. Eugene, OR: Wipf and Stock, 2011.

Tertullian. *Against Praxeas*. In *Ante-Nicene Fathers*, edited by Alexander Roberts and James Donaldson, 3:597–632. Peabody, MA: Hendrickson, 2012.

Turretin, Francis. *Institutes of Elenctic Theology*. Vol. 1, *First Through Ten Topics*. Edited by James T. Dennison Jr. Translated by George Giger. Phillipsburg, NJ: P&R Publishing, 1992.

Ursinus, Zacharias. *The Commentary of Dr. Zacharias Ursinus on the Heidelberg Catechism*. Translated by G. W. Williard. 1852. Reprint, Phillipsburg, NJ: P&R, 1985.

Secondary Sources

Allen, Michael, and Scott Swain. "The Obedience of the Eternal Son." *International Journal of Systematic Theology* 15 (2013): 114–34.

Anatolios, Khaled, ed. *Retrieving Nicaea: The Development and Meaning of Trinitarian Doctrine*. Reprint edition. Grand Rapids: Baker Academic, 2018.

Ayres, Lewis. *Augustine and the Trinity*. Cambridge: Cambridge University Press, 2010.

———. *Nicaea and Its Legacy: An Approach to Fourth-Century Trinitarian Theology*. Oxford: Oxford University Press, 2006.

Barnes, Michel René. "The Fourth Century as Trinitarian Canon." In *Christian Origins: Theology, Rhetoric, and Community*, edited by Lewis Ayres and Gareth Jones, 47–67. London: Routledge, 1998.

Barth, Karl. *Church Dogmatics*. 14 volumes. Edited by G. W. Bromily and T. F. Torrance. Peabody, MA: Hendrickson, 2010.

Bates, Matthew. *The Birth of the Trinity: Jesus, God, and Spirit in New Testament and Early Christian Interpretations of the Old Testament*. Oxford: Oxford University Press, 2015.

Bavinck, Herman. *Reformed Dogmatics*. Vol. 2, *God and Creation*. Grand Rapids: Baker Academic, 2004.

Beckwith, Carl L. *The Holy Trinity*. Wayne, IN: Luther Academy, 2016.

Beeke, Joel R., and Paul M. Smalley. *Reformed Systematic Theology*. Vol. 1, *Revelation and God*. Wheaton: Crossway, 2019.

Behr, John. *Formation of Christian Theology*. 3 vols. Crestwood, NY: St Vladimir's Seminary Press, 2001.

Bilezikian, Gilbert. "Hermeneutical Bungee-Jumping: Subordination in the Godhead." *Journal of the Evangelical Theological Society* 40, no. 1 (1997): 57–68.

Bird, Michael F. "The Coming War: Nicene Complementarians vs Homoian Complementarians." *Euangelion* (blog). Patheos, June 8, 2016. https://www.patheos.com/blogs/euangelion/2016/06/the-coming-war-nicene-complementarians-vs-homoian-complementarians/.

Bray, Gerald. *Creeds, Councils, and Christ: Did the Early Christians Misrepresent Jesus?* Downers Grove, IL: InterVarsity, 1984.

———. "The Eternal 'Subordination' of the Son?" *Unio Cum Christo* 4, no. 1 (2018): 47–63.

Boff, Leonardo. *Holy Trinity, Perfect Community*. Maryknoll, NY: Orbis, 1988.

———. *Trinity and Society*. New York: Orbis, 1988.

Butner Jr., D. Glenn. *The Son Who Learned Obedience: A Theological Case Against the Eternal Submission of the Son*. Eugene, OR: Pickwick, 2018.

Carson, D. A. *Exegetical Fallacies*. 2nd edition. Grand Rapids: Baker Academic, 1996.

———. "John 5:26: *Crux Interpretum* for Eternal Generation." In *Retrieving Eternal Generation*, edited by Fred Sanders and Scott R. Swain, 79–97. Grand Rapids: Zondervan Academic, 2017.

Coakley, Sarah. "'Persons' in the 'Social' Doctrine of the Trinity: A Critique of Current Analytic Discussion." In *The Trinity*, edited by Stephen T. Davis, Daniel Kendall, and Gerald O'Collins, 123–44. Oxford: Oxford University Press, 1994.

Craig, William Lane. "Toward a Tenable Social Trinitarianism." In *Philosophical and Theological Essays on the Trinity*, edited by Thomas McCall and Michael C. Rae, 89–99. Oxford: Oxford University Press, 2009.

———, and J. P. Moreland. *Philosophical Foundations for a Christian Worldview*. 2nd edition. Downers Grove, IL: InterVarsity, 2017.

Dolezal, James. *All That Is in God: Evangelical Theology and the Challenge of Classical Christian Theism*. Grand Rapids: Reformation Heritage Books, 2017.

———. "Trinity, Simplicity and the Status of God's Personal Relations." *International Journal of Systematic Theology* 16, no. 1 (2014): 79–98.

Duby, Steven J. *God in Himself: Scripture, Metaphysics, and the Task of Christian Theology*. Studies in Christian Doctrine and Scripture. Downers Grove, IL: IVP Academic, 2019.

Dünzl, Franz. *A Brief History of the Doctrine of the Trinity in the Early Church*. New York: T&T Clark, 2007.

Durand, Emmanuel. "A Theology of God the Father." In Gilles Emery and Matthew Levering, eds., *The Oxford Handbook of the Trinity*, 371–86. Oxford: Oxford University Press, 2014.

Emery, Gilles. *The Trinitarian Theology of St. Thomas Aquinas*. Oxford: Oxford University Press, 2010.

———. *The Trinity: An Introduction to Catholic Doctrine on the Triune God*. Washington, DC: Catholic University of America, 2011.

———, and Matthew Levering, eds. *The Oxford Handbook of the Trinity*. 1st edition. Oxford: Oxford University Press, 2014.

Erickson, Millard. *God in Three Persons: A Contemporary Interpretation of the Trinity*. Grand Rapids: Baker, 1995.

———. *Systematic Theology*. 2nd edition, Grand Rapids: Baker Academic, 1998; 3rd edition, Grand Rapids: Baker Academic, 2013.

————. *Who's Tampering with the Trinity? An Assessment of the Subordination Debate.* Grand Rapids: Kregel, 2009.

Fairbairn, Donald, and Ryan M. Reeves. *The Story of Creeds and Confessions: Tracing the Development of the Christian Faith.* Grand Rapids: Baker Academic, 2019.

Feinberg, John. *No One Like Him: The Doctrine of God.* Foundations of Evangelical Theology. Wheaton: Crossway, 2001.

Fesko, J. V. *The Trinity and the Covenant of Redemption.* Geanies House: Mentor, 2016.

Frame, John. *The Doctrine of God: A Theology of Lordship.* Philipsburg, NJ: P&R, 2002.

Frei, Hans. *The Eclipse of Biblical Narrative: A Study in Eighteenth and Nineteenth Century Hermeneutics.* New Haven: Yale University Press, 1974.

————. *The Identity of Jesus Christ: The Hermeneutical Bases of Dogmatic Theology.* Philadelphia: Fortress Press, 1975.

Giles, Kevin. *The Eternal Generation of the Son: Maintaining Orthodoxy in Trinitarian Theology.* Downers Grove, IL: IVP Academic, 2012.

————. *Jesus and the Father: Modern Evangelicals Reinvent the Doctrine of the Trinity.* Grand Rapids: Zondervan, 2006.

————. *The Trinity and Subordinationism: The Doctrine of God and the Contemporary Gender Debate.* Downers Grove, IL: IVP Academic, 2002.

————. "The Trinity without Tiers." In *The New Evangelical Subordinationism? Perspectives on the Equality of God the Father and God the Son.* Edited by Dennis W. Jowers and H. Wayne House, 262–87. Eugene, OR: Pickwick, 2012.

Goligher, Liam. "Is It Okay to Teach a Complementarianism Based on Eternal Subordination?" *Reformation 21*, June 3, 2016. https://www.reformation21.org/mos/housewife-theologian/is-it-okay-to-teach-a-complementarianism-based-on-eternal-subordination.

————. "Reinventing God." *Reformation 21*, June 6, 2016. https://www.reformation21.org/mos/housewife-theologian/reinventing-god.

Grenz, Stanley J. *The Named God and the Question of Being: A Trinitarian Theo-Ontology.* Louisville: Westminster John Knox Press, 2005.

————. *Rediscovering the Triune God: The Trinity in Contemporary Theology.* Minneapolis: Fortress, 2004.

————. *The Social God and the Relational Self: A Trinitarian Theology of the Imago Dei.* Louisville: Westminster John Knox Press, 2007.

————. *Theology for the Community of God.* Grand Rapids: Eerdmans, 2000.

Grudem, Wayne. "Biblical Evidence for the Eternal Submission of the Son to the Father." In *The New Evangelical Subordinationism? Perspectives on the Equality of God the Father and God the Son,* edited by Dennis W. Jowers and H. Wayne House, 223–61. Eugene, OR: Pickwick, 2012.

———. *Biblical Foundations for Manhood and Womanhood.* Wheaton: Crossway, 2002.

———. "Doctrinal Deviations in Evangelical-Feminist Arguments about the Trinity." In *One God in Three Persons: Unity of Essence, Distinction of Persons, Implications for Life,* edited by Bruce Ware and John Starke, 17–46. Wheaton: Crossway, 2015.

———. *Evangelical Feminism: A New Path to Liberalism?* Wheaton: Crossway, 2006.

———. *Evangelical Feminism and Biblical Truth.* Sisters, OR: Multnomah, 2004.

———. *Systematic Theology: An Introduction to Biblical Doctrine.* Revised edition. Grand Rapids: Zondervan, 1994 (appendix 6, 2000).

Gunton, Colin E. *The Promise of Trinitarian Theology.* New York: T&T Clark, 2003.

Hall, Christopher A., and Roger Olson. *The Trinity.* Grand Rapids: Eerdmans, 2002.

Hanson, R. P. C. *The Search for the Christian Doctrine of God: The Arian Controversy,* 318–81. Grand Rapids: Baker Academic, 2006.

Hill, Wesley. *Paul and the Trinity: Persons, Relations, and the Pauline Letters.* Grand Rapids: Eerdmans, 2015.

Holmes, Stephen R. "Classical Trinitarianism and Eternal Functional Subordination: Some Historical and Dogmatic Reflections." *Scottish Bulletin of Evangelical Theology* 35, no. 1 (2017): 90–104.

———. "Classical Trinity: Evangelical Perspective" and "Responses." In *Two Views on the Doctrine of the Trinity,* edited by Jason S. Sexton, 25–48 and 96–100. Grand Rapids: Zondervan Academic, 2014.

———. *Listening to the Past: The Place of Tradition in Theology.* Grand Rapids: Baker Academic, 2002.

———. *The Quest for the Trinity: The Doctrine of God in Scripture, History and Modernity.* Downers Grove, IL: IVP Academic, 2012.

———. "Three Versus One? Some Problems of Social Trinitarianism." *Journal of Reformed Theology* 3 (2009): 77–89.

Husbands, Mark. "The Trinity Is *Not* Our Social Program: Volf, Gregory of Nyssa and Barth." In *Trinitarian Theology for the Church: Scripture, Community, Worship,* edited by Daniel J. Treier and David Lauber, 120–41. Downers Grove, IL: IVP Academic, 2009.

Irons, Charles Lee. "Begotten of the Father before All Ages: The Biblical Basis of Eternal Generation According to the Church Fathers." *Christian Research Journal* 40, no. 1 (2017): 41–47.

———. "A Lexical Defense of the Johannine 'Only Begotten.'" In *Retrieving Eternal Generation,* edited by Fred Sanders and Scott R. Swain, 98–116. Grand Rapids: Zondervan Academic, 2017.

Jenson, Robert. *Systematic Theology.* Vol. 1, *The Triune God.* Oxford: Oxford University Press, 2001.

———. *The Triune Identity: God According to the Gospel.* Philadelphia: Fortress, 1982.

Johnson, Keith E. "Augustine, Eternal Generation, and Evangelical Trinitarianism." *Trinity Journal* 32 (2011): 141–63.

———. "*Imitatio Trinitatis:* How Should We Imitate the Trinity?" *Westminster Theological Journal* 75 (2013): 317–34.

———. *Rethinking the Trinity and Religious Pluralism: An Augustinian Assessment.* Downers Grove, IL: IVP Academic: 2011.

———. "Trinitarian Agency and the Eternal Subordination of the Son: An Augustinian Perspective." In *The New Evangelical Subordinationism? Perspectives on the Equality of God the Father and God the Son,* edited by Dennis W. Jowers and H. Wayne House, 108–32. Eugene, OR: Pickwick, 2012.

———. "What Would Augustine Say to Evangelicals Who Reject the Eternal Generation of the Son?" *Southern Baptist Journal of Theology* 16, no. 2 (2012): 26–43.

Jowers, Dennis W. "The Inconceivability of Subordination within a Simple God." In *The New Evangelical Subordinationism? Perspectives on the Equality of God the Father and God the Son.* Edited by Dennis W. Jowers and H. Wayne House, 375–410. Eugene, OR: Pickwick, 2012.

———. *The Trinitarian Axiom of Karl Rahner: The Economic Trinity Is the Immanent Trinity and Vice Versa.* Lewiston, NY: Edwin Mellen Press, 2006.

———, and H. Wayne House, eds. *The New Evangelical Subordinationism? Perspectives on the Equality of God the Father and God the Son.* Eugene, OR: Pickwick, 2012.

Kelly, J. N. D. *The Athanasian Creed.* London: A. & C. Black, 1964.

Kilby, Karen. "Perichoresis and Projection: Problems with Social Doctrines of the Trinity." *New Blackfriars* 81 (2000): 442.

Köstenberger, Andreas J. and Scott R. Swain. *Father, Son and Spirit: The Trinity and John's Gospel.* Downers Grove, IL: InterVarsity, 2008.

LaCugna, Catherine Mowry. *God for Us: The Trinity and Christian Life.* San Francisco: HarperSanFrancisco, 1993.

Leftow, Brian. "Anti-Social Trinitarianism." In *The Trinity: An Interdisciplinary Symposium on the Trinity,* edited by Stephen T. Davis, Daniel Kendall, and Gerald O'Collins, 203–50. New York: Oxford, 1999.

Lessing, G. E. "On the Proof of the Spirit and Power." In *Lessing's Theological Writings,* edited and translated by Henry Chadwick, 83–89. Cambridge: Cambridge University Press.

Letham, Robert. *The Holy Trinity: In Scripture, History, Theology, and Worship.* 2nd edition. Phillipsburg, NJ: P&R Publishing, 2019.

Levering, Matthew. *Scripture and Metaphysics: Aquinas and the Renewal of Trinitarian Theology.* Oxford: Blackwell, 2004.

McCormack, Bruce L. "Grace and Being." In *The Cambridge Companion to Karl Barth,* edited by John Webster, 92–100. Cambridge: Cambridge University Press, 2000.

Moltmann, Jürgen. *The Crucified God.* 40th anniversary edition. Minneapolis: Fortress Press, 2015.

———. *The Trinity and the Kingdom.* Minneapolis: Fortress, 1993.

Muller, Richard A. *Dictionary of Latin and Greek Theological Terms Drawn Principally from Protestant Scholastic Theology.* 2nd edition. Grand Rapids: Baker Academic, 2017.

———. *Post-Reformation Reformed Dogmatics.* Vol. 4, *The Triunity of God.* Grand Rapids: Baker Academic, 2003.

Ovey, Michael J. *Your Will Be Done: Exploring Eternal Subordination, Divine Monarchy, and Divine Humility.* London: Latimer Trust, 2016.

Plantinga Jr., Cornelius. *Does God Have a Nature?* Milwaukee: Marquette University Press, 1980.

———. "Social Trinity and Tritheism." In *Trinity, Incarnation, and Atonement: Philosophical and Theological Essays,* edited by Ronald J. Feenstra and Cornelius Plantinga Jr., 21–47. Notre Dame, IN: University of Notre Dame Press, 1989.

———. "The Threeness/Oneness Problem of the Trinity." *Calvin Theological Journal* 23, no. 1 (1988): 37–53.

Rahner, Karl. *The Trinity.* New York: Crossroad Publishing, 1997.

Rauschenbusch, Walter. *A Theology for the Social Gospel.* New York: Macmillan, 1917.

Reymond, Robert. *A New Systematic Theology of the Christian Faith.* 2nd edition. Nashville: Thomas Nelson, 1998.

Ritschl, Albrecht. *The Christian Doctrine of Justification and Reconciliation.* Edited and translated by H. R. Mackintosh and A. B. Macaulay. Edinburgh: T&T Clark, 1902.

Sanders, Fred. *The Deep Things of God: How the Trinity Changes Everything.* Wheaton: Crossway, 2017.

———. *The Image of the Immanent Trinity: Rahner's Rule and the Theological Interpretation of Scripture.* Issues in Systematic Theology. New York: Peter Lang, 2005.

———. *The Triune God.* New Studies in Dogmatics. Wheaton: Crossway, 2016.

Sanders, Fred, and Oliver D. Crisp, eds. *Advancing Trinitarian Theology: Explorations in Constructive Dogmatics.* Grand Rapids: Zondervan, 2014.

Sanders, Fred, and Scott Swain, eds. *Retrieving Eternal Generation.* Grand Rapids: Zondervan, 2017.

Schleiermacher, Friedrich. *The Christian Faith.* London: Bloomsbury, 2016.

———. *On Religion: Speeches to Its Cultured Despisers.* Edited by Richard Crouter. Cambridge Texts in the History of Philosophy. Cambridge: Cambridge University Press, 2007.

Sexton, Jason S. "Beyond Social Trinitarianism: The Baptist, Trinitarian Innovation of Stanley J. Grenz." *Baptist Quarterly* 44 (2012): 473–86.

Smith, Warren. "The Trinity in the Fourth-Century Fathers." In *The Oxford Handbook of the Trinity,* edited by Gilles Emery and Matthew Levering, 109–22. Oxford: Oxford University Press, 2014.

Starke, John and Bruce A. Ware, eds. *One God in Three Persons: Unity of Essence, Distinction of Persons, Implications for Life.* Wheaton: Crossway, 2015.

Swain, Scott R. "Covenant of Redemption." In *Christian Dogmatics: Reformed Theology for the Church Catholic,* edited by Michael Allen and Scott R. Swain, 107–25. Grand Rapids: Baker Academic, 2016.

———. *The God of the Gospel: Robert Jenson's Trinitarian Theology.* Downers Grove, IL: IVP Academic, 2013.

———. *The Trinity: An Introduction.* Wheaton: Crossway, 2020.

———. "The Trinity." In *Christian Dogmatics: Reformed Theology for the Church Catholic,* edited by Michael Allen and Scott R. Swain, 78–106. Grand Rapids: Baker Academic, 2016.

Tanner, Kathryn. "Social Trinitarianism and Its Critics." In *Rethinking Trinitarian Theology: Disputed Questions and Contemporary Issues in Trinitarian Theology,* edited by Giulio Maspero and Robert J. Wozniak, 368–86. New York: T&T Clark, 2012.

Thompson, Thomas R., and Cornelius Plantinga Jr. "Trinity and Kenosis." In *Exploring Kenotic Christology: The Self-Emptying of God*, edited by C. Stephen Evans, 165–89. Oxford: Oxford University Press, 2006.

Treier, Daniel J. *Introducing Evangelical Theology*. Grand Rapids: Baker Academic, 2019.

Trueman, Carl R. "Fahrenheit 381." *Reformation 21*, June 7, 2016. https://www.reformation21.org/mos/postcards-from-palookaville/fahrenheit-381.

———. "Reforming God?" *Reformed Faith and Practice* 4, no. 2 (2019): 37–52.

Volf, Miroslav. *After Our Likeness: The Church as the Image of the Trinity*. Grand Rapids: Eerdmans, 1998.

———. "Being as God Is: Trinity and Generosity." In Miroslav Volf and Michael Welker, eds. *God's Life in Trinity*, 3–12. Minneapolis: Fortress, 2009.

———. *Exclusion and Embrace: A Theological Exploration of Identity, Otherness, and Reconciliation*. Nashville: Abingdon, 1996.

———. "'The Trinity Is Our Social Program': The Doctrine of the Trinity and the Shape of Social Engagement." *Modern Theology* 14 (1998): 403–23.

Vos, Geerhardus. *Reformed Dogmatics*. Vol. 1, *Theology Proper*. Translated and edited by Richard B. Gaffin Jr. Bellingham, WA: Lexham Press, 2012–2014.

Ware, Bruce A. "Does Affirming an Eternal Authority-Submission Relationship in the Trinity Entail a Denial of *Homoousios*? A Response to Millard Erickson and Tom McCall." In *One God in Three Persons: Unity of Essence, Distinction of Persons, Implications for Life*, edited by Bruce Ware and John Starke, 237–48. Wheaton: Crossway, 2015.

———. "Equal in Essence, Distinct in Roles: Eternal Functional Authority and Submission among the Essentially Equal Divine Persons of the Godhead." In *The New Evangelical Subordinationism? Perspectives on the Equality of God the Father and God the Son*, edited by Dennis W. Jowers and H. Wayne House, 13–37. Eugene, OR: Pickwick, 2012.

———. *Father, Son, and Spirit: Relationships, Roles, and Relevance.* Wheaton: Crossway, 2005.

———. "Unity and Distinction of the Trinitarian Persons." In *Trinitarian Theology: Theological Models and Doctrinal Applications*, edited by Keith S. Whitfield, 17–62. Nashville: B&H Academic, 2019.

Warfield, B. B. "The Biblical Doctrine of the Trinity." In *The Works of Benjamin B. Warfield*. Vol. 2, 133–72. Grand Rapids: Baker Books, 1981.

Webster, John. *The Culture of Theology.* Grand Rapids: Baker Academic, 2019.

———. *God Without Measure: Working Papers in Christian Theology.* Vol. 1, *God and the Works of God.* London: Bloomsbury, 2016

Webster, John, and George P. Schner, eds. *Theology After Liberalism: Classical and Contemporary Readings.* Oxford: Blackwell, 2000.

Wellum, Stephen J. *God the Son Incarnate: The Doctrine of Christ.* Foundations of Evangelical Theology. Wheaton: Crossway, 2016.

White, Thomas Joseph. "Divine Simplicity and the Holy Trinity." *International Journal of Systematic Theology* 18, no. 1 (2016): 66–93.

———. "Intra-Trinitarian Obedience and Nicene-Chalcedonian Christology." *Nova et Vetera* 6, no. 2 (2008): 377–402.

Whitfield, Keith S., ed. *Trinitarian Theology: Theological Models and Doctrinal Application.* Nashville: B&H Academic, 2019.

Williams, Rowan. *Arius: Heresy and Tradition.* Rev. ed. Grand Rapids: Eerdmans, 2002.

Yeago, David S. "The New Testament and the Nicene Dogma: A Contribution to the Recovery of Theological Exegesis." In *The Theological Interpretation of Scripture: Classic and Contemporary Readings*, edited by Stephen E. Fowl. Malden, MA: Wiley-Blackwell, 1997.

Zizioulas, John D. *Being as Communion.* Crestwood, NY: St Vladimir's Seminary Press, 1985.

REDISCOVER THE ATTRIBUTES OF GOD

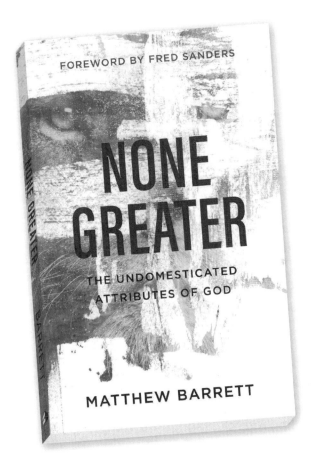

FOREWORD BY FRED SANDERS

NONE GREATER

THE UNDOMESTICATED ATTRIBUTES OF GOD

MATTHEW BARRETT

"Matthew Barrett leads us to marvel at both how much and how little we know of God."

—**TIM CHALLIES**, blogger at challies.com; author of *Visual Theology*

CREDO

MAGAZINE AND PODCAST

Credo is an online magazine published quarterly with articles, interviews, and columns on today's most important theological issues. Our desire is to see biblically-grounded, confessionally-minded, Christ-exalting reformation and transformation in the church today.

Listen to **Matthew Barrett** talk with today's top theologians about doctrines that matter.

Connect with
MATTHEW BARRETT

 @MatthewMichaelBarrett

 @MattMBarrett • @CredoMagazine

www.credomag.com